COMMUNITY CORRECTIONS

COMMUNITY CORRECTIONS
An Intersectional Approach

HAYDEN SMITH, JILL VIGLIONE,
and FAYE S. TAXMAN

cognella®
SAN DIEGO

Bassim Hamadeh, CEO and Publisher
Carolyn Meier, Publisher
Amy Smith, Senior Project Editor
Abbey Hastings, Production Editor
Jess Estrella, Senior Graphic Designer
JoHannah McDonald, Licensing Coordinator
Natalie Piccotti, Director of Marketing
Kassie Graves, Senior Vice President, Editorial

Cover image: Copyright © 2019 iStockphoto LP/KatarzynaBialasiewicz.

Printed in the United States of America.

320 South Cedros Ave., Ste. 400, Solana Beach, CA 92075

Hayden Smith

To the center of my universe:
Abigail, Leighton, and Sebastian.
You are everything to me.

Jill Viglione

To Cortland, Maddox, and Liliana.
I love you to the moon and back.

Faye Taxman

Sandy, Liz and Ian, Joe and Mariam, and Jacob and Hannah:
You make the hard work of being an academic worth it.
We can make the world a better place.

Brief Contents

Detailed Contents

Acknowledgments

A project this broad, complex, and applied requires the vantage points that only a diverse community can provide. We were fortunate to have support from the academics, practitioners, and stakeholders who afforded their insights and knowledge about community corrections. We want to thank these experts whose time, patience, and perspectives were certainly needed to see this project to completion.

First and foremost, Carolyn Henderson Meier at Cognella was instrumental in encouraging a vision for community corrections that reflects the dynamic processes occurring in the real world. Carolyn has the unique ability to disentangle an assortment of academic wishes and identify what is most salient to producing quality. Not only is Carolyn technically gifted, but she is also a genuinely nice person with a hilarious sense of humor. This makes life so much easier when faced with long nights of writing, researching, and reviewing. We are fortunate to have had Carolyn steering the ship, along with the backing of her talented team that includes Amy Smith, Alia Bales, and Jess Estrella.

We would like to highlight the work of four esteemed reviewers of our early draft, and their suggestions and recommendations for moving forward were highly valued. These professors are Dr. Michael Hollingsworth of Black Hills State University, Dr. Amber Laffin of Bemidji State University, Dr. Lisa Wanek of Wayne State College, and Dr. Angela Wartel of Lewis-Clark State College. These scholars were thoughtful and honest in their guidance, and we appreciate their willingness to participate in this project.

We would also like to thank the cadre of people who provided much needed editorial scrutiny, an often laborious, though necessary task. It is the details that matter, and the following people were essential in placing this project on sturdier ground. This includes Samuel Cheung, Paris Cloutier, Stephanie Jensen, Hyunmin Park, Lindsay Smith, Marlana Vazquez, and Amelia Wiercioch. Holly Russell deserves a particular note of thanks for her close inspection and astute observations of the project as it unfolded.

A final mention is extended to the individuals who interact with the community corrections system every day. As this book hopefully conveys, community corrections in the United States comprises a complex system made up of a diverse population of impacted individuals and staff. The authors of this book have significant experiences in research, teaching, and grant activities with community corrections, and it is through these involvements that a desire to create a better, more equitable, evidence-based, and ultimately a more just system, emerges. In line with this ethos, we thank all the administrators, officers, and individuals who interact with the community corrections system for allowing us the opportunity to explore this world.

PART I

Theoretical Orientations and Context

CHAPTER 1

An Introduction to Community Corrections

This chapter is designed to provide students an introduction to the community corrections systems in the United States. The complexity of the community corrections system is described so that students can begin to develop an appreciation of the challenges ahead. This chapter begins with the definition of community corrections, along with recent trends and the characteristics of individuals under supervision. The concept of "community" is fundamental to the community corrections system, and a discussion of how community has been studied is provided. The functions of community corrections are explained with reference to punishment philosophies (i.e., retribution, deterrence, incapacitation, rehabilitation, and restorative justice). These punishment philosophies are also described in terms of officer work, careers, and wellness, as community corrections officers face role conflict and role ambiguity that can lead to increased stress and poor physical and mental health. The four components of the community corrections system are explained as diversion, probation, intermediate sanctions, and parole. This chapter ends with a summary of the current state of the community correction system.

LEARNING OBJECTIVES

By the end of this chapter, students will be able to:

- Understand the definition, trends, and characteristics of the community corrections system.
- Describe the four main punishment philosophies of community corrections, with reference to real-world examples.
- Identify and summarize the four components of community corrections: diversion, probation, intermediate sanctions, and parole.

KEY TERMS

- Community corrections
- Diversion
- Parole
- Probation
- Punishment philosophies

CONTENT

And a step backward, after making a wrong turn, is a step in the right direction.

—Kurt Vonnegut

An Overview of the Community Corrections System

Students learning about community corrections often find themselves in a maze. This is because the community corrections system contains several challenging paradoxes. For example, while more people are being managed in the community on legal orders than any time in human history (Pearse, 2021), there has been a lack of research on best practices and policies that can lead to better outcomes. Community corrections and its staff, as well as the citizens they interact with, are largely invisible to the media, especially compared to institutional corrections (i.e., jail and prison). Additionally, the term "community corrections" is generalized and includes a range of community-based sentencing options, such as probation, parole, community service, intermediate sanctions, intensive supervision, and home detention.

IMAGE 1.1   Brown Heatley Building in Austin, TX

While these practices may link community corrections at a global level, the application of justice is dependent upon very specific geographic, linguistic, and cultural contexts (Pearse, 2021). The early history of community corrections dates as far back as 1700 England, yet in a modern-day context there has been a rapid increase in the application of technology, the bureaucratic distribution of services, and the use of the scientific method to measure the success and/or failure of programs (which is often called "evidence-based research"). To understand the community corrections system, it is necessary to develop a clear definition that provides boundaries and helps students understand processes and outcomes. This also includes the examination of data, particularly trends in probation and parole and the characteristics of clients under the supervision of these agencies.

Defining Community Corrections

A traditional definition of **community corrections** centers on "programs [that] oversee offenders outside of jail or prison" (National Institute of Justice [NIJ], n.d., para. 1). These programs are administered by agencies or courts with the legal authority to enforce sanctions (NIJ, n.d.). The traditional approach to community corrections relies on two main systems: probation and parole. **Probation** is a "court-ordered period of correctional supervision in the community, generally as an alternative to incarceration. In some cases, probation may be a combined sentence involving short periods of incarceration followed by a period of community supervision" (Oudekerk & Kaeble, 2021, p. 2). **Parole** is "a period of conditional supervised release in the community following a term in state or federal prison. Parolees include persons released through discretionary or mandatory supervised release from prison" (Oudekerk & Kaeble, 2021, p. 2). Both definitions emphasize the linkage between community corrections (i.e., probation and parole) and institutional corrections (i.e., jail and prison). Individuals may undergo correctional supervision (probation) within the community rather than jail or prison, and individuals released from prison may have a period of conditional, supervised release (parole; NIJ, n.d.).

While emphasizing the "corrections" system, this traditional definition needs revision, as it neglects the crucial role of the "community." Several key developments suggest the definition of community corrections should be broad and inclusive. First, the use of technology and bureaucracy has allowed more effective approaches to supervising individuals under proba-tion or parole supervision, collecting data, and measuring trends. For example, individuals on community corrections may now wear an ankle bracelet with a Global Positioning System (GPS) unit. Without technology like GPS, such oversight and monitoring of individuals would require additional staffing and increased costs. These technological changes are evident across multiple sectors of society and are likely to continue in the future. For example, in 2006, Wolff analyzed decades of census data for 267 occupations in 64 industries and found that worker groups categorized as "knowledge producers" and "data processors" increased 59%. In contrast, Wolff found that the worker groups categorized as "service workers" and "good-processing" declined during the same period. These data suggest that the community corrections system and the staff working in them will increasingly adopt technological advancements that are managed with bureaucratic oversight while being less involved in the basic delivery of services and goods.

Another key social change has been significant public interest in how crime and justice manifest in the community. High-profile interactions between citizens and law enforcement officers have facilitated social movements that question the current funding, structure, and philosophy that drive the entire criminal justice system. Technology has facilitated the rapid transmission of this information, and now citizens can view negative interactions between citizens and criminal justice practitioners on their phones or computers within minutes of the actual event. For example, following the murder of George Floyd by Minneapolis police, witnesses shared the video of the arrest to social media, and these images quickly became an impetus for protests. A timeline of the events surrounding George Floyd's murder reveals the rapid escalation of civil unrest that followed, with at least 140 cities erupting in violent protests leading to six deaths in the United States and waves of global protests (Taylor, 2021). Amnesty International (2020) delivered over one million signatures from around the world to U.S. Attorney General William Barr to demand justice for George Floyd. In 2021, the city of Minneapolis settled a wrongful death lawsuit with the Floyd family, with police officer Dennis Chauvin sentenced to 22.5 years in prison for two counts of murder and one count of homicide (Hayes et al., 2021).

The public now consumes and responds to major crime news regarding crime and punishment at a level unmatched throughout history, leading to real-world consequences. The George Floyd case led to lawsuits that produced substantial costs for law enforcement agencies and notable changes to criminal justice policies and practices. Much like other high-profile crime events, the George Floyd case extends far beyond the media portrayal of a one-time interaction between law enforcement and a citizen. What is often lost in this narrative is the complexity of cases like these, as these interactions are often not restricted to an isolated event. Rather, many justice-involved individuals have multiple interactions with correctional and community agencies and actors throughout their life course. For example, George Floyd had previous experiences when he was supervised on parole. George Floyd's parole experiences are vast; that is, he received housing, substance use treatment, and job placement services (Fernandez & Burch, 2021). He also delivered meals to senior citizens, mentored at-risk youth, completed a 90-day substance use program, and worked as a security guard for a homeless shelter (Fernandez & Burch, 2021). After being released from prison in 2013, George Floyd moved to Minneapolis and hoped to earn a commercial license to drive trucks, passing mandated drug and alcohol testing and other requirements while on parole.

While the media portrayal of George Floyd focuses on a negative and illegal police use of force incident, his story, like those of many other justice-involved people, is far more complex and involves repeated interactions with different aspects of the criminal justice system. It is important that we consider the role that the community corrections system plays in the lives

IMAGE 1.2   George Floyd mural outside Cup Foods at Chicago Ave. and E 38th St. in Minneapolis, Minnesota

of our citizens. The criminal justice system failed George Floyd, much like it continues to fail people every day, and community corrections is regularly involved in these cases. Interactions with criminal justice can also help people, especially the community correction system, which is literally embedded within our communities. It is important that students in criminal justice understand the role and function of community corrections, particularly as they may become academics, policymakers, and practitioners in the field.

A third justification for advancing beyond a traditional definition of the community corrections system is the complexity of programs and services now available for people under supervision in the community. For example, a review of the National Institute of Corrections (NIC, n.d.) website reveals the following "top-shelf" resources selected and endorsed by staff:

- parole
- parole boards
- caseloads
- general
- officers
- officers and firearms
- probation—drug offenders
- probation—female offenders
- probation—juveniles
- probation—LGBTI
- probation—mentally ill offenders
- probation—sex offenders
- probation—special populations and minorities
- probation—tribal
- probation—veterans
- revocation
- sanctions and rewards
- screening and assessment
- supervision

There is also an abundance of specialized databases and thousands of additional resources on community corrections topics. The complexity of programs in community corrections has produced a need to measure their effectiveness. Researchers now engage in evidence-based studies where the scientific method is used to test the effectiveness of programs, policies, and services.

This book uses a definition of community corrections as agencies that manage, oversee, and assist individuals that are adjudicated (i.e., sentenced for a criminal offense) or awaiting adjudication (i.e., pretrial) in the community in lieu of incarceration or to avoid incarceration entirely. This definition embraces a holistic approach rather than a reliance on the two primary community corrections systems (i.e., probation and parole). This includes recognition of the complexity of distributing justice in a modern-day society, including the role of intermediate sanctions as a strategy that extends beyond a single system or process. The definition also relies on an outcome that is often based on diversion—that is, the need to divert appropriate individuals away from institutional corrections (jail and prison) and into community supervision where they complete their sentence. In this context, the outcome of diversion is deemed a success. In contrast, if an individual is eligible for community corrections and they are either placed in institutional corrections (or they do not meet the obligations of their probation or parole requirements and are later sent to prison), then the outcome is considered a failure.

◊ Diversity, Equity, and Inclusion: Community

The concept of community has been described as *the* concept in social science because it conveys the sharing of norms, values, needs, interests, and goals within a particular social group or within a group linked by characteristics (Greer, 1969). The simple idea of community has been examined in social science, political commentary, and general literature (Greer, 1969). For criminology, research has examined the impact of racial oppression, economic inequality, police practices, and dysfunctional community structures. The impact of these factors has a negative effect on the community, particularly low socioeconomic communities, or communities of color. Here, the community corrections system may reinforce existing social and economic inequities that predispose people toward crime.

In this book, the term "community" reflects the work of American psychologist Urie Bronfenbrenner. Bronfenbrenner (1977) stated that community "is conceived topologically as a nested arrangement of structures, each contained within the next" much like a set of nested Russian dolls (p. 514). There are five layers to this conceptualization of community. Within the inner circle (microsystem) is the individual under supervision and those with whom they have direct, face-to-face significant relationships (Bronfenbrenner, 1979). The microsystem includes parents, siblings, romantic partners, teachers or mentors, and neighbors. The mesosystem features the interactions between these influences, and the interconnectedness or influence they have on each other. For example, an individual who takes illegal substances may experience tension between their spouse and their deviant peer group. The outer circle, or exosystem, includes contact with formal and informal social structures that influence individual behavior. Formal examples include probation, parole, health care, education, and employment, while informal examples may be linked to mass media and community resources. The macrosystem is the cultural ideologies, attitudes, and social conditions that the individual is immersed in, such as gender roles, family structures, individualism, and normative behavior. The fifth and final level of Bronfenbrenner's ecological systems theory is known as the chronosystem, which reflects a shift or transition over the life course. This may reflect historical events like growing up during a recession, a period of war, or experiencing parental divorce. The chronosystem also includes developmental changes at key transitions like entering middle school, where students adapt to puberty, evaluate their academic performance, and foster self-esteem. This nested design can be visualized by considering Figure 1.1.

When the concept of community is applied to the individuals under supervision, staff, victims, and other stakeholders, a dynamic and complex interaction emerges. This is because

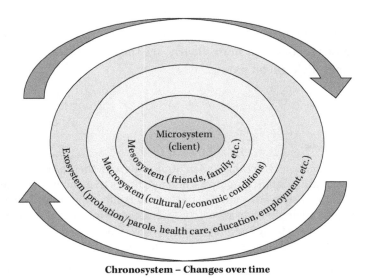

FIGURE 1.1   Community Corrections Example of Bronfenbrenner's
Conceptualization of Community

punishment is strongly related to culture. As David Garland (1990) argues, punishment and institutions like community corrections that reinforce justice and punishment shape meaning about behaviors within a cultural setting. Garland (1990) states that "punishment is shaped by broad cultural patterns which have their own origins elsewhere, but it also generates its own local meanings, values, and sensibilities which contribute—in a small but significant way—to the bricolage of the dominant culture" (p. 10). These are important factors when developing an understanding of community corrections. A more practical example can be seen here:

> The community is a place that encourages criminal activity (for instance, when offenders leave inpatient treatment, they often return to neighborhoods or social networks that promote criminal behavior). The community is also the place that heals criminality in that promoting positive communal ties is thought to be a rehabilitative force in offenders' lives. Finally, the community is something to be protected from crime. (Zozula, 2019, p. 10)

The community that an individual resides in operates within the exosystem: the external environment that can impact individual behavior. Bronfenbrenner's (1979) theory emphasizes the idea that there are important interactions between an individual and their environment. Communities have shared norms, values, needs, and other commonalities (e.g., geography, culture, religion). These shared norms, values, and needs can be useful when thinking about how to address the needs of specific groups within a community. For example, a community that values education may be more receptive to programs that improve access to education for individuals on probation or parole supervision. That is, the exosystem can directly impact the availability and accessibility of services and programs that are important to the success and well-being of various groups of individuals within a community. This is important when thinking about intersectionality and the community corrections system. To help you understand Bronfenbrenner's theory a bit more clearly, see the example in Table 1.1 that describes the application to an individual on parole.

TABLE 1.1   Bronfenbrenner's Theory Applied to an Individual on Parole

Concept	Example
Microsystem	Individual's interactions and relationships with their probation and parole officer, family, friends, employers, and neighbors that can impact their success while on supervision. For example, the level of family support an individual has can impact their ability to successfully reintegrate into society. An individual with strong familial support may be more likely to have a place to live post-incarceration and may have stronger emotional support during the reentry process.
Mesosystem	Interaction between an individual's parole requirements, employment, and community involvement. A strong mesosystem occurs where different aspects of the individual's experience in the community can coincide smoothly to support successful reintegration. For example, a weak mesosystem would occur when an individual's parole requirements interfere with their ability to successfully maintain employment.
Exosystem	External factors that could indirectly impact an individual's life include parole policies and requirements and community resources. For example, access to housing, employment, and treatment services in the community can significantly impact an individual's ability to reintegrate successfully.
Macrosystem	Cultural values, norms, and beliefs that influence the experiences of individuals on parole include public opinion towards rehabilitation and the criminal justice system as well as the emphasis on rehabilitation compared to punishment. For example, individuals residing in communities that place an emphasis on rehabilitation and support for individuals on parole may be more likely to succeed.
Chronosystem	Changes in criminal justice and parole policies over time, advancements in technology, and fluctuating societal norms. For example, changes in laws related to parole, improvements in rehabilitation and treatment programs, and changes in public opinion can impact the parole experience over time.

Communities with limited access to mental health services may have higher rates of unmet treatment needs, which could negatively impact probation and parole agencies' ability to intervene and/or link individuals under supervision to appropriate treatment. Thus, at the community level there are important variables that can interact with individual behavior that can ultimately influence the success (or failure) of supervision. Addressing the needs of specific groups within various communities requires availability and/or development of programs and services that address the unique needs of various groups. This may involve larger initiatives, such as working with local politicians, organizations, and stakeholders to address community needs.

Trends in Community Corrections

An assessment of the community corrections system over time reveals several striking trends. In the United States, the conservative drive toward the "get tough on crime" approach during the mid-1970s drastically increased contact between citizens and the criminal justice system. Punitive policies like "Three Strikes and You're Out," the War on Drugs, increased accountability, and determinate sentencing limited judges' discretion and pushed thousands of people into the criminal justice system. Evidence suggests that these mass incarceration trends disproportionately impacted people of color and those living in poverty (Harding et al., 2019). This social inequity continues today, with some families experiencing multiple generations cycling through the criminal justice system. Decades of punitive policies increased the contact between citizens and the criminal justice system while producing no measurable impact on public safety (Harding, 2019). This is because these conservative and punitive approaches failed to include consideration of underlying social and economic factors that drive crime, particularly poverty, racial discrimination, a lack of work opportunity and unsafe working conditions, a lack of health care and benefits, failing school systems, and low access to mental health treatment and effective substance use rehabilitation programs (all considered part of Brofennbrenner's (1979) exosystem).

Image 1.3

The "get tough on crime" approach to crime increased the incarcerated population by 700%, resulting in the United States having only 5% of the global population but 25% of the world's prison population (American Civil Liberties Union, n.d.). In 1975, there were almost 400,000 people housed in jail or prison, and by 2008 there was a peak of 2.3 million people (Prison Policy Initiative, 2018). Now, 1 out of every 3 Black boys born today can expect to go to prison in his lifetime, as can 1 of every 6 Latino boys—compared to 1 in every 17 White boys (American Civil Liberties Union, 2021). These trends can be seen in the three charts shown in Figure 1.2, with A documenting U.S. incarceration over time (1925–2018), B comparing incarceration rates in 15 counties, and C showing the cumulative imprisonment risk for men over time. The policies that affect mass incarceration also expand the overall scope of the justice system, including community corrections. In fact, mass incarceration has led to mass probation and parole supervision, illustrating that more people are exposed to the justice system as a result of increasing trends in punitive responses to crime. These factors are reinforced by the data presented in Figure 1.2

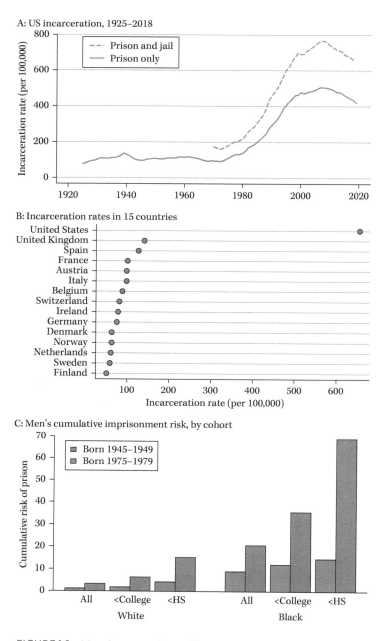

FIGURE 1.2   Mass Incarceration in Three Figures

The use of the criminal justice system to address social problems via harsh and puni-tive punishment led to a trend where both institutional corrections (i.e., jails and prisons) and community corrections (i.e., parole and probation) experienced drastic increases in population size. In addition, these populations entered the criminal justice system with physical and mental health needs far greater than their counterparts who did not interact with the criminal justice system (Franco-Parades et al., 2020). Staff working in the criminal justice system not only faced the dilemma of providing supervision and services for these individuals but also experienced their own challenges related to workplace stress, burnout, and high turnover. By the late 1990s, this reliance on the criminal justice system to address social problems began to decline. Statistical comparisons of crime rates in multiple countries showed that crime was decreasing, mostly due to social, economic, and demographic reasons (Tseloni et al., 2010).

Crime has continued to decline significantly since 2000. Between 1993 and 2019, the overall violent crime rate has decreased by 74% and property crime has decreased by 71% (Gramlich, 2020). Yet in 20 of 24 Gallup surveys conducted since 1993, at least 60% of U.S. adults have said there is more crime nationally than there was the year before, and this mistaken public opinion remains at an all-time high (Gramlich, 2020). This suggests that there is a need to educate the public (and students) on how to access data, reports, and other forms of trustworthy media to accurately assess trends in the criminal justice system. An examination of decades of reliable data does indicate one very important interaction between institutional corrections (i.e., jail and prison) and community corrections (i.e., probation and parole). In 2019, the declining incarceration rate reached 810 individuals per 100,000 adults—the lowest rate since 1995 (Minton et al., 2021). As a result, jails and prisons have moved toward a decarceration approach where nonviolent individuals, including those with mental health and/or drug addiction disorders, have increasingly been diverted away from the criminal justice system. Jails and prisons have also made efforts to decarcerate by releasing people back into the community earlier, a process that increased more during the COVID-19 pandemic. The decarceration trends presented in Figure 1.3 indicate that increased need to have a functioning probation and parole system in the United States.

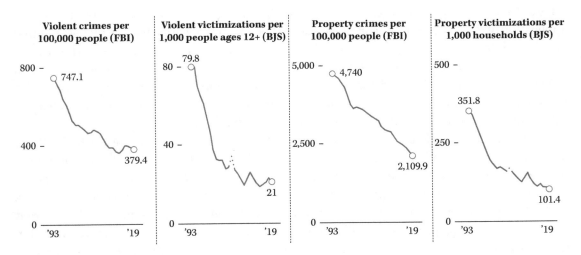

FIGURE 1.3   Trends in U.S. Violent and Property Crime, 1993–2019

Probation has followed these trends by also decreasing their populations under supervision over time, though the total number of people on probation remains very high. At year-end 2021, there were 3,745,000 people on community supervision, or 1 in 48 adults—down from 1 in 32 a decade earlier (Carson & Kluckow, 2023). This trend in community corrections was entirely due to decreases in the probation population (with a reduction of 467,300 in 2020 alone). In fact, the number of people on probation declined more rapidly than jail or prison, with declines in the probation population accounting for 65% of the overall decline in the correctional population from 2011 to 2021 (Carson & Kluckow, 2023). This decline in probation was not uniform, as probation populations decreased in 31 states; however, 18 states and the District of Columbia experienced increases in their probation populations in 2021 (Kaeble, 2023).

Changes in the total population on parole have been less drastic compared to probation. In general, the parole population has remained relatively constant, between a low of 803,200 in 2021 to a high of 878,900 in 2019 (Carson & Kluckow, 2023). However, the total number of people on parole in 2021 reflects a 7.1% decrease in the total parole population—the largest annual change since 1992 (Kaeble, 2023). Again, these changes were not uniform across the United States: 44 states plus the District of Columbia saw declines in parole populations, while six states reported an increase (Kaeble, 2023). Therefore, changes in large states, like California, can greatly influence these national trends.

Despite these parole trends, the overall composition of the correctional population remains stable. Probation consistently supervises most individuals under any form of criminal justice control. Of all people interacting with the correctional system, approximately 54% are on probation supervision, 22% incarcerated in prison, 15% on parole supervision, and 12% incarcerated in a local jail (Carson & Kluckow, 2023). This is evident in Table 1.2.

These trends indicate that community corrections represents a massive, wide-ranging, and complex system of distributing justice. This can be seen in the total inputs (entries) and outputs (exits) of the community corrections system. In 2021, probation had approximately 1,419,300 entries and 1,553,200 exits (Kaeble, 2023). There is also wide variation by state in the application of the community corrections system. For example, Georgia has the highest number of individuals on probation per 100,000 adult U.S. residents with 4,169 while New Hampshire has the lowest with 333 (Kaeble, 2023). Parole is also a system that is used frequently, with 357,000 entries and 410,200 exits documented in 2021 (Kaeble, 2023). Similar differences in the use of parole show that Arkansas has the highest number of parolees per 100,000 adult U.S. residents with 1,021, while Maine is the lowest with 2 (Kaeble, 2023).

Several caveats should be noted. From 2011–2021, available data is missing for 13%–40% of adults on probation and 6%–25% of adults on parole (Kaeble, 2023). This illustrates that there is a need for better data collection methods to understand the true impact of the system. Data collection is difficult for many reasons. For instance, an individual can enter or exit the probation system several times during a year or serve several probation sentences for different crimes. Exits (leaving probation supervision) are obviously linked to new intakes to probation (entries), though in 2021 exits outpaced entries by 133,900, making it the 13th consecutive year with more probation exits than entries (Kaeble, 2023). This illustrates changes in the probation

TABLE 1.2   Composition of the Adult Correctional System in the United States, 2011 and 2021

Correctional Population	2011		2021	
	Population	Percent of Total Population	Population	Percent of Total Population
Total[a]	6,994,500	100	5,444,900	100
Probation[b]	3,973,800	56.8	2,963,000	54.4
Prison[b,c]	1,599,000	22.9	1,204,300	22.1
Parole[b]	855,500	12.2	803,200	14.8
Local jail[d]	735,600	10.5	636,300	11.7

Note: Counts are rounded to the nearest 100 and include estimates for nonresponding jurisdictions. Details may not sum to totals due to rounding and because estimates were adjusted to exclude persons with dual correctional statuses (persons on probation or parole who were held in prisons or local jails, persons on parole who were also on probation, and prisoners who were held in local jails).

[a]Reflects probation, prison parole, and local jail counts minus persons with dual correctional statuses to avoid double counting. There were 169,300 persons in 2011 and 162,000 persons in 2021 with dual correctional statuses. Total correctional populations for 2011 and 2021 obtain standard error terms from the Annual Survey of Jails in 2011 and 2021.

[b]Population as of December 31.

[c]Persons who were under the jurisdiction of state or federal prisons.

[d]Population as of the last weekday in June. Local jail populations for 2011 and 2021 are from BJS's Annual Survey of Jails, a nationally representative sample of local jails, rather than a full census. Source: Bureau of Justice Statistics, Annual Probation Survey, Annual Parole Survey, Annual Survey of Jails, and National Prisoner Statistics program, 2011 and 2021.

Source: https://bjs.ojp.gov/document/cpus21st.pdf

populations, whereby probation agencies use procedures to move cases toward exits by recognizing that some special conditions are met by the individual, such as completing a drug class and/or the payment of court mandated fines/fees. Another trend is to cap the length of a supervision. For example, in 2020 the Minnesota Sentencing Guidelines Commission approved a cap for felony probation terms at 5 years (with the exception of homicide and criminal sex crimes), which resulted in significant reductions in probation populations (Sawyer, 2020). Reducing caps for length of probation terms often leads to increases in the number of exits from probation. While caps may serve a legal, political, or administrative function, critics of probationer caps highlight that they also greatly reduce judges' discretion in sentencing (Sawyer, 2020). This can limit a judge's effectiveness in assessing individual risks, needs, and circumstances.

While the existing data reflect the trends in the community corrections system at the state level, there is also a federal level. In 2021, the federal community supervision population was 120,400, with 49,900 entries and 55,300 exits (Kaeble, 2023). This includes 12,391 individuals on federal probation and 108,039 on federal parole (Kaeble, 2023). The historical trends of the federal system match those at the state level.

JOURNEY INTO THE FIELD: DR. FRANK CULLEN

◇◇◇◇◇◇◇◇

Full name: Francis T. Cullen

Title: Distinguished Research Professor Emeritus, School of Criminal Justice, University of Cincinnati

Dr. Francis "Frank" Cullen is one of the most respected and prominent criminological scholars of his generation. Professor Cullen received his PhD in sociology and education from Columbia University in 1979. He is a past president and fellow of both the American Society of Criminology and of the Academy of Criminal Justice Sciences. He was the recipient of the 2010 ASC Edwin H. Sutherland Award. From 2010 to 2014, he served on the Office of Justice Programs Science Advisory Board for the U.S. Department of Justice. He has published more than 300 works in the areas of criminological theory, correctional policy, white-collar crime, public opinion about crime and justice, victimology, and the organization of knowledge. Dr. Cullen is currently a distinguished research professor emeritus in the School of Criminal Justice at the University of Cincinnati. In this Journey into the Field, Dr. Cullen shares his insights on his career, the community corrections system, and the future of probation and parole.

Image 1.4

My career in criminology started with attending an inner-city high school in Boston. I was drawn to Columbia University's sociology and education doctoral program in the early 1970s. I had an elective, however, and decided to take a course in social work on "Deviance and the Social Structure" given by Richard Cloward, co-author of the classic *Delinquency and Opportunity*. I wrote a paper on labeling in education that earned a single comment—"A+ Good job"; this gave me the courage to ask Professor Cloward for a readings course on strain theory and illegitimate means. Because I read everything immediately, he asked me to write my dissertation with him 2 or 3 weeks into our course. I agreed right away and thus became a criminologist!

I am proud to reveal that I was one of the scholars who, early on, argued that correctional interventions should be "evidence-based." The evidence now yields two overriding conclusions. First, voluminous research shows that punitive community supervision is ineffective because being mean does not change the factors leading to recidivism (e.g., antisocial attitudes, low self-control). Second, effective supervision should involve three components:

- Officers should develop quality relationships with supervisees.
- The risk-need-responsivity (RNR) model should guide treatment, especially with higher risk offenders.
- Supervision should involve "environmental corrections," which focuses on reducing exposure to criminal opportunities.

I have some thoughts on the future of probation and parole. Similar to medicine, community supervision must become a profession in which officers have demonstrated expertise and embrace an ethic of care. Boilerplate conditions of supervision should be replaced by individualized supervision plans that are limited to rules shown empirically to be related to recidivism. Much like life coaches, officers should interact daily with high-risk offenders through mobile technology that sends affirming messages and serves as a hotline for those finding themselves in risky situations. Artificial intelligence is already evolving to deliver cognitive behavioral therapy, and it should be seen as a future resource for providing efficient and effective human services.

Characteristics of Individuals in Community Corrections

The characteristics of individuals on probation or parole is reflective of broader social dynamics, with young, Black men disproportionality interacting with the community corrections system. Looking at the most recent available data, the majority of individuals on probation in 2021 were primarily male and White. However, when you look at probation rates by race, Black adults actually have a higher rate, especially for those convicted of a felony, such as a violent or drug crime (Kaeble, 2023; see Figure 1.4). These characteristics have remained stable over time except for type of offense. In 2008, 50% of individuals sentenced to probation were convicted of a felony. By 2021, this number increased to 64% of individuals (with misdemeanors decreasing from 48% in 2008 to 35% in 2021; Kaeble, 2023).

The known characteristics of adults on parole demonstrate similar patterns, but Kaeble (2023) reports there is a greater percentage of males, Black individuals (37% on parole compared to 30% on probation), and Hispanic individuals (16% on parole compared to 13% on probation), as shown in Figure 1.5. Additionally, the study found there are a greater percentage of individuals on parole for a violent offense (36% compared to 26% on probation) or drug offense (30% compared to 26%). The majority of individuals on parole were sentenced to a 1 year or more in prison prior to release (93%). These characteristics in parole have also remained stable over time except for type of offense. According to Kaeble (2023), in 2008, 26% of individuals on parole were convicted of a violent crime as their most serious offense, rising to 36% in 2021, while drug offenses as most serious offense decreased from 37% to 30% in 2021.

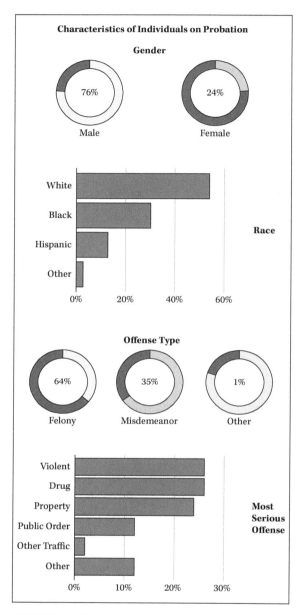

FIGURE 1.4   Characteristics of Individuals on Probation

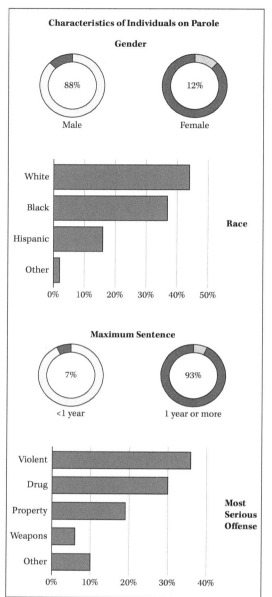

FIGURE 1.5   Characteristics of Individuals on Parole

Punishment Philosophies

There are five major **punishment philosophies** that set the blueprint for sentencing and other correctional responses to crime: retribution, deterrence, incapacitation, rehabilitation, and restorative justice. These punishments philosophies are highly influenced by social changes over time, particularly changes in economic, philosophical, and cultural approaches toward justice, law, and crime. These philosophical orientations are important because they can drive policy, decision making, and outcomes for people in the community corrections system. They often contain subconscious biases that influence the way we view crime and punishment. Generally, citizens with a politically conservative orientation tend to support retribution, deterrence, and incapacitation, while citizens with a politically liberal orientation are more likely to support rehabilitation and restorative justice. These divisions are fluid, with most citizens endorsing a mixture of these punishment philosophies in practice and more extremist views relying on one or two philosophies.

Retribution

During the early and medieval period (i.e., prior to the 17th–18th centuries), the dominant punishment philosophy was retribution (Nurjahan et al., 2013). During this time period, crime was often attributed to religious or supernatural beliefs. Retribution rests on the concept of lex talionis, which translates to "eye for any eye and tooth for a tooth." Prior to the development of formal law, retribution was used as a means of remedying "blood feuds" where private citizens enacted punishment. Over time, formal laws were written and enacted to contain uncontrolled vengeance by substituting a form of controlled retribution (Hudson, 1996). Retribution often relies on capital and corporal punishment, and the result is often a capricious distribution of justice. The focus of retributive policies is to remove discretion by matching punishment to offenses, with a focus on severity. Retribution is the only theory that is not utilitarian in nature. That is, retributive policies seek to enact punishment for punishment's sake without the pursuit of additional goals (e.g., preventing crime, providing resources and assistance to victims, etc.).

Deuxième Édition.

Dessiné par Chasselat   1823.   Gravé par Fauchery.

IMAGE 1.5   Cesare Beccaria

Deterrence

Deterrence is the dominant philosophy of the modern-day criminal justice system, though its roots start in the middle of the 19th century, during a time known as the classical period. Social changes, particularly industrialization and scientific advancement, led to the introduction of deterrence as a legal response to crime. Italian nobleman and professor of law Cesare Beccaria (1764/1986) wrote the book *On Crimes and Punishment*, where he argued that laws should protect public safety and order, not be used simply to avenge crime. Beccaria questioned the reliance on unfair trials, the use of torture, excessive sentences and fines, and the poor administration of justice. Beccaria's (1764/1986) approach to crime and punishment is summarized by his statement that "in order that any punishment should not be an act of violence committed by one person or many against a private citizen, it is essential that it should be public, prompt, necessary, the minimum possible under the given circumstances, proportionate to the crimes, and established by law" (p. 30).

Deterrence is a philosophy of punishment that endorses swift and certain punishment to discourage the criminal behavior of others. Deterrence is theoretically achieved on two levels: (a) general deterrence that is aimed at delivering punishment to an individual to prevent the public from committing crime and (b) specific deterrence that punishes the individual who committed the crime to prevent them from doing so in the future. General deterrence uses the three components of celerity (swiftness), severity, and certainty to discourage individuals from future crimes. General deterrence is based on the belief that fear of punishment leads to a reluctance to engage in crime (Siegel, 2013). Specific deterrence follows the belief that punishment inflicted on an individual will reduce their involvement in future crimes. Deterrence theory rests on the assumption that human behavior is rational.

Proponents of deterrence theory argue that crime "pays" when the benefit of the criminal act outweighs the costs (also known as a risk/reward calculation). Deterrence assumes that individuals weigh the benefits versus the risks prior to committing a crime. As such, policies that increase the costs of crime tend to increase government involvement, particularly through more rigorous police practices, prosecuting individuals more efficiently, and legislatively increasing the severity of sentencing for certain crimes (Pratt et al., 2006). Research suggests that deterrence has a limited impact on crime, including the use of the death penalty, leading to many academics arguing that the punishment philosophy of deterrence is overemphasized in the modern-day community corrections system (Pratt et al., 2006).

IMAGE 1.6 Abu Ghraib Cell Block

Incapacitation

Incapacitation is another punishment philosophy with archaic origins. *Incapacitation* refers to the physical or mental confinement of individuals to restrict their access to committing more crime. This approach includes incarceration into jail or prison, though it also includes the use of technological advancements such as the use of satellite data (GPS) to monitor individuals on "house arrest."

Incapacitation was a favored approach during the 1980s, as politicians found it more convenient to rely on mass incarceration as a response to increased crime rates. Proponents of mass incarceration highlighted research demonstrating that a subset of all individuals are responsible for committing most crime, particularly violent and serious crime (Wilson, 1983). *Selective incapacitation* is a term used to describe harsh and punitive measures directed toward this subset of more serious offenders, using the criminal justice system to monitor, incarcerate, or otherwise incapacitate those who offend at high rates. The popularity of "Get Tough on Crime" policies was reinforced by several examples of scholarly work that questioned rehabilitation. For example, Martinson (1974) examined 231 evaluations and argued that "nothing works." These evaluations included intensive supervision, psychotherapy, group therapy, vocational training, educational approaches, and medical interventions. Martinson (1974) came to the following conclusion: "With few and isolated exceptions, the rehabilitative efforts that have been reported so far have had no appreciable effect on recidivism. Studies that have been done since our survey was completed do not present any major grounds for altering that original conclusion" (p. 25).

A consequence of relying on incapacitation as a key function of the criminal justice system is that mass incarceration targets minorities and those living in poverty (Harding et al., 2019). Mass incarceration has devastating effects on some communities, leading to collateral consequences for the families of those separated from their loved ones. Social integration often declines in communities when high numbers of people are incarcerated, leading to increases in physical and mental illness, disease, and more crime in communities that are already vulnerable (Lee et al., 2014; Wildeman et al., 2013).

READING

What Works? Questions and Answers About Prison Reform
Robert Martinson

In the past several years, American prisons have gone through one of their recurrent periods of strikes, riots, and other disturbances. Simultaneously, and in consequence, the articulate public has entered another one of its sporadic fits of attentiveness to the condition of our prisons and to the perennial questions they pose about the nature of crime and the uses of punishment. The result has been a widespread call for "prison reform," i.e., for "reformed" prisons which will produce "reformed" convicts. Such calls are a familiar feature of American prison history. American prisons, perhaps more than those of any other country, have stood or fallen in public esteem according to their ability to fulfill their promise of rehabilitation.

One of the problems in the constant debate over "prison reform" is that we have been able to draw very little on any systematic empirical knowledge about the success or failure that we have met when we *have* tried to rehabilitate offenders, with various treatments and in various institutional and non-institutional settings. The field of penology has produced a voluminous research literature on this subject, but until recently there has been no comprehensive review of this literature and no attempt to bring its findings to bear, in a useful way, on the general question of "What works?". My purpose in this essay is to sketch an answer to that question.

Rehabilitation

The emergence of rehabilitation as a punishment philosophy is reflective of the advancements in science and technology that occurred during the 19th century (Nurjahan et al., 2013). *Rehabilitation* as a practice is rooted in the philosophical system of positivism, which holds that the source of knowledge comes from information that humans get from sensory experience, merged with reason and logic (Macionis & Gerber, 2011). Positivism requires the use of data that can be verified with the senses (i.e., empirical evidence); thus, positivism is based on empiricism (Macionis & Gerber, 2011). Empiricism has a strong focus on evidence—specifically, measurements that are discovered during experimentation using the scientific method.

IMAGE 1.7   Cesare Lombroso

One of the earliest examples of positivism was Italian physician and professor of medicine and psychiatry Cesare Lombroso (1835–1909). Lombroso used the empirical approach of positivism to measure the "born criminal." This approach argued that criminals have physical and mental anomalies (i.e., degeneration, in Lombroso's words) that could be identified when compared to mainstream society (Lombroso, 1876/2006). Lombroso measured the skulls of criminals and argued that there was a hereditary predisposition toward crime that can be recognized by physical defects on the skull—a practice called phrenology. Criminals were perceived to be atavistic (meaning a lower and more violent anthropological form of human), with Lombroso (1876/2006) mistakenly arguing that criminals occupy an evolutionary status somewhere between a person with mental illness and a primitive human. While vastly overstating the biological role in criminality, Lombroso and others did bring about the medical model—where individuals who commit crimes are viewed as different along biological, physical, and psychological markers. Following this approach, if the "risk factors" or differences in offender populations are addressed, then logically crime will decrease. In a modern-day context, this resulted in a movement away from the now-debunked idea of measuring the skulls of deceased criminals and toward measuring social and psychological factors that lead to crime, such as exposure to early trauma, a lack of opportunities for work, and other risks.

A dilemma facing rehabilitation is what to do with people if there is no rehabilitative treatment option. For example, this could be due to a lack of resources within a particular community or a lack of treatment for a specific condition. If crime is the product of a "sick mind," then the untreated may be subject to isolation, physical punishments, and even death. This was the premise of the National Socialist Party during the Third Reich in Germany as they cited Lombroso's work and carried out a medical-eugenic program that forced sterilizations, incarceration, and executions on criminals and people with mental illness. Fortunately, there has been an increase in awareness and education of the public about the social factors that drive crime, and eugenics is generally viewed as repulsive due to its historical application to vulnerable populations like those incarcerated, people with mental illness, LGBTQIA+ populations, and religious minority groups.

The use of rehabilitation to address crime has been aided by an increase in the bureaucratic management of individuals that can be used to divert people toward appropriate services to address risk factors. This movement has been supported by the work of two of the three founders of sociology: Karl Marx and Emile Durkheim (the other founder being Max Weber). While Marx and Durkheim have differing positions on the role of the government in punishment, they both developed the concept of the individual within society and the degrees of social cohesion—an idea that underlies rehabilitation today.

IMAGE 1.8   Karl Marx

IMAGE 1.9   Émile Durkheim

Over time, support for rehabilitation has waxed and waned. Up until the late 1960s and early 1970s, rehabilitation was viewed as an appropriate, more evidence-based method of responding to crime. Rehabilitation, with its focus on individualized treatment, requires government discretion to fit punishment to an individual rather than the crime (as is central to retribution). Rehabilitation involves components like indeterminate sentencing for judges to allow for the recognition of reform in the person, a parole board to determine who has been rehabilitated, probation and parole to provide rehabilitation within the community, a separate juvenile court system, and other practices. However, during the tough-on-crime era, many of these central components of rehabilitation came under attack.

Rehabilitation was criticized by both conservatives and liberals during this time. Conservatives believed rehabilitative polices resulted in punishments that were "soft on crime" and undermined public safety, leading to the victimization of citizens, while liberals believed rehabilitation might result in the inappropriate application of discretion and treatment of sentenced individuals, leading to a lack of procedural justice for those committing crime. The 1974 Martinson report helped to further cement the decline of rehabilitation, as it seemingly provided evidence that rehabilitative policies and programs simply did not work. It wasn't until years later in follow-up studies that researchers (including Martinson himself in 1979) concluded that those rehabilitation programs did work in many situations. However, the damage was already done, with support for rehabilitation declining in the decades to follow. The debate regarding the role of a rehabilitative punishment philosophy continues to this day; however, an extensive amount of research supports the effectiveness of rehabilitative models for community settings.

Restorative Justice

Restorative justice is "a process where all stakeholders affected by an injustice have an opportunity to discuss how they have been affected by the injustice and to decide what should be done to repair the harm" (Braithwaite, 2004, p. 28). Braithwaite (2004) adds, "With crime, restorative justice is about the idea that because crime hurts, justice should heal. It follows that conversations with those who have been hurt and with those who have inflicted the harm must be central to the process" (p. 28). Restorative justice is the broadest and most holistic approach to crime and punishment, and it operates along four foundations of respect, accountability, healing, and empathy, as shown in Figure 1.6.

Foundations of Restorative Justice

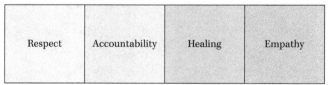

| Respect | Accountability | Healing | Empathy |

FIGURE 1.6   Foundations of Restorative Justice

While restorative justice is described as a postmodern movement (Nurjahan et al., 2013), it dates to early forms of justice used by Indigenous groups. Key academics like Howard Zehr highlight the role that the First Nations People of Canada and the Māori of New Zealand have played in developing "circle justice" (see Dorne, 2008, p. 167). Circle justice allows the victim and broader community the opportunity to express the harm done by the criminal act and provides the individual an opportunity to reenter the community without shame. Restorative justice takes place through the application of restorative practices that can be both preventative and responsive. This includes programs like victim–offender dialogue, family-group conferencing, restorative conferences, and "circles" for conflict resolution, support and accountability. These practices are designed to reduce crime and violence, improve behavior, strengthen civil society, provide effective leadership, restore relationships, increase accountability, and repair harm (Wachtel, 2012).

Restorative justice offers several potential areas for development in the field of community corrections. Restorative justice is the *only* punishment philosophy that places value on the role of community in preventing and responding to crime. This reconceptualizes justice beyond a traditional approach where the responsibility of crime prevention and response rests solely on the criminal justice agency and their staff (e.g., probation officer, parole officer,

FIGURE 1.7   The Intersection of Community, Victim, and Offender

police officer, judge, corrections officer). Instead, restorative justice requires a partnership between the criminal justice system, the offender, and the broader community. In addition, while the other four punishment philosophies are largely directed toward the offender, restorative justice recognizes the crucial role that the victim plays in proceedings. Sherman and Strang (2007) conducted a noteworthy meta-analysis of 20 years of studies on restorative justice that found positive results, particularly for victims of crime. This body of work showed that restorative justice enabled victims to return to work and normal activities sooner, reduced future verbal and physical abuse by offenders, and generated a range of positive emotions in victims (i.e., increase sense of security, trust, and self-confidence, decreased fear of crime and fear of the offender, and less anger and anxiety). However, more research is required to fully understand the role of restorative justice in community corrections, particularly for responding to serious, violent crime. Procedural justice, social integration, and the need for community partnerships continue to be key concepts in the community corrections system, which is highlighted in Figure 1.7.

◊ Officer Work, Careers, and Wellness: Punishment Philosophies

Punishment philosophies not only drive policies and programs but also influence the lives of people working in the community corrections system. Officers, staff, and other professionals working in community corrections have considerable discretion in their interactions with individuals under supervision and the sanctions that are given to them. The presence or absence of punishment philosophies held by officers can guide perceptions of people under their supervision, which in turn can influence outcomes. Take, for example, a probation or parole officer who embraces the conservative philosophies of retribution, deterrence, and incapacitation while they supervise a caseload of violent offenders. This officer may be less inclined to advocate for rehabilitative and restorative programs, and as such individuals may not receive these services. In opposition, a probation or parole officer who supports the liberal punishment philosophies may be less inclined to use "get-tough," direct, or punitive approaches with their caseload, which may result in fewer violations.

Punishment philosophies impact the physical and mental health of officers working in community corrections. While one may assume that the working lives of probation and parole officers are well defined, including the clear identification of goals, practices, and ethics, this is not the case. As far back as 1934, Reverend Ralph Gallagher addressed the National Probation Association and described the job as such: "A probation officer is in a sense a mental and moral physician. His task is to deal with the maladjusted, disorientated, and disintegrated personalities that fill our courts" (as quoted in Flynn, 1940, p. 12). Indeed, the working orientation of probation and parole officers has changed over time, and it continues to change. Officers are often left wondering if they are authoritarians, social workers, parents, psychologists, teachers, criminologists, advisors, friends, or policymakers to the people that they supervise. Unfortunately, the outcome of this confusion is low job performance, burnout, and a range of mental and physical health problems.

Over 60 years of research shows that confusion over one's mission, goals, and orientation at work leads to poor health, emotional exhaustion, and job burnout—with burnout leading to absenteeism, stress, and quitting (Allard et al., 2003). This impacts all levels of community corrections, from frontline staff to middle managers and upper administration (Kras et al., 2015). This dilemma is often based around an inherent contradiction in the job, where officers are asked to occupy both an enforcement role (via retribution, deterrence, and incapacitation) and a welfare role (via rehabilitation and restorative justice) at the same time. An *enforcement role* places value on making sure the individual is compliant and meets all their legal and organizational requirements. A *welfare role* requires the officer to provide support, guidance, and resources to motivate offenders to develop more prosocial behaviors. Differences in punishment philosophies become apparent when officers are in situations where enforcement and welfare roles become incompatible, with *role ambiguity* referring to the uncertainty that officers experience when they must decide the most appropriate course of action.

Building wellness and resiliency in officers requires an awareness of their punishment philosophies. Officers who are self-aware of their own personal philosophies will be more objective when interacting with others. Successful officers, also called protective agents, "view their role as fulfilling a dual responsibility to the offender and the community and thus aim to reconcile the therapist and police functions" (Allard et al., 2003, p. 281). There is evidence that when a probation or parole officer explains their role to individuals under their supervision, along with their orientation, the resulting officer–client relationship is improved. This can lead to the officer having more favorable attitudes toward clients, a lower sense of depersonalization, and a higher experience of professional accomplishment (Ersayan et al., 2022). The associated probation or parole agency can also build wellness and resiliency in officers, with safety training being a valuable tool to facilitate clear workplace practices (Rhineberger-Dunn & Mack, 2018). The goal with these strategies is to facilitate better decision making, which in turn will foster wellness and resiliency in officers, staff, and other professionals working in community corrections. Figure 1.8 provides a visual cue that reinforces the various dimensions of resilience.

FIGURE 1.8   Dimensions of Resilience

Diversion, Probation, Intermediate Sanctions, and Parole

There are four main strategies in the community corrections system: diversion, probation, intermediate sanctions, and parole. These are briefly discussed with reference to real-world programs and policies, with a focus on an innovative form of diversion: community courts.

Diversion

Diversion is a strategy designed to move individuals away from incarceration in jail or prison and into the community corrections system. In many cases, the risks and needs of individuals can best be addressed through community resources. Sentenced individuals may continue to experience social integration, steady employment, and family connections in the community, whereas these protective factors may vanish if they were incarcerated. Diversion strategies are more varied and available in misdemeanor cases when compared to felonies, though decades of decreasing crime rates have fueled innovative diversion strategies in numerous community corrections settings. Diversion strategies are particularly suitable for crimes where the individual is vulnerable, such as juveniles, people with mental illness, and clients who have substance use disorders. Diversion programs often feature an educational or therapeutic component designed to address individual needs. Examples include drug intervention programs, housing and welfare programs, case management programs, and crisis intervention services. Diversion is not only an ethical decision in many cases but also a financial one, as community corrections is a far less costly intervention when compared to institutional corrections. Diversion can occur at multiple points in the justice system, such as law enforcement or courts.

Law Enforcement

Law enforcement is often the first point of contact between an individual and the criminal justice system. As such, police function as an early filtering point to (a) direct people toward sanctions, punishment, and supervision or (b) divert people away toward treatment, resources, and care in the community. It has long been noted that negative outcomes occur when at-risk or vulnerable people encounter police and the need to train law enforcement for these interactions while also providing more resources and support for decision making. For example, research finds that during police interactions with people with a mental illness and/or substance use disorder, there was increased risk of police use of force and that this force produced additional injuries to all parties (e.g., citizen and police) (see Johnson, 2011). To address these challenges, diversion programs have been developed that provide police the discretion to take people who have committed a misdemeanor and who have a mental illness and/or substance use disorder to a designated center rather than to jail. This is a topic that is explored in more detail in Chapter 8: Special Populations and Caseloads. Vitale (2014) explains the use of police diversion in a modern society as such:

> Disorder can be a real threat to urban stability. Mass homelessness, untreated mental illness, and youth engaged in graffiti, performing on the subway, and dealing drugs on the street should be a concern, but the police are not the best, most cost-effective way to deal with these problems. We spend hundreds of millions of dollars a year on a revolving door criminal justice system that leaves most people worse off. (para. 11)

As described in this example, diversion practices seek to find non-punitive alternatives to respond to social problems and disorder. Importantly, diversion allows for a health-centered approach to mental illness and substance use, rather than placement in a legal or criminal setting.

Pretrial Diversion

Another area of diversion highly relevant for community corrections is pretrial diversion. Individuals placed on pretrial diversion are supervised in the community by a pretrial supervision officer (who sometimes also supervises individuals sentenced to probation as well) in lieu of incarceration while awaiting trial. Also referred to as *supervised pretrial release (SPR)*, this form of diversion is designed to protect public safety while also providing an opportunity for individuals to access programming and maintain social ties in the community (Lowenkamp & VanNostrand, 2013). Like traditional probation and parole, individuals placed on SPR must follow court-ordered conditions and report to a probation or parole officer. As opposed to pretrial detention, individuals on SPR can access community-based services, continue existing employment (or search for new employment), and maintain family and social relationships. The role of probation and parole is to (a) provide support while also monitoring court-ordered conditions and (b) ensure that the individual is present for their court date.

Community Courts

Another key diversion strategy relevant for community corrections are courts, specifically community courts. Community courts are designed to create positive working relationships between the justice system and community stakeholders, like residents, business owners, churches, schools, and social services. Community courts are neighborhood-focused problem-solving courts that address low-level crimes through collaboration with multiple stakeholders. These low-level "quality of life" offenses would traditionally be addressed by community corrections, particularly via probation and intermediate sanctions, though community courts aim to divert individuals to more appropriate solutions. The first community court began in New York City in 1993; however, they are now common throughout the United States and in international settings. While the application of community courts is varied, they rest on the following six key principles that are closely linked to restorative justice: restoring the community, bridging the gap between communities and courts, knitting together a fractured criminal justice system, helping offenders deal with problems that lead to crime, providing the courts with better information, and building a physical courthouse that reflects these ambitions (Berman, 2010).

In a fascinating ethnographic case study of a community court in New York City, Christine Zozula (2019) documented the potential for innovative approaches that could deter convicted individuals away from community corrections and into more appropriate forms of punishment and services. This approach relied on the tenants of therapeutic jurisprudence, which proposes that "encounters with legal actors present offenders with opportunities for rehabilitative changes," and restorative justice, which proposes that "justice practices should ameliorate wrongdoings and reintegrate offenders into the community" (Zozula, 2019, p. 21). Typical low-level crimes reviewed by the court include "larceny under $500, public drunkenness, trespassing, disturbance of the peace, prostitution, possession of marijuana, and interfering with an officer" (Zozula, 2019, p. 55). The court was designed to acknowledge the role of underlying issues of poverty, homelessness, alcohol addiction, substance abuse, mental illness, and gender differences. This complexity of treatment responses can be seen in the following quote:

> The Women's Diversion Program was specifically designed for women who were arrested on prostitution charges. It was a two-week outpatient program run by Greenville Community Court staff that combined mental-health counseling, substance-abuse treatment, and self-esteem-building activities (among other things). Participants in the Women's Diversion Program were afforded much more leniency than other offenders because they were viewed as less culpable for their actions than any other offender group; they were considered to be victims of male pimps and of drug and alcohol problems. (Zozula, 2019, p. 70)

Courtroom stakeholders, like the judge, lawyers and court reporters, were often bilingual, which allowed for greater connection and communication with offenders. This enabled linkages for participants to racialized and classed job training programs (Chesluck, 2007). As one can see in Figure 1.9, the structure of the community court diverts low-level individuals away from contact with community corrections.

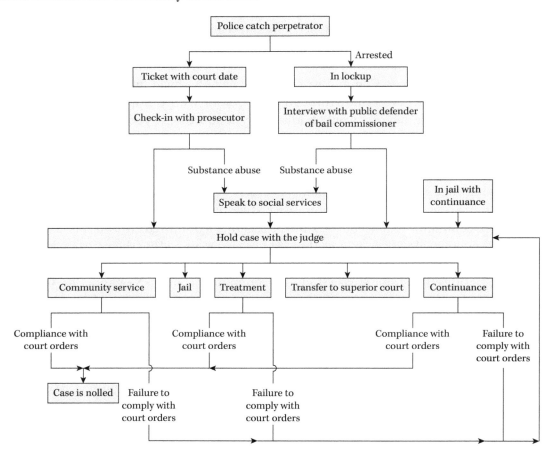

FIGURE 1.9   The Structure of a Community Court

There is certainly a need to fully measure outcomes related to community courts. Zozula (2019) and others have found that defendants, court staff, and the community shared very positive experiences about the role that community courts play in diverting low-level individuals away from community corrections and incarceration. Certainly, these people in most cases did not receive a criminal sentence or label following completion of treatment programs (e.g., alcohol/drug programs, anger management) and/or community services requirements. Zozolua (2019) found the most significant theme in participant narratives "was the humanity of the Community Court and the way the court responded to clients as individuals" (p. 98). This suggests that community courts have legitimacy as a problem-solving process in the community—one that can save taxpayer dollars, match offenders to treatments and services, and reduce the need to criminalize low-level individuals by using probation and intermediate sanctions. More research is needed to examine the gold standard of criminological research, the concept of recidivism and community courts, though this has been examined in more developed forms of diversion like mental health court, drug court, driving while intoxicated (DWI) court, domestic violence court, and sex-based offenses court (see Chapter 8: Special Populations and Caseloads). Diversion favors the categorization of people by their convicted crime, risk, and need, with community corrections serving as a key partner in these approaches.

Probation

Probation is considered a suspended sentence for which individuals are sentenced to probation in lieu of incarceration on the condition that they follow certain prescribed rules and commit no further crimes, which would result in incarceration (NIC, n.d.). Probation indicates that the individual has pled guilty or been found guilty of committing a crime by the court (distinct from diversion that may include those who are never booked into the criminal justice system). The offender then serves their sentence in the community as an alternative to incarceration. The root of the word "probation" is *testing*, which refers to a period where a person must demonstrate good behavior while under supervision. This includes mandated conditions for the individual where they are required to participate in prosocial activities (e.g., employment, education program, therapy program). Those on probation are also mandated to avoid antisocial activities (e.g., must refrain from possessing a firearm, must undergo drug and/or alcohol testing, must have no contact with victims). An individual who is not compliant with the conditions of their probation faces the risk of being incarcerated by the court. Egregious violations of probation can lead to probation being revoked completely and the potential for incarceration. Probation and the people who work in these agencies are detailed in Chapters 3 and 4.

Intermediate Sanctions

Intermediate sanctions include strategies that may fall between regular probation and incarceration, such as electronic monitoring via an ankle bracelet, community service, and intensive supervision programs. The term "intermediate" refers to the severity of the sanctions being higher than probation but less than prison (a topic discussed in Chapter 5: Intermediate Sanctions). These sanctions were created to defer costs away from institutional corrections and toward community corrections during times of rising jail and prison populations and costs. This has been expressed by Tonry and Will (1990):

> Much of the current interest in intermediate sanctions arises from political and economic pressures to devise credible punishments that can be imposed on convicted offenders for whose imprisonment the state would rather not pay. Policymakers are caught between the perceptions that the public wants criminals to be punished for their crimes but, contrariwise, does not want to pay for construction and operation of greatly increased prison capacity. (p. 1)

Parole

Parole is both a procedure by which a board administratively releases individuals from prison as well as a provision for postrelease supervision (NIC, n.d.). The root word for "parole" is *spoken word* or *promise*, as individuals on parole during the Middle Ages were asked to "give their word" that they would follow prosocial behaviors if released. This release from prison occurs prior to the completion of the sentence, as opposed to often-confused terms like "pardon," "amnesty," or "sentence commutation" where the sanction itself is removed. In the United States, different court jurisdictions specify a minimum period of incarceration that must be served until the incarcerated individual is eligible. An individual may use "time off for good behavior" (also known as "good time") to demonstrate prosocial behaviors while incarcerated as supporting evidence for early release. This can take place through a judge or parole board. If successful, individuals must comply with the conditions of the postrelease period while under supervision of a probation or parole officer. Much like probation, noncompliance by an individual on parole can lead to additional sanctions, including a return to incarcer-

Image 1.12

ation. Parole occupies a controversial role in the community corrections system—often the result of differing punishment philosophies, with critics believing it allows individuals to return to the community that pose public safety risks and supporters citing the need to provide resources and services to vulnerable people following release from prison. Parole and the people who work in these agencies are detailed in Chapters 3 and 4.

SUMMARY: THE CURRENT STATE OF THE COMMUNITY CORRECTIONS SYSTEM

The community corrections system is a massive, bureaucratic approach to distributing justice. The declining crime rates that have occurred over the last 30 years have led to more and more people being diverted from the institutional corrections system (jail and prison) and into the community corrections system, largely probation and parole. This creates an opportunity for innovative programs and policies that can meet the needs of individuals, victims, and the community. Communities of color and low-income communities are disproportionally impacted by the criminal justice system, and the trends and characteristics of those under supervision in the community corrections system reflects similar inequities. To address these complex issues, the functions of community corrections are explained with reference to punishment philosophies (i.e., retribution, deterrence, incapacitation, rehabilitation, and restorative justice). These punishment philosophies are also described in terms of officer work, careers, and wellness, as community corrections officers face role conflict and role ambiguity that can lead to poor physical and mental health. The four practical strategies of community corrections of diversion, probation, intermediate sanctions, and parole are also discussed. This introduces the community corrections system with reference to the intricacies of the system.

Scenario-Based Activities

	Case	Question(s)
1.	Officer Marks is a parole officer who believes the main goal of the correctional system should be deterrence.	How would Officer Marks likely supervise an individual on parole? What activities would they emphasize, and which activities would they deemphasize? How might their approach impact the experience of an individual on parole?
2	You are a probation officer responsible for supervising individuals who live in a low-income community with limited access to employment and education opportunities. An individual on your caseload named Darrell recently lost his job and is struggling to pay his bills.	How would you address Darrell's needs while taking into account the larger community context? What community-level resources and/or partnerships would you seek out? How would you work with other community-based stakeholders to develop a plan to address Darrell's individual needs and those of the larger community?

References

Allard, T. J., Wortley, R. K., & Stewart, A. L. (2003). Role conflict in community corrections. *Psychology, Crime & Law, 9*(3), 279–289. https://doi.org/10.1080/1068316031000093414

American Civil Liberties Union. (n.d.). *Mass incarceration.* https://www.aclu.org/issues/smart-justice/mass-incarceration

Amnesty International. (2020, October 6). *USA: Amnesty International delivers one million signatures calling for justice for George Floyd.* https://www.amnesty.org/en/latest/press-release/2020/10/usa-amnesty-international-delivers-one-million-signatures-calling-for-justice-for-george-floyd/

Beccaria, C. (1986). *On crimes and punishments.* Hackett Publishing. (Original work published 1764)

Berman, G. (2010). *Principles of community justice: A guide for community court planners.* Center for Court Innovation. https://www.courtinnovation.org/sites/default/files/Communitycourtprinciples.pdf

Braithwaite, J. (2004). Restorative justice and de-professionalization. *The Good Society, 13*(1), 28–31. https://doi.org/10.1353/gso.2004.0023

Bronfenbrenner, U. (1977). Toward an experimental ecology of human development. *American Psychologist, 32*(7), 513–531. https://doi.org/10.1037/0003-066X.32.7.513

Bronfenbrenner, U. (1979). *The ecology of human development experiments by nature and design.* Harvard University Press.

Carson, E. A., & Kluckow, R. (2023). *Correctional populations in the United States, 2021 – Statistical Tables. Bureau of Justice Statistics.* https://www.ojp.gov/ncjrs/virtual-library/abstracts/correctional-populations-united-states-2021-statistical-tables

Chesluck, B. (2007). *Money jungle: Imagining the new Times Square.* Rutgers University Press.

Dorne, C. K. (2008). *Restorative Justice in the United States.* Pearson Prentice Hall.

Ersayan, A. E., Çankaya, B., Erdem, G., Broers, N. J., & de Ruiter, C. (2022). The link between attitudes toward probationers and job burnout in Turkish probation officers. *Journal of Community Psychology, 50*(2), 727–741. https://doi.org/10.1002/jcop.22673

Fernandez, M., & Burch, A. S. (2021, April 20). George Floyd, from "I want to touch the world" to "I can't breathe." *The New York Times.* https://www.nytimes.com/article/george-floyd-who-is.html

Flynn, F. T. (1940, February). Training for the probation profession. Federal Probation, 4(1) 11–14.

Franco-Paredes, C., Ghandnoosh, N., Latif, H., Krsak, M., Henao-Martinez, A. F., Robins, M., Barahona, L. V., & Poeschla, E. M. (2021). Decarceration and community re-entry in the COVID-19 era. *The Lancet Infectious Diseases, 21*(1), E11–E16. https://doi.org/10.1016/S1473-3099(20)30730-1

Garland, D. (1990). *Punishment and modern society: A study in social theory.* University of Chicago Press.

Gramlich, J. (2020, November 20). *What the data says (and doesn't say) about crime in the United States.* Pew Research Center. https://www.pewresearch.org/fact-tank/2020/11/20/facts-about-crime-in-the-u-s/

Greer, S. (1969). *The concept of community: Readings with interpretations.* New York.

Harding, D. J. (2019, June 21). Do prisons make us safer? *Scientific American.* https://www.scientificamerican.com/article/do-prisons-make-us-safer/

Harding, D. J., Morenoff, J. D., & Wyse, J. J. (2019). *On the outside: Prisoner reentry and reintegration.* University of Chicago Press.

Hayes, M., Macaya, M., Wagner, M., & Rocha, V. (2021, April 20). *Derek Chauvin guilty in death of George Floyd: Live updates.* CNN. https://edition.cnn.com/us/live-news/derek-chauvin-trial-04-20-21/index.html

Hudson, B. A. (1996). *Understanding justice: An introduction to ideas, perspectives and controversies in modern penal theory.* Open University Press.

Johnson, R. R. (2011). Suspect mental disorder and police use of force. *Criminal Justice and Behavior, 38*(2), 127–145. https://doi.org/10.1177/0093854810388160

Kaeble, D. (2023). *Probation and parole in the United States, 2021.* Bureau of Justice Statistics. https://bjs.ojp.gov/sites/g/files/xyckuh236/files/media/document/ppus21.pdf

Kras, K. R., Rudes, D. S., & Taxman, F. S. (2015). Managing up and down: Community corrections middle managers' role conflict and ambiguity during organizational change. *Journal of Crime and Justice, 40*(2), 173–187. https://doi.org/10.1080/0735648X.2015.1085889

Lee, H., Wildeman, C., Wang, E. A., Matusko, N., & Jackson, J. S. (2014). A heavy burden: The cardio-vascular health consequences of having a family member incarcerated. *American Journal of Public Health, 104*(3), 421–427. https://doi.org/10.2105%2FAJPH.2013.301504

Lombroso, C. (2006). *Criminal man* (M. Gibson & N. H. Rafter, Trans.). Duke University Press. (Original work published 1876).

Lowenkamp, C. T., & VanNostrand, M. (2013). *Exploring the impact of supervision on pretrial outcomes.* Laura and John Arnold Foundation.

Macionis, J. J., & Gerber, L. M. (2011). *Sociology* (7th ed.). Pearson.

Martinson, R. (1974). What works? Questions and answers about prison reform. *The Public Interest, 35*, 22–54.

Minton, T. D., Beatty, L. G., & Zeng, Z. (2021). *Correctional populations in the United States, 2019—Statistical tables.* Bureau of Justice Statistics. https://bjs.ojp.gov/sites/g/files/xyckuh236/files/media/document/cpus19st.pdf

National Institute of Corrections. (n.d.). *Probation and parole.* Retrieved October 1, 2023, from https://nicic.gov/projects/probation-and-parole

National Institute of Justice. (n.d.). *Community corrections.* Retrieved October 1, 2023, from https://nij.ojp.gov/topics/corrections/community-corrections

Nurjahan, K. J., Mohammed, J. I., Banarjee, S., & Paul, M. (2013). Philosophy of punishment in criminology: A historical review. *Journal of Media and Social Development, 1*(1), 79–94.

Oudekerk, B., & Kaeble, D. (2021). *Probation and parole in the United States, 2019.* Bureau of Justice Statistics. https://bjs.ojp.gov/sites/g/files/xyckuh236/files/media/document/ppus19.pdf

Pearse, M. (2021). Managing offenders in the community in the 21st century. In P. Birch & L. A. Sicard (Eds.), *Prisons and community corrections: Critical issues and emerging controversies* (pp. 230–245). Routledge.

Pratt, T. C., Cullen, F. T., Blevins, K. R., Daigle, L. E., & Madensen, T. D. (2006). The empirical status of deterrence theory: A meta-analysis. In F. T. Cullen, J. P. Wright, & K. R. Blevins (Eds.), *Taking stock: The status of criminological theory* (pp. 367–395). Transaction Publishers.

Prison Policy Initiative. (2018). *States of incarceration: The global context 2018.* https://www.prisonpolicy.org/global/2018.html

Rhineberger-Dunn, G., & Mack, K. Y. (2019). Impact of workplace factors on role-related stressors and job stress among community corrections staff. *Criminal Justice Policy Review, 30*(8), 1204–1228. https://doi.org/10.1177/0887403418787227

Sawyer, L. (2020). Sentencing Guidelines Commission approves 5-year felony probation cap. *Star Tribune.* https://www.startribune.com/sentencing-guidelines-commission-votes-to-approve-5-year-felony-probation-cap/566852112/

Sherman, L. W., & Strang, H. (2007). *Restorative justice: The evidence.* International Institute for Restorative Practices. http://www.iirp.edu/pdf/RJ_full_report.pdf

Siegel, L. (2013). *Criminology: Theories, patterns, and typologies* (11th ed.). Wadsworth, Cengage Learning.

Taylor, D. B. (2021). George Floyd protests: A timeline. *The New York Times.* https://www.nytimes.com/article/george-floyd-protests-timeline.html

Tonry, M., & Will, R. (1990). *Intermediate sanctions.* Office of Justice Programs. https://www.ojp.gov/ncjrs/virtual-library/abstracts/intermediate-sanctions

Tseloni, A., Mailley, J., & Garrell, G. (2010). Exploring the international decline in crime rates. *European Journal of Criminology, 7*(5), 375–394. https://doi.org/10.1177/1477370810367014

Vitale, A. S. (2004). The neoconservative roots of the broken windows theory. *Gotham Gazette.* https://www.gothamgazette.com/index.php/opinion/5199-neoconservative-roots-broken-windows-policing-theory-nypd-bratton-vitale

Wachtel, T. (2012). *Defining restorative.* International Institute for Restorative Practices. https://www.iirp.edu/pdf/Defining-Restorative.pdf

Wildeman, C., Lee, H., & Comfort, M. (2013). A new vulnerable population? The health of female partners of men recently released from prison. Women's Health Issues, 23(6), 335–340. https://doi.org/10.1016/j.whi.2013.07.006

Wilson, J. Q. (1983). *Thinking about crime* (Rev. ed.). Basic Books.

Wolff, E. N. (2006). The growth of information workers in the U.S. economy, 1950–2000: The role of technological change, computerization, and structural change. *Economic Systems Research, 18*(3), 221–225. https://doi.org/10.1080/09535310600844193

Zozula, C. (2019). *Courting the community: Legitimacy and punishment in a community court.* Temple University Press.

Image Credits

CHAPTER 2

Theoretical Approach

Intersectionality

This chapter introduces students to the theoretical approach of intersectionality. This begins with an introduction of intersectionality and a focus on the definition, components, and application to the community corrections system. Intersectionality as applied to community corrections has roots in criminological critical theories, with prime examples being radical and conflict theories, feminism, labeling theory, peacemaking criminology, and queer (LGBTQIA+) criminology. Intersectionality is employed as a framework that can link these perspectives, making it suitable to the complexity of the community corrections system. The complexity facing the community corrections system is best captured by three case studies that highlight the intersection of factors like gender, race, socioeconomic status, early childhood trauma, and crime.

LEARNING OBJECTIVES

By the end of this chapter, students will be able to:

- Describe the intersectionality framework in terms of definition, components, and application to the community corrections system.
- Understand the basic tenets of critical criminological theories.
- Synthesize the complexity of individual risks and needs.

KEY TERMS

- Best practices
- Critical theories
- Decarceration
- Intersectionality
- Victim–offender mediation (VOM)

CONTENT

Intersectionality allows us to focus on what is most important at a given point in time.

—bell hooks

Intersectionality

Intersectionality is defined as a methodology for studying "the relationships among multiple dimensions and modalities of social relationships and subject formations" (McCall, 2005, p. 1171). In 1989, Professor Kimberlé Williams Crenshaw wrote an influential article where the framework of intersectionality was more fully developed. Crenshaw argued that a range of factors merged to create social and political identities that lead to advantage (i.e., privilege) and disadvantage (i.e., discrimination). These determinants include factors like gender, caste, sex, race, class, sexuality, religion, disability, and physical appearance. There are three aspects to the framework: structural, political, and representational intersectionality (Crenshaw, 1991). *Structural intersectionality* refers to the impact of social structures working together to define the experiences of people. For example, Crenshaw (1991) explored how class, race, and gender structures in society impact how women of color experience victimization such as rape and intimate partner violence. These structural issues do not necessarily move in the same direction. For example, Pedulla (2014) examined social stereotypes of Black men who are gay, rejecting the label of the "double disadvantage" of race and sexuality. Instead, Pedulla suggested that common negative stereotypes of Black men being threatening, aggressive, and criminal may be offset by stereotypes of gay men being effeminate and weak. Such stereotypes exist in our society, especially when we are discussing justice, vulnerable populations, and health. As a result, structural issues create intersecting social identities that are complex and dynamic.

IMAGE 2.1   Kimberlé Crenshaw

Political intersectionality centers on the lack of political discourse and effective policy that can address privilege and discrimination. Crenshaw (1989) states, "I have chosen this title as a point of departure in my efforts to develop a Black feminist criticism because it sets forth a problematic consequence of the tendency to treat race and gender as mutually exclusive categories of experience and analysis" (p. 139). Early waves of feminism have been criticized for separating women and women of color into two subordinate groups. For example, the 1913 Woman Suffrage Procession was the first large-scale suffragist parade in U.S. history and was designed to provide voting rights to women. While advocating for women's rights, there was considerable resistance to the inclusion of Black women, including calls for segregated units within the march ("Colored Women in Suffrage Parade," 1913, p. 2; see also King, 1988). Similar criticisms of early feminism's exclusion of Black women were echoed during political and civil rights movements such as the Equal Pay Act of 1963, Title IX, and *Roe v. Wade*. These movements often centered on advancing the social status of White, western, heterosexual, middle-class women at the expense of other groups (McCall, 2005). *Representational intersectionality* refers to the convergence of stereotypes in cultural presentations, particularly negative media portrayals that reinforce sexist and racist themes. Representational intersectionality is often used in communications studies of music, film, and internet sources. Media representations are an important, though often inaccurate, means by which people develop perceptions of crime and punishment.

Intersectionality provides an analytic lens that can be used to examine the influence of various social forces simultaneously. This is particularly salient in the context of community corrections—a large, dynamic aspect of the criminal justice system where the social position of those involved (whether as clients, staff, or the public) are essential considerations. The origins of intersectionality in critical sociology, feminist studies, and critical race studies suggest that interlocking systems of power can impact those who are privileged or marginalized in society. However, Crenshaw (1989) adds that "conceptions of race and sex become

IMAGE 2.2   Official Program from the Woman Suffrage Procession, Washington, D.C., in 1913

grounded in experiences that actually represent only a subset of a much more complex phenom-enon" (p. 140). The goal with intersectionality is *egalitarianism*, which is a political philosophy designed to provide people in society equal rights based on the doctrine that humans are equal in fundamental worth or moral status (Gowdy, 1998). Policy solutions that promote egalitar-ianism involve the decentralization of power, the strengthening of existing civil rights, and the use of political and social reform to address existing inequalities. Crenshaw (1989) states,

> It is not necessary to believe that a political consensus to focus on the lives of the most disadvantaged will happen tomorrow in order to recenter discrimination discourse at the intersection. It is enough, for now, that such an effort would encourage us to look beneath the prevailing conceptions of discrimination and to challenge the complacency that accompanies belief in the effectiveness of this framework. By so doing, we may develop language which is critical of the dominant view and which provides some basis for unifying activity. The goal of this activity should be to facilitate the inclusion of marginalized groups for whom it can be said: "When they enter, we all enter." (p. 167)

Intersectionality has a focus on the interconnected processes that occur between social categories, like gender, race, or class, and the resulting interdependent systems of discrimi-nation or disadvantage. While originally applied toward legal theory, its application has been extended toward understanding processes throughout the criminal justice system. Within community corrections, an intersectional lens can amplify the strengths of social resources, potentially maximizing the community aspect of the system to rehabilitate, address health

JOURNEY INTO THE FIELD: DR. CREAIG DUNTON

◇◇◇◇◇◇◇◇

Full name: Creaig Dunton

Title: Associate Professor of Criminal Justice and Director of Gender and Women's Studies Minor, Western New England University

Dr. Creaig Dunton is an associate professor and researcher in the Department of Criminal Justice and Criminology at Western New England University. His expertise is in the areas of victimization, gender studies, sexual violence, and community corrections. This published work has appeared in academic journals, such as *Violence and Victims*, *Criminal Justice and Behavior*, and the *International Journal of Offender Therapy and Comparative Criminology*. As a professor, Dr. Dunton engages with students on topics related to intersectionality, gender studies, and the

Image 2.3

criminal justice system. He has won several esteemed teaching awards while continuing to study the intersection of gender, race, and community corrections. Dr. Dunton recently became the director of the Gender and Women's Studies minor at Western New England University, where he developed several key initiatives to engage students (many of whom will enter the criminal justice workforce). In this Journey into the Field, Dr. Dunton discusses intersectionality in the context of community corrections.

I entered the field of criminal justice as a researcher and professor following undergraduate studies in psychology and criminal justice. Having academically transitioned from a generalist to specializing in victims' studies and its relationship to gender and sexuality, my teaching has reflected this study of intersectionality. In addition to my position as an associate professor of criminal justice, this transition has also led to me taking on the role of director of the Women and Gender Studies minor, as well as teaching courses in Violence Against Women, Corrections, and developing a course on LGBTQ+ Issues in Criminal Justice.

As America has begun a course correction from a punitive to a more medicalized approach to substance use, the number of nonviolent drug offenders being brought into the system has been reduced all around. Women had frequently been subject to these punitive policies, so this is a step in the right direction. However, the intersectionality with gender, race, and social class is still problematic, with the requirements of community corrections (e.g., fees, meetings, drug testing) being especially burdensome on women of color who may be a sole childcare provider. Community supervision is of course necessary, but it need not be an additional form of punishment. The availability of mental health and substance use counseling is also an excellent approach to reducing recidivism and bettering society for all.

Issues such as fees for probation and parole need to be eliminated, as they create a significant financial burden and further negatively impact rehabilitation. Additionally, fees provide additional stressors that severely hinder progress regarding mental health or substance use treatment, which should be at the center of any community correctional efforts. Again, this form of criminalizing poverty is especially difficult for single mothers whose struggles are significantly exacerbated by this. An awareness of intersectionality, as well as an increased allocation of funding for mental health resources, is one of the best ways we have of achieving this goal.

needs, and reinforce public safety. However, an intersectional lens also requires us to examine the inequalities and entrenched biases in the community corrections system, as these weaknesses limit the distribution of justice in our society.

Critical Theories of Crime

It is important to note that intersectionality is not a theory but rather a qualitative analytic framework. Yet, with its focus on systems of power, particularly the differences in social status that privilege and discrimination bring and the resulting interaction between citizens and the criminal justice system, intersectionality rests on a number of critical criminological theories. **Critical theories** challenge the traditional approaches to understanding law, crime, and justice. These theories are diverse in their theoretical explanations and methods, though they share commonality in examining how factors like disadvantage, inequality, and power relations influence the causes of crime, how people who engage in crime are labeled, and the response of the criminal justice system. Critical theories endorse strategies of diversion, decarceration, and deinstitutionalization, making them highly compatible to the community corrections system and setting the groundwork for intersectionality.

The concept of diversion was addressed in Chapter 1 and will remain a key aspect throughout the book, as it argues for diverting appropriate individuals away from the community corrections system and into the care they need. **Decarceration** refers to policies and practices that reduce the amount of people who are in custody, incarcerated, or under supervision. As McMahon (1992) states, "in the corrections context, the concept of decarceration is used in analyzing the interrelationships of prisons with alternatives such as probation, parole, community service orders, diversion schemes, temporary absence, and other community programs" (p. 29). Deinstitutionalization aims to reform restrictive and coercive places like jails, prisons, and mental health hospitals to place individuals in the care of the community. Chapter 8 provides more information on previous errors with deinstitutionalization while also affirming its potential for success when applied correctly.

Critical theorists argue that harsh, punitive responses to crime with incarceration, isolation, and removal of rights limit any effective rehabilitative effect for the individual while also excluding the community from active participation in justice. These critical theories justify the use of diversion, decarceration, and deinstitutionalization, which has obvious implications for the community corrections system. Here, the community corrections system can perform more effectively if the complexity of factors like race/ethnicity, age, health status, socioeconomic inequality, education, neighborhood trauma exposure, and education are effectively addressed. While these critical theories are over 100 years old, with origins in Karl Marx's view of social inequality, more recent critical approaches have included a focus on race, gender, sexuality, and the community (Long, 2016). Several critical criminological theories will now be briefly explained with reference to the community corrections systems.

Radical and Conflict Theories

Radical theory is rooted in the work of Karl Marx, though it is interesting to note that Marx actually wrote very little about crime and criminal justice. Marxism is based on the idea that social conflict occurs as a result of the political structure, particularly the class relations that reflect the political, economic, and legal realities of societies. Marx was critical of capitalistic society, which he argued held intrinsic conflicts. A famous maxim of Marx, as documented in *Manifesto of the Communist Party,* is the statement that "the history of all hitherto existing society is the history of class struggles" (Marx & Engels, 1848/2004, p. 85). According to Marx, the capitalist mode of production divided people into a minority who own the means of production (i.e., the bourgeoisie) and the majority who produce goods and services (i.e., the proletariat).

Within a capitalistic society, the proletariat do not own land or property and thus only have their labor to offer. This produces a social contradiction whereby the bourgeoisie exploit and oppress the proletariat, which ultimate leads to a class struggle that can produce social upheaval and revolution (Gregory & Stuart, 2003). Marxism argues that for this reason, capitalism represents an economically unsustainable structure, with the prediction that socialism was inevitable. Despite the lack of specific reference to criminal justice, Marxism does provide insight into social factors that may influence crime. For example, the exploitation of working classes by the bourgeoisie may meet the current definition of white-collar crime. The working class also contains the "lumpenproletariat," which Marx describes as social outcasts of criminals, vagabonds, and prostitutes. Indeed, today's criminal justice system disproportionately impacts people who face economic, educational, and occupational hardships. The presence of these hardships, often in combination with one another, challenges populations under the supervision of the community corrections system and the staff who are responsible for supervising and helping them.

In 1916, William Bonger published *Criminality and Economic Conditions*, which introduced a focus on criminal justice within radical theory. Bonger argued that crime was largely a rational response to a capitalistic system that rewarded greed, egotism, and competition (rather than collaboration). As a result, people in lower classes of society were criminalized and punished more frequently and severely compared to people in higher socioeconomic classes. This line

IMAGE 2.4   Karl Marx

of reasoning received a boost during the 1960s and 1970s—a period in which citizens questioned the function of the social institutions, including the criminal justice system. Later works like William Chambliss's (1964) *A Sociological Analysis of the Law of Vagrancy* and Richard Quinney's (1970) *The Social Reality of Crime* lead to the emergence of the radical school as an accepted criminological theory used to explain the social and economic forces that impact crime.

Conflict theory uses a similar lens as radical theory in the belief that the law is defined by powerful groups in society to control working class groups. However, conflict theory argues that these processes are not only found in capitalistic countries but rather are root dynamics in all large-scale contemporary societies. To conflict theorists, there will always be a competitive process in society whereby values, interests, and behaviors are governed by the powerful as a means of social control. Conflict theory suggests that that power is not necessarily generated by social class but rather should be considered by the segment or group the individual identifies with (e.g., a political division between "liberals" and "conservatives" or differences based on social groupings). While radical criminology is centered in the ideological approach of Karl Marx, conflict theorists test the tenants of their assumptions using real-world data and empirically based research. As Bernard (1981) states, "Marx's theory was a theory of history, not a theory of human behavior" (p. 364).

In a book titled *Theoretical Criminology*, George Vold (1958) argued that groups naturally form in society because of common interests and needs, with collective action representing one key expression of power. However, each group may have interests and preferences that overlap; thus, the law serves as a tool to reinforce self-interest. When people engage in behaviors that the powerful viewed as a threat, these behaviors are labeled as deviant and/or criminal, with the criminal justice system serving as a means of oppressing the actions of minority groups. A similar approach to conflict theory was used by Austin Turk (1969) in *Criminality and Legal Order*, where he highlights the enormous power exercised by social institutions like the criminal justice system. Turk reveals that while some conflict may be beneficial to society, the functions of authoritarian decision makers such as police, judges, and lawyers are typically dictated by more powerful groups. For community corrections, interactions with law enforcement, courts, and institutional corrections (i.e., jail and prison) systems and staff are part of daily work tasks. In many of these interactions, the authority figure (i.e., probation or parole officer) may neglect to fully realize that the person under their supervision could face challenges because of their upbringing, culture, language, and experiences. Rather than a simple separation of rich versus poor, conflict theory highlights that individuals are influenced by a range of factors that can limit their success when engaging with the criminal justice system.

A criticism of both radical and conflict theory is the portrayal of criminal activity as the product of the justified expression of less powerful groups. Jock Young (1986) suggests that crime is often intraclass and intraracial, and by focusing exclusively on power dynamics, there has been a tendency of radical and conflict theories to downplay the severity of street crime. Young (1997) termed this movement as "left realism" and noted:

> There is no evidence that absolute deprivation (e.g., unemployment, lack of schooling, poor housing, and so forth) leads automatically to crime. Realist criminology points to relative deprivation in certain conditions as being the major causes of crime; i.e., when people experience a level of unfairness in their allocation of resources and utilize individualistic means to attempt to right this condition. ... To say that poverty in the present period breeds crime is not to say that all poor people are criminals. Far from it: most poor people are perfectly honest and many wealthy people commit crimes. Rather, it is to say that the rate of crime is higher in certain parts of society under certain conditions. (pp. 30–31)

Left realism rejects the notion of criminal behavior as an expression of social warriors. That is, those in poverty rarely challenge the powerful but are more likely to target and victimize other socially disadvantaged people in their own community. While recognizing the influence of power dynamics in society, left realists highlight the real harm and pain experienced by victims of crime. Jock Young (1997) and others found that the lower class, particularly low socioeconomic status and minorities groups, were doubly victimized, by both the powerful (i.e., white-collar crime) and by predatory street crime. As such, they are the victims of both the powerful and the disempowered (Young, 1997). Left realism reinforces radical views that theory should "create an adequate explanation of crime, victimization, and the reaction of the state" (Young, 1986, p. 25).

For community corrections, left realism provides insight into the overlap between committing a crime and being victimized, as a substantial portion of the population on probation and parole supervision often have experiences with both dynamics. This can be captured by the phrase "hurt people, hurt people," as trauma inflicted on individuals increases the risk that they will subsequently inflict trauma on others. The role of trauma in community corrections populations has received additional attention from researchers, with evidence-informed practices such as trauma-informed care (TIC) detailed in Chapter 7.

Feminism

Critical theories of crime often reference feminism, as gender is one of the most enduring and disproportionate facets of crime. However, progress for women in society has been unequal. The first and second waves of feminism have been criticized as excluding women of color, women of low socioeconomic status, and women who are immigrants from the communal experiment, political discourse, and subsequent social changes. Crenshaw (1989) found that "the paradigm of sex discrimination tends to be based on the experiences of white women; the model of race discrimination tends to be based on the experiences of the most privileged Blacks" (p. 151). These exclusions were recognized by criminologists who noted that while crime committed by males was decreasing over time, there was a pattern of increasing involvement of women in the criminal justice system. For example, in 1980 there were 26,378 women housed in federal prison, state prison, and jail, and by 2016 that population increased to 213,722 (Cahalan & Parson, 1986; Carson, 2018). Between 2006 and 2016, the sentenced female population in prison alone increased from 103,337 to 105,683 while at the same time the sentenced male prison population decreased from 1,401,261 to 1,353,850 (Carson, 2018).

Several key books written by feminist criminologists highlighted the intersection of gender and crime. This includes *Sisters in Crime* by Freda Adler (1975) and *Women and Crime* by Rita James Simon (1975). These academic approaches recognized the status and roles of women in society. According to these perspectives, women experience inequality through a lack of rights related to education, employment, and politics. While women commit fewer crimes than men, feminist criminology examines the delinquent and the criminal behavior of girls and women through the lens of a patriarchal system with references to expectations of gender roles and

IMAGE 2.6   2017 Women's March Rally in Washington, D.C.

the experience of abuse from men (Daly & Chesney-Lind, 1988; Simpson, 1989). This includes recognition of the different pathways toward crime that women and men experience (Daly, 1992; Richie, 1996). These pathways have a direct impact on the criminal justice system. For example, approximately 62% of women in state prison report having minor children, compared to about 51% of men, but 77% of mothers reported that they were the daily caregiver for their child(ren) before incarceration, compared to 26% of fathers (Glaze & Maruschak, 2010). The relationship between mothers and their minor children has been found to be a crucial component of successful reentry outcomes, particularly those involving linkages to probation and parole (Mignon & Ransford, 2012; Rose & LeBel, 2017).

Traditional theories and criminal justice practices have long ignored the unique needs of women, perhaps due to crime and victimization overwhelmingly involving men. For women under community corrections supervision, their progress toward meeting goals will frequently include needs related to pregnancy, family relationships, childcare, and mental health. There is an increasing recognition surrounding the importance for training, resources, and practices that are sensitive to these needs and the unique pathways toward (and away from) crime. The topic of gender and gender-responsive programs is more fully explored in Chapter 7.

Labeling Theory

Another theoretical approach that is associated with critical criminology is labeling theory. *Labeling theory* posits that deviancy and antisocial behavior is not inherently criminal but rather a reflection of mainstream society's rejection of violations of standard cultural norms (Becker, 1963; Mead, 1934). Labeling theory was developed from sociologist Emile Durkheim's functionalist approach that recognizes that the purpose of the deviant and criminal label is to maintain societal order; however, it contends that the label inadvertently results in more deviance and more criminal behavior (Erikson & Puritans, 1966). This is because negative labels such as "juvenile delinquent," "offender," "criminal," "convict," and "ex-inmate" carry weight and can be internalized by the individual. This can produce a self-fulfilling prophecy as people become those labels. Becker (1963) argued that those in positions of moral authority, such as legislators, create the rules and laws defining what is deviant. From a functionalist perspective, moral authority would exist even in a "society of saints," and behaviors outside the social norms would be met with punishment to preserve social order.

According to labeling theory, deviance consists of two categories: primary and secondary. *Primary deviance* refers to the initial act of deviancy, which could extend from dressing in a nonconforming manner to serious acts of crime. At the time primary deviance occurs, an individual has not been labeled as a deviant. Rather, primary deviance involves recognition of the violation of a social norm. *Secondary deviance* occurs in subsequent deviant and/or criminal acts and is at the center of labeling theory (Lemert, 1951). When an individual violates the law, they are labeled a criminal even when they have been law-abiding at any other time. Therefore, while correcting an individual's behavior is the primary purpose of punishment, the individual is instead stigmatized and placed in the category of the "other" (Erikson & Puritans, 1966). This engagement with the criminal justice system can fuel further acts of crime, as the individual begins to accept the label. Lemert (1967) states that secondary deviancy can become a "means of defense, attack, or adaptation" to the problems created by deviant labeling (p. 17).

This represents several considerations for community corrections. For juveniles engaged in deviancy and/or crime, Matsueda (1992) found that the way youth viewed themselves was linked to how their parents and others viewed them and their behavior. These "reflected appraisals" by others could strongly influence developing levels of self-esteem and self-concept. For those involved in the justice system in general, they can be stigmatized (or not) by involvement with the community corrections systems, suggesting that the approach taken by probation and parole agencies and their staff is influential on the people they supervise. For example, modified labeling theory examines how labeling specifically affects individuals with mental health disorders, including their decisions to seek or avoid treatment (Link et al., 1989). Indeed, research on people with mental health disorders who have been hospitalized indicates that the vast majority feel "devalued and discriminated against" (Markowitz, 1998, p. 339). Other authors have commented that labeling theory is closely aligned with the community corrections endorsement of rehabilitation (Cullen & Jonson, 2014).

Labeling theory in community corrections is often centered on consideration of the choice of words (or labels) that are applied to those engaged in deviant and/or criminal acts. For example, in an article for community corrections officers, John Hegger (2015) writes that the use of negative labels by probation and parole officers can have profoundly negative effects on clients, as they may adopt these labels as part of their self-esteem. This echoes Matza's (1969) earlier quote that "to be cast as a thief, as a prostitute, or more generally, a deviant, is to further compound and hasten the process of becoming that very thing" (p. 18). Hegger (2015) states that "probationer" may be a more appropriate term for someone under the supervision of probation—and one that can be removed when they successfully complete their probation sentence. Hegger (2015) suggests that "client" or "justice-involved individual" may also be appropriate, writing:

> The goal of community corrections is to break down barriers, to assist individuals with changing their mindset and getting them to "buy in" to the fact that they can make it through their supervision successfully. Officers spend hours trying to break down defensive walls during the first few interactions with an individual that has been placed on supervision. It only takes a few moments to destroy all of that hard work an officer has done, and put the client back on the defense again. (para. 3)

IMAGE 2.7 Historical Image of Alice Caush

Labelling theory provides insight into the conceptual processes of negative labelling while also creating awareness and sensitivity to words that may be stigmatizing and demeaning. Labels indeed carry weight, and a criminal record can be an impediment to relationships, employment, housing, and other important social resources. These are important considerations when probation and parole officers interact with people under supervision.

Peacemaking Criminology

In 1991, Hal Pepinsky and Richard Quinney developed peacemaking criminology as a means of explaining that crime and suffering are reflective of broader social differences in power. Peacemaking criminology is influenced by the nonviolent philosophies of Gandhi, Dr. Martin Luther King Jr., and elements of Zen Buddhism and Quakerism (Quinney, 1991). It is also most aligned with restorative justice practices that rely on collaborative partnerships that highlight the role of the community in addressing crime. To Pepinsky and Quinney, human existence is characterized by suffering, with crime being a particularly salient expression of this suffering. This begins with recognition that the criminal justice system tends to rely on violence as a means of stopping violence, which may be viewed as illogical. Indeed, the failures of the "Get Tough on Crime," "War on Drugs," and "War on Terrorism" in terms of both costs and any real impact suggest that traditional approaches might cause more harm than good. Peacemaking criminologists suggest that the use of violence to solve violence is counterproductive, as it also excludes the voice of victims, the individuals who committed a crime, and the broader society or community. Pepinksy, Fellman, and Neuman (1999) explain that:

> People cannot talk, listen together, and fight one another at the same time. Peacemaking is a matter of injecting doses of conversation into our social space-conversation that embraces the greatest victims and the most powerful oppressors of the moment at the same time. The sooner dialogue begins, the less likely explosive and violent relations will develop. The sooner the dialogue commences, the sooner power imbalances will be mediated, and the sooner peace will be made. (p. 616)

Image 2.8

Peacemaking criminology has policy implications that extend beyond criminal justice to more encompassing themes of human experience and society. Fuller (2003) offers the following principles for peacemaking: nonviolence (with physical force identified as being counterproductive), social justice (maximizing fairness and equality in all aspects of criminal justice and society), inclusion (encouraging stakeholder participation), correct means (rejecting coercion and discrimination), comparable knowledge (transparency in policy development and implementation), and the categorical imperative (follow the maxim "first do no harm"). These principles aim to reinforce peaceful approaches to crime responses, particularly through compassion and service, and the raising of awareness of alternative approaches toward addressing crime. In many ways, peacemaking criminology is perfectly suited for community corrections, given the connection between this form of criminal justice and the community. Braswell et al. (2001) highlight this in the suggestion that,

> The emphasis on community justice is not on the punishment of the offender, but the restoring of the relationship between the offender and victim, as well as maintaining order and social and moral balance in the community. Community justice therefore has a broader mandate than the traditional criminal justice system. (p. 141)

◊ Diversity, Equity, and Inclusion: Victim–Offender Mediation (VOM)

While peacemaking criminology may at first appear to be a "touchy-feely" or an abstract approach to crime, it features real-world applications that can be profound, practical, and transformative. One key area involves increased recognition of victims of crime and their families and loved ones. Victims have long been a disregarded component of the criminal justice system. For example, the original description of the criminal justice system consisting of police, courts, and corrections neglects any mention of victims. In the current criminal justice system, victims continue to have very little inclusion. Victim involvement is essentially limited to three aspects: a witness or victim account during a police response to a crime, a victim impact statement (VIS) read in court, and appearances or written accounts presented at parole hearings. However, these opportunities are limited by jurisdiction and the nature of the crime, and none are legally guaranteed. Victims are similarly excluded from engagement with the community corrections system, which is surprising when one considers that the individual who committed the crime and the victim may still reside in the same house, same neighborhood, or same community. In the case of a violent crime where the victim died, victimization extends to the family who are often left with numerous unanswered questions that can lead to depression, anger, and frustration. The individual who committed the crime may also experience guilt, remorse, and confusion over the criminal event and wish to provide answers or express contrition to the family. Peacemaking theory suggests that this unresolved negative emotion is a barrier to addressing justice in the community.

One method of addressing these needs involves face-to-face meetings between the individual who committed the crime and the victim (or victims' family). These interactions are a direct policy implication of peacemaking criminology, and they are termed as **victim–offender mediation (VOM)**. Other terms include victim–offender reconciliation, community dispute resolution, community reparation, family group conferencing, youth mediation, and sentencing circles. The first VOM began in Kitchener, Ontario, during the early 1970s when a probation officer convinced a judge that two juveniles convicted of vandalism should meet the victims of their crimes. VOM has since developed into a standard feature of many of the community corrections agencies of Canada, Australia, and the United States. The desired outcome of VOM is simply that "victims and offenders are able to develop creative and long-lasting resolutions to their difficulties" (Fuller, 2004, p. 85).

This effort toward conflict resolution is distinct from other justice interactions such as child custody or divorce hearings where the goal is a legal outcome. Rather, VOM centers on dialogue that is aimed to produce forgiveness, intro- spection, and change. In some VOM outcomes, there may be a reparation plan to provide financial compen- sation to the victim, doing work for the victim and their family, or engaging in acts of community service. Such rep- aration plans are not based in court ruling, and they must be mutually agreeable to all parties. While early examples

Image 2.9

of VOM usually focused on individuals convicted of a crime for the first time, youth involved in delinquency, and less serious crimes (e.g., property crime or minor assaults), the use of VOM has been extended to more serious, violent crimes in recent years.

In the context of community corrections, VOM begins with the training of officers and mediators, along with support from probation and parole administrators. These interactions can be sensitive and potentially traumatic, therefore requiring a competent approach by staff that is reinforced by teamwork within an agency. Trained staff are responsible for identifying willing parties for the VOM, and then they must prepare each party independently prior to the face-to-face meeting. This is to provide an outline of the procedure, guide expectations, and address any potentially negative emotions, such as risk of revictimization that may occur as a result of recounting the possibly traumatic, criminal event. During the victim–offender meeting, the victim (and/or their family) and the individual who committed the crime discuss the crime itself, including the impact of the crime on their lives and their feelings about it. A skilled mediator can move these feelings toward acceptance, resolution, and conflict reduction.

There is considerable evidence that VOM produces favorable outcomes. In one metanalysis of VOM used for juveniles, there was evidence that "the data regarding reduction of recidi- vism, the high levels of victim and offender experience of satisfaction and fairness in the VOM process, and high rates of restitution agreement completion supports the use of VOM as an empirically supported intervention" (Bradshaw et al., 2006, p. 94). According to Hansen and Umbreit (2018), 40 years of VOM practice and research show that,

> Victims and offenders are more satisfied with the process and outcomes than with the courts, they are more likely to draft and complete restitution agreements, they derive psychosocial benefits, the process is less expensive, crime victims are more likely to receive apologies from offenders, and offenders are less likely to recidivate. (p. 99)

Students who would like to learn more about VOM can search the internet for videos of real- world examples, many showing intense and emotional interactions. Students should begin this research with recognition of the unique role of victims. Rather than being relegated to powerless positions in a traditional model of justice, victims and their families are placed in a more direct and powerful role. (Note: Even the term "VOM" places the word "victim" before the word "offender.") Students should also search for videos that include members of the broader community, with examples including justice within Indigenous tribes and groups. A final mention must include student expectations, as they will likely find videos where a physically intimidating individual who committed a crime meets with victims and their families who appear small, frail, and weak; students are often surprised to find at the end of the VOM that the victims and their families remain calm and composed while the individual becomes very emotional and distressed (usually because enormous amounts of guilt have been released). This highlights the complexity of crime occurring in the community and the potential for alternative approaches to remediation.

Queer (LGBTQIA+) Criminology

Criminological theories often reflect the experiences of dominant groups in society and rely on historical, political, and cultural assumptions about crime and criminal justice populations. Critical criminological theories often address the gaps in knowledge about groups that are unique in their demographic portrait (e.g., gender, race, sexual orientation). As Woods (2017) explains, "in the criminological literature, there is little attention to lesbians, bisexuals, and transgender people, and even less attention to intersectional issues involving LGBTQ identity and race, ethnicity, class, and gender" (p. 135). In response, the criminal justice experiences of lesbian, gay, bisexual, transgender, queer, questioning, intersex, asexual, and more (LGBTQIA+)

Image 2.10

people has been included under the broad umbrella of "queer criminology." This approach tends to focus on the intersection between LGBTQIA+ people as both those committing crimes and victims within the criminal justice system, as well as the experiences of LGBTQIA+ people in other roles such as working as probation and parole officers.

LGBTQIA+ identity and its relation to the criminal justice system have occupied an often conflicting and confusing role in our society. For example, in 1952 the American Psychiatric Association's *Diagnostic and Statistical Manual of Mental Disorders* (*DSM-1*) listed homosexuality as a mental disorder. Additionally, sexual acts between consenting LGBTQIA+ people were often labeled deviant and even criminal, resulting in some LGBTQIA+ people seeking inappropriate medical and psychiatric treatment to alter their sexual orientations and gender identities. This included severe interventions, such as electroshock treatment, castration, and lobotomy. In the United States during this time, the act of sodomy was deemed a felony in every state with a punishment of imprisonment and/or hard labor, with the law disproportionately aimed at LGBTQIA+ groups (Canaday, 2008). In contrast, in 1957 England, the Committee on Homosexual Offenses and Prostitution released the "Wolfenden Report" that concluded that criminalization was an inappropriate response to private consensual same-sex conduct and prostitution. The 1980s introduced a movement toward antidiscrimination that aimed to "move discussions about LGBT identity and crime away from viewing LGBT people as *deviant* sexual *offenders* toward viewing them as innocent and *nondeviant* hate crime *victims*" (Woods, 2017, p. 130).

Today, significant discrimination remains for LGBTQIA+ populations with regard to serving in the military, seeking employment, and adopting children—among other issues. There has also been the reemergence of conversion therapy, which uses unscientific and potentially dangerous methods in an attempt to alter an individual's sexual orientation. The American Psychiatric Association (2010) opposes conversion therapy because it disseminates unscientific views about sexual orientation that lead to social harm, and it remains an unethical practice for mental health professionals. At the international level, engagement in same-sex sexual behavior still carries risk of contact with the criminal justice system. Queer criminology acknowledges this long-term discrimination and oppression in the context of the unique pathways toward crime that LGBTQIA+ populations occupy. This interaction is often facilitated by a range of factors that increase the risk of interaction with the community corrections system. The effects of discriminatory

Image 2.11

practices, family rejection, and abuse have produced estimates of 20%–40% of homeless youth being LGBTQIA+, which increases risk of sexual, physical, and verbal victimization (Woods, 2017). This pattern becomes more severe in vulnerable LGBTQIA+ populations, such as people of color, transgender people, undocumented people, people living with HIV, and people with low-income (Woods, 2017).

Queer criminology has relevance for the community corrections system with practical approaches to addressing the unique risks and needs of this population. This begins with training probation and parole officers in best practices for addressing LGBTQIA+ groups, including openness to creating safe spaces, inclusive language, and recognition of nontraditional relationships. Agency officers benefit from understanding the impact of hate crimes on the broader community, as they are often in a position to minimize the social isolation and discrimination experienced by LGBTQIA+ people. This may require partnerships with public health and mental health agencies to maximize outcomes.

Intersectionality Case Studies

Critical theories of crime "are centered on capitalism, stratification and inequality, patriarchy, modernity, war making, and monolithic approaches to crime" (Barlow & Kauzlarich, 2010, p. 128). Beyond the five critical theories presented here, there is a range of critical approaches including though not limited to rural criminology, cultural criminology (including media studies), postmodern criminology, masculinities and crime, green/environmental criminology, convict criminology, and white-collar crime (crimes of the powerful). One pervasive theme in all critical criminological theories is the role of power in various criminal justice systems, including the inequitable distribution of justice. Community corrections is one component of the criminal justice system that can reflect broader societal power relationships and inequalities (including discrimination, oppression, and other harms). While critical theories have developed from basic origins, they are now a major subdiscipline in the field of criminology, though one criticism has been a lack of integration. As such, critical theories share goals and are diverse in breadth and scope, though they are often applied in isolation.

Intersectionality offers utility, as it allows the combination of various critical theories to better explain how multiple factors merge to influence crime and the community corrections system. While this explanation is theoretical, real-world **case studies** are provided to highlight intersectionality. The following case studies are based on composites of real-world profiles, and they have been reviewed for accuracy by experts in criminology and law, probation and parole officers, and by people who have been on probation and parole supervision. These case studies reflect the diversity and complexity of people who interact with the community corrections systems. As you read each case study, you should consider the significance of the critical theories listed above. Intersectionality reflects the nuances of the risks and needs found in each person's unique circumstances.

Case Study 1: Jasmine

Jasmine is a Hispanic transgender women who is 30 years of age, and she resides in Chicago, Illinois.

Image 2.12

Jasmine was born in Chicago to undocumented immigrant parents from Mexico. Jasmine was identified as male at birth and given the name José. José's childhood was relatively good, though his father was often away from the house working long hours in construction while his mother had varied jobs such as cleaning houses and babysitting. José was often left at home with his three sisters, and he enjoyed their company, love, and affection. José's sisters were responsible for most of the caregiving, including cleaning the house and cooking meals. From an early age, José was taught to fear law enforcement, as they could break the family apart. He also learned that the family unit had a strong cultural connection to other undocumented families in the neighborhood. During his childhood, José was more comfortable with traditional female activities like dressing up in his sisters' clothing, playing with their makeup, and watching media that his sisters enjoyed.

During kindergarten, José was yelled at by a teacher for going to the girl's bathroom at school. It was the first time that he realized he was different from other boys. At school he continued to enjoy the company of girls more than boys, and he was more comfortable engaging in games with girls. He was a conscientious student who enjoyed school and a tight-knit home life. This pattern continued for several years with several indications of gender fluidity, such as at age 7 when José refused to cut his hair and expressed being more comfortable wearing his sisters' clothing. When José was 9, his father Alejandro injured his back on a construction site and was forced to stay at home on rest for a month. During this time, Alejandro noticed his son's behaviors and he became very critical and angry. Alejandro would verbally abuse José and call him names. Alejandro also blamed his wife, Maria, and his three daughters who he believed had caused these behaviors. Yet, José was confused, as while he was born a male, he never felt like he was meant to be in a male body. José did not understand his father's anger and he increasingly felt threatened and vulnerable. Alejandro returned to work after the month, but this led to a constant battle, with Alejandro attempting to force José to have a girlfriend, wear traditional masculine clothing, and act "a certain way."

By age 15 the situation in the house was very stressful, and José reacted by becoming more comfortable with his gender fluidity and developing friendships with students at school who identified as being gay or bisexual. This infuriated Alejandro, who told José to leave the house. At age 16, José left the house, much to the distress of his mother and sisters. José would say, "I love my dad, but he is a very traditional person." José then lived with a female friend from school who identified as a lesbian; her name was Juanita. Juanita also faced social isolation, as her family had rejected her, and she sold marijuana as a means of having her own apartment.

This was a confusing time for José because on one hand he was embracing his predominantly feminine gender identity and presentation, though on the other hand he faced isolation from his family, which produced symptoms of anxiety, panic disorder, and obsessive-compulsive behaviors. José expressed that he felt most "normal" when presenting as a female and that it was only when other people said he was not normal that he had a problem. It was during this time that José changed his personal pronoun from "he" to "she" and changed his name to "Jasmine." Jasmine told friends, "My name is Jasmine, a name which I picked for myself to become the wonderful transgender woman I am today."

At age 20, Jasmine had little in terms of work. When she applied for a job, she felt that she was not even considered due to the potential employer guessing her transgender status. Jasmine would frequent the local gay and lesbian bar, as it was a place where she felt safe and respected. On one evening visit to the bar, a man paid for all her drinks and offered her money to go home and sleep with him. Jasmine thought about her need to make money and agreed. Jasmine met the man several times after, and each time he paid for sex. The man had several friends who would also contact Jasmine to pay for sexual encounters. Between the ages of 20 and 30, Jasmine increasingly turned to sex work to make money, afford housing, and buy clothing. In fact, Jasmine was surprised by the significant money she could make from sex work. Jasmine practiced safe sex and used online advertisements to attract new clients. Despite having some safety precautions in place, on one occasion Jasmine was raped by a client. She felt unable to contact law enforcement and instead visited her mother and sisters in a state of distress. Jasmine's father returned home during this event, and he banned Jasmine from visiting their home. This left Jasmine in a state of hopelessness and with feelings of abandonment. Jasmine continued to engage in sex work until she was caught in a police sting operation that targeted online prostitution. Answering her door one day, Jasmine was arrested and placed in jail, where she encountered conflicting and mixed policies over whether to place her in the male or female units. As staff were deciding, Jasmine's attorney posted her bond, and she was released.

Jasmine attended a court proceeding for her charge of prostitution. Due to having no prior prostitution-related offenses, this was a class-A person misdemeanor offense. She received the mandatory minimum penalty of a $2,500 fine, and the judge gave Jasmine a probation sentence in lieu of a jail sentence (which could have been up to 12 months of incarceration in a county jail). The misdemeanor probation sentence did not require regular visits to the probation office, but rather Jasmine had to pay the $2,500 in fines and follow several standard rules of probation (i.e., obey all laws, obtain permission from the probation office before changing home address or leaving the state, and to not illegally possess, use, or sell any narcotic drug, controlled substance, counterfeit substance, or related paraphernalia). Jasmine was not a drug user and she felt she could abide by all these conditions, except for the one condition regarding continued engagement in prostitution. The last 10 years of sex work had protected Jasmine from homelessness. Nonetheless, she had been informed by the judge that a new charge of prostitution would constitute a felony conviction, with a mandatory minimum fine of $5,000 separate from any other sentence imposed. The judge and her attorney were clear when they told Jasmine that a new prostitution charge would likely result in a period of incarceration.

Jasmine wanted to comply with the requirements, though she could not see another way to make money and survive. Jasmine remained very uncertain and anxious about her future.

Case Study 2: Tamika

Tamika is an African American, heterosexual female who is 55 years of age, and she resides in the Bronx, New York.

Tamika was born in upstate New York to a Trinidadian father, Ronaldo, and an African American mother, Lauren. Tamika had a stable, middle-class upbringing along with her two sisters and one brother. Her father worked as a schoolteacher at a nearby middle school, and her mother worked as a bookkeeper

Image 2.13

for the school district. Tamika recalls these early years as enjoyable, and she held a strong connection to the community through her parents' active involvement in the local church. When Tamika was 8 years of age, her father passed away unexpectedly. Shortly after this event, Lauren moved with her three children to the Bronx, New York, to be near Tamika's grandmother for assistance with childcare. This move was also connected to Lauren finding new work as a bookkeeper. Tamika described this time as an adjustment period, as upstate New York had more rural areas compared to the urban boroughs of New York. Despite these changes in her life, Tamika excelled at school and was placed in advanced classes for mathematics. When Tamika was in high school, she started dating Marcus. Marcus was a gang member, though Tamika never saw him engage in violence or criminal activities. For several years, they had a stable relationship, and then Tamika discovered she was pregnant. During this time, Marcus became more involved in gang activities to support his new child. Tamika gave birth to a girl and received help with childcare from both her mother and grandmother. Due to this assistance with childcare, Tamika was able to take classes in bookkeeping and retain employment for a large company in Manhattan working on budgets and managing money.

When the baby was 2 years old, police arrested Marcus on a charge of attempted murder, which was related to his gang affiliation and peer associations. Police raided Tamika's house, which caused her toddler and mother significant distress. They discovered a handgun and one pound of cocaine hidden in a closet. Tamika was detained for questioning at the police station, but she was released when Marcus accepted responsibility for the illegal firearm and drugs. Tamika supported Marcus during his legal hearings, though he was ultimately found guilty of the attempted murder charge. Tamika was resentful about the fact that Marcus stored the weapon that almost killed someone in her house, along with drugs that could have harmed their child. However, she remained in love with Marcus, as he was the father of their child. Marcus received a 10-year prison sentence for his crime, with a mandatory minimum of

7 years to be served before parole could be considered. During the initial 2 years of Marcus's incarceration, Tamika visited the prison routinely despite finding it emotionally taxing. Marcus experienced depression after incarceration but seeing Tamika and their daughter kept him connected to the outside world.

In a relatively short time, Tamika's grandmother and mother both passed away, leaving her with little childcare support. At the same time, Tamika received a promotion at work that enabled her more access and control over the company budget. Tamika felt significant pressure from supporting Marcus and his incarceration, maintaining a job, and now a need to pay for quality childcare (particularly finding someone trustworthy to drop off and pick up her child from school). After several attempts to identify a child caretaker, Tamika felt frustrated and realized she needed to budget a higher amount of money to get better help. The amount she needed for childcare made her think about moving away from the New York area, though Marcus's prison was located close to her home, and she wanted to keep that connection between Marcus and their daughter. Marcus added to these pressures, as he wanted to fight his case and needed $1,000 more to pay for a lawyer. Tamika felt very lost without the social support of her mother and grandmother.

One day at work, Tamika realized that she had considerable control over the way in which the company funds were recorded. This centered around a 3-day delay between the time the company's weekly budget was first documented and when it was finalized. Being short of money, Tamika used this 3-day period to take $1,000 to pay for the lawyer. Tamika later used money from her personal account to put the money back into the company funds. Tamika continued to engage in similar actions with the company budget, and while she recognized it as technically being a crime, she did not see the harm, as the money was always replaced in time. This led to Tamika opening several mock accounts to move the company's money around and cover her own financial needs. When Marcus needed more legal services, Tamika withdrew $3,500 from the company account and into her personal fund. While at work one day, Tamika was arrested by police for embezzlement. The company had been monitoring her activities, and the company attorney had initiated the charge in conjunction with the NYC prosecutor's office.

Tamika was surprised to learn that a theft or embezzlement of property valued at more than $3,000 is third-degree larceny—that is, a Class D felony in the state of New York. An individual convicted of this class of offense faces up to 7 years in state prison. Tamika was booked into a local jail but released following a short bond hearing. The judge considered various facts of the case and gave Tamika a probation sentence. This included placement on formal probation for 1 year with regular reporting to her probation officer. As part of the probation sentence, Tamika had to perform 50 hours of community service, repay the value of the money embezzled, and advise the probation officer of any access to a computer and/or bookkeeping work. Failure to complete probation carried the risk of incarceration in prison. Tamika has completed half of her probation sentence, but she struggles to balance paying the company back while also looking for new work (and with a criminal record) and continuing to support her daughter and Marcus.

Case Study 3: William

William is a White, heterosexual male who is 20 years of age and resides in Baton Rouge, Louisiana.

William's childhood was turbulent, featuring constant drug and alcohol use by his young parents. While pregnant, William's mother, Veronica, smoked cigarettes, drank alcohol, and ingested cocaine. William was born prematurely and experienced physical health problems that resulted in several weeks in the neonatal intensive care unit (NICU) at the hospital. During this time, he displayed symptoms of fetal alcohol syndrome, such as being far below average height and weight, hyperactivity, and heart and kidney problems. Medical staff contacted police and social work professionals who met with Veronica, and she confirmed her use of alcohol and illegal substances while pregnant. Veronica was diagnosed with postpartum depression during her time in hospital. Doctors kept Veronica in hospital, as she continued to experience anxiety and depression, including moments of suicidal thoughts. Authorities decided to inspect the home before allowing Veronica to leave the hospital. Here they found William's father, Kenneth, dealing drugs in a ramshackle house with no electricity. There was also evidence of family pets not being looked after.

Authorities petitioned the court to have William placed in foster care, and the judge agreed. William was placed in a foster care home that was stable, comfortable, and with several siblings. During this time, Veronica would stop taking drugs for short periods of time and petition the court for custody. However, home visits by social workers with interviews showed that she could not provide a safe home. Visits were restricted to one weekend a month, though they would often unsettle William. The foster parents were older, and William had a good childhood until the age of 5, at which point both foster parents passed away. William was then placed in a group home setting in foster care. This environment was very turbulent and hazardous, with physical and emotional abuse occurring frequently in the group home. During these early schooling years, William was bullied by his classmates. William had several characteristics of fetal alcohol syndrome that remained, such as being smaller than other children his age, having delayed development in fine motor skills, and significant deficits in social behavior. His clothes were often dirty and needed mending, which would further add to the bullying.

During his school years leading up to adolescence, William reported the emergence of strong feelings of anger, frustration, and sadness. He would withdraw from peers and teachers and expressed a strong desire to be "left alone." While he was rarely invited to parties and social gatherings, he did attend one school party at age 15 where alcohol was available. William proceeded to get "black out" drunk, and he woke up in a nearby field the next morning. This led to William increasingly using alcohol as a coping mechanism. William's goal was to remain unnoticed in school, and he joined a small group that was known to engage in drug use. This included the use of pills stolen from the medicine cabinets of parents, alcohol use, and huffing inhalants like paint fumes. These binge sessions would increase following supervised visits by his mother, Veronica. Following high school, William worked in a grocery store stocking shelves and performing other menial duties. During this time, his use of substances increased to hard drugs, particularly cocaine and methamphetamine. To supplement his addiction, William would steal products from the grocery store and trade them for drugs. This also involved purposely leaving boxes of incoming products on the store loading dock to have his friends take them. During one of these episodes, William was arrested by local police, as they had been alerted by the store manager and the store was under surveillance. William was immediately fired from his job and prosecuted.

William was given a court-appointed attorney, as he faced charges of internal theft of a total value over $10,000. William's attorney recognized his alcohol and drug use issues and provided this information to the judge. The prosecutor recognized William as a first-time nonviolent individual convicted of a crime, and she was agreeable to a less severe sentence. The judge ruled that William would be placed on probation for 3 years, and during that time he would be liable for paying his former employer $150 a month in restitution. The county probation office was responsible for monitoring payment, and they were also required to ensure William attended an alcohol and drug addiction program. William's probation sentence was dependent on him completing both requirements (i.e., financial restitution and completion of the drug/alcohol program).

Without employment (and with a criminal record), William struggled to find housing, and he was forced to move in with his biological mother, Veronica. Veronica continued to use illegal drugs in the house, which made it difficult for William (as he was concerned about the urine testing requirements of his probation). Overwhelmed with stress, William visited a friend who had alcohol and cocaine. William binged on alcohol and drugs for several days. While driving home, William passed out and his car drifted into oncoming traffic, leading to a large accident that took the life of a man. William failed a field sobriety test and was immediately arrested. He did not remember anything from the accident, though he felt tremendous guilt upon seeing the man's family in the courtroom.

Following a plea deal, William received the charge of vehicular manslaughter with gross negligence. William can still recount the moment the judge said, "Gross vehicular manslaughter while intoxicated, with a minimum sentence of 7 years." While incarcerated, William had no visitors from family, and he lost the few friends and social connections that he had. Following release after 7 years, William was placed on parole, and he meets regularly with his parole officer. William has expressed concern about his future, and he often self-labels his status as being an "offender" who is on parole supervision. William meets regularly with his parole officer who has been helping him apply for a welding training program offered by the local community college. William appears to be at a crossroads, where his life can move toward more antisocial criminal activity or more prosocial outlets. With little social support, few friends, and a lack of employment, William risks further interactions with the community corrections system (including the risk of not completing the requirements of the parole sentence). However, William remains optimistic that he can meet his goals.

◊ Officer Work, Careers, and Wellness: Best Practices

These cases reveal the complexity of individuals under supervision of the community corrections system. They are not intended to portray every type of individual or scenario, as this would produce a wide-ranging list of individual backgrounds, pathways to crime, and probation or parole conditions. However, it does reflect the typical activities of those working in the community corrections system. The risks and needs presented by those under supervision can often overwhelm staff working in community corrections, many of whom may struggle to meet public safety mandates while addressing the risk and needs of an individual under supervision (as discussed in Chapter 4). Officers may be unsure of the correct course of action or how to best create a treatment plan for the individuals under their supervision. This can emerge as a component of officer discretion, as probation and parole officers have considerable latitude in the decision-making processes in community corrections. For example, Arluke (1969) conducted surveys of parole agencies as early as 1956 and 1969 and found that parole rules were unrealistic, unenforceable, and not standardized in any way (see also Travis & Latessa, 1984). Supervision rules appeared too numerous and unpredictable, thus leading to officers making consideration discretionary decisions. Arluke (1969) concluded:

> Some parole conditions are moralistic, most are impractical, others impinge on human rights, and all reflect obsolete criminological conceptions. On the whole they project a percept of a man that does not exist. Nevertheless, prisoners are required to sign the agreement, obviously with many reservations, before being paroled. The most tangible result is the growing number of violations of the conditions imposed. (p. 269)

Without clear guidelines and decision-making support from their agency, officers may experience role conflict and ambiguity, job stress, burnout, and other negative outcomes to their mental health (and working life). Officers face an overwhelming complexity of social problems that cannot be solved by individual decisions and intuition. What is needed to protect officers' health is training that promotes evidence-based policy and practice. The National Institute of Corrections (2017) states that "evidence-based policy and practice is focused on reducing individual risk, which in turn reduces new crime and improves public safety" (p. 3). Evidence based practices are validated by research and in the field, though they are often directed at broad agency policies, programs, and practices. When applied to decision-making of officers, a more applied term is "**best practice**" which is a method or technique that has been generally accepted as superior to other known alternatives because it often produces results that are superior to those achieved by other means and complies with legal or ethical requirements (see U.S. Department of Health and Human Services, 2003). Best practice can serve as a tool that can guide community corrections officer's decision making, thus reducing areas of confusion, or eliminating outright errors. Probation and parole officers can consider five focal areas that reinforce best practices: assessment, treatment, monitoring and drug testing, co-occurring disorders (i.e., addressing concurrent substance use and mental health disorders), and relapse prevention (Williams, 2007). These focus areas have remained constant over time and continue to occupy the attention and energy of officers.

Best practices are constantly being updated in response to social, criminological, and research-based considerations. For example, the National Institute of Corrections (2017) has a dedicated page with the latest approaches to best practices, with a significant amount of information aimed at community corrections. Best practices are valuable for several reasons. In terms of avoiding negative outcomes, the use of best practices can reduce recidivism and minimize lawsuits for the agency. With regard to maximizing positive outcomes, best practices improve officer wellness and resilience and promote a successful workplace culture. The link between best practices and the endorsement of evidence-based practices reputable organizations like the National Institute of Corrections can be viewed in Figure 2.1

National Institute of Corrections 8 Principles of Evidence-Based Practice
- Assess Risk and Needs
- Enhance Motivation to Change
- Target Interventions
- Skill Training with Directed Practice
- Increase Positive Reinforcements
- Engage Ongoing Community Support
- Measure Relevant Processes & Practices
- Measurement Feedback

FIGURE 2.1   National Institute of Corrections 8 Principles of Evidence Based Practice

More specific examples include the Council of State Governments Justice Center's (2011) outline of 10 steps for officer best practices broken into three stages, with the goal of reducing recidivism.

Stage 1: Setting the agenda for change

1. Engage and inform key stakeholders about the activities and goals of the probation and/or parole agency.
2. Review and evaluate current departmental policies and practices to determine which are effective and reduce recidivism.
3. Analyze data collected in departmental evaluations, determine actions in response, and develop a mechanism for overseeing change.

Stage 2: Redesigning departmental policies

4. Improve probationer screening and assessment processes.
5. Align supervision plans with screening and assessment results.
6. Redesign incentive and sanctioning strategies.
7. Develop recidivism-reduction training.

Stage 3: Implementing procedures to ensure quality and monitor progress

8. Develop and implement a process- and outcome-accountability system to measure performance on an ongoing basis.
9. Revise the personnel evaluation system to reinforce agency-wide recidivism-reduction efforts.
10. Review progress and set goals for continuous improvement.

This comprehensive approach to policy and practice must be reinforced through the tenets of public administration—that is, good leadership, effective workplace culture, appropriate standardization, and use of just rules. It is important to note that implementation of best practices within an agency can be time consuming, complex, and may take several years to complete and maintain. This may also include partnerships with other criminal justice systems, like institutional corrections and courts. This complexity is presented in Figure 2.2 which portrays the implementation of best practices in a probation system.

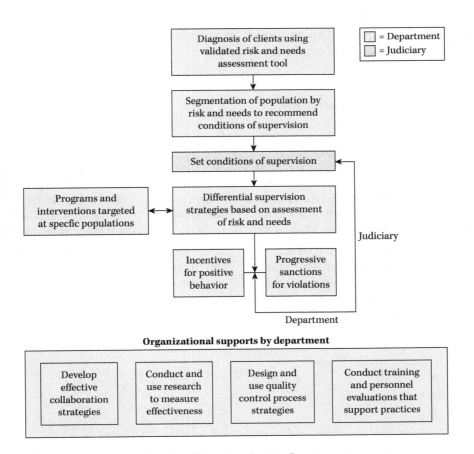

FIGURE 2.2   Multi-level Model of Probation System Components

SUMMARY: INTERSECTIONALITY AND THE COMMUNITY CORRECTIONS SYSTEM

In a recent interview with Professor Kimberlé Crenshaw, she reflected:

> Intersectionality is a lens through which you can see where power comes and collides, where it interlocks and intersects. It's not simply that there's a race problem here, a gender problem here, and a class or LBGTQ problem there. Many times, that framework erases what happens to people who are subject to all of these things. (Columbia Law School, 2017, para. 4)

Intersectionality as applied to community corrections has roots in criminological critical theory, with examples being radical and conflict theories, feminism, labeling theory, peacemaking criminology, and queer (LGBTQIA+) criminology. These theoretical approaches can be combined using an intersectional framework to better understand processes in community corrections. While theoretical and abstract, these approaches are rooted in real-world policies. For example, victim–offender mediation (VOM) is a practice that emerged from critical theory. The complexity facing the community corrections system is best captured by three case studies that highlight the intersection of factors like gender, race, socioeconomic status, early childhood trauma, and of course criminality.

Scenario-Based Activities

	Case	Question(s)
1.	You are a parole officer in a busy parole agency with large caseloads. You find yourself stressed and burned out, often making decisions with your intuition and little support from your supervisor or other officers.	What steps would you take to develop an understanding of best practices for your work? Where would you find these materials? How would you use them in your workplace? Do you think they would help lower your stress levels?
2	A probation agency has been approached by a community organization seeking to create a victim–offender mediation (VOM) program. Many of the people they would like to include would be under the supervision of the probation agency.	What are the potential benefits and risks for this program? How could you measure the program's effectiveness over time?

References

Adler, F. (1975). *Sisters in crime: The rise of the new female criminal*. McGraw-Hill.

American Psychiatric Association. (2010). *Position statement: Therapies focused on attempts to change sexual orientation (reparative or conversion therapies)*. https://web.archive.org/web/20110407082738/http://www.psych.org/Departments/EDU/Library/APAOfficialDocumentsandRelated/PositionStatements/200001.aspx

Arluke, N. R. (1969). A summary of parole rules— thirteen years later. *Crime & Delinquency, 15*(2), 267–274.

https://DOI.org/10.1177/001112876901500208 Barlow, H. D., & Kauzlarich, D. (2010). *Explaining crime: A primer in criminological theory.* Rowman & Littlefield Publishers.

Becker, H. (1963). *Outsiders: Studies in the sociology of deviance.* Free Press.

Bernard, T. J. (1981). Distinction between conflict and radical criminology. *Journal of Criminal Law and Criminology, 72*(1), 362–379. https://DOI.org/10.2307/1142914

Bonger, W. A. (1916) *Criminality and economic conditions.* Little, Brown.

Bradshaw, W., Roseborough, D., & Umbreit, M. S. (2006). The effect of victim offender mediation on juvenile offender recidivism: A meta-analysis. *Conflict Resolution Quarterly, 24*(1), 87–98. https://DOI.org/10.1002/crq.159

Braswell, M., Fuller, J., & Lozoff, B. (2001). *Corrections, peacemaking and restorative justice: Transforming individuals and institutions.* Routledge.

Cahalan, M. W., & Parsons, L. A. (1986). *Historical corrections statistics in the United States, 1850–1984.* U.S. Department of Justice, Bureau of Justice Statistics. https://www.bjs.gov/content/pub/pdf/hcsus5084.pdf

Canaday, M. (2008, September 3). We colonials: Sodomy laws in America. *The Nation.* https://www.thenation.com/article/archive/we-colonials-sodomy-laws-america/

Carson, A. (2018). *Prisoners in 2016.* Bureau of Justice Statistics. https://www.bjs.gov/content/pub/pdf/p16.pdf.

Chambliss, W. J. (1964). A sociological analysis of the law of vagrancy. *Social Problems, 12*(1), 67–77. https://DOI.org/10.2307/798699

Chesney-Lind, M., & Morash, M. (2013). Transformative feminist criminology: A critical re-thinking of a discipline. *Critical Criminology, 21*, 287–304. https://DOI.org/10.1007/s10612-013-9187-2

Colored women in suffrage parade. (1913, March 2). *The Times Dispatch.* https://chroniclingamerica.loc.gov/data/batches/vi_sepia_ver01/data/sn85038615/00296020011/1913030201/0362.pdf

Columbia Law School. (2017). *Kimberlé Crenshaw on intersectionality, more than two decades later.* https://www.law.columbia.edu/news/archive/kimberle-crenshaw-intersectionality-more-two-decades-later

Committee on Homosexual Offences and Prostitution. (1957). *Report of the Committee on Homosexual Offences and Prostitution.* Her Majesty's Stationery Office.

Council of State Governments Justice Center. (2011). *A ten-step guide to transforming probation departments to reduce recidivism.* Bureau of Justice Assistance, U.S. Department of Justice.

Crenshaw, K. (1989). Demarginalizing the intersection of race and sex: A black feminist critique of antidiscrimination doctrine, feminist theory and antiracist politics. *University of Chicago Legal Forum, 1*, 139–167.

Crenshaw, K. (1991). Mapping the margins: Intersectionality, identity politics, and violence against women of color. *Stanford Law Review, 43*, 1241–1299.

Cullen, F. T., & Jonson, C. L. (2014). Labeling theory and correctional rehabilitation: Beyond unanticipated consequences. In D. P. Farrington & J. Murray (Eds.), *Empirical tests of labeling theory: Advances in criminological theory* (Vol. 18, pp. 63–85). Transaction Publishers.

Daly, K. (1992). Women's pathways to felony court: Feminist theories of lawbreaking and problems of representation. *Southern California Review of Law and Women's Studies, 2*(1), 11–52.

Daly, K., & Chesney-Lind, M. (1988). Feminism and criminology. *Justice Quarterly, 5*(4), 497–538. https://DOI.org/10.1080/07418828800089871

Erikson, K., & Puritans, W. (1966). *A study in the sociology of deviance.* Cambridge University Press.

Fuller, J. (2003). Peacemaking criminology. In M. D. Schwartz & S. E. Hatty (Eds.), *Controversies in critical criminology* (pp. 85–95). Anderson.

Glaze, L. E., & Marushak, L. M. (2010). *Parents in prison and their minor children.* Bureau of Justice Statistics. https://www.bjs.gov/content/pub/pdf/pptmc.pdf

Gowdy, J. (1998). *Limited wants, unlimited means: A reader on hunter-gatherer economics and the environment.* Island Press.

Gregory, P. R., & Stuart, R. S. (2003). *Comparing economic systems in the twenty-first century* (7th ed.). Cengage Learning.

Hansen, T., & Umbreit, M. (2018). State of knowledge: Four decades of victim–offender mediation research and practice: The evidence. *Conflict Resolution Quarterly, 36*(2), 99–113. https://DOI.org/10.1002/crq.21234

Hegger, J. (2015). *How terminology affects the cycle of recidivism: Labeling someone as an "offender" can actually cause more harm than good.* https://www.corrections1.com/probation-and-parole/articles/how-terminology-affects-the-cycle-of-recidivism-gVORCn31zkOgMVdu/

King, D. K. (1988). Multiple jeopardy, multiple consciousness: The context of a Black feminist ideology. *Signs: Journal of Women in Culture and Society, 14*(1), 42–72. http://www.jstor.org/stable/3174661

Lemert, E. M. (1951). *Social pathology: A systematic approach to the theory of sociopathic behavior.* McGraw-Hill.

Lemert, E. M. (1967). *Human deviance, social problems, and social control.* Prentice Hall

Link, B. G., Cullen, F. T., Struening, E. L., Shrout, P. E., & Dohrenwend, B. P. (1989). A modified labeling theory approach to mental disorders: An empirical assessment. *American Sociological Review, 54*(3), 400–423. https://DOI.org/10.2307/2095613

Long, M. A. (2016). Critical criminology. In W. G. Jennings (Ed.), *The encyclopedia of crime and punishment* (pp. 1–7). Wiley-Blackwell. https://DOI.org/10.1002/9781118519639.wbecpx148

Markowitz, F. E. (1998). The effects of stigma on the psychological well-being and life satisfaction of persons with mental illness. *Journal of Health and Social Behavior, 39*(4), 335–347. https://DOI.org/10.2307/2676342

Marx, K., & Engels, F. (2004). *Manifesto of the Communist Party.* https://www.marxists.org/archive/marx/works/1848/communist-manifesto/index.htm (Original work published 1848)

Matsueda, R. L. (1992). Reflected appraisals, parental labeling, and delinquency: Specifying a symbolic interactionist theory. *American Journal of Sociology, 97*(6), 1577–1611. https://DOI.org/10.1086/229940

Matza, D. (1969). *On becoming deviant.* Prentice Hall.

McCall, L. (2005). The complexity of intersectionality. *Journal of Women in Culture and Society, 30*(3), 1771–1800.

McMahon, M. (1992). *The persistent prison? Rethinking decarceration and penal reform.* University of Toronto Press.

Mead, G. H. (1934). *Mind, self, and society.* University of Chicago Press.

Mignon, S. I., & Ransford, P. (2012). Mothers in prison: Maintaining connections with children. *Social Work in Public Health, 27*(1–2), 69–88. https://DOI.org/10.1080/19371918.2012.630965

National Institute of Corrections (2017). *Evidence-based practices in the criminal justice system: An annotated bibliography.* https://nicic.gov/evidence-based-practices-criminal-justice-system-annotated-bibliography

Pedulla, D. S. (2014). The positive consequences of negative stereotypes: Race, sexual orientation, and the job application process. *Social Psychology Quarterly, 77*(1), 75–94. https://psycnet.apa.org/DOI/10.1177/0190272513506229

Pepinksy, H.E., Fellman, G., & Neuman, J. (1999). Rambo and the Dalai Lama: The compulsion to win and its threat to human survival. *Contemporary Sociology, 28*(5), 616–617. https://DOI.org/10.2307/2655054

Pepinsky, H. E., & Quinney, R. (1991). *Criminology as peacemaking.* Indiana University Press.

Quinney, R. (1970). *The social reality of crime.* Little, Brown.

Quinney, R. (1991). *Journey to a far place.* Temple University Press.

Richie, B. E. (1996). *Compelled to crime: The gender entrapment of battered black women.* Psychology Press.

Rose, S. J., & LeBel, T. P. (2017). Incarcerated mothers of minor children: Physical health, substance, and mental health needs. *Women & Criminal Justice, 27*(3), 170–190. https://DOI.org/10.1080/08974454.2016.1247772

Simon, R. J. (1975). *Women and crime.* Lexington Books.

Simpson, S. S. (1989). Feminist theory, crime, and justice. *Criminology, 27*(4), 605–631. https://10.1093/obo/9780195396607-0013

Travis, L. F., & Latessa, E. J. (1984). "A summary of parole rules—Thirteen years later": Revisited thirteen years later. *Journal of Criminal Justice, 12*(6), 591–600. https://DOI.org/10.1016/0047-2352(84)90116-8

Turk, A. T. (1969). *Criminality and legal order.* Rand McNally.

U.S. Department of Health and Human Services. (2003). Administration for children and families program announcement. *Federal Register, 68*(131).

Vold, G. (1958). *Theoretical criminology.* University of Delaware Press.

Williams, T. H. (2007). What works? Evidence-based practices in parole and probation. *Journal Of Community Corrections, 16*(4), 5–7.

Woods, J. B. (2017). LGBT identity and crime. *California Law Review, 105,* 668–734.

Young, J. (1986). The failure of criminology: The need for a radical realism. In R. Matthews & J. Young (Eds.), *Confronting crime* (pp. 4–30). SAGE.

Young, J. (1997). Left realism: The basics. In B. MacLean & D. Milovanovic (Eds.), *Thinking critically about crime* (pp. 28–36). The Collective Press.

CHAPTER 3

Probation and Parole

This chapter focuses on the key elements of the probation and parole systems. This begins with probation, which is the largest component of the correctional system—far surpassing parole, jails, and prison populations. The history of probation in the United States is explored with reference to the early advancements made by John Augustus. This moves toward an examination of the modern-day probation system, where systematic functions, goals, and processes are discussed. Parole is the most severe and punitive form of community corrections, as it is designed to address the risks and needs of individuals released from prison. Historical efforts at parole were largely experimental and born out of necessity in early penal colonies. This included influential prison administrators such as Alexander Maconochie (Van Diemen's Land and Norfolk Island), Sir Walter Crofton (the Irish mark system), and Zebulon Reed Brockway (Elmira Reformatory). An overview of probation and parole systems across the United States is discussed, along with key issues, challenges, and practices.

LEARNING OBJECTIVES

By the end of this chapter, students will be able to:

- Describe definitions, functions, and processes that drive the modern-day parole and parole systems in the United States.
- Identify leading historical figures in community corrections and how their work influenced the development of the modern community corrections system.
- Summarize how parole decisions are made, including the types of information considered when making these decisions.

KEY TERMS

- John Augustus
- Parole
- Probation
- Recognizance
- Zebulon Reed Brockway

I've been completely fascinated with history because it tells everything about what's going to happen next because it's cyclical, everything repeats in general.

—Emilie Autumn

Probation

The vast majority of people who are convicted of crimes spend their sentences in the community under supervision, with most being placed on probation. People (and the media) often use the words "probation" and "parole" interchangeably, though they are distinct systems. As a rule, probation represents an alternative method of rehabilitation as ordered by a court and typically as a means of avoiding a sentence to jail or prison (i.e., institutional corrections). Individuals convicted of both felony and misdemeanor offenses are under probation supervision in the United States. Those sentenced to probation avoid incarceration but are subject to a probational period that can carry house arrest, fees, admittance to a rehabilitation center, and/or the completion of programmatic requirements that address issues like anger management, mental health, or drug/alcohol addiction. Today, probation represents the largest, most bureaucratic, and expansive component of the entire criminal justice system. Restated, if an individual is convicted of a crime, the most common of all correctional responses is probation, making the public much more likely to have interactions with probation when compared to other forms of justice.

JOURNEY INTO THE FIELD: DIRECTOR SUSAN GAGNON

◇◇◇◇◇◇◇◇

Full name: Susan L. Gagnon

Title: Director of Adult Community Corrections, Maine Department of Corrections

Director Susan Gagnon began her career with the Maine Department of Corrections as a juvenile probation officer where she encountered at-risk youth with significant risks and needs. In 2007, Director Gagnon was promoted to regional correctional manager where she was responsible for supervising and coaching a team of probation officers. This work included a focus on evidence-based practices and current correctional practices. In 2011, she became a regional correctional administrator for the state of Maine, supervising a nine-county division within the Department of Corrections of juvenile probation officers. She then transferred to the adult division of probation and parole in 2013 and coordinated all functions of a seven-county region, including programming, recruitment, and policy development. This career path then moved to becoming part of the ex-

ecutive leadership team for the commissioner of the Department of Corrections when she became the director of adult community corrections in 2019. Ms. Gagnon served as the chief administrator of community corrections for a 16-county division in the state of Maine. This work involved developing and implementing policies and initiatives, supporting the goals and objectives of the department, and providing guidance to the community stakeholders about the mission of the department. Director Gagnon has been active in engaging in partnerships with other agencies, serving as coordinator for the parole board and executive clemency board in the state of Maine and as a board member with the New England Council on Crime and Delinquency. In many ways, Director Gagnon is the epitome of the modern-day community corrections staff member, having worked from being a frontline probation officer to an administrative director of a large state agency. These experiences were shared in the following Journey into the Field.

I began my career in community corrections in 1997 when I was hired as a juvenile community corrections officer. Over the years, I have held various roles within the juvenile division, including juvenile community corrections officer (JCCO), field training officer, and regional correctional manager. Finally, in 2013, I transferred to the adult division of community corrections as a regional correctional administrator. My former supervisor, who had taken on the role of associate commissioner of the Maine Department of Corrections, recruited me to transfer given the shift in philosophy that the adult division was undertaking. I had expertise in implementing evidence-based practices, coaching and mentoring of staff, as well as training and policy development from my time in the juvenile division, which is the direction the adult division was moving toward.

For probation to be effective, departments need to be willing to look at data and current trends and adjust as necessary. To simply say, "This is the way we have always done it" is no longer acceptable. Maine has developed a new model of corrections, promoting the well-being and safety of everyone—staff and clients included. This also ensures our clients see less barriers as they engage in rehabilitative-focused services. This philosophy is focused on normalizing and humanizing our work in corrections.

I often say it's an exciting time to be in corrections, and I truly believe that humanizing our interactions with clients will result in much better outcomes, resulting in safer communities and more positive and safer working environments for staff. Departments should be data-driven, people-focused, continue to engage community partners, and provide education on the role the department plays in a client's success.

A Brief History of Probation

Understanding probation begins with a review of the term itself and historical foundations. The root word of **probation** is the Latin verb *probare*, which means "to prove" or "to test." This reflects the historical origins of probation as a form of judicial reprieve. During the Middle Ages in England and other parts of Europe, justice was distributed in a capricious and harsh manner. Standard punishments for crimes included branding, flogging, mutilation, and public hanging. Torture was regularly applied indiscriminately to both adults and children, with citizens having little legal representation or recourse. During King Henry VIII's reign, there were 200 crimes punishable by death, with many related to minor offenses. Such capricious forms of justice were illogical, as they encouraged people to commit greater offenses rather than minor ones, as there was no differentiation or standardization in the resulting punishment.

As England moved toward modernity during the 1800s, these legal approaches were questioned and adjusted. Progressive developments included a reduction in inhumane punishment along with increases in royal pardons, benefit of clergy, and judicial rulings. Judges were able to offer increased protection from overly harsh sentences, often through new legal terms like "sanctuary," "suspended sentences," and "judicial reprieve." One key progressive idea during this period was the practice of "binding over for good behavior," which was a form of temporary release during which people convicted of a crime could take measures to secure royal pardons or reduced incarceration sentences. They would then have to "prove" good behavior while being in the community. The evolution of a form of justice that valued probation occurred gradually. For example, in 1876 Frederic Rainer of the Church of England Temperance Society (CETS) donated five shillings toward "reclaiming drunkards" from the court; this involved the use of two missionaries to work with magistrates to release individuals on the condition that they were monitored by the missionary and accept guidance (The Guardian, 2007). Several years later this was expanded to eight missionaries who provided open homes and shelters to those convicted of a crime, along with vocational training and residential work.

Yet, it was not until the Probation of Offenders Act of 1907 that missionaries gained the official status of "officers of the court"—a title that was later changed to "probation officers" (The Guardian, 2007). The Probation of Offenders Act allowed courts the opportunity to suspend punishment and discharge individuals if they entered a recognizance of between 1 and 3 years, with the condition that they would be supervised by a person named in the "probation order." This led to the professionalization of probation in 1913 with the establishment of the National Association of Probation Officers, though there was a continued religious orientation with a focus on individuals avoiding alcohol, engaging in work, and attending church.

IMAGE 3.2 "The Drunkard's Progress," by Nathaniel Currier

In the United States, there was a similar movement away from harsh and capricious forms of justice and toward more balanced and rehabilitative approaches. A driving force was the work of scholars from the Age of Enlightenment, such as Cesare Beccaria. While the field of criminology did not exist during this period, Cesare Beccaria is considered an influential criminologist and economist whose writings were ahead of his time (Tittle et al., 2011). Beccaria endorsed an approach to justice that centered on deterrence, which remains the bedrock of the modern-day criminal justice system (see Chapter 1).

Beccaria (1764/2009) argued for reform of the criminal justice system in his classic text titled *On Crimes and Punishments.* This included the notion that severity of punishment should be limited to only what is necessary and the abolition of torture and capital punishment. These reforms were based on the concept of the social contract, where citizens surrendered some personal freedoms to protect the common good. According to Beccaria, when an individual commits a crime, they have breached the social contract, and they should be subjected to a predetermined and logically arranged system of punishments that deter future criminal conduct. If the punishment was overly harsh or capricious, then the criminal justice system failed, and there would be a reliance on tyranny, barbarity, and inequality.

The effect of Beccaria's work on the American criminal justice system was profound. After being translated into English in 1767, *On Crimes and Punishments* was read by statesmen such as John Adams and Thomas Jefferson and incorporated into the U.S. Constitution.

These ideas also guided the development of the American probation system. U.S. courts were now able to suspend a sentence for defendants based on a lack of evidence or to reinstate the case later—concepts that are taken for granted today. Judges were given more discretion to dismiss minor technicalities that could unfairly impact the defendant. New practices that paved the way for early probation included early forms of bail known as "good aberrance" or "security for good behavior." These allowed defendants the opportunity to pay a fee as a form of a guarantee they would engage in prosocial behavior in the community. The combination of the court being able to suspend a sentence and the early use of recognizance where a defendant avoided or delayed incarceration represent the early forms of probation.

IMAGE 3.3 The United States Constitution

Recognizance is a particularly important concept, as without recognizance there would be no probation system. **Recognizance** as a concept has remained stable over time, originally defined as follows:

> A conditional pledge of money undertaken by a person before a court which, if the person defaults, the person or their sureties will forfeit that sum. It is an obligation of record, entered into before a court or magistrate duly authorized, whereby the party bound acknowledges (recognizes) that they owe a personal debt to the state. A recognizance is subject to a "defeasance"; that is, the obligation will be avoided if person bound does some particular act, such as appearing in court on a particular day, or keeping the peace. (Chisholm, 1911, p. 958)

John Augustus (Early Probation in the United States)

Early probation in the United States is credited to the work of **John Augustus** and his work in advocacy for vulnerable populations. John Augustus was born in 1785 in Woburn, Massachusetts, and he is known as the "Father of Probation" (Fields, 2012). Like earlier efforts that centered on alcohol, Augustus was a member of the Washington Total Abstinence Society, a group that argued that rehabilitative and religious efforts directed at "poor drunks and petty criminals" were preferable over harsh mandatory sentences and incarceration (Fields, 2012, p. 17). These "Washingtonians" favored moral therapy, empathy, and understanding as a primary approach to rehabilitation. A rehabilitative orientation guided John Augustus, and he was a successful businessman who had the means and status to influence bail decisions. In 1841, Augustus witnessed a court case involving a "drunkard," and in lieu of a usual 30-day sentence to the House of Correction, Augustus petitioned the court to defer the sentence for 3 weeks while he personally supervised the man. Augustus provided housing and a job while the defendant signed a pledge that he would stay out of trouble and cease drinking. At the end of the 3-week sentence, the judge, being convinced of the man's reform, imposed a fine of one cent plus court costs of $3.76 (Fields, 2012).

IMAGE 3.4   Plaque about John Augustus on the Boston Public Schools Headquarters

John Augustus went on to serve almost 20 years as a volunteer probation officer, with a focus on helping individuals find housing, employment, and education. By 1858, Augustus provided bail for 1,946 men and women (Augustus, 1852/1972). His work went far beyond alcohol consumption, and Augustus engaged in supervising individuals convicted of other acts of deviancy and criminality while also being an advocate for juvenile justice, offering bail for children accused of delinquency. Augustus was selective of the cases he took and considered factors like the individual's personality, age, and the place of the crime prior to arguing for the individual to be released under his supervision in the community, representing an early system of presentence investigation and risk assessment.

Augustus was often controversial, with many Boston organizations and politicians supporting his work but with opposition from law enforcement officials who often preferred a focus on punishment rather than rehabilitation. Augustus' early work paved the way for probation as we know it today. His efforts led to the creation of groups of volunteer probation officers, often recruited from various churches, with some police officers being reassigned to serve in probation as well. As the popularity of this emerging probation system grew, the job of a probation officer became a more formal, paid, and respected position. Early on, employed probation officers worked directly for judges and often had a background in law enforcement. As a result, the "dual-role" conflicts between welfare needs and law enforcement practices were entrenched in probation work from the very beginning.

The impact of John Augustus on probation cannot be overstated. He was the first person to apply the term "probation" to a working system, he was the first true probation officer, and prestigious awards like the "Order of Augustus" are still given to outstanding probation and parole officers at annual conferences. Augustus's distinct approach to juveniles led to

IMAGE 3.5 Massachusetts Washington Total Abstinence Society

the first juvenile court being established in Chicago in 1899, and today all states have both juvenile and adult probation. The legacy of John Augustus is evident in the philosophical orientation of the modern-day probation system—one that features a rehabilitative approach balanced with public safety, classification based on demographic and social factors (e.g., age, gender), an ordered approach centered in procedural justice and fair decision making, and interactions between probation and other criminal justice systems such as courts, jails, and prisons.

Modern-Day Probation

The Bureau of Justice Statistics defines modern-day probation as "a court-ordered period of correctional supervision in the community, generally as an alternative to incarceration. In some cases, probation may be a combined sentence involving incarceration followed by a period of community supervision" (Oudekerk & Kaeble, 2021, p. 2). The Bureau of Justice Statistics has been responsible for collecting administrative data on probation agencies in the United States since 1980 via the Annual Probation Survey (Kaeble, 2021). These surveys provide information on the total number of adults on state and federal probation each year and the characteristics of these individuals. While informative, these data and reports provide a partial viewpoint of proba-

IMAGE 3.6 Seal of the South Carolina Department of Probation, Parole and Pardon Services

tion. This is because probation systems are highly variable in their manifestation. For example, the administrative structure of probation agencies varies by geographic location, with some states having probation and parole merged into a single agency, other states having distinct agencies, and others having probation administered by the judiciary. Additionally, some states feature large, centralized bureaucracies with probation and parole merged with jails, while other states are more disparate and have state-administered and locally administered probation systems operating independently.

The diversity of administrative structure is further increased by the diversity in the job requirements of staff. In general, probation officers are peace officers who have limited law enforcement capabilities; however, many have significant overlap with the court system and engage in social work and community welfare activities. In the United States, most probation agencies have armed probation officers, though there is wide divergence in arrest powers, the type of weapon that can be carried, and law enforcement classification. Some state probation agencies feature different job classifications for probation officers based on the county in which they work, with some counties having probation officers serve entirely as peace officers with no law enforcement capacities, no authority to carry a weapon, and no arrest powers.

The scope of probation across the United States is large in both the size of agencies and areas of their responsibilities. As a result, probation agencies frequently operate as bureaucracies, with specialized units for different types of individuals and needs, with one key area involving individuals who abscond. *Absconding* refers to "the conduct of a person who, while under probation or parole supervision, fails to comply with the requirement to report periodically and otherwise maintaining contact with the supervising agency" (Abadinsky, 2012, p. 1). This may result in a probation or parole violation and a warrant being issued for the individual on supervision. Due to local law enforcement often having other priorities than warrant enforcement for probation, there has been an increase in the use of specialized units within probation that serve this function. Examples include The Pennsylvania Board of Probation and Parole's Fugitive Apprehension Search Team and the New York State Division of Parole's Absconder Search Unit. These specialized units may work independently or partner with law enforcement to conduct surveillance, carry firearms, and ultimately engage in an arrest of the absconder. In this capacity, these specialized units operate with an entirely law enforcement orientation.

The specialization of units in probation extends beyond absconders to include a range of community engagement activities, juvenile population services, and victim resources. The largest probation agency is the County of Los Angeles Probation (n.d.), followed by the New York City Department of Probation (n.d.). The following case study of Los Angeles Probation shows its magnitude.

The County of Los Angeles Probation's 2018 annual report indicates that it has 5,364 probation employees, with two thirds sworn officers, and offering services in 50 area facilities. This indicates that the County of Los Angeles Probation office contains approximately 10% of all probation officers in the entire United States. The 2018 annual budget for the County of Los Angeles Probation was $1,001,687,000. This funding included (a) $32.1 million dollars for adult reentry programs, (b) $13 million dollars for clients from state prison systems now under county probation in need of temporary housing, employment, and system navigation services, and (c) $3.2 million dollars for partnerships designed to address at-risk youth. Such a large enterprise requires the support of staff from a variety of areas, as described here:

> As the largest probation services agency in the United States, the Los Angeles County Probation Department requires extensive internal day-to-day services to keep it running smoothly. From landscaping, maintenance, and mail distribution to computer systems, financial resources, and employee wellness, the men and women who work behind the scenes make up the Department's Administrative Service Bureau (ASB). ASB is comprised of the Professional Accountability Bureau, Information Systems Bureau, Budget and Fiscal Services Unit, the Human Resources Division, Management Services, and the Contracts and Grants Management unit. ASB prepares and monitors the Department's budgets, provides examinations and facilitates recruitments and hiring of staff, operates the Return-to-Work Program's administration, provides payroll services, conducts employee relations, and civil service advocacy. Additionally, ASB manages facility services and provides ancillary services throughout the Department. (County of Los Angeles Probation, 2018, p. 57)

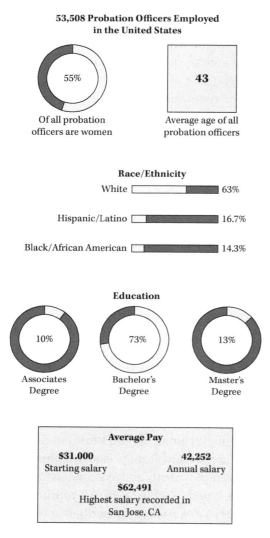

FIGURE 3.1   Probation Officers Employed in the United States

While data on the demographic characteristics of probation officers are largely absent from academic studies, Zippia's (2023) search of the Bureau of Labor Statistics data, U.S. Census Bureau data, and career websites indicates that there are there are over 53,508 probation officers currently employed in the United States. In terms of gender, Zippia found that 54.6 % of all probation officers are women, while 45.4% are men. They reported the average age of an employed probation officer is 43 years old, and the most common race and ethnicity reported is White (63.0%), followed by Hispanic/Latino (16.7%) and Black/African American (14.3%). Despite decades of decreases in probation populations, the career outlook for probation officers remains stable, with most officers employed by governmental agencies and a small subset working in private forms of probation. Zippia reports the average starting salary of probation officers is currently $31,000, with an average annual salary of $47,252. The highest probation officer salary was recorded in San Jose, California, at $62,491. Pay differentials may be influenced by education level, with 10% of probation officers having an associate degree, 73% having a bachelor's degree, and 13% having a master's degree. According to Zippia, this reflects an educated workforce, with approximately 96% of all probation officers having an education higher than a high school diploma. These characteristics can be seen in Figure 3.1 which provides a portrait of probation officers.

◊ Diversity, Equity, and Inclusion: Net Widening in Probation

A major concern for probation is whether the system is being applied appropriately. This perspective acknowledges that city, state, and federal governments often favor the use of probation over incarceration, as it is a more cost-effective option. By using probation instead of jail or prison, costs related to housing, health care, and security are offset to the local community, including the individual, their friends and family, and their employer. As a result, the expansion of probation as a means of social control can lead to people entering the community corrections system who would otherwise have received a lesser punishment (e.g., fine) or to individuals on probation supervision receiving more punitive sanctions than they normally would. The expansion of probation resembles a well-known quote from the 1989 movie *Field of Dreams*, which states, "If you build it, they will come" (though this is a misnomer, as the original quote was "If you build it, he will come"). This quote captures the idea that constructing, and adequately staffing probation agencies, creates a need to fill them with people under supervision. As a result, the driving force behind probation risks becoming an economic decision, rather than the actual criminal behavior of people. This is termed *net widening* or *widening the net*, which describes an expansion of justice administration that results in a greater number of people being placed on probation (and other forms of community corrections). Net widening can refer to the basic expansion of probation to meet the movement away from institutional corrections (i.e., to reduce jail and prison populations), and it can also include probation increasing in line with "get-tough" movements that increase all forms of criminal justice contact, from probation to prison.

Net widening rests on the faulty assumption that researchers can accurately predict future dangerousness every time. What is known, however, is that the best predictor of future behavior is often past behavior. As such, there is a cadre of items that can be useful in predicting arrest or future involvement in the justice system, such as age of first arrest, number of times on supervision, and number of times incarcerated. Even with these factors in mind, Tonry (2019) cautions that for every two "true positives" of predictions of dangerousness there are three "false positives" and that these errors rapidly increase contact between minority populations and the criminal justice system. Tonry (2019) states that even for basic factors like criminal history of the individual, these predictions of dangerousness are "inflated for black and other minority individuals by deliberate and implicit bias, racially disparate practices, profiling, and drug law enforcement that targets minority individuals and neighborhoods" (p. 439).

By applying an intersectional approach, we can see that net widening, with its reliance on faulty predictions of future dangerousness, disproportionately impacts minority individuals and low-income individuals. The modern-day probation system has significant racial and socioeconomic disparities, with Black people being more than 2.6 times more likely than White people to be placed on probation (Bradner et al., 2020). Black people represent around 13% of the total population and yet they constitute 30% of those under probation supervision (Bradner et al., 2020). These differences are lower than the racial differences in institutional corrections, as minority individuals are more likely to be sentenced to incarceration in jail and prison. However, once placed under the supervision of probation, Black individuals receive a higher number of probation conditions, and they remain on probation for longer than White individuals with similar backgrounds and offense histories

Image 3.7

(Kimchi, 2017). These differences extend throughout probation, with Black individuals having more technical violations, higher rates of rearrest, higher risk of incarceration, and greater chances of being revoked for violations than White individuals (Jannetta et al., 2014; Phelps, 2018; Steinmetz & Anderson, 2016).

Indeed, a review of existing research found that Black individuals are 18%–66% more likely than White individuals to have their probation revoked and 4.3 times more likely to be sentenced to prison for a probation revocation (Eaglin & Solomon, 2015; Kimchi, 2017). These historical and structural disadvantages can manifest in minority and low-income communities where there are few resources, little mentorship from older males, and a concentration of disadvantage. The likelihood of failure to successfully complete probation can also increase when probation officers are not adequately trained to recognize and respond to challenges faced by specific racial, ethnic, and socioeconomic groups under their supervision (Frankel, 2020). This is particularly important, as probation officers have considerable discretion in how they respond to individual noncompliance, with officer training linked to the decision to support individuals versus applying punitive sanctions.

A Brief History of Parole

In contrast to probation, individuals enter **parole** only after a period of incarceration in a state institution or federal institution. This refers to prison, as incarceration in jail does

not qualify to receive parole; instead, they would enter probation supervision. Parole has two main features: (a) a parole board that reviews individuals in prison for release based on their progress during the period of incarceration and (b) supervision officers to oversee and assist people released from prison in the community. Parole is a particularly intriguing system, as many of the original tenets of parole remain intact today. Also, these early efforts were largely experimental and born out of necessity during a remarkable time in history. First, it is key to understand that the term "parole" derives from the French word for "word" or "promise." This reflects a code or standard of honor between the individual who committed a crime and the community. Parole also refers to a reward system that is embedded in the prison system, where prosocial, compliant, and restorative behaviors displayed while incarcerated can lead to early release and reintegration into society. While these behaviors reassure authorities of a lowering

IMAGE 3.8   A Probation Officer Outside the District Court of Maryland of risk in the individual, parole serves as a monitoring mechanism designed to bolster public safety—one that is far more cost-effective than long-term incarceration. Parole is associated with a range of inherent problems, with conservative critics often citing high-profile crime incidents (e.g., an individual committing a murder or other serious crime while out on parole) as justification for its ineffectiveness. Liberal critics have also opposed parole, calling for the abolition or severe reduction of the parole system, and deeming it racially biased, expensive, and ineffective. While these debates continue, for incarcerated individuals parole represents a crucial means of early release from prison and a return to society.

Returning to the origins of parole, the mid-1800s represented the progressive era of criminal justice reform. In England and other European countries, the application of harsh and excessive punishment resulted in a lack of places where individuals could be housed. Authorities were resorting to using abandoned caves, makeshift buildings, and local lockups to house people awaiting trial. One method of incarceration was the use of decommissioned ships that were moved to harbors to serve as floating prisons or "hulks." These prison hulks had deplorable conditions and were rife with abuse, violence, disease, and death. With no end in sight for increasingly overcrowded, dangerous, and harsh incarceration options, there emerged technological advancements in sailing and navigation that produced the most active period of Earth exploration on record.

With this new exploration came the development of the penal colony or exile colony, where individuals were transported to remote locations, typically an island or distant colonial territory. The British Empire established penal colonies in Australia, the United States (i.e., Maryland, Virginia, Georgia), Bermuda, and India. France sent individuals to the United

IMAGE 3.9   The Norfolk Island Convict Settlement at Kingston, 1848

States (i.e., Louisiana), French Guiana (i.e., Devil's Island), and New Caledonia. Penal colonies were also established in Mexico and various countries in South America. People sent to these colonies included a mix of male and female criminals, political dissidents, the poor (i.e., debtor prisons), and low-level lawbreakers who were arrested for misdemeanors like drunkenness and petty theft.

In these colonies, a small group of governors and leaders were often compelled to create a fair process of justice, whereby a large group of incarcerated people would be released and reintegrated into the community. These colonies were attempting to create a functional society that relied heavily on the labor of people who were formerly incarcerated. Moreover, these leaders had considerable discretion in their approaches to releasing people, as penal colonies were in remote locations far from the control and influences of centralized monarchies, bureaucracies, and authorities. There are three key occurrences during this early period that have greatly influenced the modern-day parole system. This includes Alexander Maconochie in Van Diemen's Land and Norfolk Island, Sir Walter Crofton and the Irish mark system, and Zebulon Reed Brockway (Elmira Reformatory).

Alexander Maconochie (Van Diemen's Land and Norfolk Island)

Alexander Maconochie (1878–1860) has been credited as being the "Father of Parole." Maconochie was born in Scotland and served in the Napoleonic Wars, where he was a prisoner of war for 3 years (1811–1814). During this time, Maconochie endured forced marches in the cold and other indignations that later inspired his reforms of the penal system. Returning to the United Kingdom, Maconochie became the first professor of geography and a founder of the Royal Geographical Society (Fields, 2012). Maconochie was offered the position of secretary to Lieutenant Governor Franklin in Van Diemen's Land (now Tasmania), a task that enabled him to develop his progressive ideas about incarceration. Van Diemen's Land was an island prison colony with a harsh environment, extreme isolation, and a reputation for being inescapable.

Between 1836 and 1839, Maconochie balanced an approach of punishing individuals for their crimes while simultaneously training them for future employment in governmental positions. He rejected the use of cruelty in punishment, arguing that such measures do a disservice to the victim and broader society, and he began the use of labor tasks rather than time sentences and moral education as a means of individuals working toward release. Maconochie (1838) wrote an influential report on convict discipline to the English parliament titled *Thoughts on Convict Management and Other Subjects Connected with the Australian Penal Colonies*. In this report, Maconochie argued that consideration of the best methods of transitioning individuals from "convict status" to citizens was not only an ethical issue but a cost-effective strategy for these emerging penal societies. Maconochie (1838) stated:

> The expense of the Penal Colonies is at present enormous—partly from the prevailing system of mere coercion in them, partly from the unproductiveness of every descrip-tion of labor under this system, partly from the crime which it directly generates, and partly from the large police, and other public checks and establishments, which the repression and punishment of this crime render necessary. A system of training, on

the contrary, could only be effective in proportion to its successful adaptation of moral influence to its object—and any system founded in large measure on moral influence must be less expensive than one of mere physical restraint. (pp. 15–16)

Following his success in Van Diemen's Land, Maconochie was appointed superintendent of Norfolk Island, a penal colony island home to the most incorrigible individuals. Norfolk Island, like Van Diemen's Land, also had a reputation for cruel, abusive, and degrading conditions. Maconochie imported his own practices of punishment and reform, with the implementation of the "marks system" that allowed individuals to serve their sentence in stages where good behavior led to increased trust and responsibility and with the ability for people to use marks to purchase food and other items. Importantly, marks earned through hard work and good behavior could be leveraged into shortened prison sentences and early release. These "earned release credits" remain a feature of the modern-day criminal justice system.

The innovations crafted by Alexander Maconochie reformed the penal colonies of both Van Diemen's Land and Norfolk Island, though both experienced returns to harsh and brutal methods when Macon-ochie returned to England in 1844. When he tried to

IMAGE 3.10   Alexander Maconochie

implement these reformed penal practices in England, they were viewed as being too lenient and futile, and ultimately, they failed. Alexander Maconochie's reforms were largely forgot-ten until discovered and reexamined years later. Maconochie's model is now central to the mission, philosophies, and practices of parole, particularly the credo of punishing for the past and training for the future. John Barry (1967) summarized that "Maconochie was a pioneer in penal reform, and suffered the fate of men in advance of their times. His concepts and many of his practical measures are now the basis of Western penal systems" (p. 1).

Sir Walter Crofton (The Irish Mark System)

Sir Walter Crofton (1815–1897) is known as Alexander Maconochie's ideological heir because he transformed the mark system and other penal reforms into a more standardized format in Ireland. While Maconochie often receives more academic attention, this is largely due to him being more active in publishing and promoting his own penal reforms. Yet, it was Crof-ton's efforts that produced a more extensive and long-lasting implementation of these ideas, including a working model of parole that has been adopted in multiple countries (Morris, 2002). Sir Walter Crofton served as the chairman and then governor of the Board of Directors of Convict Prisons for Ireland. In these capacities, he instituted a three-stage process where individuals moved from strict supervision toward increasing freedom and finally conditional release. The first stage centered on moralistic and isolation techniques, with the individual

IMAGE 3.11   Historical Image of Edward Shevlin

serving 8–9 months in solitary confinement and given only minimal rations for the first few months. During this stage, it was hoped that the incarcerated person would link productive labor with increased rations, with the goal being that work became viewed as a privilege rather than a burden.

In Crofton's second stage, individuals were required to demonstrate prosocial behaviors toward work, school, and obedience in public works while in prison. This stage featured four levels (Levels A–D), with a strong emphasis on reinforcing self-discipline through prison labor. An individual could act in accordance with these moralistic values and be moved away from the general population and towards Level A, or they could remain in the lower levels and serve their entire sentence. Crofton's third and final stage continued to rely on moralistic approaches, as these individuals were moved from prison to an "intermediate" prison, which in modern terms most resembles a halfway house. To calculate these early releases, prison administrators documented individual displays of prosocial attitudes and efforts toward personal reform with a credit system or "marks." The desired outcome was for individuals to receive a "ticket of leave," which was an official document of parole that allowed for certain freedoms. Under Maconochie, a ticket of leave could also result in transportation to Australia, where the individual would continue their sentence as an indentured servant before obtaining their freedom. Under Crofton's Irish mark system, a ticket of leave or "ticket of license" justified increased freedoms during incarceration coupled with the potential for early release from prison and reentering society.

A ticket of leave was a form of conditional release that gradually provided autonomy in daily tasks, like running errands in the community and attending church services. While housed in the community, these individuals who were formerly incarcerated were now under the supervision of an inspector who verified employment status, periodically visited their place of residence, and had the authority to return the individual to prison if they violated good-conduct requirements. These inspectors are the equivalent of modern-day parole officers. The revocation of parole (i.e., returning the individual to prison) also included violations like associating with known criminals or failing to report to work. Once the period of the original sentence expired, the individual was fully restored to free society, and they were no longer supervised by authorities. The Irish mark system's elements of conditional release, parole inspectors, and halfway houses remain fundamental components of the modern-day parole system. It is worth noting that Sir Walter Crofton's greatest contribution to community corrections is his advancing of Alexander Maconochie's mark system for granting early release into a process where continued supervision occurs after release, thus giving parole the essential responsibility of monitoring the perceptions, behaviors, and experiences of formerly incarcerated individuals (Morris, 2002).

Zebulon Reed Brockway (Elmira Reformatory)

Zebulon Reed Brockway (1827–1920) has been labeled the "Father of Prison Reform" and "Father of American Parole." Brockway had an extensive career in corrections that was documented in his own writings and in public advocacy. Beginning as a correctional officer in Connecticut in 1848, he worked in various capacities in New York and Michigan prisons and ultimately became the superintendent of the New York Penitentiary in 1854. Brockway advocated for a medical model of criminology, where criminal behavior was viewed as a treatable disease. During Brockway's time in Michigan, he advocated for a system designed to educate and change individuals rather than simply punish and isolate them. This began with a program at the Michigan House of Corrections where individuals ages 16–21 received vocational skills and educational classes, with rewards for good behavior.

As a prison superintendent, Brockway had the legislative power to attempt to establish the country's first indeterminate sentencing system. *Determinate sentencing* refers to judges sentencing an individual to a specific time (e.g., 5-year sentence), with no discretion by authorities for good behavior exhibited by the individual and little legal discretion afforded the sentencing authority. As a result, "determinate" refers to the sentence being determined, with little to no room to change or alter the sentence. In contrast, *indeterminate sentencing* denotes that the sentence is a range rather than a fixed period (e.g., 3- to 5-year sentence). "Indeterminate" indicates that the sentence is not determined, that good behaviors by the individual could

IMAGE 3.12   Zebulon Reed Brockway Interviewing New Arrivals at the New York State Reformatory

reduce the sentence, and that judges have more latitude to recognize extenuating circumstances surrounding the criminal event (e.g., limited mental capacity, social constraints of abuse and poverty, etc.).

In 1869, Brockway drafted a law to codify the use of indeterminate sentencing as a standard practice and advocated its use at the national level. One year later, he presented an influential paper on the principles of indeterminate sentencing at the Cincinnati Prison Congress. Brockway's (1912) law provided a mandatory 3-year sentence for "common prostitutes" but with conditional release subject to the "managing authorities of the house of correction" (p. 108). Brockway described this system as "the first attempted practical application in America of the profound principle of the indeterminate sentence system, which substitutes both in the laws and in prison practice reformatory in place of the usual punitive regime" (as cited in Beha, 2008, p. 790).

Despite these successes, Brockway was frustrated when Michigan—and later the Supreme Court—failed to pass legislation that allowed him to fully implement his system of indeterminate sentencing. To Brockway, this legal decision reduced the capacity for incarcerated people to engage in good behavior. While Brockway resigned when his reforms in Michigan failed, several significant social and professional changes would bring his parole techniques back into relevancy. First, society during this period underwent significant scientific advancement, particularly with the linkage that Charles Darwin identified between biology and the environment. Crime was soon viewed as a moral disease that required the application of a new discipline called the "social sciences" to rehabilitate individuals. This movement was bolstered by a post–Civil War effect where returning soldiers demonstrated changes to their physical and mental health that required therapy rather than harsh discipline or religious guidance. While personally a religious man, Brockway endorsed this scientific approach, and

IMAGE 3.13   Lockstep in Auburn Prison

he argued that jails and prisons should function in a fundamentally therapeutic role that safely links people back into the community. Brockway (1912) wrote:

> Reformation of prisoners which affords adequate measure of public protection from their future crimes must include rehabilitation, by which is meant reabsorption of reformed individuals into the mass of industrious orderly inhabitants, putting out of sight completely, if gradually, from the common recollection and from any degrading self-consciousness, the former fault and imprisonment. (p. 78)

A second impetus for change was the prison congress of 1870 in Cincinnati, titled The National Congress on Penitentiary and Reformatory Discipline. For the first time in American history, prisons were being asked to function as rehabilitative institutions, there was a movement toward a scientific approach to the "disease" of crime, and this reform required the use of a professionalized, bureaucratic management approach that could be standardized. As part of this reform, the Irish mark system was integrated into prison systems, thus establishing the key elements of parole. The Cincinnati Congress produced 41 principles for prison, signifying the establishment of what became the medical model of rehabilitation in American corrections.

This new scientific approach also moved toward a calculation of justice, whereby the sentence of an individual was indeterminate with a calculation of the punishment of incarceration being long enough for the rehabilitative processes of education, therapy, and medical treatment to take effect. A new prison was needed to demonstrate the mark system was capable of linking the self-interest of individuals to being released early to their improved behavior while incarcerated, making prisons realize their full rehabilitative potential.

IMAGE 3.14   Elmira Reformatory in Elmira, New York

With great enthusiasm for a new model of incarceration, Zebulon Brockway was positioned as the superintendent of Elmira Reformatory. Brockway adapted the Irish mark system into progressive stages where individuals could demonstrate a commitment to work, educational and trade programs, physical activity, and good behavior to be considered for conditional release with supervised parole. Elmira Reformatory held individuals convicted of a crime for the first time and who were between the ages of 16 and 30 (as it was argued this age group would be more amenable to prosocial changes in behavior). The use of seriousness of the offense and age represented one of the first efforts to calculate the risk of the individual, as these individuals were perceived to be midway between (a) juveniles involved in delinquency and housed in juvenile houses of refuge and (b) adults incarcerated in state prisons. Brockway himself conducted individualized interviews with new residents to create treatment plans for each person housed at Elmira. The application of individualized treatment plans for individuals remains an essential component of parole today.

Elmira's progressive system was bolstered by a law codified in 1877 that authorized a 5-year indeterminate sentence and included the discretion of the board of managers employed by the prison to accept or reject parole. At Elmira, a three-grade system was instituted, with new intakes placed in the middle grades. These individuals were evaluated for performance in school, work, and behavior, and if successful they were moved to the first grade, where they would receive extra privileges. Another 6-month evaluation on the same criteria could earn the individual eligibility for parole. A failure to meet school, work, or behavioral expectations resulted in a demotion to a lower level, with the third-grade level leading to the most punitive responses (e.g., wearing a red suit, movement via lockstep, and no correspondence or visitation privileges). Basic education was provided with advanced classes in geography, bookkeeping, physiology, ethics, and psychology taught by professors from nearby universities. Trades were taught in the industrial school, and they included hollow-ware manufacture, shoemaking, iron works, and brush making.

While successful, Elmira was far from perfect. Unfortunately, Brockway had not completely abandoned the use of Christian moral education and hard labor as a means of addressing behavior. In 1893, John Gilmore, a former resident of Elmira, was before a judge on charges, and he requested to be sent to state prison rather than be returned to the Elmira Reformatory. Gilmore testified that he had been brutally beaten at Elmira, a claim which ultimately led to an investigation by the State Board of Charities. This investigation discovered that select residents of Elmira were afforded power over others, leading to abuse, neglect, and sexual violence. While Elmira had demonstrated effectiveness with parole, there was ample evidence of the use of harsh physical punishment, forced labor, long-term solitary confinement, refusal of medical care, and starvation as forms of punishment. This investigation led to the following conclusion:

> The final report of the committee, released on 14 March 1894, was unequivocal; its findings were unanimously endorsed by the ten members of the New York State Board of Charities: That the charges and the allegations against the general superintendent

Z.R. Brockway of "cruel, brutal, excessive, degrading and unusual punishment of the inmates" are proven and most amply sustained by the evidence, and that he is guilty of the same. (Pisciotta, 1994)

Brockway retired at the age of 72 facing considerable criticism, with new managers opting to share the authority, responsibility, and decision making for Elmira, thus removing the autonomy of a single leader. New officers and teachers arrived, special powers for a handful of individuals were removed, and individual classification was expanded to include social, economic, psychological, biological, and moral factors. However, the essential components of the modern-day parole system survived intact. Brockway (1912) later wrote an autobiography on his 50 years in prison service where he stated:

Release of prisoners was constantly urged by outsiders on the ground that one or another had already been "punished enough," but there were of course different ideas of just what is "enough." Prisoners came imbued with the idea that they were imprisoned for punishment, and this idea, until it could be removed, proved a hindrance to their interest and progress in the means adopted for reformation. (p. 167)

Modern-Day Parole

The modern-day parole system is generally identified by two processes; that is, first, an individual is released from prison, and second, the formerly incarcerated individual is supervised in the community. More specifically, the Bureau of Justice Statistics definition of modern-day parole is "a period of conditional supervised release in the community following a term in state or federal prison. Parolees include persons released through discretionary or mandatory supervised release from prison" (Oudekerk & Karble, 2021, p. 2). Parole can result from a determinate sentence in which a preset prison sentence is completed, and the individual is then released under supervision of a parole agency. Parole can also occur in indeterminate sentences that include a minimum prison sentence followed by a range of years that the individual can continue to be incarcerated. Once within this range, a paroling authority has the authority to release the individual. This indeterminate sentencing process is termed "discretionary parole," with the discretion of release moving from the authority of the court to a parole authority.

Parole now occupies a unique position in the contemporary criminal justice system. Since 2011, the parole population has been relatively stable. Probation populations have been decreasing appreciably since 2019 (see Table 3.1). In fact, during 2021 there was a 7.1% reduction in the total parole population—the largest change in nearly 30 years (Kaeble, 2023). However, continued reliance on parole makes this component of the criminal justice system distinct, as more consistent, larger decreases have been recorded in the national crime rate, total incarceration rate, and the overall community corrections supervision rate. These trends are linked, as a reliance on parole has increased individuals under supervision as populations are shifted away from institutional corrections (i.e., jail and prison). In short, states have become more aggressive in utilizing parole to reduce prison populations, which has been compounded by changes in parole decision making regarding parole revocation. These trends in community supervision populations can be viewed in Figure 3.2.

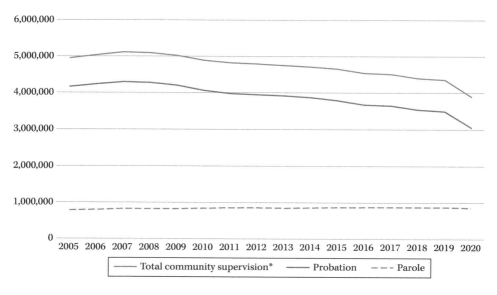

FIGURE 3.2   Trends in Community Supervision Populations (Kaeble, 2023)

Basic activities of the parole agencies are fundamentally influenced by differences in structure and goals. Parole agencies are much like probation agencies in terms of their considerable variation in size, scope, and function. Currently, there is only one data source on parole agencies: Bonczar's (2008) report for the Bureau of Justice Statistics titled *Characteristics of State Parole Supervising Agents, 2006*. While outdated, this one-time data collection provides insights into the structure of parole at the national level, and it highlights key considerations for understanding parole processes.

This begins with recognition that parole agencies are diverse in size and function. At the national level, parole is dominated by several very large, bureaucratic state entities. Five state parole agencies account for almost half of all adults under supervision—that is, California (109,080 adults on parole), Texas (104,280), Pennsylvania (80,640), New York (39,800), and Arkansas (23,830), excluding adults supervised by county parole offices (Kaeble, 2023). As such, increases in the reliance of parole can be influenced by legal and policy changes located in only a few states. There are also differences in function, with about half of parole agencies having a role in determining who gets released to parole, setting the conditions of supervision, or conducting revocation hearings (Bonczar, 2008). Boncza (2008) adds that approximately 77% of parole agencies were administered by a state-level department of corrections, with 16% serving as independent parole agencies and 8% being other (such as a department of public safety). Table 3.1. provides more data from the National Institute of Justice on this topic.

TABLE 3.1 Number of State Adult Parole Supervising Agencies, Offices, and Adult Parole and Probation Population, by Type of Agency, June 30, 2006

Type of Agency	Number of Parole Agencies	Number of Parole Agency Offices[a]	Adult Parole Population		Adult Probation Population	
			Number	Percent	Number	Percent
Agency Administration[b]	52	2.287	660.959	100%	1,200,570	100%
Department of Corrections	38	1,804	454,387	69%	920,203	77%
Independent parole agency	11	369	162,329	25%	190,021	16%
Other[c]	3	114	44,243	7%	90,346	8%
Population served[b]						
Parolees	17	503	391,543	59%	~	~
Parolees and probationers	35	1,784	269,416	41%	1,200,570	100%

~Not applicable.
[a]Parole offices that comprised the 52 agencies on June 30, 2006, including administrative offices, regional offices, and all separate suboffices, such as field offices; includes estimates for Illinois, Wisconsin, and Virginia.
[b]Excludes local parole supervision agencies in Alabama and Pennsylvania
[c]Includes the Arkansas Department of Community Corrections, the Nevada Department of Public Safety, and one response representing Oregon's county-based parole system.

Source: Bonczar, 2008

Parole is also like probation in that both systems are understudied, especially with a lack of data that documents the key characteristics of the workforce. In 2006, there were an estimated 65,000 full-time and 2,900 part-time workers employed by the 52 state parole supervising agencies (note that the term "workers" refers to a range of job descriptions; Bonczar, 2008). More current data by Zippia (2023) show that there are currently 6,950 full-time parole officers in the United States. With the increasing reliance on parole services, Zippia expects the growth rate to expand by 3% between 2018 and 2028, producing 3,000 job opportunities at the national level. According to this data, approximately 52% of parole officers are women, and the average age is 43 years old. Zippia also reported that (a) approximately 75% of parole officers have a bachelor's degree, with criminal justice being the most common major, followed by psychology, sociology, and social work; (b) almost 15% have a master's degree; and (c) 8% have an associate's degree. The average national salary for a parole officer is $45,474, with the

6,950 Full-Time Parole Officers in the United States

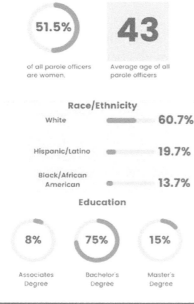

51.5%
of all parole officers are women.

43
Average age of all parole officers

Race/Ethnicity

White ▬▬▬ **60.7%**

Hispanic/Latino ● **19.7%**

Black/African American ● **13.7%**

Education

8%
Associates Degree

75%
Bachelor's Degree

15%
Master's Degree

Average Pay

$31,000
Starting salary

$45,474
Annual salary

$64,567
average salary in California, highest paying state

Adapted from Zippa (2022)

FIGURE 3.3   Parole Officers in the United States

highest average salary recorded in California at $64,567, according to Zippia. The portrait of parole officers at the national level is shown in Figure 3.3 which follows.

Prison Release: Parole Boards

There are several key decision points in the parole system: determining whether an individual should be released on parole, identifying the conditions of parole supervision, and determining whether any individual has successfully or unsuccessfully completed their parole term. Parole boards represent one authority that is responsible for making these decisions, with issues of the need for transparency discussed in Chapter 4. *Parole boards* "are governing bodies whose members are appointed officials. Their main job is to determine when an individual housed within a prison is eligible for release and, when that time comes, to determine if he or she is fit to return to society" (Falconer, 2012, p. 286). Parole boards often define the conditions or requirements of a parole period. If these conditions are met, then the parole board will release the parolee from being on parole. If these conditions are not met, then the parole board will revoke the parolee's rights, which can lead to placement in an alternative program, extension of the parole term, or returning the individual to prison. Parole boards weigh factors like prior criminal history with other data, like the reports of parole officers or correctional officers, the type of new crime that was committed, and overall risk that the individual displays. Parole board decisions are often restricted by guidelines that remove their discretion.

Parole boards have received criticism for being influenced by media and politics rather than procedural justice, equity, and fairness. When an individual on parole commits a crime, the media is apt to condemn the parole board's decision to release the individual. In one example, Massachusetts's entire parole board resigned after a released parolee shot and killed a police officer near Boston (see Shaw, 2012). The media highlighted the fact that the parole board had voted for the release of the individual despite his three life sentences. These concerns can lead parole boards to lean toward conservative decisions that keep individuals incarcerated who would not commit future crime (false positives) rather than release those deemed noncriminal who go on to commit crime (false negatives). This approach overinflates the risk presented by the individual (whose risk is often difficult to fully predict), as at the group level, risk in

IMAGE 3.15   President Hoover Meets With His Newly Created Enforcement Commission, 1929

parolees may be low and more predictable. For example, one California-based study tracked 860 people convicted of homicide and sentenced to life who were released on parole for up to 16 years (Weisberg et al., 2011). In the years following their release, only five individuals (less than 1%) had been returned to prison or jail because of new felonies, indicating a very low rate of recidivism.

Individuals are typically politically appointed to serve on a parole board. However, the President's Crime Commission produced the recommendation that parole boards avoid political appointees and move towards using correctional professionals (Little, 1967). This has been a sluggish process, with entire parole boards replaced when a new governor or political official is elected (Falconer, 2012). Some states have adopted civil service or merit systems for parole board membership, where education and expertise are required, and political officials are not eligible. Falconer (2012) states that parole boards tend to range from three to 19 members, with the national average of seven parole board members.

The degree of involvement of the parole board differs by the legal mandates. If the jurisdiction is bound by indeterminate sentencing, then the board is responsible for parolee eligibility dates and other restrictions. Once an individual is eligible for parole, the board will hold a hearing

What Information Does a Parole Board Consider?

? Crime Characteristics

? Criminal History

? Institutional Reports

? Mental Health

? Physical Health

? Remorse

? Risk of Recidivism

? Victim Input

FIGURE 3.4 Information Considered by Parole Board

or a series of hearings before making a parole ruling. When individuals are incarcerated, these hearings take place in an assigned area of a prison. The parole board receives a range of materials that include, though are not limited to, crime characteristics (e.g., criminal history, sex offense status, violent crime, recidivism), a presentence investigation form, institutional reports of prosocial behavior (e.g., education, therapy, and programs) and antisocial behavior (e.g., misconduct, nonengagement in programs), and physical and mental health reports. These variables can be summarized into a Salient Factor Score (SFS) that include six measures: prior convictions and adjudications, prior commitments (30 or more days), age at current offense, recent amount of time the individual was commitment-free, technical violations, and drug dependency. The hearing process that follows may include a hearing examiner who interviews the individual up for parole and writes a report. Victims of crime and their families and friends may also participate in parole hearings. This can occur either in person or by correspondence that may include presentation of a victim impact statement (VIS) outlining the harm the crime caused them and the need to grant or reject parole for the individual. Figure 3.4 provides a list of the materials that are typically compiled by a correctional officer or parole officer, who then interacts with law enforcement, correctional agencies, and victim groups.

Individuals who seek parole have rights throughout the process. As such, due process often centers on reasonable requirements if parole is approved or justifications for a parole denial. For example, this may include the individual up for parole's access to a representative before and during the hearing, the inclusion or exclusion of relevant materials, inaccuracies or procedural issues during the hearing, and the length of time the parole board took to provide a written ruling on the parole decision. Parole officers have a legal duty to provide the parole board will all relevant information, including their own views on parole recommendations (Lyons & Jermstad, 2013). This also includes the release criteria should parole be approved that is both reasonable and achievable for the released individual. Due to parole denial being "an area of considerable litigation" (Lyons & Jermstad, 2013, p. 253), many state laws and agency policies mandate at least a minimum standard of providing reasons for parole denial. This information should provide the individual with areas they can address to increase their likelihood of receiving parole at their next hearing date.

There are several prominent criticisms surrounding parole boards that jeopardize their future use. First, parole boards still contain political appointees, with proceedings often occurring in secret and with no external reviews of decision making. In addition to various assessments and other materials on the individual, parole boards may also consider hearsay, rumor, and other forms of information. Parole boards and their members have no legal obligation to be transparent, and in some jurisdictions, they have unlimited discretion. As Schwartzapfel (2015) argues, "few others in the criminal justice system wield so much power with so few professional requirements and so little accountability." This lack of transparency can be seen in Figure 3.5 which reveals which states have public, mixed, or secret parole board procedures.

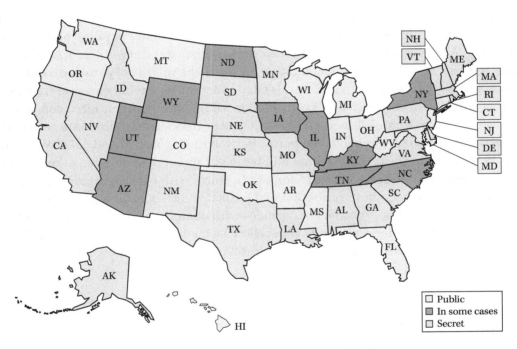

FIGURE 3.5   States where Parole Board Decisions are Public, Mixed, or Secret

Second, there is little understanding of how parole board members make decisions. Schwartzapfel (2015) found that in 24 states, boards need not disclose what material they relied upon to reach their decisions, citing court rulings that incarcerated people have no due process right to parole. There is also evidence that the final decision is largely shaped by victim input. This is a rare exception in the criminal justice system where the victim's input is direct and central to outcomes. Third, to counteract these weaknesses, parole boards have been increasingly tasked with using parole guidelines to score individual risk to the community. However, these risk assessment tools are often unstandardized between jurisdictions (some being valid, while others are outdated), confusing to untrained and inexperienced board members, or simply not used at all.

The Landscape of Probation and Parole Across the United States

Across the country, there are variations in the availability of and function of various community supervision agencies. For example, probation can operate at both the federal level as well as the local, county, and state level (or a combination of these). For parole, the Sentencing Reform Act of 1984 passed by Congress eliminated federal parole for all offenses committed after November 1, 1987. Despite this abolition of parole, individuals are often sentenced to supervised release following their incarceration where they often are supervised for around 6 months in the community. Calls for the abolition of parole have been heard in nearly every state among pressures to move to a less discretionary system of determinate sentencing. As the general view toward the criminal justice system shifted to a "tough-on-crime" perspective and faith in rehabilitation declined, the validity of parole was questioned by both liberals and conservatives. Liberals cited concerns for similar cases receiving vastly different outcomes due to high levels of discretion, while conservatives voiced concerns over perceived leniency of parole boards. As a result, states also began to eliminate parole. There are currently 16 states that abolished parole between 1976 (Maine) and 2000 (Wisconsin), while 19 states limit the types of crimes eligible (e.g., Connecticut does not allow parole for those convicted of murder or capital felonies). In states with parole, 29 have agencies that supervise individuals on both probation and parole, while six have separate agencies for probation and parole supervision. For agencies with combined probation and parole populations, individual officers typically supervise caseloads that contain individuals under both probation and parole supervision. Table 3.2 provides a breakdown by states on how parole and probation systems operate.

TABLE 3.2   Breakdown of Parole/Probation Systems in the United States

State	Probation/Parole Combined	Separate Agencies	Probation Only	No Parole/Date Abolished
Alabama	X			
Alaska	X			
Arizona	-	-	X	1994
Arkansas	X			
California			X	1977
Colorado	X			
Connecticut		X		
Delaware			X	6/30/1990

State	Probation/Parole Combined	Separate Agencies	Probation Only	No Parole/Date Abolished
District of Columbia		X		
Florida			X	10/1/1983
Georgia		X		
Hawaii		X		
Idaho	X			
Illinois			X	1978
Indiana			X	1977
Iowa	X			
Kansas			X	7/1/1993
Kentucky	X			
Louisiana	X			
Maine			X	1976
Maryland	X			
Massachusetts		X		
Michigan	X			
Minnesota			X	1982
Mississippi	X			
Missouri	X			
Montana	X			
Nebraska	X			
Nevada	X			
New Hampshire	X			
New Jersey	X			
New Mexico			X	1979
New York	X			
North Carolina			X	1994
North Dakota	X			
Ohio			X	1996
Oklahoma	X			
Oregon			X	1989
Pennsylvania		X		
Rhode Island	X			

(continued)

State	Probation/Parole Combined	Separate Agencies	Probation Only	No Parole/Date Abolished
South Carolina	X			
South Dakota	X			
Tennessee		X		
Texas	X			
Utah	X			
Vermont	X			
Virginia			X	1995
Washington			X	1994
West Virginia	X			
Wisconsin			X	2000
Wyoming	X			

◊ Officer Work, Careers, and Wellness: Caseloads

It is evident that the daily activities of probation and parole officers can be challenging, and they must engage in different activities that are labor intensive, complex, and rest on the development of a trusting and transparent officer–client relationship. Parole and probation work practices are highly influenced by the number of individuals that have been assigned to each officer, which is termed their "caseload." Research indicates that high caseloads not only detract from the quality of officer–client interactions and subsequent outcomes for people under supervision but also directly impact the officer (e.g., quality of work, job stress, job satisfaction). In a recent study of 3,000 case inspections and 2,000 interviews with frontline probation officers, Ball et al. (2021) found that caseloads of over 50 individuals greatly impaired the quality of probation work. Participating probation officers clearly linked high caseloads to overwhelming stress, sleeplessness, and fear of making serious mistakes through overwork. During interviews, they voiced concerns like the following:

> I got really stressed at one point and emailed my manager saying I can't manage and was having panic attacks before I came into the building. But I was advised they couldn't reduce the caseload. (Ball et al., 2021, p. 23)

> The role has become unmanageable, it is a hostile environment, some days I feel the stress of the job will cause a premature death for me. Numerous staff shortages; a job that was done by two people is now done by one. (Ball et al., 2021, p. 24)

This issue of large caseloads and officer stress emerged in President Lyndon Johnson's 1965 address to the U.S. Congress, where he emphasized the need for rehabilitation, services, and reintegration in the criminal justice system. Heralding an era of liberalism, Johnson enacted the Presidents Commission, which called for "the establishment of a blue ribbon panel to probe fully and deeply into the problems of crime in our Nation" (Mackenzie, 2001, p. 6). This panel produced several key recommendations for community corrections that impacted officer duties, including the need for probation and parole officers to develop new approaches to reintegrating individuals into the community, increasing treatment and interventions in the community, documentation that all releasees from corrections receive adequate supervision, and a reduction of caseloads to an average ratio of 35 individuals per probation or parole officer (Little, 1967). However, by the "get-tough" conservative era of the early 1990s, the average adult supervision caseload ballooned to 117 individuals per probation or parole officer (Camp & Camp, 1995).

To address both officer effectiveness and wellness, estimates of appropriate average caseloads have been identified and endorsed by professional organizations like the American Probation and Parole Association (APPA, 2013). The goal of resulting recommendations is to provide estimates of what constitutes a caseload level that maximizes supervision while minimizing officer stress. Burrell (2006) provides the following recommendations for caseload standards in Table 3.3.

TABLE 3.3   Recommended Caseload Standards for Probation and Parole

Standard	Case Type	Cases-to-Staff Ratio
Adult caseload standards	Intensive	20:1
Adult caseload standards	Moderate to high risk	50:1
Adult caseload standards	Low risk	200:1
Adult caseload standards	Administrative	No limit? 1,000?
Juvenile caseload standards	Intensive	15:1
Juvenile caseload standards	Moderate to high risk	30:1
Juvenile caseload standards	Low risk	100:1
Juvenile caseload standards	Administrative	Not recommended

Consideration of individual risks and needs can impact these recommendations or caseloads. Low-risk individuals may only require a bureaucratic approach where the officer documents their progress and provides no other services, programs, or interventions. This allows for higher caseloads per officer, with some jurisdictions creating entirely administrative caseloads of upwards of 200 low-risk individuals. In contrast, moderate- to high-risk individuals often require significantly more supervision, have greater interactions with other criminal justice systems (e.g., court, institutional corrections, community partners), and possess a constellation of risks and needs that are challenging to address. As a result, caseloads consisting of a greater number of higher risk clients will be more time consuming to supervise. Some jurisdictions use an innovative approach to assign a point value to each risk level (e.g., high risk is 20 points, moderate risk 10, and low risk 5 points). Case assignments are then determined using mathematical equations to ensure that each caseload does not go over set point-level limits.

SUMMARY: PROBATION AND PAROLE

To understand probation and parole systems, it is valuable to explore the origins, developments, and key figures in history. Displaced populations of "convicts" who were often shipped from England and incarcerated in penal colonies created a crisis. With few correctional officers compared to incarcerated people, parole was the product of experimentation, innovation, and necessity. As this movement expanded toward the United States, key influencers like Alexander Maconochie, Sir Walter Crofton, and Zebulon Reed Brockway expanded the basic principles of probation and parole. The modern-day probation and parole system in the United States is enormously complex, expensive, and bureaucratic. Officers who work in these systems must balance the risks and needs of justice-involved individuals, often balancing large caseloads while maintaining professionalism and avoiding burnout. Across the United States, the ways in which probation and parole are structured vary, with some operating under one agency and others independently. Regardless of structure, there remains controversy about the effectiveness of probation and parole supervision and parole boards. Often based on political differences, there are calls to either support these agencies and officers with increased funding or to abandon the notion of probation and parole entirely.

Scenario-Based Activities

	Case	Question(s)
1	Mark was sentenced to 15 years in prison for armed robbery. He served 10 years of his sentence and is now eligible for parole. During his time in prison, Mark participated in a cognitive behavioral program and began GED classes. He received no misconducts, and prison staff reported him as compliant.	Pretend you are a member of the parole board reviewing Mark's case. What factors would you consider when deciding whether to grant Mark's parole? How would you determine Mark's potential risk for recidivism and possibility for success while on parole?
2	A law was passed 3 years ago that made it easier for judges to sentence individuals convicted of a crime to probation instead of prison time. The goals of this law were to reduce the number of people incarcerated for nonviolent offenses and to save money on corrections costs. Since the law has been in place, some argue that it has led to "net widening."	Pretend you are a criminal justice policymaker tasked with examining this issue of net widening. Answer the following questions: What is net widening, and how does it occur? What are the potential consequences of net widening, both for individuals on probation and for the criminal justice system as a whole? What policy solutions could be implemented to address the issue of net widening while still achieving the original goals of this law (reducing incarceration and saving money)?

References

Abadinsky, H. (2012). Absconding. In S. M. Barton-Bellessa (Eds.), *Encyclopedia of community corrections* (Vol. 1, pp. 1–3). SAGE Publications. https://doi.org/10.4135/9781452218519

American Probation and Parole Association. (2013). *Effective responses to offender behavior: Lessons learned for probation and parole supervision.* American Probation and Parole Association. https://perma.cc/DBQ9-QNNG

Augustus, J. (1972). *John Augustus: First probation officer.* Patterson Smith. (Original work published 1852)

Ball, K., Buckley, L., & Moore, R. (2021). *Caseloads, workloads and staffing levels in probation services.* Her Majesty's Inspectorate of Probation. https://www.justiceinspectorates.gov.uk/hmiprobation/wp-content/uploads/sites/5/2021/03/Caseloads-and-Workloads-RAB-LL-designed-RM-amends-Mar-21.pdf

Barry, J. V. (1967). *Maconochie, Alexander (1787–1860).* Australian Dictionary of Biography, National Centre of Biography, Australian National University. https://adb.anu.edu.au/biography/maconochie-alexander-2417/text3207

Beccaria, C. (2009). *On crimes and punishments* (G. R. Newman & P. Marongiu, Trans.). Transaction Publishers. (Original work published 1764)

Beha, J. J. (2008). Redemption to reform: The intellectual origins of the prison reform movement. *Annual Survey of American Law, 63,* 773–793.

Bonczar, T. P. (2008). *Characteristics of state parole supervising agencies, 2006.* U.S. Department of Justice, Bureau of Justice Statistics. https://bjs.ojp.gov/content/pub/pdf/cspsa06.pdf

Bradner, K., Schiraldi, V. N., Mejia, N., & Lopoo, E. (2020). *More work to do: Analysis of probation and parole in the United States, 2017–2018.* https://academiccommons.columbia.edu/doi/10.7916/d8-hjyq-fg65

Brockway, Z. B. (1912). *Fifty years of prison service: An autobiography.* University of Michigan Press.

Burrell, B. (2006). *Caseload standards for probation and parole.* American Probation and Parole Association. https://www.appa-net.org/eweb/docs/APPA/stances/ip_CSPP.pdf

Camp, G. M., & Camp, C. (1995). *The corrections yearbook 1995: Probation and parole.* Criminal Justice Institute.

Chisholm, H. (Ed.). (1911). Recognizance. In *Encyclopedia Britannica* (Vol. 22, 11th ed.). Cambridge University Press.

County of Los Angeles Probation (n.d.). *Homepage.* https://probation.lacounty.gov/

County of Los Angeles Probation. (2018). *County of Los Angeles Probation annual report.* https://probation.lacounty.gov/wp-content/annual-report/?page=1

Eaglin, J., & Solomon, D. (2015). *Reducing racial and ethnic disparities in jails: Recommendations for local practice.* Brennan Center for Justice, New York University School of Law.

Falconer, S. M. (2012). Parole boards and hearings. In S. M. Barton-Bellessa (Ed.), *Encyclopedia of community corrections* (Vol. 1, pp. 286–290). SAGE Publications. https://doi.org/10.4135/9781452218519

Fields, C. B. (2012). Augustus, John. In S. M. Barton-Bellessa (Ed.), *Encyclopedia of community corrections* (Vol. 1, pp. 17–18). SAGE Publications. https://doi.org/10.4135/9781452218519

Frankel, R. (2020). *Revoked: How probation and parole feed mass incarceration in the United States.* ACLU Human Rights Watch.

Gray, M. K., Fields., M., & Maxwell, S. R. (2001). Examining probation violations: Who, what and when. *Crime and Delinquency, 47*(4), 537–557. https://doi.org/10.1177/0011128701047004003

The Guardian. (2007, May 2). *Timeline: A history of probation: 100 years and counting of probation services.* https://www.theguardian.com/society/2007/may/02/crime.penal

Jannetta, J., Breaux, J., & Ho, H. (2014). *Examining racial and ethnic disparities in probation revocation: Summary findings and implications from a multisite study.* Urban Institute https://www.urban.org/research/publication/examining-racial-and-ethnic-disparities-probation-revocation

Kaeble, D. (2021). *Annual Probation Survey and Annual Parole Survey.* Bureau of Justice Statistics. https://bjs.ojp.gov/data-collection/annual-probation-survey-and-annual-parole-survey

Kaeble, D. (2023). *Probation and Parole in the United States, 2021.* Bureau of Justice Statistics. https://bjs.ojp.gov/sites/g/files/xyckuh236/files/media/document/ppus21.pdf

Kimchi, A. (2017). Investigating the assignment of probation conditions: Heterogeneity and the role of race and ethnicity. *Journal of Quantitative Criminology, 35*(4), 715–745. https://doi.org/10.1007/s10940-018-9400-2

Little, A.D. (1967). *Preliminary report to the President's Commission on Law Enforcement and Administration of Justice Precedent to Drugs and Narcotics Report.* U.S. Department of Justice, Office of Justice Programs. https://www.ojp.gov/ncjrs/virtual-library/abstracts/preliminary-report-presidents-commission-law-enforcement-and

Lyons, P., & Jermstad, T. (2013). *Civil liabilities and other legal issues for probation/parole officers and supervisors.* U.S. Department of Justice. National Institute of Corrections Accession No. 027037. https://nicic.gov/civil-liabilities-and-other-legal-issues-probationparole-officers-and-supervisors-4th-edition

Maconochie, A. (1838). *Thoughts on convict management: And other subjects connected with the Australian penal colonies.* Good Books.

MacKenzie, D. L. (2001). *Sentencing and corrections in the 21st century: Setting the stage for the future.* U.S. Department of Justice, Office of Justice Programs. https://www.ojp.gov/ncjrs/virtual-library/abstracts/sentencing-and-corrections-21st-century-setting-stage-future

Morris, N. (2002). *Maconochie's gentlemen: The Story of Norfolk Island & the roots of modern prison reform.* Oxford University Press. https://doi.org/10.1093/oso/9780195146073.002.0001

New York City Department of Probation. (n.d.). *Homepage.* https://www1.nyc.gov/site/probation/index.page

Oudekerk, B., & Kaeble, D. (2021). *Probation and parole in the United States, 2019.* U.S. Department of Justice, Office of Justice Programs. https://bjs.ojp.gov/content/pub/pdf/ppus1718.pdf

Phelps, M. S. (2018). Mass probation and inequality: Race, class, and gender disparities in supervision and revocation. In J. T. Ulmer & M. S. Bradley (Eds.), *Handbook on punishment decisions: Locations of disparity* (pp. 43–65). Routledge. https://doi.org/10.4324/9781315410371

Pisciotta, A. W. (1994). Benevolent repression: Social control and the American reformatory-prison movement. NYU Press.

Schwartzapfel, B. (2015, July 11). How parole boards keep prisoners in the dark and behind bars. The Washington Post (July 11th, 2015). https://www.washingtonpost.com/national/

the-power-and-politics-of-parole-boards/2015/07/10/49c1844e-1f71-11e5-84d5-eb37ee8eaa61_story.html?utm_term=.23be58509ecb

Shaw, J. W. (2012). Parole guidelines score. In S. M. Barton-Bellessa (Ed.), *Encyclopedia of community corrections* (Vol. 1, pp. 294–295). SAGE Publications. https://doi.org/10.4135/9781452218519

Steinmetz, K. F., & Anderson, J. O. (2016). A probation profanation: Race, ethnicity, and probation in a Midwestern sample. *Race and Justice*, 6, 325–349. https://doi.org/10.1177/2153368715619656

Tittle, C., Botchkovar, E., & Antonaccio, O. (2011). Criminal contemplation, national context, and deterrence. *Journal of Quantitative Criminology*, 27, 225–249. https://doi.org/10.1007/s10940-010-9104-8.

Tonry, M. (2019). Predictions of dangerousness in sentencing: Déjà vu all over again. *Crime and Justice*, 48, 439–482. https://doi.org/10.1086/701895.

Weisberg, R., Mukamal, D., & Segall, J. D. (2011). *Life in Limbo: An examination of parole releases for prisoners serving life sentences with the possibility of parole in California*. Stanford Criminal Justice Center.

Zippia. (2023, July 21). *Probation officer demographics and statistics in the U.S.* https://www.zippia.com/probation-officer-jobs/demographics/

Image Credits

PART II

Functions of Community Corrections

CHAPTER 4

Probation and Parole Officer Work

Probation and parole agencies occupy a dual function of having both a law enforcement orientation and a social welfare orientation. This can create role conflict in probation and parole officers, which can impact work performance, wellness, and resiliency. The daily activities of probation and parole officers include considerable interaction with other criminal justice systems, such as police, courts, jails, and prisons. These daily activities include investigation, documentation, and monitoring individuals' progress on court-ordered supervision conditions. A key element is the probation/parole officer–individual on supervision relationship, with best practices centered on the fostering of a working alliance. Growing emphasis on core correctional practices and the risk-need-responsivity (RNR) model shapes the expectations and responsibilities of these officers. Violation procedures may present challenges, especially when there is an emphasis on punishing noncompliance without recognizing and incentivizing positive behaviors. The work of a probation and parole officer is complex, though crucial for the functioning of the community corrections system.

LEARNING OBJECTIVES

By the end of this chapter, students will be able to:

- Understand the daily activities of probation and parole officers, including the impact of role conflict and high caseloads.
- Identify and explain probation and parole conditions for individuals that influence success and failure to complete the supervision sentence.
- Synthesize and explain core correctional practices and their importance for probation/ parole supervision.

KEY TERMS

- Core correctional practices
- Presentence investigation report (PSIR)
- Revocation
- Risk-need-responsivity (RNR) model
- Supervision conditions
- Technical violations

Probation and Parole Officer Responsibilities
◊ Journey into the Field: Mr. Jaime Barrera
Daily Activities of Probation and Parole Officers
Day in the Life of a Probation Officer
Presentence Investigation Report
Monitoring Compliance—Supervision Conditions
Core Correctional Practices
The Risk-Need-Responsivity (RNR) Model
The Officer—Individual on Supervision Relationship
◊ Officer Work, Careers, and Wellness: Role Conflict
Violations and Revocations
Prison Return: Parole Revocation
◊ Diversity, Equity, and Inclusion: Technical Violations
Summary: Probation and Parole Officer Work
Scenario-Based Activities

Talent is cheaper than table salt. What separates the talented individual from the successful one is hard work.

—Stephen King

Probation and Parole Officer Responsibilities

The responsibilities of probation and parole officers are diverse both between and within agencies; however, there are shared commonalities that can be examined throughout the community corrections system. This can be understood by examining these commonalities at various levels. At the broadest level are the mission statements and goals of specific state or local probation and parole agencies. The responsibilities of probation and parole officers are often split between the dual functions of a law enforcement orientation (where officers focus on surveillance, control, and punitive responses to probation or parole violations) and a social welfare orientation (where officers attempt to meet individual needs in education, social services, jobs, mental health, and therapeutic interventions). The degree to which these orientations are embedded within each probation or parole officer, each probation or parole agency, and the broader community can determine the daily practices that impact individuals on supervision.

At the community level, probation and parole officers have the responsibility of reinforcing public safety by reducing the recidivism of individuals under supervision. At the individual level, probation and parole officers are responsible for considerable investigation, documentation, and interaction with other criminal justice systems (i.e., police, courts, jails, prisons). While probation and parole officers often have considerable discretion over the individuals they supervise, including decisions to return noncompliant individuals to prison, there is evidence that the fostering of a good probation/parole officer–supervisee relationship is a key effective means of meeting goals.

When examining the work that probation and parole officers perform, it is common for people to rely on negative media portrayals, myths, and stereotypes. However, an intersectional approach suggests that the important job of supervising individuals while they are on probation and parole can be challenging, complex, and rewarding. Officers come to work with a range of personal life experiences and demographic characteristics, they have different motivations and approaches for the individuals they supervise. Officers also leave their daily work activities to go home to family, friends, and the community they serve. This is not to suggest that criticisms or limitations of current practices should be ignored but rather that one should consider the challenge of reinforcing public safety via surveillance and supervision while also removing barriers to treatment, health care, and services for individuals on supervision. Tonry and Will (1990) highlight this dynamic in the following quote:

> Please don't misunderstand us. We don't mean to disparage probation officers, probation departments, or judges who sentence offenders to probation. The view of probation as "doing nothing" is overstated and oversimplified. There are thousands of conscientious probation officers, too often overworked and underpaid, and there are many well-run probation programs in which probation supervision is meaningful and probation conditions are enforced. However, there are also many probation offices in which caseloads are enormous and budgets are inadequate and in which supervision is not meaningful and conditions are not enforced. (p. 1)

Probation and parole officers are asked to address a range of complex social problems, while often remaining invisible or having their work dismissed. Yet, every day in the United States these officers, and the agencies that employ them, engage in crucial community functions and face challenges in the fair application of justice. These topics require further exploration.

IMAGE 4.1   A Parole Officer Interviews a Drug-Related Offense Probationer

JOURNEY INTO THE FIELD: MR. JAIME BARRERA

◇◇◇◇◇◇◇

Full name: Jaime Barrera

Title: Community Supervision Officer, Hidalgo County Community Supervision and Corrections Department

Officer Jaime Barrera grew up in the very small town of Lasara, Texas, and he graduated from Raymondville High School in 1991. In 1996, Mr. Barrera graduated from the University of Texas–Pan American with a bachelor's of science degree in criminal justice. During his college education, Officer Barrera engaged in internship activities with the Alamo Police Department in Alamo, Texas. Officer Barrera then attended the University of Texas Systems Police Academy in 1999 and worked as a university police officer for the University of Texas–Pan American Police Department between 1999 and 2002. In 2002, he joined the Hidalgo County Community Supervision and Corrections Department where he has worked ever since. In these 20 years

Image 4.2

of service, Officer Barrera has worked with regular caseloads, intense supervision caseloads, pretrial diversion caseloads, reduced risk program caseloads, and virtual supervision caseloads. His current position is a community supervision officer with the Hidalgo County Community Supervision and Corrections Department in the virtual supervision program. When not at work, Officer Barrera enjoys spending time with his wife Yolanda (a teacher in Edinburg, Texas) and his children, Michael, Alyssa, and David. In the following Journey into the Field, Officer Barrera reflects on his pathway to a career in community corrections and his expectations for the future.

I first got into probation work by researching what would happen to people who I arrested as a police officer way back in 1999. I wanted to be more involved in the process of helping people via a social work (supervision and treatment) mentality. My career has changed since 2002, when I became a probation officer, by means of seeing people on probation succeed (getting it right). I routinely keep in mind my purpose to help others.

My opinion regarding probation work is based on 20+ years of experience in working with people under supervision in Texas. Probation works when taken as an opportunity to get it right and succeed in life. Current policies, practices, and rules work for the most part. Continued use of what works or best practices plus improving them will only result in success. Rewarding good behavior works by keeping in mind that the probation population is so diverse. Working out the severity of punishment is key.

The future of probation will continue to be shaped by changes that take place in society (legislation, case law, and probation departments). The use of technology and a methodology that works with special programs can maximize outcomes. Proper diagnosis plus supervision and treatment can mean influencing the future behavior of people on supervision to reduce recidivism. Officers must be given guidance without removing discretion. Violations do take place in this line of work, and the response makes a difference. We can get there by adapting to what works now and what will be required for the future.

Daily Activities of Probation and Parole Officers

The mission statements and goals of probation and parole agencies should be reflected in the daily activities of their probation and parole officers. However, these daily activities are not fixed and often fluctuate between a law enforcement and social welfare approach to supervision. Additionally, the daily activities of a probation or parole officer may change dramatically as their careers advance. For example, a person may begin their career in a security or frontline probation or parole officer capacity, then they may gravitate toward the intensive supervision of high-risk individuals that requires a law enforcement orientation, or perhaps they become a case manager or program manager for individuals with special needs or mental health issues that suits a social welfare orientation. Advanced career paths may move these officers into purely administrational positions where they manage entire components of probation or parole agencies, or even become the director or chief of an agency—both of which are heavily influenced by political, community, and budgetary considerations and involve very little direct interaction with individuals on supervision.

When examining the daily activities of most probation and parole officers, there is recognition that the work involves managing large caseloads of individuals under supervision, documentation and writing reports, and participating in court proceedings. Court proceedings are a focal point for probation and parole officers, as they are often required to testify in court using evidence such as behavioral reports, witness and victim statements, and progress reports on the completion of any court-mandated requirements. This requires effective caseload management, as probation and parole officers may be responsible for monitoring the progress of people under their supervision (see a more in-depth discussion of caseloads in Chapter 3). These caseloads are typically lower when more intense supervision is necessary, such as for high-risk individuals convicted of a sex offense, youth with drug addictions, and people with histories of violence. Officers who supervise lower risk individuals often have higher caseloads, as they may rely more on infrequent telephone check-ins and other less intrusive forms of supervision. Probation and parole officers are often required to balance and blend law enforcement and social work responsibilities. In terms of law enforcement, the daily activities of probation and parole officers center on reinforcing public safety and security. Officers review case files of individuals and they have direct knowledge of the types of offenses that individuals committed, the frequency with which these were committed, and the risk factors associated with offending. Probation and parole officers are responsible for documenting the progress of individuals over time, particularly in terms of legal requirements that must be completed during the supervision period (e.g., drug addiction programs, financial payments). Officers routinely interact with other criminal justice systems, such as submitting reports to courts and referrals to jails and prisons.

The law enforcement function relies on promoting accountability in individuals through surveillance, mainly in terms of where they live, working status, known associates, and attendance of programs. Many daily activities of officers are built around a law enforcement approach to public safety, as discussed above. When the individuals under supervision fail to meet these conditions, the probation or parole officer is responsible for implementing sanctions that can range from providing a warning, to increasing reporting requirements, or filing a motion to revoke (termed revocation). A revocation is a failed probation or parole sentence, and it is the most undesirable outcome (see Chapter 10 for a more thorough discussion of probation and parole outcomes). As such, probation and parole officers have considerable discretion in terms of punitive responses to individual noncompliance. The probation or parole officer may partner with law enforcement agencies and other officials to gather information about an individual on supervision, including the collection and dissemination of criminal history and financial data. The officer may also collaborate with other agencies to issue subpoenas, execute warrants, and track absconders. These diverse roles and responsibilities are evident in Figure 4.1.

In contrast to law enforcement activities, the daily tasks of probation and parole officers may also feature a social work orientation. Here, the officers aim to remove barriers or obstacles that hinder the chances of supervisee success. There is a strong relationship between addressing obstacles during supervision and future desistance from crime by individuals (Farrall, 2012). This includes providing periodic feedback to the individual regarding their progress on conditions such as attendance at programs for mental health and drug addiction. Helping individuals

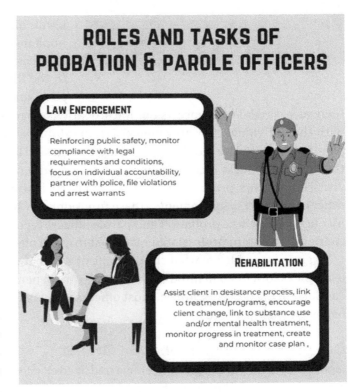

FIGURE 4.1

find and maintain employment is also considered part of the role. The social work role emphasizes the need to be empathetic and compassionate while helping individuals fulfill the conditions of supervision.

Probation and parole officers are tasked with supporting the needs of individuals on their caseload, particularly by referring suitable individuals to drug treatment, domestic violence classes, mental health evaluations and therapies, anger management interventions, and other community services. This may also include the use of outside agencies that provide treatments, employment resources, and educational options. Similar strategies such as referral to counseling or group meetings are often used by probation and parole officers to address substance abuse, though drug testing may also be mandated by the court as an additional requirement. In some agencies, probation and parole officers are responsible for administering drug and alcohol testing.

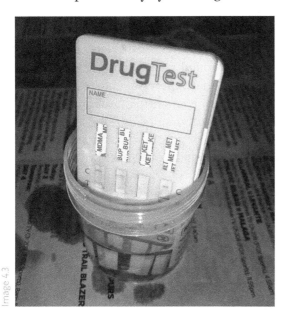

Image 4.3

Among their daily tasks, probation and parole officers are often expected to create and implement a supervision plan, also referred to as a "case plan." *Supervision plans* are tailored to the individual and should lay out specific goals for the individual to achieve to support their success while on supervision. The probation or parole officer should work collaboratively with the individual they are supervising to establish, monitor, and update the supervision plan. Officers are also required to keep up-to-date and accurate records for each individual on their caseload. These records include details regarding all contacts with the supervisee, office visits, home visits, program attendance and participation, drug testing dates and results, and other established requirements. These functions rely heavily on partnerships with community agencies, where probation and parole officers receive training, refer individuals on their caseload, maintain professional relationships, and offer assistance and input where needed.

To give you an idea of what the daily life of a probation and parole officer might be, see the example below. Keep in mind that this may vary depending on the agency and the individual caseload of the officer; however, most officers will engage in the key duties and tasks outlined below on a regular basis.

Day in the Life of a Probation Officer

Jessica Martin is a probation officer in a midsized city. She has worked for her current probation agency for 5 years. The agency balances a law enforcement and social welfare orientation, with a cultural standard of referring to an individual under supervision as a "client." She supervises a general caseload of 100, which has a mix of individuals assessed as low, moderate, and high risk. Her typical workday is from 9:00 a.m. until 5:00 p.m. The following is an example of a typical day in the life of Officer Martin.

9:00 a.m.	Arrive at the office, turn on computer, and check email and respond to any emergent messages; prints schedule for the day and reviews case files for clients she will meet with.
9:30 a.m.	First scheduled contact with a newly released individual who is on probation for drug possession. Because this is the intake appointment, it will last longer than a typical contact. During this appointment, Officer Martin will: • Introduce herself, her role as a probation officer, and the goals of probation. • Review conditions of supervision and answer any questions the individual may have. • Update client's case file with relevant information (e.g., contact information, photographs, description of tattoos). • Conduct risk and needs assessment (this will likely be the longest part of the contact). • Conduct urinalysis. • Discuss next steps, answer questions, and set a date for a home visit and next office contact. After the meeting is over, Officer Martin enters in her case notes describing the nature of the contact with the client, including what was discussed, paperwork that was completed, and demeanor of the client. She inputs the date for the home visit and next office visit.
10:30 a.m.	Appointments with existing clients begin. Officer Martin has three clients on her schedule this morning. The first two show up on time and take about 15 minutes each. In these meetings, Officer Martin reviews whether there have been any changes (e.g., new address, change in employment), new contact with law enforcement, and any substance use. She congratulates one of her clients who recently completed a cognitive behavioral program. She plans to attend the program graduation next week. One of the clients was due for a drug test, so Officer Martin walked her to the bathroom for an observed urinalysis. In this office, officers stand outside of the bathroom and watch clients provide a sample through a glass window in the bathroom.
	After the client leaves the sample, Officer Martin labels it and uses a dipstick to test the urine. After a few minutes, the sample comes back negative for all substances. Officer Martin lets the client know and then returns to her office to wait for her third client. While she waits, she enters case notes for the two clients she just met with. After 10 minutes, Officer Martin calls the third client who has not shown up yet. The client answers and says they forgot about the meeting. Officer Martin reminds them that attending their appointments is a required part of their supervision conditions. Because this is their first missed appointment, she offers them the opportunity to reschedule for tomorrow. Officer Martin finishes updating her case notes on her computer until lunch.

(continued)

12:00 p.m.	Lunch time. Officer Martin has a lot of paperwork to catch up on, so she eats at her desk while working. She prints off case file information and addresses for her field work this afternoon.
1:00 p.m.	Officer Martin leaves the office to conduct four home visits. Her agency does not have any cars, so she drives her personal vehicle. She drives to the furthest client first, which is 35 minutes away. When she arrives, she scopes out the outside of the home and neighborhood. The client is expecting her and welcomes her into his home. Once inside, Officer Martin asks the client to show her around his apartment. They walk briefly through each room in the house.
	During this time, Officer Martin is looking for any signs of noncompliance (e.g., drugs, drug paraphernalia) as well as reviewing the general living conditions. After the walk-through, she and the client sit down in the living room to talk. This client has been searching for employment for a few months. Officer Martin asks how the job search has been going. The client informs her he has an interview later in the week. Officer Martin congratulates him on this and asks him if he has prepared how he will talk about his criminal history and the fact that he is on probation. She practices with him and gives him advice. At the end of their conversation, she reminds him of his next office visit.
	This home visit took about 30 minutes. Officer Martin travels to her next two clients who live in the same neighborhood about 15 minutes away. She conducts a similar check-in with each of these clients, both taking 30 minutes. She drives 5 minutes to her final client for a surprise home visit. When she arrives, no one answers the door. She plans to try again later in the week. She drives the 15 minutes back to the office.
3:40 p.m.	Officer Martin updates her case notes from the three successful home visits and one attempted home visit. She does not get a chance to finish, so she saves her notes to complete tomorrow.
4:00 p.m.	Officer Martin attends a meeting with probation officers and supervisors in her agency to discuss a new policy their agency is implementing next week.
5:00 p.m.	Officer Martin heads home for the day.

Presentence Investigation Report

Within some probation systems, officers are tasked with preparing a **presentence investigation report (PSIR)** that provides a link between probation and the court. That is, prior to sentencing, the probation agency may be tasked with completing a PSIR, which is a legal document that presents the findings from an investigation into the legal and social background of a person convicted of a crime to determine if there are extenuating circumstances that should influence the severity or leniency of a criminal sentence. The PSIR is generally used for felony cases. The PSIR report consists of both legal and extra-legal information about the individual. Extra-legal information often reflects socioeconomic characteristics of the individual and/or the community, particularly financial stability, marital status, housing, education, and other resources that can influence available solutions. While not exhaustive, the Table 4.1 features the typical variables used in a PSIR:

TABLE 4.1   Presentence Investigation Report Information

Legal Information	Extra-legal Information
Juvenile record	Probation officer recommendations
Adult record	Gang affiliation
Previous court record	Background and ties to the community
Probation/parole history	Substance use disorder history
Mitigating and aggravating circumstances	Physical health
Official version of offense	Mental health
Plea bargain	Financial circumstances
Custody status	Employment history
Pending cases	Education history
Previous cases	Medical history
Recommendation summary	Victim impact statement
Fines and restitution	Marital history
Sentencing options	Military record
Sentencing recommendations	Evaluative/needs summary

Source: Table adapted from Alarid & Montemayor, 2010

Probation officers begin the PSIR with a review of relevant documents. This includes court filings, plea agreements, previous reports from criminal justice agencies, educational records, financial records, validation of previous/current employment, and previous/current engagement in social services, programs, and treatment centers. Legal information regarding the chronology of the individual's case is examined, which moves from the criminal history of the individual (using national crime databases) to the details of the criminal offense (using police reports and other materials). In recent years, advancements in technology have allowed officers the ability to identify, request, and examine a range of computerized records from various jurisdictions. The PSIR may also be relevant for institutional corrections, as jail and prison staff may use the report for assignment of inmate housing, assignment of programs and services, and release date (including reentry strategies).

Probation officers will also conduct a presentence investigation that requires interviewing all relevant parties. Interview skills are valuable, as officers may be interacting with law enforcement, court personnel, and correctional staff, as well as the victim/s, the individual's family, present/current employers, school officials, medical and mental health professionals, and others (Bunzel, 1995). The PSIR centers on the probation officer writing a report for the court. This requires that officers be trained and proficient in report writing, including professionalism in conducting the PSIR in a detached, dispassionate, and impartial manner. An initial draft is disclosed to the individual and relevant attorneys for their review, which allows for the identification of missing or erroneous information and for discussion of tentative findings and implications. The final report written by the probation officer will include all relevant legal and extra-legal information, along with a mathematical system of allocating points in relation to existing sentencing guidelines. For example, a criminal history points system originally developed by the United States Sentencing Commission is frequently used by probation officers to calculate a score for the individual in an unbiased and uniform manner across different jurisdictions. While the PSIR can be a time-consuming and complex task, the primary duty of the probation officer can be summarized as such:

> The probation officer is responsible for the preparation of all sections of the presentence report. In this endeavor the officer is an independent reporter to the court about the offense and the defendant, and also provides an analysis of how that information applies to the sentencing guidelines. The probation officer does not reinvestigate the offense or conviction. (U.S. Probation Office, 2009, p. 4)

The format of the PSIR varies between jurisdictions, including international differences, though they will contain the components discussed. Additionally, agency policies surrounding the completion of PSIRs vary. For example, some agencies have dedicated probation officers who solely complete PSIRs, while other agencies disperse PSIR assignments amongst all officers.

Monitoring Compliance—Supervision Conditions

A key component of probation and parole work is monitoring compliance with **supervision conditions**, or requirements imposed either by the court, parole board, or supervision agency. Most supervision agencies can impose restrictions if they do not violate liberty restrictions. Individuals who are placed on probation or parole supervision are often required to complete a number of conditions before their supervision term is over. It is estimated that individuals on probation are required to comply with an average of 10–20 conditions (Roth et al., 2021). Standard conditions include (a) reporting regularly to an assigned probation/parole officer and/or allowing unannounced visits from the officer; (b) avoiding additional law violations; (c) finding and maintaining employment; (d) not possessing drug, alcohol, pornographic material, or weapons; (e) participating in court-ordered programs such as anger management or drug/alcohol desistance courses; and (f) paying any monthly supervision fees, drug testing fees, treatment fees, restitution, and/or other financial sanctions. Supervision conditions may include situational considerations of risk, like avoiding gang membership or relationships with people who have criminal records, curfews, and notification of address changes or movements out of state.

2022 Florida Statutes

Title XLVIICRIMINAL PROCEDURE AND CORRECTIONS
Chapter 948PROBATION AND COMMUNITY CONTROL
SECTION 03 Terms and conditions of probation.

948.03   Terms and conditions of probation.—
(1) The court shall determine the terms and conditions of probation. Conditions specified in this section do not require oral pronouncement at the time of sentencing and may be considered standard conditions of probation. These conditions may include among them the following, that the probationer or offender in community control shall:

(a) Report to the probation officer as directed. Such reporting requirements may be fulfilled through remote reporting if approved by the relevant probation officer, the relevant county probation authority or entity, or the Department of Corrections and if the court has not excluded the possibility of remote reporting by the defendant in his or her order of probation. If the Department of Corrections or a county probation authority or entity elects to authorize remote reporting, it must adopt and make available remote probation reporting policies.

(b) Permit the probation officer to visit him or her at his or her home or elsewhere.

(c) Work faithfully at suitable employment insofar as may be possible.

(d) Remain within a specified place.

(e) Live without violating any law. A conviction in a court of law is not necessary for such a violation of law to constitute a violation of probation, community control, or any other form of court-ordered supervision.

(f) Make reparation or restitution to the aggrieved party for the damage or loss caused by his or her offense in an amount to be determined by the court. The court shall make such reparation or restitution a condition of probation, unless it determines that clear and compelling reasons exist to the contrary. If the court does not order restitution, or orders restitution of only a portion of the damages, as provided in s. **775.089**, it shall state on the record in detail the reasons therefor.

(g) Effective July 1, 1994, and applicable for offenses committed on or after that date, make payment of the debt due and owing to a county or municipal detention facility under s. **951.032** for medical care, treatment, hospitalization, or transportation received by the felony probationer while in that detention facility. The court, in determining whether to order such repayment and the amount of the repayment, shall consider the amount of the debt, whether there was any fault of the institution for the medical expenses incurred, the financial resources of the felony probationer, the present and potential future financial needs and earning ability of the probationer, and dependents, and other appropriate factors.

(h) Support his or her legal dependents to the best of his or her ability.

(i) Make payment of the debt due and owing to the state under s. **960.17**, subject to modification based on change of circumstances.

(j) Pay any application fee assessed under s. **27.52**(1)(b) and attorney's fees and costs assessed under s. **938.29**, subject to modification based on change of circumstances.

(k) Not associate with persons engaged in criminal activities.

(l) 1. Submit to random testing as directed by the probation officer or the professional staff of the treatment center where he or she is receiving treatment to determine the presence or use of alcohol or controlled substances.

Florida Senate, "Terms and Conditions of Probation," 2023 Florida Statutes, 2022.

2. If the offense was a controlled substance violation and the period of probation immediately follows a period of incarceration in the state correctional system, the conditions must include a requirement that the offender submit to random substance abuse testing intermittently throughout the term of supervision, upon the direction of the probation officer.

(m) Be prohibited from possessing, carrying, or owning any:
1. Firearm.
2. Weapon without first procuring the consent of the probation officer.

(n) Be prohibited from using intoxicants to excess or possessing any drugs or narcotics unless prescribed by a physician, an advanced practice registered nurse, or a physician assistant. The probationer or community controllee may not knowingly visit places where intoxicants, drugs, or other dangerous substances are unlawfully sold, dispensed, or used.

(o) Submit to the drawing of blood or other biological specimens as prescribed in ss. **943.325** and **948.014**, and reimburse the appropriate agency for the costs of drawing and transmitting the blood or other biological specimens to the Department of Law Enforcement.

(p) Submit to the taking of a digitized photograph by the department as a part of the offender's records. This photograph may be displayed on the department's public website while the offender is under court-ordered supervision. However, the department may not display the photograph on the website if the offender is only on pretrial intervention supervision or if the offender's identity is exempt from disclosure due to an exemption from the requirements of s. **119.07**.

(2) The enumeration of specific kinds of terms and conditions does not prevent the court from adding thereto such other or others as it considers proper. However, the sentencing court may only impose a condition of supervision allowing an offender convicted of s. **794.011**, s. **800.04**, s. **827.071**, s. **847.0135**(5), or s. **847.0145** to reside in another state if the order stipulates that it is contingent upon the approval of the receiving state interstate compact authority. The court may rescind or modify at any time the terms and conditions theretofore imposed by it upon the probationer. However, if the court withholds adjudication of guilt or imposes a period of incarceration as a condition of probation, the period may not exceed 364 days, and incarceration shall be restricted to either a county facility, or a probation and restitution center under the jurisdiction of the Department of Corrections.

Image 4.4

Criticisms of probation and parole include recognition that there is very little research evidence that supports the efficacy of conditions. Judges have wide discretion in assigning conditions, and this can emerge in vague requirements of "associating with good people" and "avoiding bad habits" that can be unrelated to the individual's circumstances and/or offense. Such vagueness increases the risk of an individual failing probation or parole and has led some experts to doubt whether they themselves could be successful on supervision (Frankel, 2020). Supervision conditions can also be conflicting, which reduces compliance and individual success. For example, individuals may be required to remain employed while simultaneously reporting to probation or parole officers and attending treatment programs that may interfere with their work schedule.

When compared to international systems of probation, probation and parole conditions within the U.S. system are often described as being uniquely punitive, "with longer terms, a much higher average number of conditions, a greater emphasis on enforcement and control, less supportive assistance, higher revocation rates, and a greater reliance on incarceration to punish noncompliance" (Roth et al., 2021, p. 3). Probation and parole conditions are influenced by punishment orientations that fluctuate over time (see Chapter 1 for a description of punishment philosophies). While probation and parole have historically followed a rehabilitative philosophy with officers occupying a social worker role, this changed during the "get tough on crime" movement of the late 1970s and 1980s. During this period, probation and parole mimicked institutional corrections with the emergence of "intensive supervision probation." Intensive supervision probation (ISP) features a drastic increase in supervision of the individual and the use of severe restrictions (see more about ISP in Chapter 5). This may include the use of several probation officers to supervise one individual, more frequent visits to probationer

IMAGE 4.5   Senator Zellnor Y. Myrie Speaking at a Press Conference for the "Clean Slate" Bill, 2021

residences, employment and treatment locations, or the requirement of house arrest for the individual. While ISP is directed toward the increased monitoring of medium- to high-risk individuals, research indicates that it tends to increase rather than decrease violations and revocations (Gendreau et al., 2000; Phelps, 2015; Vera Institute of Justice, 2013). Evidence can be seen in successful probation completion rates dropping from 80% to 60% during the 1980s, with a 60% completion rate now remaining consistent for decades (American Probation and Parole Association, 2013).

Core Correctional Practices

Probation and parole supervision integrates elements of risk management with an emphasis on moderating risk factors through conditions of supervision. Risk management centers on identifying, assessing, and mitigating potential risks of an individual on probation or parole. This process includes the use of risk assessment to identify risk levels, as well as unique dynamic risk factors. *Risk factors* are characteristics that increase the likelihood or probability that an individual will engage in crime-related behaviors (Farrington, 2007; Ullich & Coid, 2011). There are eight factors that have consistently been supported in the literature as being risk factors for criminal behavior: antisocial attitudes, antisocial associates, a history of antisocial behavior, antisocial personality pattern, problems at home, problems at school or work, problematic leisure circumstances, and substance abuse (Andrews & Bonta, 2010a; 2010b). These factors will be explored throughout this chapter.

As early as 1980, scholars like Andrews and Kiessling introduced key dimensions into core correctional practices that were relevant to probation and parole, with an emphasis on the quality of the interpersonal relationship between officer and individual. This approach highlighted the probation and parole officer characteristics of being respectful, open, warm, mature, understanding, genuine, non-blaming, flexible, reflective, and bright (Andrews, 2011). These characteristics were valuable even in relationships where mandated requirements could make interactions difficult for supervisees, such as routine appointments, drug testing, and at-home visits from officers. In a meta-analysis that included 273 studies, Dowden and Andrews (2004) found that **core correctional practices** were based on the following five dimensions:

- Effective use of authority: Staff use a "firm-but-fair" approach with an emphasis on procedural justice.
- Appropriate modeling and reinforcement: Staff demonstrate behavior and reward individual adherence. Staff provide effective disapproval and use a structured learning process; positive reinforcements are powerful in changing behaviors.
- Problem solving: Staff assist individuals in goal setting, evaluating options, and implementing plans.
- Effective use of community resources: Staff advocate for individuals in the community (i.e., at work, school, etc.).
- Quality of interpersonal relationships: Staff has rapport with individuals and uses skilled communication.

These five dimensions required probation and parole officers to initiate a number of steps in order to develop a working alliance—namely, the building of rapport; development of respect and empathy; use of authority only when necessary; defining and modeling attitudes, behaviors, and skills for supervisees; providing opportunities for individuals to self-identify problems, barriers, or challenges that they face; and the creation of a working alliance to address deviant or criminal behavior (including the avoidance of antisocial peers). Core correctional practices therefore merge the law enforcement and social work roles to guide officers to treat individuals with respect during the accountability process.

Image 4.6

The Risk-Need-Responsivity (RNR) Model

The most dominant approach guiding policies and practices surrounding identification of and response to individual risk is the **risk-need-responsivity (RNR) model**. Practices aligned with this model have been shown to reduce individual recidivism by up to 35%, even in high-risk populations (Andrews & Bonta, 2010a; see Chapter 6 for a more in-depth discussion of correctional practices aligned with the RNR model). The RNR model is used by agencies to decide which individuals should receive services, the appropriate areas that rehabilitation services should target (e.g., substance abuse, family problems), and the cognitive social learning strategies that can reduce criminal behavior. The RNR model emphasizes three principles at the core of effective programming:

Risk Principle

Individuals differ in their risk of recidivism; therefore, different kinds of interventions and controls are appropriate. When the risk is low, interventions may be unreasonable and can increase risk. For higher risk individuals, intensive interventions are likely necessary to produce change in behavior. This principle dictates "who" should receive treatment.

Need Principle

Every individual naturally has their own set of dynamic risk factors or criminogenic needs, such as antisocial attitudes, antisocial associates, antisocial personality patterns, family/marital relationships, leisure time (or lack thereof), and substance abuse. When targeted via appropriate interventions, reductions in recidivism are possible. Interventions should target these individual needs for best results. This principle dictates "what" should be targeted in treatment.

Responsivity Principle

Behavioral and cognitive behavioral interventions have been shown to improve outcomes. Officers can use cognitive techniques in their interactions with individuals on supervision.

Image 4.7

Effective interactions and interventions should be tailored to individual characteristics such as age, gender, cognitive abilities, and/or motivation (see Andrews & Bonta, 2010b; Andrews et al., 1990a, 2011). The responsivity principle dictates "how" treatment should be delivered.

The logic of the risk principle is that actuarial risk assessments can more reliably predict criminal behaviors when compared to the subjective assessments of officers. That is, statistical techniques can improve the prediction of the risk that an individual presents, as these methods rely on data-driven formulas that identify higher risk individuals. This is similar to car insurance in that costs are determined by the individual's driving record (e.g., number of accidents, number of traffic violations.) and age (e.g., higher premiums for younger people, who are more likely to have accidents). Actuarial risk tools use similar methods to more accurately predict future involvement in the legal system.

The RNR framework clarifies that individuals who are higher risk need more surveillance and treatment. Yet, in reality some community corrections agencies may actually focus more on lower risk individuals simply because such individuals are easier to deal with. This is a "cream of the crop" method, as agencies want to show that their supervision practices produce the best results. However, this is counterproductive, as oversupervising low-risk individuals produces smaller outcomes and wastes agency resources, and there is evidence that increased supervision of these populations may in fact lead to increases in future crime (Andrews & Bonta, 2010a). The risk principle minimizes services for low-risk individuals and directs intensive services to the higher risk individuals where more progress can be made. The risk principle also encourages the separation of low- and high-risk individuals so they do not interact with each other.

The need principle describes what should be treated. To best reduce recidivism, interventions and programs should address criminogenic and noncriminogenic needs (see Table 4.2). Criminogenic needs focus on the "central eight" factors linked to offending: criminal history, procriminal attitudes, antisocial personality, procriminal associates, education/employment deficits, family/martial variables, substance abuse, and leisure/recreation pursuits. Individuals under supervision may also have noncriminogenic needs, such as self-esteem, emotional discomfort, mental health disorder, lack of ambition, history of victimization, fear of official punishment, and lack of physical activity. While the noncriminogenic needs will not directly reduce criminal behavior, they do affect how stable the individual is and the likelihood that they will comply with the conditions of supervision.

TABLE 4.2   Criminogenic and Noncriminogenic Needs

Criminogenic	Noncriminogenic
History of criminal behavior	Self-esteem
Procriminal attitudes (thoughts, values, and sentiments supportive of criminal behavior)	Vague feelings of emotional discomfort (anxiety, feeling blue, and feelings of alienation)
Antisocial personality (low self-control, hostility, adventurous pleasure seeking, disregard for others, callousness)	Major mental disorder (schizophrenia, depression)
Procriminal associates	Lack of ambition
Social achievement (education, employment)	History of victimization
Family/marital (marital instability, poor parenting skills, criminality)	Fear of official punishment
Substance abuse	Lack of physical activity
Leisure/recreation (lack of prosocial pursuits)	Housing instability
	Food instability

Source: Andrews & Bonta, 2010a, p. 46

The final component of the RNR model is the responsivity principle. Responsivity centers on presenting the treatment and interactions between the officer and the individual on supervision in a style and mode that is appropriate to the abilities and learning orientation of the individual. Much like students in a classroom may be more responsive to verbal, visual, or other modes of communication, individuals differ in their learning style, motivation, abilities, and strengths. As such, treatments should be tailored to maximize these individual orientations. Responsivity can be divided into general responsivity and specific responsivity. *General responsivity* applies to all individuals regardless of their behavior and emphasizes the importance of cognitive and behavioral social learning interventions that enable good outcomes. This includes the facilitation of a working alliance between the officer and supervisee, where a productive relationship based on warmth, respect, and collaboration is developed (see next section in this chapter). This also includes probation or parole officers modeling and reinforcing prosocial behaviors and effective problem-solving skills. *Specific responsivity* considers the presence or absence of personal strengths and social factors in applying behavioral interventions. Specific responsivity seeks to remove barriers related to learning style, personality, motivation, and biosocial (e.g., gender, race) characteristics while maximizing strengths in these domains. It may also include cultural awareness, such as the inclusion of elders in tribal justice parole mandates and requirements. Tribal justice and the need for cultural competency in officers can be seen in Chapter 7.

While the RNR framework does not directly consider issues related to housing, food, transportation, and basic needs, recent studies (Taxman & Smith, 2020) have noted that these factors can be either stabilizers (contribute to helping the person be productive in the community)

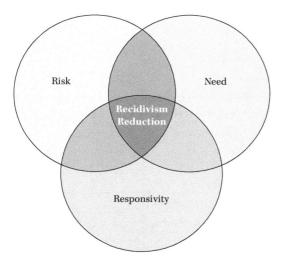

FIGURE 4.2   Risk-Need-Responsivity Model

or destabilizers (creating problems for individuals in the community). Experts suggest these factors should be added in a fourth principle to the RNR model that specifically addresses social determinants of health. Further work is needed to redefine the RNR model to accommodate the range of needs that may impact individuals on probation or parole supervision. The intersection of risk, need, and responsivity is displayed in Figure 4.2.

The Officer–Individual on Supervision Relationship

The daily activities of probation and parole officers include numerous duties, though routine visits with individuals assigned to their caseload is one of the most important. During these meetings the probation or parole officer will monitor and assess the progress of the individual. This is also the time in which the officer and individual under supervision will develop a working relationship. This relationship is very important to the success of completing a community supervision sentence. As Farrall (2004) highlights:

> During one calendar year there are 8,760 hours, of which one third of these (let's say) would be spent asleep—leaving 5,840 hours of "wakefulness." Of the 5,840 hours the probationer is awake, he or she would spend about one third of 1 percent of this time with his or her officer. (p. 175)

The interactions between the officer and the individual under supervision can be transformative. While the actual time spent in these interactions is small, Cornacchion and colleagues (2016) found that officers can create memorable messages that are meaningful and inspiring to those under supervision. A trusting relationship, agreement on treatment goals, and consensus on the tasks, programs, or services can also facilitate positive relationships (DeLude et al., 2012).

The officer–individual on supervision relationship frequently centers on topics of risk and need that may at first glance appear mundane. Typical challenges facing individuals under supervision include employment, housing, interpersonal relationships, family conflict, antisocial peer groups, drug and alcohol abuse, mental illness, and poverty or financial difficulties. However, these issues often represent very significant barriers to success for people on supervision. For example, Farrall (2004) recruited 199 probationers in six different probation services and followed them and their supervising officers through the course of their probation term. The confluence of these issues emerged in the accounts of these

Image 4.8

probation officers following meetings with their assigned probationer, as seen by the following officer reflections:

> I think that he is more at risk of getting back into heavy drug use and re-offending—in terms of stealing—because he has gone back to where he knows a lot of drug-using people. That was why he left in the first place, to get away from that scene. (Farrall, 2004, p. 199)

> [His mental health] is still a problem, but now dormant. It is there, but he got employment. If he loses the job, the depression will come back. Psychiatric service help is still in the pipeline, but it is up to the service to contact him. He got the job himself [and] he's bloomed. It raised his self-esteem and financial "muscle." He threw himself into work. (Farrall, 2004, p. 122)

> We looked at some of his past instances of losing his temper. But this got sidetracked by him losing his accommodations and job. These then became the focus of the work. He walked out of his job after a conflict at work. He doesn't see it as a problem. (Farrall, 2004, pp. 123–124)

The risk factors that individuals under supervision face can often be daunting, and lead to probation and parole agencies having poor outcomes as measured by high failures in completion rates and continued recidivism. This can create a cynical view in individuals on supervision that probation or parole is nothing more than a means of a government agency charging fees to increase revenues. Such cynicism is compounded when one considers that individuals may receive interventions "relatively late in the chain of cumulative continuity" (Moffitt, 1993, p. 415), resulting in these collective risk factors overwhelming the individual. It is common for the immediate duties of probation and parole officers to receive their attention. This includes tasks such as writing reports, meeting with individuals, documenting attendance in programs, making phone calls, and interacting with their colleagues and other criminal justice practitioners. However, activities that are more challenging, such as addressing social issues like poverty, unemployment, discrimination, health conditions, and unstable housing, may improve the officer–individual on supervision relationship and produce more positive outcomes.

An emerging practice for probation and parole officers is the use of a strength-based approach for addressing the needs of individuals. This approach acknowledges that individuals have existing strengths that can be emphasized to support their success on supervision. For example, goals for individuals on supervision that have a strong support system already in place may include maintaining those relationships, while those without a support system may need to work toward building a support system of individuals who are not involved in the criminal justice system. Using a strengths-based approach, officers focus on the strengths of each individual while working toward identifying and removing obstacles that can lead to further offending. This practice relies on the development of the personal and social capital that individuals may already possess. This also includes providing individuals with quality, evidence-based programs that can maximize these strengths. Current examples of such programs are discussed later in this book, though they currently include cognitive behavioral therapy, basic skills courses, and family-centered activities.

Traditional approaches directed toward individuals on community corrections supervision tend to rely on combative, moralistic, or authoritarian relationships, which fail to produce any meaningful or successful outcomes. These approaches avoid consideration of intersectionality in which supervision populations may have a constellation of risks and needs, diverse backgrounds and experiences, and a need for cultural competency to understand their perspective. In response, probation and parole agencies have moved toward an officer–individual on supervision relationship that is characterized by a working alliance. Adopted from the field of psychology, a *working alliance*, also known as a "helping alliance" or "therapeutic alliance," is defined as "a mutual understanding and agreement about change goals and the necessary tasks to move toward these goals along with the establishment of bonds to maintain the partners' work" (Bordin, 1994, p. 130). Training staff on the best practices for facilitating a working alliance with individuals is now an integral feature of core correctional practices and RNR.

IMAGE 4.9   Training of Trainers

A good probation/parole officer–individual on supervision relationship can produce several successful outcomes. For example, Tatman and Love (2010) studied individuals on supervision in six different parole sites, where 253 individuals were randomly assigned to a parole officer–therapist–individual collaborative intervention and 227 individuals were randomly assigned to supervision as usual. The collaborative intervention emphasized the values of caring, fairness, trust, and toughness. Those individuals who received the intervention had much higher ratings of the officer–individual on supervision relationship and had lower violation rates and fewer drug use days than the control group (Tatman & Love, 2010). Similarly, an analysis of serious and violent individuals on parole found that their negative perceptions of the officer–individual on supervision relationships were linked to higher recidivism, while perceptions of a positive relationship lowered the individual's likelihood of recidivism (Chamberlain et al., 2018). Several studies on the relationship between officers and individuals on probation found that when there was a strong, positive relationship, individuals were more likely to follow supervision conditions and had fewer arrests (Kennealy et al., 2012). There is also evidence that a positive officer–individual relationship can lead to avoidance of health risks, such as lowering engagement in risky sexual behaviors (Green et al., 2013), and drug use (Blasko et al., 2015). To be effective, probation and parole officers must occupy a dual-role function (i.e., law enforcement and social welfare) while developing productive working alliance relations that are "firm, fair, and caring," as there is clear evidence this leads to good outcomes (Kennealy et al., 2012, p. 501).

◊ Officer Work, Careers, and Wellness: Role Conflict

In 1956, Ohlin and colleagues noted that parole officers experienced complexity in their work with individuals on supervision. They created a typology of three orientations of staff working in community corrections. First is the *punitive officer*, who relied on threats, punishment, and control when interacting with individuals, with the goal of being "the guardian of middle-class community morality" (Ohlin et al., 1956, p. 215). The punitive orientation relied heavily on the surveillance of individuals, with justifications of protecting the community rather than a focus on individual needs. Second is the *protective officer*, who moved between protecting the community and reinforcing the needs of the individual, mainly by providing direct assistance, lecturing, and expressions of praise and blame. Third, the *welfare worker* centered on a large influx of professionals trained in social work following World War II. These welfare workers held the view that the protection of community was only possible through the rehabilitation of the individual, with threats and other external forms of coercion being viewed as temporary and ineffective.

When these social workers were newly employed as parole officers, they often experienced a conflict between the knowledge, skills, and techniques of their professional training and the existing culture within the parole agency (see Chapter 11 for more on agency culture). The result was an identity crisis, where dual roles emerged. Ohlin et al. (2016) explain: "on the one hand, he tries to offer a caseworker's sympathetic understanding and help; on the other, he is the agent of law and respectability" (p. 261). This conflict produced a lack of effectiveness between the parole officer and the individual on supervision, the parole agency, and the broader community. Many social workers responded by leaving the field of parole altogether or remaining in the field but being "unhappy" (Ohlin et al., 2016, p. 222).

Role conflict has been defined as the expectation "to provide both treatment and supervision services which have opposed philosophies" (Sigler & McGraw, 1984, p. 28). Similarly, it has been defined as "the apparent incompatibility of the welfare and enforcement roles" that officers face (Allard et al., 2003, p. 4). Role conflict is not limited to different orientations between types of officers, nor is limited to officers with backgrounds in social work, but rather role conflict is a workplace risk linked to a range of poor health outcomes in probation and parole officers. Role conflict is often a personal dilemma—one that requires the officer to adjust their own perceptions and behaviors to cope in the workplace. For example, in a study that included Australian parole agents, researchers found that parole officers who experienced role conflict had higher rates of emotional exhaustion (Allard et al., 2003). This emotional exhaustion carried the risk of experiencing generalized stress, such as feeling overextended at work and a lack of emotional resources when interacting with individuals (Whitehead & Lindquist, 1986). Emotional exhaustion can also lead to a range of physical and mental health issues (e.g., tension, anxiety, physical fatigue, and insomnia), personal problems (e.g., drugs and alcohol abuse, marital and family conflict), and workplace issues (e.g., deterioration in the quality of care provided by staff, low morale, absenteeism, and high turnover (see Allard et al., 2003)).

A possible solution to role conflict is for probation and parole agencies to develop and train officers using more standardized approaches to addressing the risks and needs of individuals under supervision. This centers on probation and parole agencies developing clear mission statements that can then direct officer roles and responsibilities. As Fearn (2012), states, "Once clearly defined objectives are established, several other commonly cited negative issues may be more easily dealt with as well, such as improving recruitment, training, and retention strategies to correspond more closely to these stated objectives" (p. 218). This may include an increase in pay to match expertise and education related to these objectives, as well as efforts to create more positive public perceptions of the important work that community corrections officers do.

Violations and Revocation

Approximately 66% of individuals on probation and 69% of individuals on parole will successfully complete their supervision terms (Kaeble, 2021). However, even those who successfully complete probation or parole supervision may experience violations of supervision. There are two main types of violations: a technical violation and a new offense. **Technical violations** represent noncompliance with a court-ordered supervision condition; however, this behavior is not typically considered illegal (e.g., not attending treatment). The most frequent violation is the failure to report to a probation officer (Gray et al., 2001; Pettus-Davis & Kennedy, 2020). Probation and parole officers typically have vast discretion in determining whether and how they respond to a technical violation. However, if they decide to file a formal violation, they will typically complete paperwork like the example report shown on the next page.

A violation of supervision conditions can result in a wide range of responses, from adjusting the conditions of parole supervision to assignment of additional of programs, trainings, and classes, and different forms of incarceration (i.e., reporting centers, short jail stays, new prison sentence). This tends to follow a pattern of graduated responses that range from verbal or documented warnings from a probation or parole officer to a formal legal ruling by the courts. There is less discretion for probation and parole officers when determining responses to a new offense, with many being referred for a revocation hearing and thus be addressed by the courts. However, an individual may still have a new arrest, typically for a minor crime, and still complete a successful probation. Current estimates of the total probation population's failure to complete probation include 14% being revoked to incarceration and 20% exiting for other or unknown reasons (Kaeble, 2021). In total, around 30% of the 1.8 million people placed on supervision will fail their probation period each year (Bradner et al., 2020). Estimates of failure to complete parole include 23% being revoked to incarceration and 8% exiting for other or unknown reasons (Kaeble, 2021).

When an individual under supervision violates the conditions of supervision (i.e., noncompliant), their probation or parole officer must decide how to respond. Probation and parole officers typically have a great deal of discretion in determining how they respond to technical violations. They can respond informally without notifying the court or they could file a formal violation with the court. If a formal violation is filed, a violation hearing will be held where a

Probation Violation Recommendation Report

TO: District attorney
FROM: PROBATION DEPARTMENT
    123 Supervision Way
    Anywhere, U.S.A.
    (123) 123-1234

RE: Louis DeGarza (#123456)

CASE INFORMATION:

Case Number: 2023JK000456A

ID Number: 123456

Original Offense: Battery   **Offense Degree:** 1st Degree Misdemeanor

Date of Probation Sentence: 01/01/2023

Supervision Term: One Year Probation

Fine: $500

Deferred Case: Yes ☐   No ☒

Termination Date: 12/31/2024

Supervising Officer: Jessica James

Defendant Address: 123 Mulberry Lane City, ST   **Phone #:** (111) 222-3333

Motion to Revoke Yes ☒   No ☐

Officer Jessica James instructed the defendant on conditions of probation on 01/08/2023.
Eligible for Electronic Monitoring Yes ☒ No ☐
Eligible for Substance Abuse Treatment Facility Yes ☒ No ☐
Eligible for Mental Health Treatment Facility Yes ☐ No ☒
Eligible for Other Special Programs Yes ☐, Specify: _____ No ☒
If the court continues the defendant on probation supervision, probation recommends:
SUBSTANCE USE TREATMENT FACILITY

OFFICER COMMENTS: DeGarza (#123456) has not been compliant with their supervision conditions. He has failed to report for two office visits in May (05/01/2023 and 05/15/2023). He showed up for his appointment on 06/01/2023 but he tested positive for opioids. He also tested positive for opioids on 03/12/2023. He was referred for substance use evaluation and was identified as eligible for treatment.

Supervising Officer Name: Jessica James   **Date:** 06/01/2023

(PLEASE PRINT)

Supervising Officer Signature: *Jessica James*

Supervisor Signature: *Robin Garza*

Date Approved: 06/02/2023

Example probation violation report, created by authors

judge will determine whether the supervision term will be revoked, modified, or continued. When one considers that a substantial number of individuals on probation or parole will not complete their supervision terms, it is important that scholars understand what counts as a success or failure. Table 4.3 table provides definitions of key terms related to probation and parole completion:

Prison Return: Parole Revocation

Revocation indicates that the individual has demonstrated poor performance through non-compliance, technical violations, or criminal activity that invalidates the parole conditions. This is described as a "failure to abide by the terms or conditions of supervision may result in revocation of parole" (Falconer, 2012, p. 286). If a revocation leads to a return to prison, then deliberations will lead to ruling on whether any of the parole sentence served will be credited and what the new prison sentence will be (i.e., a shorter fixed sentence or a requirement to

IMAGE 4.10 Idaho State Correctional Institution

complete the entire original sentence). Between 1980 and 2000, parole revocations nationally increased from 18% to 34% (Falconer, 2012). By 2005, 47% of all individuals entering the California prison system were the result of parole revocations, which is higher than the 38% of individuals entering the prison system due to a new felony conviction (Falconer, 2012). This indicates the regular use of parole revocation and its effect on incarceration.

Parole revocation hearings are protected by the Due Process Clause of the Fourteenth Amendment. Parole agencies represent an arm of the court, and when parole revocation is considered, the liberty of the individual is in jeopardy. These constitutional protections were

TABLE 4.3 Key Terms Related to Probation and Parole Completion

Key Term	Definition
Probation or parole violation	Noncompliance with any of the conditions of supervision constitutes a probation or parole violation, which can lead to sanctions or revocation. Violations are commonly divided into two categories: technical violations and new offense violations. *Technical violations* involve noncompliance with supervision conditions that are not in themselves illegal (e.g., failing to report to a probation officer, failing to pay fees, drinking alcohol, etc.), while *new offense violations* involve conduct that constitutes a crime.
Detainer or hold	Detainers, often referred to as "holds," are orders requiring that people charged with violating supervision be held in jail. When a detainer is lodged, there is no possibility of release unless it is lifted, either by the judge presiding over the violation, or, in some places, by the probation/parole officer. Even if someone was charged with both a violation and a new offense and a different judge ordered their release in the new case, they would remain in jail while the detainer was in place.
Violation hearing	Proceedings on probation violations are initiated by a probation officer filing a notice of violation or motion to revoke probation to the court. For parole violations, parole officers also initiate proceedings; however, they file notice with the parole board. The U.S. Supreme Court has held that two hearings are necessary for probation and parole violations: a preliminary hearing to determine if there is probable cause that a violation occurred and a final hearing to decide whether the person violated probation and what should happen. Due process is extremely limited at these hearings.
Sanction	Sanctions could include modifying supervision conditions, extending the supervision term, or a period of incarceration, usually in jail, with supervision continuing afterward. In many jurisdictions, probation/parole officers are given the authority to impose "administrative" sanctions (i.e., sanctions that do not require approval by a judge), including "short" jail sentences, without instituting formal violation proceedings in court.
Revocation	Revocation is the most severe penalty for a violation, involving the termination of the sentence to probation supervision and the imposition of a new or previously suspended sentence. Revocation almost always results in a sentence involving incarceration, often to prison for people on probation for felonies, and is usually more severe than the sentence that someone not on probation would have received. In some jurisdictions where the judge previously suspended a specific sentence, only that sentence can be imposed on revocation, while in others, the sentence on revocation can be anything up to the maximum for the original offense. It is also possible that individuals can receive a revocation and be continued on community supervision. Their supervision terms are often extended for a longer period. For individuals on parole, revocations typically result in the return to incarceration to complete the remainder of their original sentence.

Source: Roth et al., 2021, p. 4

the result of the Supreme Court ruling in *Morrissey v. Brewer* (1972). Morrissey served a 7-year prison sentence in Iowa State Penitentiary. Morrissey was paroled in 1968, and 7 months later he was arrested as a parole violator and placed in the county jail. One week later, the Iowa Board of Parole reviewed the case, including the parole officer's written report, and revoked Morrissey's parole. Morrissey was returned to the Iowa penitentiary. He challenged the ruling by asserting that he received no hearing prior to revocation of his parole.

The Supreme Court deliberated on the case, and they provided for two procedural requirements. First, the court ruled that when an individual is arrested and detained, usually at the direction of their parole officer, there is a requirement to conduct a minimal inquiry into information, sources, and circumstances of the arrest (*Morrissey v. Brewer*, 1972). At the preliminary hearing the court recommended that the individual be allowed to appear and speak on their behalf and bring any relevant documentation or witnesses (e.g., letters, documents, or individuals who can provide information to the hearing officer). Second, a revocation hearing includes additional protections. The legal standard during a revocation hearing is to determine probable cause, and as such, an individual has the right to confront and cross-examine an adverse witness. This is known as a "Morrissey Hearing," with the Supreme Court listing the following minimum requirements of due process:

> Written notice of the claimed violations of parole; Disclosure to the parolee of evidence against him; Opportunity to be heard in person and to present witnesses and documentary evidence; The right to confront and cross-examine adverse witnesses (unless the hearing officer specifically finds good cause for not allowing confrontation); A "neutral and detached" hearing body such as a traditional parole board, members of which need not be judicial officers or lawyers; And a written statement by the factfinders as to the evidence relied on and reasons for revoking parole. (*Morrissey v. Brewer*, 1972, p. 489)

◊ Diversity, Equity, and Inclusion: Technical Violations

It is reasonable to predict that when an individual on probation or parole commits a new crime that is serious, violent, or involves sexual assault, then a revocation is likely. However, in most cases, a failure to complete the conditions of supervision results in a technical violation. Recommitment to prison or receipt of punitive sanctions can even result from relatively minor technical violations of probation or parole conditions. This may include violations like breaching curfew or not reporting a change of address. In some parole agencies, up to 16% of individuals on supervision have been reincarcerated due to a failed drug test (Bonczar, 2008). Another method of understanding this dynamic is to consider that for every person on parole who is returned to prison for committing a new crime, two people on parole are returned to prison for a technical violation (Kaeble & Alper, 2020). In fact, almost half of all state prison admissions are the result of violations of probation or parole, with one quarter of these admissions being the result of a technical violation (Council of State Governments Justice Center, 2019).

Image 4.11

Not only is responding to technical violations through incarceration expensive but there is a significant body of research that reveals racial, ethnic, and socioeconomic disparities in these technical violations. Even when controlling for demographic and legal variables, Black adults are between 50% and 100% more likely to be charged with parole violations compared to their parole counterparts of other races (Steen & Opsal 2007; Steen et al., 2013). Young, male individuals of color are routinely shown to have the greatest risk of revocation (Steen & Opsal, 2007; Steen et al., 2013). Black and Latinx people are also more likely than other racial or ethnic groups to remain on parole for longer periods of time (Eaglin & Solomon 2015). Perhaps most alarming is that Black adults on parole supervision are more likely to be returned to prison for a technical violation, which further adds to racial and ethnic disparities in incarceration (Vito et al., 2012).

These effects are cumulative, with Black and Hispanic individuals being more likely to be placed on parole supervision compared to White individuals (6.8 and 2.5 times, respectively), more likely to be detained for parole violations (12 and 4 times, respectively), and more likely to be incarcerated (5 times and 30%, respectively; see Bradner et al., 2020). These racial and ethnic differences for individuals on parole and/or probation can be found by examining the Relative Rate Index (RRI), as shown in Figure 4.3. The RRI allows us to compare the occurrence of a particular event between different groups, allowing us to assess the relative frequency of such an event happening in one group compared to another group. More specifically, we can compare the rate of an event in one group to the rate of an event in another group. If the value is greater than 1, it suggests the event is more likely to occur, whereas if it is less than 1, the event is less likely to happen compared to the second group. As you can see in Figure 4.3, the RRI demonstrates that Black adults are 2.64 times more likely to be placed on probation and 3.89 times more likely to be on parole compared to White adults. The RRI results are even higher for Hispanic groups, who are 2.74 times more likely to be placed on probation and nearly 5 times more likely to be placed on parole compared to White adults. These RRI values are presented in Figure 4.3.

The responses to technical violations committed by individuals under probation and parole supervision illustrate the significant discretion that officers have. This suggests that different outcomes may be due to the decision making of the probation or parole officer and reinforced by the punishment orientation of the probation or parole agency. In fact, role orientations can impact both the development of relationships and the decisions officers make. One early study found that New York parole officers who held punishment orientations were more likely to

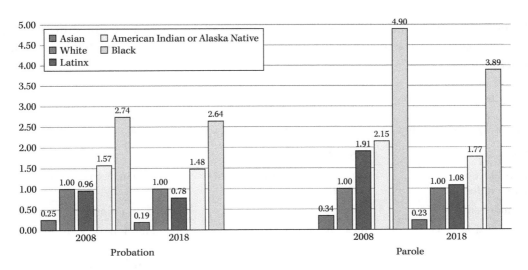

FIGURE 4.3   Relative Rate Index for Probation and Parole Supervision, 2008 and 2018

Sources: Kaeble and Alper 2020, Table 1, Appendix Tables 4 and 8; U.S. Census Bureau 2011; U.S. Census Bureau 2020.

cite individuals on parole for technical violations and recommend revocation (Dembo, 1972). Rehabilitative-orientated parole officers were less likely to have caseloads of individuals on parole with technical violations and recommended fewer revocations. A punishment orientation has been linked in other studies to a greater likelihood for parole officers to pursue revocations for individuals on supervision (Steiner et al., 2011). Probation and parole officers who adhered to a hybrid approach, integrating law enforcement and rehabilitative approaches, had lower violation rates compared to those adhering solely to law enforcement or rehabilitative orientations (Paparozzi & Gendreau, 2005). Officers who engaged in a hybrid approach were more likely to form quality relationships with individuals on their caseloads (Kennealy et al., 2012).

To address these disparities, many supervision agencies have developed graduated response matrices, which are guidelines as to how to respond to situations when an individual complies or does not comply with the supervision conditions. The goal of these matrices is to provide structure and consistency across decisions about how to handle typical situations such as: (a) delivering an incentive when individuals are drug-free, pay their fines/fees, do community service, or other signals of progress or (b) providing a sanction when individuals are not complying with their conditions. In practice, agencies often focus more on sanctions as opposed to incentives. This is problematic, as research suggests sanctions have little to no impact on outcomes, while incentives can improve success. Wodahl and colleagues (2011) found that implementing incentives or rewards at a greater ratio compared to sanctions (4:1 ratio) was most effective at reducing recidivism and violations.

Table 4.4 and Table 4.5 provides examples of graduated incentives and sanctions used by Utah Department of Corrections. Typically, these guidelines would be used in conjunction with a list that categorizes different violations into different levels of seriousness and accomplishes into levels based on difficulty/significance. When a violation or accomplishment occurs, the supervising officer can review the guidelines for appropriate, intermediate responses to swiftly respond.

TABLE 4.4   Graduated Incentives (Sentencing Guidelines, Form 9)

These are guidelines only. They do not create any right or expectation on behalf of the offender.		
Level 1	**Level 2**	**Level 3**
Up to 30% community service reduction	Up to 50% community service reduction	Reduction in degree of conviction
Eliminate curfew	Voucher	Early termination
Accomplishment certificate/recognition	Recommend fine reduction	Fine reduction
Voucher	Approval to serve as peer mentor	Transfer to court/lower probation
Awards	Reduce substance/alcohol screening	Any lower level incentive
Reduce curfew length	Any lower level incentive	
Redeem 5 success chips		
Public recognition		
Positive reports		
Success chip(s)		
Written recognition		
Verbal recognition		

Source: Utah Department of Corrections, 2015, p. 3

TABLE 4.5   Graduated Sanctions (Sentencing Guidelines, Form 10)

These are guidelines only. They do not create any right or expectation on behalf of the offender.		
Level 1	**Level 2**	**Level 3**
Up to 60-day curfew	Request court/BOPP sanction	1–3 daily jail sanction (max 5 days/30 days)
Travel restrictions	Up to 90-day curfew	Hearing before court/BOPP
Structured living	Up to 72 hours home restriction	Community correctional center
Increased supervision	Treatment resource center	GPS electronic monitoring
Require change in residence	Up to 16 hours community service	
Revision of case action plan		
Increased reporting/testing		

Level 1	Level 2	Level 3
Community accountability board		
Workshops		
Assignments		
Family meeting		
Problem-solving report		
Mentoring program		
Develop risk-avoidance plan		
Letter of apology		
Thinking report		
Payment schedule adjustment		
Verbal warning		

Source: Utah Department of Corrections, 2015, p. 5

Critics have argued that the use of incarceration as a response to noncriminal, technical violations should be abandoned. For example, Bradner and colleagues (2020) suggest that even short periods of incarceration are highly disruptive to economic status, employment, housing, family dynamics, and social relationships. Bradner et al. (2020) propose:

> People under community supervision should not be incarcerated, even for short-term holds, unless they are accused of having engaged in criminal activity. In cases where criminal activity is suspected, policymakers should require judicial review before a person is incarcerated, with the same level of due process proceedings that would be expected for a member of the public who is not on probation or parole. Policymakers should also require that revocation proceedings only follow after, not in place of, full criminal proceedings and conviction. This ensures appropriate due process, and avoids unnecessary incarceration. (p. 14)

If disparities regarding technical violations for individuals under supervision are measured and continue, additional solutions at the agency level can include training, education, and policies designed to address inequitable outcomes for individuals on probation and parole. Other actions could be policies such as earned release, which allows individuals the opportunity to reduce supervision periods through compliant and prosocial behavior (Bradner et al., 2020), and reducing or individualizing supervision conditions. Technical violations represent a specific issue that is reflective of broader dilemmas facing community corrections—one that will take considerable research, investment, and deliberation to remedy.

SUMMARY: PROBATION AND PAROLE OFFICER WORK

Frontline probation and parole officers are the cornerstone of the community corrections system. Probation and parole officers maintain the dual roles of law enforcement and surveillance and social work, which can present challenges in their work when orientations are in conflict. These officers are responsible for supervising the conditions of supervision for individuals on probation or parole. The daily activities of probation and parole officers are a direct reflection of the agency's mission, goals, and procedures. This often features the use of technical skills such as writing a presentence investigation report (PSIR) that will be shared with courts and other criminal justice agencies. It may also involve punitive responses to noncompliance, such as the application of technical violations and revocations. To promote behavior change and assistance, probation and parole officers are encouraged to follow core correctional practices. The most popular forms of these practices are rooted in the risk-need-responsivity (RNR) model that has demonstrated success in reducing recidivism, even in the most challenging populations.

Scenario-Based Activities

	Case	Question(s)
1.	Steven is on probation for theft. He has been doing well for the past 4 months. However, Steven's probation officer recently received a report that he was seen leaving a store without paying for an item. Steven's probation officer suspects Steven violated the terms of his probation and may need to face consequences.	Pretend you are Steven's probation officer. What steps would you take to investigate this potential probation violation? How would you balance the need to hold individuals on your caseload accountable for their actions while also helping them successfully complete probation? What factors would you consider when determining the appropriate response to a probation violation?
2	Alexa is a high-risk individual on probation supervision for a drug-related offense. Alexa is new to probation and needs a case plan created that is guided by the risk-need-responsivity (RNR) model.	Pretend you are Alexa's probation officer. How would you apply the RNR model to develop a case plan for Alexa? What specific factors would you prioritize in designing her case plan? How would you ensure the interventions you recommend are appropriate for her risk and needs? How would you ensure your case plan is responsive to her individual characteristics and circumstances? How would you measure Alexa's progress and adjust the case plan as needed to ensure it is effective in reducing her risk of reoffending? Finally, what challenges might you encounter in applying the RNR model to Alexa's case? How might you address these challenges?

References

Allard, T. J., Wortley, R. K., & Stewart, A. L. (2003) Role conflict in community corrections. *Psychology, Crime & Law, 9*(3), 279–289. https://doi.org/10.1080/1068316031000093414

Andrews, D. A. (2011). The principles of effective correctional programs. In E. J. Latessa & A. M. Holsinger (Eds.), *Correctional contexts: Contemporary and classical readings* (pp. 228–237). Oxford University Press.

Andrews, D. A., & Bonta, J. (2010a). *The psychology of criminal conduct* (5th ed.). Anderson Publishing. https://doi.org/10.4324/9781315721279

Andrews, D. A., & Bonta, J. (2010b). Rehabilitating criminal justice policy and practice. *Psychology, Public Policy and Law, 16*(1), 39–55. https://doi.org/10.1037/a0018362

Andrews, D. A., Bonta, J., & Hoge, R. D. (1990a). Classification for effective rehabilitation. *Criminal Justice and Behavior, 17*(1), 19–52. https://doi.org/10.1177/0093854890017001004

Andrews, D. A., Bonta, J., & Wormith, J. S. (2011). The risk-need-responsivity (RNR) model: Does adding the good lives model contribute to effective crime prevention? *Criminal Justice and Behavior, 38*(7), 735–755. https://doi.org/10.1177/0093854811406356

Bunzel, S. (1995). The probation officer and the federal sentencing guidelines: Strange philosophical bedfellows. *Yale Law Journal, 104*(4), 930–955. https://doi.org/10.2307/797109

Blasko, B. L., Friedmann, P. D., Rhodes, A. G., & Taxman, F. S. (2015). The parolee–parole officer relationship as a mediator of criminal justice outcomes. *Criminal Justice and Behavior, 42*(7), 722–740. https://doi.org/10.1177/0093854814562642

Bonczar, T. (2008). *Characteristics of state parole supervising agencies, 2006*. Bureau of Justice Statistics. https://bjs.ojp.gov/library/publications/characteristics-state-parole-supervising-agencies-2006

Bordin, E. S. (1994). Theory and research on the therapeutic alliance: New directions. In A. O. Horvath & L. S. Greenberg, (Eds.), *The working alliance: Theory, research, and practice* (pp. 13–37). John Wiley.

Bradner, K., Schiraldi, V. N., Mejia, N., & Lopoo, E. (2020). *More work to do: Analysis of probation and parole in the United States, 2017–2018*. https://doi.org/10.7916/d8-hjyq-fg65

Brockway, Z. R. (1912). *Fifty years of prison service: An autobiography*. Charities Publication Committee.

Chamberlain, A. W., Gricius, M., Wallace, D. M., Borjas, D., & Ware, V. M. (2018). Parolee–parole officer rapport: Does it impact recidivism? *International Journal of Offender Therapy and Comparative Criminology, 62*(11), 3581–3602. https://doi.org/10.1177/0306624X17741593

Cornacchione, J., Smith, S. W., Morash, M., Bohmert, M. N., Cobbina, J. E., & Kashy, D. A. (2016). An exploration of female offenders' memorable messages from probation and parole officers on the self-assessment of behavior from a control theory perspective. *Journal of Applied Communication Research, 44*(1), 60–77. https://doi.org/10.1080/00909882.2015.1116705

Council of State Governments Justice Center. (2019). *Confined and costly: How probation & parole violations fill prisons and drive costs*. The Council of State Governments Justice Center. https://csgjusticecenter.org/confinedandcostly/

Davis, G. F. (1964). A study of adult probation violation rates by means of the cohort approach. *The Journal of Criminal Law, Criminology, and Police Science, 55*(1), 70–85. https://doi.org/10.2307/1140455

DeLude, B., Mitchell, D., & Barber, C. (2012). Probationer's perspective on the probation officer-probationer relationship and satisfaction with probation. *Federal Probation, 76*(1), 35–39.

Dembo, R. (1972). Orientation and activities of the parole officer. *Criminology, 10*(2), 193–215. https://doi.org/10.1111/j.1745-9125.1972.tb00554.x

Dowden, C., & Andrews, D. A. (2004). The importance of staff practice in delivering effective correctional treatment: A meta-analytic review of core correctional practice. *International Journal of Offender Therapy and Comparative Criminology, 48*(2), 203–214. https://doi.org/10.1177/0306624X03257765

Eaglin, J., & Solomon, D. (2015). *Reducing racial and ethnic disparities in jails: Recommendations for local practice.* Brennan Center for Justice.

Falconer, S. M. (2012). Parole boards and hearings. In S. M. Barton-Bellessa (Ed.), *Encyclopedia of community corrections* (Vol. 1, pp. 286–290). SAGE Publications. https://doi.org/10.4135/9781452218519

Farrall, S. (2012). *Rethinking what works with offenders.* Routledge. https://doi.org/10.4324/9781003143789

Farrington, D. P. (2007). Origins of violent behavior over the life span. In D. J. Flannery, A. T. Vazsonyi, & I. D. Waldman (Eds.), *The Cambridge handbook of violent behavior and aggression* (1st ed., pp. 19–48). Cambridge University Press. https://doi.org/10.1017/9781316847992.002

Fearn, N. E. (2012). Job satisfaction in community corrections. In S. M. Barton-Bellessa (Ed.), *Encyclopedia of community corrections* (Vol. 1, pp. 217–218). SAGE Publications. https://doi.org/10.4135/9781452218519

Frankel, R. (2020). *Revoked: How probation and parole feed mass incarceration in the United States.* ACLU Human Rights Watch.

Gendreau, P., Goggin, C., Cullen, F. T., & Andrews, D. A. (2000). The effects of community sanctions and incarceration on recidivism. *Forum on Corrections Research, 12*(2), 10–13.

Gray, M. K., Fields., M., & Maxwell, S. R. (2001). Examining probation violations: Who, what and when. *Crime and Delinquency, 47*(4), 537–557. https://doi.org/10.1177/0011128701047004003

Green, T. C., Johnson, J., Harrington, M., Pouget, E. R., Rhodes, A. G., Taxman, F. S., O'Connell, D. J., Martin, S. S., Prendergast, M., & Friedmann, P. D. (2013). Parole officer–parolee relationships and HIV risk behaviors during community supervision. *AIDS and Behavior, 17*, 2667–2675. https://doi.org/10.1007/s10461-011-0081-1

Kaeble, D. (2021). *Probation and parole in the United States, 2020.* Bureau of Justice Statistics. https://bjs.ojp.gov/library/publications/probation-and-parole-united-states-2020

Kaeble, D., & Alper, M. (2020). *Probation and parole in the United States, 2017–2018.* U.S. Department of Justice, Office of Justice Programs, Bureau of Justice Statistics. https://www.bjs.gov/content/pub/pdf/ppus1718.pdf

Kennealy, P. J., Skeem, J. L., Wodahl, S. M., & Eno Louden, J. (2012). Firm, fair, and caring officer–offender relationships protect against supervision failure. *Law and Human Behavior, 36*(6), 496–505. https://doi.org/10.1037/h0093935

Moffitt, T. E. (1993). Adolescence-limited and life-course-persistent antisocial behavior: A developmental taxonomy. *Psychological Review, 100*(4), 674–701. https://doi.org/10.1037/0033-295X.100.4.674

Morrissey v. Brewer, 408 U.S. 471 (1972). https://www.oyez.org/cases/1971/71-5103

Ohlin, L. E., Piven, H., & Pappenfort, D. M. (1956). Major dilemmas of the social worker in probation and parole. *National Probation and Parole Association Journal, 3*, 211–225.

Paparozzi, M., & Gendreau, P. (2005). An intensive supervision program that worked: Service delivery, professional orientation, and organizational supportiveness. *The Prison Journal, 85*(4), 445–466. https://doi.org/10.1177/0032885505281529

Pettus-Davis, C., & Kennedy, S. (2020). *Going back to jail without committing a crime: Early findings from a multi-state trial.* Florida State University, Institute for Justice Research and Development. https://doi.org/10.13140/RG.2.2.28409.83048

Phelps, M. S. (2013). The paradox of probation: Community supervision in the age of mass incarceration. *Law and Policy, 35*(1–2), 51–80. https://doi.org/10.1111/lapo.12002

Roth, A., Kajeepeta, S., & Boldin, A. (2021). *The perils of probation: How supervision contributes to jail populations.* Vera Institute of Justice. https://www.vera.org/downloads/publications/the-perils-of-probation.pdf

Sigler, R. T., & McGraw, B. (1984). Adult probation and parole officers: Influence of their weapons, role perceptions and role conflict. *Criminal Justice Review, 9*(1), 28–32. https://doi.org/10.1177/073401688400900105

Steen, S., & Opsal, T. (2007). Punishment on the installment plan: Individual-level predictors of parole revocation in four states. *The Prison Journal, 87*(3), 344–366. https://doi.org/10.1177/0032885507304526

Steen, S., Opsal, T., Lovegrove, P., & McKinzey, S. (2013). Putting parolees back in prison: Discretion and the parole revocation process. *Criminal Justice Review, 38*(1), 70–93. https://doi.org/10.1177/0734016812466571

Steiner, B., Travis, L. F., Makarios, M. D., & Brickley, T. (2011). The influence of parole officers' attitudes on supervision practices. *Justice Quarterly, 28*(6), 903–927. https://doi.org/10.1080/07418825.2010.539246

Tatman, A. W., & Love, K. (2010). An offender version of the Working Alliance Inventory–Short Revised. *Journal of Offender Rehabilitation, 49*(3), 165–179. https://doi.org/10.1080/10509671003666560

Taxman, F. S., & Smith, L. (2020). Risk-need-responsivity (RNR) classification models: Still evolving. *Aggression and Violent Behavior, 101459*, 1–11. https://doi.org/10.1016/j.avb.2020.101459

Tonry, M., & Will, R. (1990). *Intermediate sanctions.* National Institute of Justice. https://www.ojp.gov/pdffiles1/Digitization/126865NCJRS.pdf

Ullrich, S., & Coid, J. (2011). Protective factors for violence among released prisoners—Effects over time and interactions with static risk. *Journal of Consulting and Clinical Psychology, 79*(3), 381–390. https://doi.org/10.1037/a0023613

U.S. Probation Office. (2009). The presentence investigation report: A guide to the presentence process. https://www.ncwp.uscourts.gov/sites/default/files/general/Guide_to_the_Presentence_Process.pdf

Vera Institute of Justice. (2013). *The potential of community corrections to improve safety and reduce incarceration.* https://perma.cc/M2T3-TKUV.

Vito, G. F., Higgins, G. E., & Tewksbury, R. (2012). Characteristics of parole violators in Kentucky. *Federal Probation, 76*(1), 58–59.

Weisberg, R., Mukamal, D., & Segall, J. D. (2011). *Life in Limbo: An examination of parole releases for prisoners serving life sentences with the possibility of parole in California.* Stanford Criminal Justice Center.

Whitehead, J. T., & Lindquist, C. A. (1986). Correctional officer job burnout: A path model. *Journal of Research in Crime and Delinquency, 23*(1), 23–42. https://doi.org/10.1177/0022427886023001003

Wodahl, E. J., Garland, B., Culhane, S. E., & McCarty, W. P. (2011). Utilizing behavioral interventions to improve supervision outcomes in community-based corrections. *Criminal Justice and Behavior, 38*(4), 386–405. https://doi.org/10.1177/0093854810397866

Image Credits

CHAPTER 5

Intermediate Sanctions

This chapter introduces students to intermediate sanctions. Students are provided with a description of the history of intermediate sanctions to enhance their understanding surrounding the reasons why these alternative punishments grew in popularity over time. This includes an examination of the continuum of punishment as a means of understanding the goals of punishment and intermediate sanctions and to assess whether these punishments achieve their goals. Students are introduced to different categories of intermediate sanctions, including the least intensive enhancements to standard probation (i.e., drug testing, financial sanctions, and community service), intensive supervision programs, those that partially contain individuals (i.e., curfews, electronic monitoring, house arrest, and day reporting centers), those that require full containment (i.e., boot camps, halfway houses, and work release), and lastly treatment programming. Next, a discussion is provided of the challenges surrounding application and use of intermediate sanctions, including the complexities they introduce for the work of probation/parole officers. Finally, the chapter ends with an overview of the research on the effectiveness of intermediate sanctions, with a spotlight on the racial disparities in intermediate sanctions.

LEARNING OBJECTIVES

By the end of this chapter, students will be able to:

- Describe the goals, purpose, and types of intermediate sanctions with reference to emerging technologies.
- Identify the challenges associated with intermediate sanctions.
- Synthesize the research evidence supporting the use of intermediate sanctions.

KEY TERMS

- Electronic monitoring
- Intensive supervision programs (ISPs)
- Intermediate sanctions
- Sentencing guidelines
- Treatment programming

The public has a right to know what kind of monitoring the government is doing, and there should be a public discussion of the appropriate trade-offs between law enforcement and privacy rights.

—Adam Cohen

Intermediate Sanctions

Intermediate sanctions refer to a continuum of punishments and responses that fall between probation on one end (the more "lenient" punishment) and prison on the other (the more severe punishment). While intermediate sanctions may be assigned during sentencing, some jurisdictions leave it to the probation or parole agency to add restrictions to a standard probation or parole supervision and therefore assign an intermediate sanction(s). The overarching purpose of intermediate sanctions is to provide multiple options to respond to individuals who have been accused of or convicted of committing criminal acts. Intermediate sanctions offer options to the system that are outside of the prison and jail walls and expand *how* punishments can be delivered in the community. The more possible sentences are available, the greater likelihood an appropriately proportionate response can be selected. For example, if probation and prison are the only two possible sentences, the result may be that individuals either receive a sentencing that is too harsh (e.g., prison) or receive a sentence that does not adequately address the needs of society and/or the individual (e.g., probation). Intermediate sanctions provide a mechanism to promote surveillance, treatment, individual accountability, and responsibility through sentences that are less restrictive than incarceration but more restrictive than probation. In doing so, the goal is to preserve incarceration for individuals who are a danger to society or who committed heinous crimes requiring severe sentences. As Tonry (1998) states, "intermediate sanctions have been seen as a way both to reduce the need for prison beds and to provide a continuum of sanctions that satisfied the just deserts concern for proportionality" (p. 101).

Figure 5.1 below illustrates a continuum of conditions and tools that define intermediate sanctions. Intermediate sanctions can be applied in the form of "enhanced conditions" where additional requirements are added to the supervision term when standard supervision is considered too lenient. In this application, the addition of intermediate sanctions intensifies the probation or parole sentence. These enhancements are often used with the goal of reducing the risk of future involvement with the legal system and/or to address the needs of the individual. Enhancements designed to be rehabilitative (e.g., requirement to attend cognitive behavioral therapy) are more often applied for individuals with a higher degree of need (e.g., characterized by unmet social and psychological needs). Probation and parole agencies can deploy various tools to create a tailored approach for the individual and their circumstances.

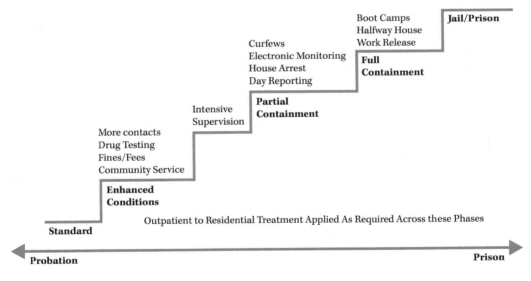

FIGURE 5.1   A Continuum of Conditions

These enhancements of supervision conditions include tools such as drug testing, fines and fees, contacts with the officer, treatment services, and specialized programs that serve the public safety goals of preventing recidivism and improving a person's quality of life. These various tools can be mixed and matched to create a program like intensive supervision or to add to a particular setting like work release and outpatient therapy. For example, an individual can be sentenced to work release but also have requirements for fines/fees, community service, outpatient treatment, and probation supervision. Besides enhanced conditions, intermediate sanctions include a range of specific interventions, including intensive probation supervision, interventions that result in partial containment of the individual (e.g., curfews, electronic monitoring, house arrest, day reporting), those that result in full containment (e.g., boot camps, halfway house, work release), and incarceration in jail or prison. As illustrated in Figure 5.1, the severity and intensity of punishment increase as the level of containment and temporary isolation from the community increases.

History of Intermediate Sanctions

The emergence of intermediate sanctions can be traced back to the 1960s and 1970s when rehabilitation was the primary emphasis, but there were simultaneous pressures for account-ability and liberty restrictions. As a result, community corrections gained popularity as a means of keeping individuals convicted of nonviolent offenses in the community. During this time, individuals were placed in programs such as halfway houses and treatment facilities as opposed to prison. In these community-based programs, they could maintain critical ties to the community and social networks, receive education and employment training, search for and acquire employment, and receive treatment services.

The original focus on rehabilitative intermediate sanctions began to turn in the 1970s with the larger shift towards a "tough-on-crime" approach. Tonry (1999) provides three explanations for the resulting shift toward more punitive intermediate sanctions. First, as previously discussed, there was an overarching decline in support for rehabilitation in general as a primary goal of punishment. Second, an increased focus on just deserts emerged, emphasizing the need for increased proportionality in punishment and more options to ensure that the punishment fits the crime. Third, as the "tough-on-crime" ideology spread, proponents pushed for less use of probation. As discussed in Chapter 2, the punishment philosophies of deterrence, retribution, and incapacitation were emphasized, and prison populations soon boomed. With these expansions in prison populations came astronomical costs and overcrowding, which fueled calls for punitive punishment options in the community.

Support for intermediate sanctions continued to increase in the 1980s. Prison overcrowding had reached crisis levels across the United States, particularly in the South where federal courts found several prison systems to be in violation of the eighth amendment (i.e., cruel and unusual punishment). In these rulings, the courts determined these states had two options: build new prisons or develop a system of alternative punishments in the community that could reduce prison crowding. Due to the mass construction of new prisons not being financially viable, emphasis shifted to developing less expensive, nonincarceration-based responses to crime. During this transition, a highly influential study published by the RAND Corporation examined the use of probation for individuals convicted of a felony (Petersilia et al., 1985). The study found that individuals convicted of serious felonies were sentenced to probation at excessive rates that overburdened probation staff (i.e., with caseloads over 100 or more being common). As a result, these individuals were not adequately supervised, and nearly two thirds were rearrested within 3 years, many for serious offenses. Chapter 3 reinforces how large case-loads, especially those consisting of many high-risk, high-needs individuals, can negatively impact the mental health of officers, increase job stress, and disrupt the work environment. This RAND study brought to light the immense pressure placed on the probation system to supervise large populations, also demonstrating the need for alternative approaches.

The push for alternatives was further strengthened in Morris and Tonry's (1990) influential book *Between Prison and Probation: Intermediate Punishments in a Rational Sentencing System.* Morris and Tonry illustrated the stringent limitations placed on judges to deliver appropriate punishment, due mainly to a lack of options beyond prison or probation. Morris and Tonry (1990) wrote that "imprisonment is used excessively; probation is used even more excessively; between the two is a near vacuum of purposive and enforced punishments" (p. 3). The total reliance on prison probation created numerous challenges that were sure to create poor outcomes. For example, judges with little flexibility or choices, were often forced to issue sentences that were not proportionate either for the offense or the individual. In response, Morris and Tonry (1990) outlined a conceptual framework for developing a graduated system of punishment that relied on a range of options. The authors argued that a continuum of punishments could better match individuals to sanctions based on the seriousness of the offense and based on facilitating change (rehabilitation). It was through this approach that sentencing systems could be more rational and would better serve victims and the justice system.

Following these major events, jurisdictions started to build their own system of intermediate sanctions that allowed for more tailored sentencing, including options such as house arrest, electronic monitoring, and intensive supervision. These alternatives to incarceration were designed to take place in the community, be more punitive than standard probation, and be less punitive and expensive than prison. The expectation was that as intermediate sanctions grew, prison populations would decline because judges would sentence more people to alternatives. Additionally, it was expected that these alternatives would reduce recidivism, including subsequent offenses and prison commitments. Intermediate sanctions also became a catch-all term used to describe anything that resulted in more intensive programming (e.g., intensive probation supervision, day reporting centers). In some jurisdictions, agencies applied additional intermediate sanctions (e.g., drug testing, GPS monitoring) in response to noncompliance with probation conditions. As we will discuss later in this chapter, the original goals of intermediate sanctions were to reduce recidivism and to reduce the use of incarceration, but these goals have not been fully achieved for a number of reasons.

JOURNEY INTO THE FIELD: DIRECTOR JERRY ADGER

◇◇◇◇◇◇◇

Full name: Jerry B. Adger

Title: Director of the South Carolina Department of Probation, Parole, and Pardon Services

Director Adger has had an extensive career spanning over 40 years, specializing in law enforcement tactics, program management, strategic planning, and achieving organizational goals. He began his career with the Federal Bureau of Investigations as a fingerprint analyst. He then worked for the South Carolina Law Enforcement Division for 23 years, followed by the South Carolina Department of Juvenile Justice (DJJ) in December 1999 to direct the newly established Office of the Inspector General. He is South Carolina's first nationally certified inspector general, receiving his certification at the American University in Washington, DC, through the Inspectors General Institute. In 2003, he was appointed to the position of deputy director, in which he served for 8 years. During his tenure, he gained a national reputation for his work transforming the treatment of young women at Willow Lane, a gender-responsive facility. In 2011, he was appointed as inspector general for the South Carolina Department of Corrections.

(Image 5.)

Director Adger is an adjunct professor in the School of Criminology and Criminal Justice at the University of South Carolina. He holds a Master of Criminal Justice degree and a Bachelor of Arts degree in psychology from the University of South Carolina. Director Adger is married, has two sons, and resides in Columbia, South Carolina. In the following Journey into the Field, Director Adger provides insight into his career avenues and his views on the important role that community corrections have in supervising individuals.

After spending 23 years with the South Carolina Law Enforcement Division, in December of 1999 I accepted a position with the South Carolina Department of Juvenile Justice (DJJ) and subsequently was promoted to the deputy director of rehabilitative services. In 2015, Governor Nikki Haley appointed me to the position of director of the South Carolina Department of Probation Parole and Pardon Services (PPP), a position that I currently hold today. After 46 years in state government, I've gone from enforcing the laws of the state of South Carolina as a SLED Agent (South Carolina Law Enforcement Division), to leading the way in promoting the mission in preparing individuals under supervision to becoming productive citizens.

Probation and parole are critical components of the criminal justice system. Historically, the trend has been to incarcerate individuals who violated state and/or federal laws. Today, the trend has shifted to reducing the incarceration rate across the United States. This is in part due to the cost of incarceration and the need to find more effective modalities and strategies in dealing with nonviolent criminal behavior. Therefore, more people are given probation or released from prison with conditions. It is the role of the probation and parole agencies to supervise and hold accountable those who are released to supervision in the community. A holistic approach with wraparound services will benefit all involved. Supervision that is offender-driven with individualized treatment plans will meet specific demands.

In the state of South Carolina, I can tell you that the future is bright for probation and parole. The optimism comes from the work that has been done at PPP over the past 8 years in better preparing probation agents who have the responsibility of supervising individuals released to community supervision. Simply put, PPP has adopted what I call a "medical model" in its approach to better serve the indivduals under supervision. Under this model, PPP has moved from a high caseload to a more manageable caseload. By reducing each agent's caseload, more time can be spent on the individuals who require the attention. Furthermore, under this model, specific cases are assigned based on the conviction of a specific offense (specialized caseloads). At PPP, there are three categories involving specialized caseloads: Sex Offender, Domestic Violence, and Mental Health. Each specialized caseload has a maximum ratio to ensure that the attention needed for each individual under supervision can be applied. Furthermore, specific training is required for each agent relative to the specialized caseload that they have been assigned. It is my opinion that PPP in South Carolina is in a much better position to assist and effectively supervise each individual using the model described above. It is the agency's mission to prepare individuals under our supervision in becoming productive citizens without comprising public trust.

Sentencing Guidelines

While every state and/or local community corrections system implemented some form of intermediate sanctions, the type and application varied. Currently, twenty-seven states have some form of sentencing guidelines to promote more consistent, uniform, and proportionate sentencing practices. These guidelines focus on specifying who should be sent to prison rather than who should receive intermediate sanctions. **Sentencing guidelines** create a routine method for identifying an appropriate sentence so that similarly situated individuals would receive similar sentences. However, not all state sentencing guidelines include specific systems for formalizing and regulating the use of intermediate sanctions. Sentencing guidelines also rely on objective data such as the offense and criminal history; yet, determining an appropriate intermediate sanction often requires consideration of case-specific factors, making them more challenging to regulate. States such as Michigan, Oregon, Pennsylvania, and Washington have made efforts to structure and regulate the use of intermediate sanctions (Frase, 2005). For example, view the Basic Sentencing Matrix used in Pennsylvania in Figure 5.2. Here, you can see they use the seriousness of the offense and criminal history to generate a "Prior Record Score" shown in the columns of the table. The rows represent the level of seriousness of offense. Within the body of the table, the matrix provides the minimum range of a possible sentence. For less serious offenses committed by individuals with minimal criminal history, a restorative sanction may be recommended. Restorative sanctions (RS) represent the intermediate sanctions available in the state.

At the federal level, intermediate sanctions, sometimes referred to as "alternative sentences," are now built into the federal guidelines system and are available to all individuals except those facing mandatory minimum prison sentences or to noncitizens facing deportation (United States Sentencing Commission, 2009). As shown in Figure 5.3, the federal guidelines

Level	OGS	Prior Record Score						RFEL	REVOC	AGG/MIT
		0	1	2	3	4	5			
LEVEL 5	14	72-SL	84-SL	96-SL	120-SL	168-SL	192-SL	204-SL	SL	~/-12
	13	60-78	66-84	72-90	78-96	84-102	96-114	108-126	240	+/- 12
	12	48-66	54-72	60-78	66-84	72-90	84-102	96-114	120	+/- 12
	11	36-54	42-60	48-66	54-72	60-78	72-90	84-102	120	+/- 12
	10	22-36	30-42	36-48	42-54	48-60	60-72	72-84	120	+/- 12
	9	12-24	18-30	24-36	30-42	36-48	48-60	60-72	120	+/- 12
LEVEL 4	8	9-16	12-18	15-21	18-24	21-27	27-33	40-52	NA	+/- 9
LEVEL 3	7	6-14	9-16	12-18	15-21	18-24	24-30	35-45	NA	+/- 6
	6	3-12	6-14	9-16	12-18	15-21	21-27	27-40	NA	+/- 6
LEVEL 2	5	RS-9 P2 (225-250)	1-12	3-14	6-16	9-16	12-18	24-36	NA	+/- 3
	4	RS-3 P1 (100-125)	RS-9 P2 (225-250)	RS-<12 P2 (300-325)	3-14	6-16	9-16	21-30	NA	+/- 3
	3	RS-1 P1 (50-75)	RS-6 P1 (150-175)	RS-9 P2 (225-250)	RS-<12 P2 (300-325)	3-14	6-16	12-18	NA	+/- 3
LEVEL 1	2	RS (25-50)	RS-2 P1 (75-100)	RS-3 P1 (100-125)	RS-4 P1 (125-150)	RS-6 P1 (150-175)	1-9	6- <12	NA	+/- 3
	1	RS (25-50)	RS-1 P1 (50-75)	RS-2 P1 (75-100)	RS-3 P1 (100-125)	RS-4 P1 (125-150)	RS-6 P1 (150-175)	3-6	NA	+/- 3

Restorative Sanctions (RS) are non-confinement sentence recommendation (204 Pa.Code §303.9(f))
Guilt without further penalty (42 Pa.C.S. § 9723)
Fines (18 Pa.C.S. § 1101) including Fines/Community Service Guidelines (204 Pa.Code § 303.14(a)(4))
Communtiy Service (range of hours), including Fines/Community Service Guidelines (204 Pa.Code § 303.14(a)(4))
Restitution (18 Pa.C.S. § 1106)
Probation (42 Pa.C.S. §§ 9722, 9763(b)), including recommendations for duration of probation
    P1: 1 year   P2: 2 years   **Probation as Restorative Sanction = Recommended aggregate term not to exceed <u>5 years</u>.**

Confinement sentence recommendations (204 Pa.Code § 303.9(e)) are ranges of minimum terms in months
Confinement in state faciilty (§ 303.9(e)(1))
Confinement in county faciilty (§ 303.9(e)(2), (3))
Probation with restrictive conditions (§ 303.9(e)(2), (3)) are CIP programs (42 Pa.C.S. Chapter 98), subject to the following recommendations:
    Sentencing guidelines . Duration of restrictive conditions and confinement recommended not to exceed sentence range.
    DUI mandatory minimum requirement . Duration of restrictive conditions and confinement equivalent to mandatory minimum requirement.
    Clinical evaluation . Diagnostic evaluation of dependency on alcohol and other drugs consistent with clinically prescribed treatment.
    RNR assessment . Validated assessment of risk, needs, and responsivity may guide decisions related to: intensity of intervention, use of restrictive conditions, and duration of community supervision.

    Probation supervision period = Recommended aggregate term not to exceed <u>10 years</u>.

Omnibus Offense Gravity Score (OGS) assignments. See Omnibus policy (§ 303.3(f)) and OGS assignments (§ 303.15):
    M3 = OGS 1   M2 = OGS 2   M1 = OGS 3
    F3 = OGS 5   F2 = OGS 7   F1 = OGS 8   F1 (maximum>20 years) = OGS 10

FIGURE 5.2 Pennsylvania Basic Sentencing Matrix

SENTENCING TABLE
(in months of imprisonment)

Offense Level	Criminal History Category (Criminal History Points)					
	I (0 or 1)	II (2 or 3)	III (4, 5, 6)	IV (7, 8, 9)	V (10, 11, 12)	VI (13 or more)
1	0–6	0–6	0–6	0–6	0–6	0–6
2	0–6	0–6	0–6	0–6	0–6	1–7
3	0–6	0–6	0–6	0–6	2–8	3–9
4	0–6	0–6	0–6	2–8	4–10	6–12
5	0–6	0–6	1–7	4–10	6–12	9–15
6	0–6	1–7	2–8	6–12	9–15	12–18
7	0–6	2–8	4–10	8–14	12–18	15–21
8	0–6	4–10	6–12	10–16	15–21	18–24
9	4–10	6–12	8–14	12–18	18–24	21–27
10	6–12	8–14	10–16	15–21	21–27	24–30
11	8–14	10–16	12–18	18–24	24–30	27–33
12	10–16	12–18	15–21	21–27	27–33	30–37
13	12–18	15–21	18–24	24–30	30–37	33–41
14	15–21	18–24	21–27	27–33	33–41	37–46
15	18–24	21–27	24–30	30–37	37–46	41–51
16	21–27	24–30	27–33	33–41	41–51	46–57
17	24–30	27–33	30–37	37–46	46–57	51–63
18	27–33	30–37	33–41	41–51	51–63	57–71
19	30–37	33–41	37–46	46–57	57–71	63–78
20	33–41	37–46	41–51	51–63	63–78	70–87
21	37–46	41–51	46–57	57–71	70–87	77–96
22	41–51	46–57	51–63	63–78	77–96	84–105
23	46–57	51–63	57–71	70–87	84–105	92–115
24	51–63	57–71	63–78	77–96	92–115	100–125
25	57–71	63–78	70–87	84–105	100–125	110–137
26	63–78	70–87	78–97	92–115	110–137	120–150
27	70–87	78–97	87–108	100–125	120–150	130–162
28	78–97	87–108	97–121	110–137	130–162	140–175
29	87–108	97–121	108–135	121–151	140–175	151–188
30	97–121	108–135	121–151	135–168	151–188	168–210
31	108–135	121–151	135–168	151–188	168–210	188–235
32	121–151	135–168	151–188	168–210	188–235	210–262
33	135–168	151–188	168–210	188–235	210–262	235–293
34	151–188	168–210	188–235	210–262	235–293	262–327
35	168–210	188–235	210–262	235–293	262–327	292–365
36	188–235	210–262	235–293	262–327	292–365	324–405
37	210–262	235–293	262–327	292–365	324–405	360–life
38	235–293	262–327	292–365	324–405	360–life	360–life
39	262–327	292–365	324–405	360–life	360–life	360–life
40	292–365	324–405	360–life	360–life	360–life	360–life
41	324–405	360–life	360–life	360–life	360–life	360–life
42	360–life	360–life	360–life	360–life	360–life	360–life
43	life	life	life	life	life	life

Zone A — Offense Levels 1–8
Zone B — Offense Levels 9–11
Zone C — Offense Levels 12–13
Zone D — Offense Levels 14–43

November 1, 2016

FIGURE 5.3 Federal Guidelines per Offense Level and Criminal History assign points to an individual's offense level and criminal history. The total score correlates to a sentence range as specified in four specific zones on the grid (Zones A to D). Individuals whose scores land in Zone A are eligible for probation, an intermediate sanction, or a prison sentence of up to 6 months based on judicial discretion. Those who land in Zone B will likely face incarceration in prison; however, judges can fully or partially substitute prison time with a confinement-based intermediate sanction, such as home detention. Individuals in Zone C can serve half of the identified time in prison and the remaining half in a confinement-based intermediate sanction. Lastly, those in Zone D are not eligible for any alternative sentences.

Both state and federal guidelines attempt to increase consistency in terms of who is eligible for intermediate sanctions. However, they provide little guidance to judges in determining the specific factors they should consider in determining who should receive them and when. As Engen and colleagues (2003) put it, existing guidelines provide "windows of discretion" that permit decision makers the ability to consider factors outside of the sentencing guidelines. This level of discretion creates challenges surrounding the use of intermediate sanctions, which is discussed later in this chapter.

Types of Intermediate Sanctions

Intermediate sanctions were originally used to supervise an individual convicted of a nonviolent offense in the community to promote rehabilitation and reintegrative goals. As the political landscape changed and punishment philosophies shifted to a "tough-on-crime" approach, more punitively focused intermediate sanctions similarly gained traction. While today there is a wide range of intermediate sanctions available, the majority take place in the community, usually with a probation or parole officer responsible for overseeing the intermediate sanction. In fact, probation and parole agencies often apply many intermediate sanctions as enhancements or "add-ons" to standard supervision conditions (often in response to noncompliance or the needs of an individual).

Along the continuum of intermediate sanctions, there are both control- and treatment-oriented enhancements that are designed to increase the intensity of the punishment in response to the severity of the offense, risk of the individual, and/or needs of the individual. Some sanctions, such as intensive supervision or boot camps, are more control or containment oriented but they may also include treatment components. Treatment-oriented interventions are offered to facilitate behavior change, while control-oriented components focus on controlling, containing, and monitoring individual behavior. Control-focused intermediate sanctions often focus on restrictions in two areas: spatial/liberty and financial. *Spatial and liberty restrictions* emphasize limiting the geographical areas an individual can move within (e.g., curfews, house arrest, electronic monitoring). *Financial restrictions* include a range of fines, fees, restitution, and other financial related requirements. Lastly, intermediate sanctions may involve psychological components, such as evaluations for substance use and mental health, drug testing, and treatment services. These can be used alone or in conjunction with other intermediate sanctions.

Probation with Enhanced Conditions

In the following sections, we will explore the various tools probation and parole agencies can apply to enhance supervision conditions. In most cases, the number of additional tools applied equates to an increased intensity of conditions and requirements.

Drug Testing

Drug testing, or the analysis of urine or blood to detect illicit substance use or the use of breathalyzers for alcohol use, is common in most probation agencies. Many agencies have policies that require individuals on supervision to undergo drug testing to signal that illicit drug use will not be tolerated, to assess compliance with conditions of release, and to monitor the individual's behavior. Research studies have found that drug testing does not reduce recidivism or provide a mechanism to gauge the effectiveness of drug treatment (O'Connell et al., 2016). Instead, it is a tool used primarily to control behavior and to hold individuals accountable per supervision conditions. Best practices for drug testing include random testing so that the individual under supervision cannot regulate their drug use in advance of a known test day. Clinical research suggests that drug testing should be used only to inform treatment and not to punish an individual. Despite this research, drug testing results are commonly used to monitor and punish individual behavior (Jarvis et al., 2018; Reichert, 2020).

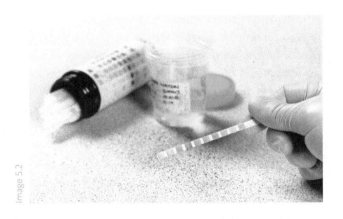

Image 5.2

Financial Sanctions

Individuals sentenced for a crime may be ordered to pay (or repay) for the harms resulting from criminal behavior. Financial sanctions are meant to hold an individual accountable while also addressing the harm caused. There are three common types of financial sanctions an individual under community supervision might have to pay: restitution, fines, and fees. *Restitution* is a type of financial penalty that is directed at repayment toward individuals or communities with the amount, at least theoretically, matching the severity of the behavior and harm done. There are additional types of financial penalties that are designed to be more focused on accountability. These include having the individual pay a fine and/or fees associated with being on supervision and/or in treatment. Fines are a punishment that constitutes part of the total financial penalty assessed for committing a crime. Typically, restitution and fines are determined by the court.

Administrative agencies like probation or parole and the related treatment organizations in the community can set fees to cover their services. Some treatment agencies use a sliding scale to determine the amount of the fee each individual can pay. Probation and parole agencies tend to use a flat fee that is imposed regardless of the hardship it might place on an individual. Many supervision agencies charge a monthly fee for being on supervision that can range from $10 a month to upwards of $150 a month. Other agencies charge a flat fee for a year (ranging from $150 to $4,600; Brett et al., 2020). These fees may be directed back to the probation or parole agency (which can be used to pay for operational expenses), the judiciary, or the general revenue fund of a state or local government. Fees are designed to enhance punishment by imposing a financial penalty in addition to liberty restrictions that are associated with community supervision. Over the last few decades, various fees (e.g., fines, fees for service, fees to be on supervision) have escalated, as well as an increase in the amount/type of organizations and services requiring fees, such as drug testing and treatment. In response, probation and parole agencies are now realizing that fees can be excessive, and some states, like Massachusetts, no longer allow fees for those under supervision.

Most probation and parole agencies lack a process for determining the amount of financial liability an individual should be accountable for, including whether the individual can afford to pay the financial penalty. Few agencies offer assistance for those who cannot afford the financial penalty, which increases the likelihood those individuals will violate a condition of probation or parole. It is merely expected that the individual would have the funds to pay financial sanctions, even with combined costs of fees, fines, and restitution that range from an average of $500 to $4,600 a year, depending on the jurisdiction and the sentencing judge (Link, 2023). The lack of consistent and standardized practices for determining financial sanctions means that individuals convicted of the same offense with similar circumstances might receive vastly different financial penalties depending on the sentencing court or jurisdiction by whom they are supervised.

When individuals do not pay their financial sanctions, they may not be allowed to complete probation (even if their sentence has expired) and they may be subject to supervision revocation or return to prison. These financial penalties place tremendous pressure on individuals

Image 5.3

on probation or parole. Those on probation or parole are often low-income and have unstable employment, making financial requirements an even more substantial burden. In a study by Ebony Ruhland (2021), individuals on community supervision reported that they often paid these financial penalties before paying their rent or purchasing food. These individuals also admitted that given the steep consequences associated with failing to pay these financial penalties, they were more likely to engage in illegal or illicit activities to obtain money.

Community Service

Unpaid labor is another form of accountability used by the community corrections system. This is termed *community service*, and individuals are generally assigned to a particular agency to assist for a given number of hours. Community service can consist of stuffing envelopes, painting, cleaning up a highway or park, or working for just about any type of organization that could use volunteer or "free" labor. The majority of community service work involves manual labor; slightly more than half also use public or social service work. In a recent study by Picard and colleagues (2019) up to 65% of sentences include community service, but there have only been two national evaluations of the effectiveness of these approaches. Most courts report that they use community service as an alternative to a fine (54%) or to repair harm to the community (49%). This national survey also found that community service tends to be required of those who are not convicted of more serious crimes. That is, the majority who receive community service are those with a first offense and/or youth under 18 years old. Service agencies often have limits on the type of person who can perform community services, particularly in regard to those with prior convictions, mental health diagnoses, and/or those with disabilities. Individuals with domestic violence offenses are also less likely to be offered community service compared to other individuals. Figure 5.4 highlights the impact that different characteristics have on eligibility for community service.

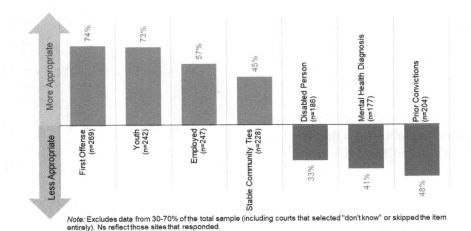

Note: Excludes data from 30-70% of the total sample (including courts that selected "don't know" or skipped the item entirely). Ns reflect those sites that responded.

FIGURE 5.4 Impact of Select Defendant Characteristics on Eligibility for Community Service Mandates

The impact of community service as a sanction is not well understood. There is little research that examines whether participating in community service reduces recidivism, increases a person's sense of responsibility, or effectively repairs harm to the community. One U.S. study examined community service in lieu of a jail sentence (Lee et al., 2013). This study found that community service participants were less likely to recidivate compared to those incarcerated in jail. Bouffard and Muftić (2007) compared the use of fines versus community service as sentences for individuals convicted of low-level offenses. They found that individuals who were sentenced to community service had lower recidivism rates compared to those who received fines only. However, there are no existing studies of the effectiveness of community service as part of a probation or parole sentence. Table 5.1 provides a list of types of community service individuals on probation or parole might engage in. Keep in mind, the type of community service opportunities available to individuals on supervision will also depend on their mandated conditions of probation or parole.

TABLE 5.1 Types of Community Service Opportunities

Type of community service	Examples
Environmental cleanup	Clean up local park: trash removal, trail maintenance, planting trees
Nonprofit organizations	Food banks, homeless shelters, animal shelters, community centers
Neighborhood improvement	Neighborhood cleanup, graffiti removal, community garden maintenance
Senior citizen support	Run errands, assist with household chores, provide transportation
Educational support	Tutor, mentor, help with after-school programs

Intensive Supervision Programs

Intensive supervision programs (ISPs) are the most-used intermediate sanction and have been referred to as the "cornerstone of the intermediate sanctions movement" (Petersilia, 1998, p.5). Under intensive supervision programs, individuals meet with their officers more frequently than they would on standard supervision. Early ISPs began in the 1960s, based on the idea that smaller caseload sizes would lead to increased ability of

probation and parole officers to both monitor and provide services, which could potentially lead to reductions in recidivism. In the 1980s, a renewed focus on ISPs resulted out of a need to address widespread prison-crowding issues. These programs were focused on providing a community-based mechanism for monitoring and surveillance, with little focus on the provision of treatment and services. They served both as an alternative for lower risk individuals who previously would have been incarcerated and as a means to supervise higher risk individuals on probation more closely.

The state of Georgia developed the first well-publicized ISP. In this program, they assigned 25 individuals under probation supervision to a team of two probation officers (Tonry & Will, 1990). One officer specialized as a surveillance officer, who focused on close monitoring, while the other officer served as a probation officer, who had legal authority over the case and focused on counseling. This ISP was focused on frequent meetings between officers and individuals on supervision (sometimes up to five times per week), community service, employment, and education. Additionally, individuals in the ISP had to pay a supervision fee to cover program expenses. In their own evaluation of the program, Georgia reported that ISP participants were much more successful, with less than 5% recidivism rates, stable employment, and high compliance with restitution requirements (Petersilia & Turner, 1993). The Georgia corrections commissioner at the time, David Evans, even went so far as to claim that ISP prevented the expense of building two prisons. This early ISP program gained a lot of national attention. The *New York Times* called Georgia's ISP program "the future of American corrections" (see Petersilia, 1999, p. 11).

The program received positive attention from probation staff who believed it allowed them to do their job the way it was intended to be done and supporters believed the program could effectively reduce prison crowding while enhancing public safety and promoting rehabilitation in a cost-effective manner. Similar ISPs began spreading across the country, starting in states like Illinois, Massachusetts, New Jersey, and Florida. Between 1985 and 1995, ISPs vastly expanded across the country, with hundreds of new programs implemented. Despite their popularity, studies examining these new ISPs found most did not achieve their goals. First, Petersilia (1998) found that very few individuals actually participated in ISPs, estimating that around 10% of adults on community supervision participated. Second, for those who did participate, the intensity of the program was much less than originally intended and outlined in Georgia's first program, likely due to vastly insufficient funding to maintain low caseloads (typically 25:2 with frequent visits). Petersilia estimates that most officers eventually moved back to one to two visits per month.

In 1993, Petersilia and Turner conducted the largest national study of ISPs which involved the random assignment of over 2,000 individuals to either ISP or traditional probation in 13 jurisdictions. This study found individuals who participated in an ISP had no differences in arrests but had slightly more technical violations and were more likely to return to prison or jail compared to those on regular probation. These findings have been echoed in many following examinations of ISP, with the consensus that ISPs resulted in closer surveillance, which in turn produced more technical violations. When those technical violations were detected, probation officers responded punitively, often resulting in revocations to prison. As a result, these programs did not reduce costs and in many areas ended up costing more. A meta-analysis conducted by Gendreau et al. in 2000 examined 47 studies of ISPs, concluding that ISP could actually increase recidivism by 6% compared to traditional supervision. Research on participant experiences in ISPs found they viewed ISPs as more punitive compared to incarceration (Spelman, 1995). In a review of ISPs, this generation of ISPs were termed "mean" punishments because of the focus on containing individuals, stacking on conditions, and requiring little involvement of therapeutic treatments (Taxman et al., 2020).

Later iterations of ISPs emphasized the importance of integrating rehabilitative components. That is, ISPs that included treatment and services alongside increased supervision were more effective compared to traditional ISPs. Research suggests that individuals who participated in both rehabilitative activities (e.g., drug treatment, community service, employment) had recidivism rates 10%–20% lower than those who did not participate in rehabilitative activities (Gendreau et al., 2000; Petersilia & Turner, 1993). Drake and colleagues (2009) identified 11 treatment-oriented ISPs, which produced a 17% reduction in recidivism on average leading to cost savings of nearly $20,000 per participant. These ISPs that integrate treatment with supervision are referred to as more "meaningful" ISPs (Taxman et al., 2020). While research supports this model of ISP to be more effective, there is evidence that in practice, many agencies focus more heavily on surveillance (Latessa & Lovins, 2019).

In summary, the research on ISPs suggests that increased surveillance increases technical violations, does not reduce recidivism, and does not reduce prison crowding; however, when combined with treatment, ISPs may be more effective. When ISPs do not address risk factors associated with recidivism and rather focus on control, surveillance, and the threat of punishment, they do not reduce prison crowding (Petersilia, 1999), do not save money (Drake et al., 2009), and do not reduce recidivism (Gendreau et al., 2000; Lipsey, 2009). Experts agree that ISPs that seek only to control and punish will likely fail. Rather, ISPs should seek to integrate core correctional practices that intentionally and systematically seek to address individual risk factors through rehabilitative interventions.

Partial Containment

The following are strategies to provide more intensive oversight and monitoring of an individual, primarily to limit physical movement (i.e., a spatial penalty) or to provide structure. The goal is to constrain an individual to some extent while also allowing some movement. The goal of partial containment strategies is to help the individual learn to restructure their movements in the community.

Curfews

Curfews are a frequent tool used to limit the movement of an individual by imposing a time restriction when the individual cannot be out of their residence. Curfews are generally used as a tool to restrict the activities of an individual. They are favored tools for juveniles on supervision, but curfews are often used for adults on supervision as well. Some curfews are intensified by a restraining order, which is a court order to preclude a person from visiting a particular area or from being near a particular person. The curfew generally requires an individual to abide by stipulated rules; however, probation and parole officers can intensify the curfew through the use of house arrest, electronic monitoring, requiring the individual to call the probation office, or other means to verify that the individual is following the probation orders.

Electronic Monitoring

During the same time ISPs grew in popularity, so did an interest in leveraging technology to supervise individuals in the community. Early forms of **electronic monitoring** systems first emerged in the early 1980s, primarily to monitor curfew restrictions. Several companies developed systems that used ankle-worn radio transmitters with programmable receivers connected to hardwired telephone lines. In the 1990s, technology advanced and global position systems (GPS) technologies came onto the market, with some created specifically for law enforcement and correctional use. GPS tracking now provided agencies with the ability to track individuals in real time, representing a massive change to supervision practices. The GPS software monitored the individual's location through remote collection of location data from the GPS receiver. The data is then transmitted through software, which the probation or parole officer can view from any device (e.g., computer) with an active internet connection. Officers are typically able to identify restricted areas where the individual cannot travel, as well as specific times the individual is required to be somewhere (e.g., at their home, school, work).

Modern versions of electronic monitoring use software that can send alerts to officers for any noncompliance with prespecified requirements. Additionally, many GPS programs allow the probation and parole officers to view individual movements on a map over a specified period of time. In addition to GPS, there is also radio frequency (RF) technology, which monitors an individual's presence or absence from a fixed location rather than continuous, 24/7 tracking. These devices are more commonly used for individuals sentenced to house arrest or those who are subject to curfews. RF technology requires the individual to wear an ankle bracelet and place a home monitoring unit in their home. Like GPS, RF alerts probation and parole officers of a violation. In practice, there are challenges associated with GPS and RF technology, including signal receiving and transmission failures. These failures are often due to a range of technological issues (e.g., broken charging device), cellular network disruptions, and physical and/or environmental interferences (e.g., physical structure blocking a satellite).

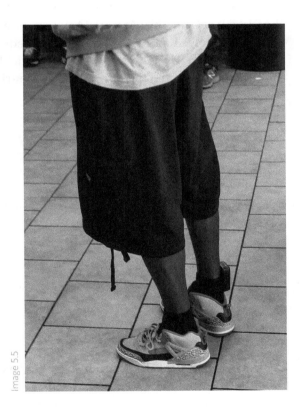

Image 5.5

There are several goals associated with electronic monitoring. First, electronic monitoring can be used as an intermediate sanction to divert individuals who may need closer supervision from incarceration. This may help to alleviate prison crowding or reduce the need to construct new prisons or jails. Second, electronic monitoring can help probation and parole officers conduct surveillance of their caseloads in a more efficient manner. Officers are frequently required to track the movements of individuals on supervision, and technology provides a mechanism to automate this process. As opposed to manually verifying whether individuals are where they are supposed to be, these software systems can monitor locations and flag violations 24/7.

The use of GPS is particularly salient for individuals on supervision with serious crimes such as a sex offense, given the legal restrictions on where these individuals can live, work, and travel. For these reasons, the popularity of electronic monitoring has grown substantially across the United States. Electronic monitoring has grown as an option for supervising higher risk parolees in the community, monitoring individuals pretrial, and to release lower risk individuals from jail to the community. Additionally, some probation and parole agencies use electronic monitoring for monitoring special caseloads more closely, such as those convicted of substance use, driving while intoxicated, and domestic violence (a population that is explored in more detail in Chapter 8). Currently, electronic monitoring occurs in all 50 U.S. states and the District of Columbia. At least 44 states passed legislation authorizing electronic monitoring of justice-involved individuals, with some requiring lifetime monitoring for those convicted of a sex offense. From 2005 to 2015, there was a 140% increase in the number of active electronic monitors as presented in Figure 5.5 (Pew Charitable Trusts, 2016).

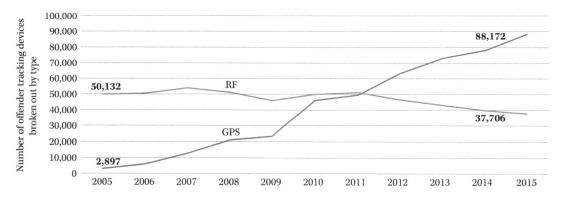

FIGURE 5.5   Electronic Monitoring Technology GPS and RF, 2005–2015

Electronic monitoring is often suggested as a more desired alternative to incarceration that allows individuals to remain in their communities. Proponents suggest its use allows the justice system to promote public safety, rehabilitation, and to prevent absconding. However, research on the effectiveness of electronic monitoring suggests that it is costly, impedes rehabilitation, and can exacerbate systemic harms (Kilgore et al., 2018). For example, a study conducted on federal probation found that those on electronic monitoring were more likely to receive a technical violation but were not more likely to be arrested for a new offense, indicating that the technology was more aligned with supervision conditions than recidivism goals

(Sainju et al., 2018). A meta-analysis conducted by Gendreau and colleagues (2000) identified slightly higher recidivism rates among individuals under electronic monitoring compared to those not monitored. Like the research on ISP, there is some evidence that recidivism can be reduced when electronic monitoring is combined with programs that specifically address an individual's criminogenic needs (Gendreau et al., 2000). However, one study found that rehabilitation plus electronic monitoring was only effective for high-risk individuals and not for low-risk individuals (Bonta et al., 2008).

Critics argue that electronic monitoring adds additional restrictions to already restrictive probation and parole sentences, setting them up for failure. Additional criticisms of electronic monitoring include the following arguments:

- Electronic monitoring exacerbates systemic harms: It exacerbates systematic racism, as Black people are more likely to be placed on electronic monitoring compared to White people. It discriminates against people with disabilities that may make it more difficult to comply with complex requirements associated with electronic monitoring. Electronic monitoring worsens economic and housing inequalities, as individuals on supervision must pay for the devices that could cost hundreds of dollars per month.
- Electronic monitoring impedes rehabilitation: It interferes with employment, education, family responsibilities, interferes with privacy, and encourages intrusive searches/ monitoring of household members.
- Electronic monitoring is costly: Electronic monitoring can cost between $547.50 and $17,555 per year (Weisburd et al., 2021), much of which is charged to the individual under supervision, and the increase of violations associated with electronic monitoring means more people are incarcerated, also increasing the costs substantially. Although this is hard to estimate, research suggests states spend over $9.3 billion annually imprisoning people for supervision violations, with $2.8 billion for technical violations (The Council of State Governments, 2019).

House Arrest

House arrest (also referred to as "home confinement") serves to remove an individual from the community without the use of prison or jail. House arrest can be used in the front end of the corrections system, serving as a diversion from incarceration, or it can be used in the back end of the system, with individuals released from incarceration early into home confinement program. In some states, house arrest is used in lieu of detention pretrial. While the application of house arrest has been in existence for centuries, it became highly prevalent during the 1970s and 1980s. During this time, house arrest programs focused on individuals convicted of driving under the influence and minor property crimes. House arrest has since expanded to include a wide range of offenses and individuals on supervision.

Since the advancement of electronic monitoring, the use of house arrest has continued to increase. Today, it is very common for individuals to be sentenced to house arrest, with electronic monitoring used to monitor compliance. In many situations, individuals under house

Image 5.6

arrest are allowed to leave their homes to go to work, receive medical care, or attend religious services. The use of electronic monitoring ensures that the individual always remains in their home, except for special permission to attend certain activities.

Research on the effectiveness of house arrest programs is limited, but available evidence suggests its impact on recidivism is limited and that it may have similar negative consequences (i.e., net widening, creating more violations). One study of house arrest programs in Arizona found the program was expensive and had revocation rates twice that of parolees not under house arrest (Palumbo et al., 1992). However, more extensive and rigorous research is needed to fully evaluate the impacts of house arrest.

Day Reporting Centers

Day reporting centers are modified halfway houses or work release centers that provide structure for a short period of time (3–8 hours a day). However, day reporting centers do not allow individuals to reside at the facility, and the individuals cannot sleep there. Some day reporting centers offer educational and/or therapeutic services, while others offer shower services, laundry service, access to email, and/or a variety of programs. Research on day reporting centers finds they are not effective at reducing recidivism, but they do offer opportunities for individuals to be in a secure setting for a period of time.

Full Containment

Some intermediate sanction programs require the person to be fully contained in a facility and participate in specific programming. The model uses short periods of containment to intensify the punishment.

Boot Camps

Boot camps (also referred to as "shock incarceration") are short-term incarceration programs designed to mimic a military training program. Key features of boot camps include physical training and exercises, manual labor, drill and ceremony, and strict discipline. Boot camps mirror a quasi-military environment—from the physical appearance of correctional officers and inmates (e.g., uniforms, shaved heads), language used (officers use military titles, inmates may be grouped in squads), to punishment for misconduct (e.g., push-ups). When inmates complete the program, a graduation ceremony is typically held with family members in attendance.

While the basic premise behind boot camps is consistent across programs, there are differences in the emphasis on physical requirements (e.g., training and labor) and rehabilitative programming (e.g., education, treatment). Like house arrest, boot camps can also operate

FIGURE 5.7   U.S. Navy Boot Camp, 1980

as front-end diversion or back-end prison release programs. An individual can be directly sentenced to a boot camp by a judge, or they can be identified by correctional staff as a good candidate for participation.

Boot camps originated in the 1980s and quickly became popular. The first boot camps opened in Georgia in 1983 and spread throughout both adult and juvenile correctional systems (although juvenile boot camps are less focused on hard labor and are required to provide education). Today, there are boot camps in the federal, state, and local systems across the United States. Despite their popularity, they are a less commonly used form of intermediate sanctions. These programs have been criticized widely for their harsh approach and lack of focus on rehabilitation. Empirical research suggests that boot camps are not effective either, with a meta-analysis of 26 boot camp evaluations finding no impacts on recidivism (Wilson et al., 2005), a recent review confirming boot camps did not reduce recidivism rates (Taxman et al., 2020), and others finding the programs do not save money when compared to other alternatives (MacKenzie, 1995).

Halfway Houses and Work Release

Besides intensive services in the community, intermediate sanctions also include structured arrangements to limit their movement and to ensure that individuals are monitored more. In these programs, individuals often work during the day (or some period at night) and/or participate in structured programming. These programs can occur in halfway houses or work release centers but often are called a variety of things: group residences, restitution centers, sober living homes, or transitional housing. Regardless of the label, residents are often there for short periods of time and can receive therapeutic services of varying nature (see the Treatment Programming section), are monitored, and receive necessities (e.g., food, shelter).

These residential settings offer structure and discipline for the purpose of helping individuals to establish new living patterns. Halfway houses and work release centers are similar in that individuals are allowed to leave the facility to go to work but must reside in the facility at all other times. The size of the facility may vary from small residential (8–20 people) to larger facilities (up to several hundred people). A halfway house and/or work release center can be operated by state corrections departments, probation and parole offices, federal agencies, or private nonprofits. Some states have regulations overseeing halfway houses, while the majority do not. The Federal Bureau of Prisons has residential reentry centers (RRCs), which include halfway houses and work release centers. Typically, the individual is responsible for their own room and may have responsibilities in the facility such as preparing meals, cleaning, and/or laundry. The underlying theory is that these places can serve to transition individuals into the community by providing not only a residence but also a place to work, learn new skills, and learn to be a productive member of the community.

The residential centers can also serve as therapeutic centers. Some halfway houses serve as recovery residences, such as sober living houses or recovery homes. Their goal is to provide a safe and healthy living environment that promotes recovery from alcohol and drugs. The services provided include case management, self-help groups, traditional group therapy, and individual counseling. The services can be peer-run, monitored by a house manager or senior resident, supervised by a variety of staff, and/or provided by a service provider. Often, the houses are provided in conjunction with self-help groups, outpatient treatment, or other community services.

It is estimated that on an average day, 45,143 men and 6,834 women live in these residential, structured settings. Many centers require individuals to pay fees for staying in the house, but some are funded by the city, county, or state agencies, while the federal government funds the RRCs. Very few studies have been done on the effectiveness of halfway houses or work release centers. Halfway houses or work release centers are often criticized for being poorly managed, with some labeled "houses of crime."

Treatment Programming

Many programming efforts also include a myriad of treatment programs that are designed to address substance use or mental illness. These programs can be offered in conjunction with residential programming (described above), either by the staff of the probation agency, contractual staff, or in partnership with treatment agencies. Given that over half of the individuals involved in probation have substance use disorders, mental illness, or co-occurring disorders, treatment is a common addition to conditions of supervision. The complexities surrounding supervision of individuals with mental illness and who use substances is further explained in Chapter 8.

When considering **treatment programming**, there are four things to consider: (a) dosage or the frequency and length by which the services are offered (e.g., total number of hours someone spends in a treatment program); (b) the type of sessions (i.e., individual, one-on-one versus group sessions); (c) physical location of services; and (d) the orientation of the program.

Dosage refers to how many sessions with a clinician or provider an individual participates in as well as how frequent the sessions are. A common dosage for an individual on community supervision is one group session a week for 60 to 90 minutes, but the treatment can also be offered multiple times a week, biweekly, monthly, or quarterly. In other words, depending on the provider and/or the probation and parole system, services are offered on a variety of schedules. Programs can be classified by the dosage level: Low-intensity services are 100 hours or less, medium-intensity services are 101–200 hours; and high-intensity services are over 201 hours (Sperber et al., 2013). The more problem behaviors a person has, the more likely the

IMAGE 5.8   Group Therapy Session Room at the National Problem Gambling Clinic

person should receive more intense services and thus a greater dosage. There are a number of issues related to dosage, including determining the appropriate number of hours each program requires, how many weeks long should a program be, and what type of support services are needed to improve the intensity of programming.

The *type of sessions* refers to whether the treatment is offered as individual sessions or in a group setting. Individual sessions are one on one with a treatment provider and are often integral in addressing trust issues and developing an effective working relationship between the provider and individual. However, individual sessions are considered a luxury because they are more expensive for individuals and more time intensive for staff. Group sessions, however, became the favored technique because (a) 8–15 individuals can be treated at the same time; (b) group settings provide a therapeutic opportunity for individuals to provide feedback to

one another; and (c) the group can be used to challenge misperceptions and/or misbehaviors (e.g., group members can hold each other accountable). Research suggests that males tend to do better in group sessions, while females (who may have additional trust and relationship issues compared to their male counterparts) do better in individual sessions. As discussed in Chapter 4, these considerations are critical for developing effective officer–individual on supervision relationships.

IMAGE 5.9   Group Therapy at the U.S. Disciplinary Barrack

Case management services are often needed to supplement or complement clinical services, given the needs of individuals. Case management provides additional support to obtain normal everyday materials to thrive. For example, these sessions often focus on assessing individual needs, referring to services, and addressing issues like housing, transportation, food, and employment.

In recent years, peer navigation services have also emerged to augment traditional treatment services. *Peer navigation* refers to individuals with lived experience (e.g., having prior substance use disorder, having been in prison or in the legal system, or both) serving as a mentor and guide for an individual in a similar situation. The peer navigator brings the credentials of having similar experiences and characteristics with the individual on supervision or in prison, and therefore the peer can serve as a credible role model. Peer navigators have been successfully used in mental health treatment settings. In correctional settings like jail and prison, the role of a peer has been controversial, given there is little interest in having one justice-involved individual have influence over another and concerns about possible negative influences. While recent research supports the use of peer navigators with justice-involved individuals, this is a relatively new concept that remains understudied.

A third consideration for treatment has to do with the physical location of the program or service. Individual and group sessions can be offered in any setting: prison, jail, the community, a halfway house, work release centers, day reporting programs, a clinic, or a probation office. In the substance use field, there is a distinction between "outpatient" and "inpatient" programs (see Table 5.2). This is a distinction as to whether the program occurs in a clinic or community setting (outpatient) or in a residential facility (inpatient). While it is typically assumed that a residential facility offers a greater dosage and more intensive services, prior research suggests the services are often less intensive (such as weekly or even monthly) or nonclinical (e.g., Alcohol or Narcotics Anonymous groups). As a result, the setting of treatment may not determine the dosage or intensity of services. However, research does suggest that treatment is most effective in the community compared to an incarceration-type setting. The key differences between outpatient and inpatient treatment is provided in Table 5.2.

The final consideration for treatment centers around the orientation of the program itself. A *therapeutic orientation* refers to the purpose, goals, and style of therapy or services offered. The term *therapeutic* refers to services that are designed to be clinical to help individuals change their attitudes and/or behaviors. The following list details commonly used programs with therapeutic orientations. It is important to note that not all of these programs are evidence-based, nor are they all considered best practices for reducing recidivism and/or other behaviors (e.g., substance use). Each of these programs can be offered in individual, group, and/or family sessions.

- *Self-support:* These are peer-driven services that focus on key principles of behavior change. Generally, these services are offered as "meetings" and require the participant to identify a "sponsor" or support person to help them make behavioral change (e.g., Alcoholics Anonymous).

TABLE 5.2   Outpatient Versus Inpatient Treatment

	Outpatient	Inpatient
Setting	Clinic, hospital, community-based treatment center	Residential facility, hospital
Level of care	Less intensive, flexible schedule	More intensive, 24/7 care is possible although research suggests may be weekly/monthly
Dosage	Several hours per week	Several weeks to months
Level of supervision	Minimal	Constant
Flexibility	High; depending on program availability, can typically accommodate daily routine	None; requires a full break in daily routine
Structure	Less structured, often self-paced	Highly structured, daily schedules
Support	Relies heavily on individual's social support system	Support from staff and other program participants
Cost	Generally, more affordable	Often expensive

- *Motivational enhancements:* This is typically a short-term program designed to address the motivation to change. Generally, this is a precursor to treatment programs to encourage an individual to be ready for the program.
- *Contingency management:* Contingency management uses rewards and incentives to encourage behavioral change. Individuals often work with a counselor to identify goals and steps needed to achieve those goals. They will then be rewarded when they accomplish various steps. This process uses incentives to activate behavior and thinking changes.
- *Psychoanalysis and psychodynamics:* This is a type of talk therapy where the focus is on the unconscious thoughts and/or analyzing factors in one's past.
- *Behavioral therapies:* These programs are designed to focus on negative behaviors and replace them with positive ones.
- *Cognitive therapies:* These therapies are designed to focus on thought processes and decision making with an emphasis on promoting more prosocial behaviors.
- *Cognitive behavioral therapy (CBT):* This is one of the most common types of programs offered to individuals on probation/parole. CBT attends to attitudes, values, and behaviors that are problematic with a focus on promoting improved decision making and addressing thoughts that fuel negative feelings and behaviors. CBT programs focus on getting individuals to understand how their thinking impacts their behaviors and encourage thinking in a prosocial manner to produce prosocial behavior.
- *Therapeutic milieu:* This is the process of using the living environment to generate changes in their values, attitudes, and/or behavior by having a structured social culture. The therapeutic milieu is generally done in a residential setting where residents

subscribe to a certain set of rules focused on serving the community. The process involves learning the rules and the promotion of leadership values.

- *Humanistic therapy:* This form of therapy is focused on helping a person develop an appreciation for the uniqueness of their own human experiences and that of others. Typical types are gestalt (examine your life in the present moment), individual-centered therapy (Rogerian therapy with a focus on the individual), and existential therapy (allowing each person to define their own meaning of life).
- *Integrative therapy:* This type of therapy uses a mix of approaches to help the individual with complex issues.

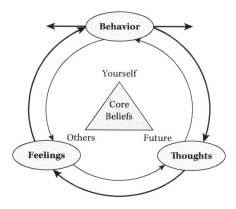

FIGURE 5.6   Tenets of Cognitive-Behavioral Therapy

Of these various approaches, just two have enough evidence indicating their effectiveness to be deemed an evidence-based treatment: cognitive behavioral therapy (CBT) and contingency management. Studies have consistently found that CBT and contingency management are effective in reducing drug use, improving social functioning, and changing attitudes. In terms of reducing recidivism, research finds the combination of using CBT and incentives at twice the rates of using sanctions is a best practice for justice-involved populations (Mowen et al., 2018). Figure 5.6 provides a visual approach to understanding the link between core beliefs and behavior, feelings, and thoughts, which are essential components of CBT and contingency management.

Challenges with Intermediate Sanctions

While the original intent of intermediate sanctions was to solve the problem of prison overcrowding and massive financial strain associated with incarceration while offering a community-based sanction that held individuals accountable for their behavior, their use is not without problems. Experts note at least three major issues. First, a major challenge with intermediate sanctions is determining who and when to assign them as punishment. Remember, the assignment of intermediate sanctions often happens within the courts at the sentencing phase. While sentencing guidelines provided a clear attempt to shift away from discretionary decision making through legal stipulations regarding which individuals are eligible for intermediate sanctions, they do not legally define who should receive them. As a result, court actors (e.g., judges) must incorporate additional information to help make these decisions.

Steffensmeier and colleagues' (1998) focal concerns theory aids our understanding of how court actors (in this example, judges) make decisions like assignment of intermediate sanctions. This perspective suggests that court actors make discretionary punishment decisions by weighing three focal concerns: individual blameworthiness, individual dangerousness, and practical constraints and consequences of the sentence (e.g., individual amenability to treatment, family/employment status). The focal concerns perspective suggests that court actors aim for a rational decision-making process, but in the face of organizational constraints (e.g., large caseloads, incomplete information about individuals, lack of resources), decision making becomes characterized by "bounded rationality." This means that court actors, such as judges, must make critical sentencing decisions (e.g., whether to

IMAGE 5.10   Miles Ehrlich, Judge

apply an intermediate sanction or incarcerate) with too little information for judging the future risk of an individual. As a result, judges may consider "perceptual shorthands" to aid decision making, such as race, gender, and age (Steffenmeier et al., 1998). The use of these factors in decision making may produce disparities in the application of punishment. That is, individuals convicted of similar crimes with similar backgrounds may receive different punishments. This is in direct conflict with the retributive approach to punishment, as discussed in Chapter 1.

A second related challenge is a wide variation in the design and application of intermediate sanctions across jurisdictions. This results in vastly different levels and types of punishment applied for similar individuals based solely on geographical differences and variations in the design of a particular intermediate sanction. These differences may be further amplified based on the availability of resources and funding within a particular locale. This possibility for differences in punishment for similar individuals convicted of similar crimes also violates just deserts. Third, a major challenge with intermediate sanctions is that they may promote net widening. As discussed in Chapter 3, net widening carries risk of reinforcing racial, ethnic, and social disparities in community corrections.

It is clear that intermediate sanctions often involve increased requirements, surveillance, and monitoring, which in turn can lead to increased opportunities for noncompliance and increased detections of that noncompliance. As a result, more individuals may be ultimately sent to jail or prison due to the practices of intermediate sanctions. This is particularly problematic, as prior to the advancement of intermediate sanctions, these individuals might have received probation instead. For these reasons, it is critical to conduct rigorous research studies on the effectiveness of intermediate sanctions.

◊ Officer Work, Careers, and Wellness: Managing Punishment and Supervision Conditions

The growth in popularity of intermediate sanctions resulted in changes in the responsibilities of probation and parole officers. Traditionally, the officer's individual responsibilities involved conducting face-to-face contacts, monitoring employment, and checking on the living arrangements of the individual. With additional conditions to monitor, officer roles transformed to bill collector (for financial penalties), urine collector (or observer, as many probation and parole officers have to physically enter the bathroom with an individual while they provide a sample) for drug testing, assessor for collecting data on individual risk and need factors, provider for administering treatment sessions via individual or group meetings, monitor of technology for electronic monitoring, and curfew validator for curfews and house arrest. These are just a few of the newer roles and responsibilities of officers. This creates a situation where probation and parole officers must "wear many hats," with each of these responsibilities bringing their own challenges to the job. For example, Ruhland (2020) found that officers often perceive their role as a bill collector as one that strains the supervision experience, forcing them to focus on collecting money rather than engaging in other compliance or rehabilitation services. In Ruhland's (2020) study, she provides excerpts from probation officer accounts discussing their concerns:

> I will tell you it's something that's pushed very hard … I mean it's how our department is funded. And we depend on collection of fees. So monthly … our officers are under a lot of pressure to do whatever we can to collect fees. Period. End of story. And it's a very important … the collection of fees, it's a priority. (pp. 54–55)

Officers in Ruhland's (2020) study emphasized how much time and energy they spent discussing, documenting, and tracking the fines and fees of the individuals on their caseloads. Further, officers discussed how it was a challenge to balance this bill collector role with that of being an enforcer and social worker as well. As a result, officers often felt strain from managing multiple expectations that often took away from their ability to help individuals on their caseloads.

Effectiveness of Intermediate Sanctions

The research on intermediate sanctions suggests that increasing restrictions and requirements geared toward monitoring and surveilling compliance does not result in lower rates of recidivism. In fact, in many cases we see increases in recidivism and technical violations when individuals are subjected to more severe punishment, an outcome that is primarily due to punitive intermediate sanctions. The more restrictions and punishments placed on individuals in the community corrections system, the more burdensome the punishment is. In the field of social work, practitioners are trained that individuals should not be given more than three requirements, as this is usually what one person can handle at a time. As mentioned earlier in this chapter, in the era of intermediate sanctions, supervision conditions can mount to well over this number, with an average of 17! The high number of supervision conditions and requirements creates pressure and tension, with those experiencing supervision often perceiving the system as "hard" and "trying to get me." There is even evidence that justice-involved individuals may prefer a term of incarceration rather than community supervision due to the strenuous and restrictive nature of the process (Spelman, 1995).

However, research suggests that intermediate sanctions can be effective if they are used in conjunction with therapeutic, rehabilitative programming (Alm, 2016). Therapeutic features help individuals to learn social skills to manage their behavior and problem-solving skills to improve their decisions. For example, if individuals have a supervision fee but the person would like new clothing, the therapeutic skills approach would emphasize personal responsibility to pay the fee first. Improved outcomes are possible if that programming adheres to the risk-need-responsivity (RNR) model discussed in Chapter 4. In a study of 55 intermediate sanctions in Ohio, Lowenkamp et al. (2006) found that when programs focused on higher risk individuals, providing more intensive supervision *and* treatment, recidivism was reduced by 15% on average. For programs that did not adhere to these principles, recidivism increased by 13%. As noted by Taxman et al. (2020), intermediate sanctions emerged in the "mean" era of probation when the emphasis was on social control. However, the advance of the RNR framework introduced a "meaningful" era of supervision where the goals were on individuals achieving success and using the probation period to make meaningful change in their quality of life that affects offending and drug use behaviors.

◊ Diversity, Equity, and Inclusion: Racial Disparities in Intermediate Sanctions

In the United States, 75.8% of the population is White, 18.9% is Hispanic or Latino, 13.6% is Black, 6.1% is Asian, 1.3% is American Indian and Alaska Native, and 0.3% is Native Hawaiian and Other Pacific Islander (United States Census Bureau, 2021). However, in 2020, the probation population was 30% Black and 13% Hispanic while the parole population was 37% Black and 16% Hispanic (Kaeble, 2021). In contrast, White individuals made up only 54% of probation and 44% of the parole populations. These frequencies suggest that White individuals are underrepresented in the community corrections system, while Black and Hispanic individuals are overrepresented. There are many studies exploring the racial disparities associated with sentencing outcomes. For example, a wealth of research finds that compared to White defendants, Black and Hispanic defendants are more likely to receive severe sentences (even for similar crimes and similar mitigating/aggravating factors; see King & Light, 2019; and Steffensmeier et al., 1998). Franklin and colleagues (2017) examined 10 years of sentencing data to assess differences in the types of individuals who were offered intermediate sanctions as compared to prison or standard probation. They found that young Black males were more likely to receive prison sentences than intermediate sanctions or probation in the U.S. federal system.

In addition to disparities in sentencing, research also examines the impact of race on probation or parole supervision experiences and outcomes. Intermediate sanctions provided the opportunity to use community sanctions with added liberty restrictions to intensify the probation/parole experience (e.g., drug testing, electronic monitoring, curfews). This results in many conditions broadly applied rather than tailored to an individual's circumstance. This high number of conditions creates a restrictive environment where being in full compliance can be challenging, even for individuals who are trying their best. As discussed earlier in this chapter, studies on intensive supervision, for example, have found that increased conditions usually result in more technical violations or unsuccessful completion from supervision (Taxman et al., 2020). There have been several studies examining racial disparity issues in parole violations. One study by Mechoulan and Sahuguet (2015) examined violation patterns in states using the National Corrections Reporting Program (NCRP), which collects data on individuals under correctional supervision in all U.S. states. This study found that there was a 12% difference in the probability of violation, with Black parolees having an average violation rate of 44% and White parolees having a violation rate of 32% for states with indeterminate sentencing laws (i.e., the parole board can release an individual early due to good conduct in prison). In these states, Black parolees were more likely to be returned to prison for a violation.

Research conducted by Jannetta et al. (2014) for the Urban Institute studied probation violations in Dallas County (Texas), Iowa's Sixth Judicial District (SJD; Iowa), Multnomah County (Oregon), and New York City (New York). They found Black individuals were revoked at higher rates compared to similarly situated White or Hispanic individuals. In their research, between 51% and 80% of the differences in revocation rates could be explained by characteristics of the individual such as risk level, offense type, and age, with 20% to 49% of the disparity attributed to an individual's race (Jannetta et al., 2014). While more research on the impact of racial disparities in sentencing and supervision outcomes is needed, the existing research suggests race has impacts on different decision points throughout the criminal legal system and may determine who receives an intermediate sanction, what type of sanction they receive, and whether they receive a supervision violation and/or revocation.

SUMMARY: FUTURE OF INTERMEDIATE SANCTIONS

While intermediate sanctions have gained popularity as a cost-saving, effective alternative to incarceration, research suggests these goals have not been realized in practice. However, issues of overutilizing prison and probation remain pressing challenges. There is a critical need to understand how the current system of intermediate sanctions can be reworked to address the aforementioned challenges. For example, improvements in tools to promote consistency and reduce disparities in decision making at the sentencing stage are needed. To prevent net widening, more data-driven policies are needed to determine who truly needs more than probation to promote public safety. And for those for whom probation is not appropriate, intermediate sanctions should incorporate rehabilitative principles in line with the RNR model. While not an easily solved problem, lack of resources for community-based supervision and treatment remains a critical challenge. Correctional programs can only do so much with limited resources. These financial constraints should be considered in determining guidelines for determining who and when intermediate sanctions should be used.

Scenario-Based Activities

	Case	Question(s)
1.	Alex was recently placed in an intensive supervision program after receiving his second conviction. As part of this program, he has to meet with his probation officer four times a week, submit to regular drug testing, complete 200 hours of community service, maintain active employment, and pay $60 per month in supervision fees.	What is the intermediate sanction Alex received? How does this intermediate sanction aim to address Alex's offense and reduce the likelihood he will recidivate? What challenges would you anticipate facing in implementing and enforcing this intermediate sanction?
2	Pretend you are a probation officer responsible for supervising Tasha, a 30-year-old single mother of two children. Tasha has a history of substance use and has been mandated by the court to attend drug treatment and participate in a parenting program on top of the general supervision conditions.	Thinking about supervising Tasha, what approach/approaches do you think you would need to use to effectively manage her case? How could you balance the need to enforce compliance with probation conditions while also providing support and resources for rehabilitation? What challenges might you face in trying to achieve multiple goals as a probation officer? What techniques might you use to overcome those challenges?

References

Alm, S. S. (2016). HOPE probation: Fair sanctions, evidence-based principles, and therapeutic alliances. *Criminology & Public Policy, 15*(4), 1195–1214. https://doi.org/10.1111/1745-9133.12261

Bonta, J., Rugge, T., Scott, T. L., Bourgon, G., & Yessine, A. K. (2008). Exploring the black box of community supervision. *Journal of Offender Rehabilitation, 47*(3), 248–270. https://doi.org/10.1080/10509670802134085

Bouffard, J. A., R Muftić, L. R. (2007). The effectiveness of community service sentences compared to traditional fines for low-level offenders. *The Prison Journal, 87(2)*, 171–194. https://doi.org/10.1177/0032885507303741

Brett, S., Khoshkhoo, N., & Nagrecha, M. (2020). *Paying on probation: How financial sanctions intersect with probation to target, trap, and punish people who cannot pay.* Criminal Justice Policy Program, Harvard Law School. https://finesandfeesjusticecenter.org/articles/financial-sanctions-intersect-with-probation/

Drake, E. K., Aos, S., & Miller, M. G. (2009). Evidence-based public policy options to reduce crime and criminal justice costs: Implications in Washington State. *Victims and Offenders, 4*(2), 170–196. https://doi.org/10.1080/15564880802612615

Engen, R. L., Gainey, R. R., Crutchfield, R. D., & Weis, J. G. (2003). Discretion and disparity under sentencing guidelines: The role of departures and structured sentencing alternatives. *Criminology, 41*(1), 99–130. https://doi.org/10.1111/j.1745-9125.2003.tb00983.x

Franklin, T. W., Dittmann, L., & Henry, T. K. S. (2017). Extralegal disparity in the application of inter-mediate sanctions: An analysis of U.S. District Courts. *Crime & Delinquency, 63*(7), 839–874. https://doi.org/10.1177/0011128715607533

Frase, R. (2005). State sentencing guidelines: Diversity, consensus, and unresolved policy issues. *Columbia Law Review, 105*, 1190–1232. Available at https://scholarship.law.umn.edu/faculty_articles/507

Gendreau, P., Goggin, C., Cullen, F. T., & Andrews, D. A. (2000, May). The effects of community sanctions and incarceration on recidivism. *Forum on Corrections Research, 12*(2), 10–13.

Jannetta, J., Breaux, J., & Ho, H. (2014). *Examining racial and ethnic disparities in probation revocation: Summary findings and implications from a multisite study.* Urban Institute. https://www.urban.org/sites/default/files/publication/22746/413174-Examining-Racial-and-Ethnic-Disparities-in-Probation-Revocation.PDF

Jarvis, M., Williams, J., Hurford, M., Lindsay, D., Lincoln, P., Leila, G., Luongo, P., & Safarian, T. (2017). Appropriate use of drug testing in clinical addiction medicine. *Journal of Addiction Medicine, 11*(3), 163–173. https://doi.org/10.1097/ADM.0000000000000323

Kaeble, D. (2021, December 16). *Probation and parole in the United States, 2020.* Bureau of Justice Statistics.

Kilgore, J., Sanders, E., & Hayes, M. (2018). *No more shackles: Why we must end the use of electronic monitors for people on parole.* The Center for Media Justice: Open Society Institute.

King, R. D., & Light, M. T. (2019). Have racial and ethnic disparities in sentencing declined? *Crime and Justice, 48*(1), 365–437. https://doi.org/10.1086/701505

Latessa, E. J., & Lovins, L. B. (2019). Privatization of community corrections. *Criminology & Public Policy, 18*(2), 323–341. https://doi.org/10.1111/1745-9133.12433

Lee, C. G., Cheesman, F. L., Rottman, D. B., Swaner, R., Lambson, S., Rempel, M., & Curtis, R. (2013). *A community court grows in Brooklyn: A comprehensive evaluation of the Red Hook Community Justice Center.* National Center for State Courts.

Link, N. W. (2023). Paid your debt to society? Court-related financial obligations and community super-vision during the first year after release from prison. *Corrections: Policy, Practice, and Research*, 8(3), 202–218. https://doi.org/10.1080/23774657.2021.1878072

Lipsey, M. W. (2009). The primary factors that characterize effective interventions with juve-nile offenders: A meta-analytic overview. *Victims and Offenders*, 4(2), 124–147. https://doi.org/10.1080/15564880802612573

Lowenkamp, C. T., Pealer, J., Smith, P., & Latessa, E. J. (2006). Adhering to the risk and need principles: Does it matter for supervision-based programs? *Federal Probation*, 70(3), 3–8.

MacKenzie, D. L., Brame, R., McDowall, D., & Souryal, C. (1995). Boot camp prisons and recidivism in eight states. *Criminology*, 33(3), 327–358. https://doi.org/10.1111/j.1745-9125.1995.tb01181.x

Mechoulan, S., & Sahuguet, N. (2015). Assessing racial disparities in parole release. *The Journal of Legal Studies*, 44(1), 39–74. https://doi.org/10.1086/680988

Morris, N., & Tonry, M. (1991). *Between prison and probation: Intermediate punishments in a rational sentencing system.* Oxford University Press.

Mowen, T. J., Wodahl, E., Brent, J. J., & Garland, B. (2018). The role of sanctions and incentives in promoting successful reentry: Evidence from the SVORI data. *Criminal Justice and Behavior*, 45(8), 1288–1307. https://doi.org/10.1177/0093854818770695

O'Connell, D. J., Brent, J. J., & Visher, C. A. (2016). Decide your time: A randomized trial of a drug testing and graduated sanctions program for probationers. *Criminology & Public Policy, 15*(4), 1073–1102. https://doi.org/10.1111/1745-9133.12246

Palumbo, D. J., Clifford, M., & Snyder-Joy, Z. K. (1992). From net widening to intermediate sanctions: The transformation of alternatives to incarceration from benevolence to malevolence. In J. M. Byrne, A. J. Lurigio, & J. Petersilia (Eds.), *Smart sentencing: The emergence of intermediate sanctions* (pp. 229–244). SAGE Publications.

Petersilia, J. R. (1998). *Community corrections: Probation, parole, and intermediate sanctions.* Oxford University Press.

Petersilia, J. (1999). A decade of experimenting with intermediate sanctions: What have we learned? *Justice Research and Policy, 1*(1), 9–23. https://doi.org/10.3818/JRP.1.1.1999.9

Petersilia, J., & Turner, S. (1993). Intensive probation and parole. *Crime and Justice, 17,* 281–335. https://doi.org/10.1086/449215

Petersilia, J., Turner, S., Kahan, J., & Peterson, J. (1985). *Granting felons probation: Public risks and alternatives.* Rand.

Pew Charitable Trusts. (2010). *Collateral costs: Incarceration's effect on economic mobility.* https://www.pewtrusts.org/-/media/assets/2016/09/collateral_costs_report.pdf

Pew Charitable Trusts. (2016). *Use of electronic offender-tracking devices expands sharply.* https://www.pewtrusts.org/en/research-and-analysis/issue-briefs/2016/09/use-of-electronic-offender-tracking-devices-expands-sharply

Picard, S., Tallon, J. A., Lowry, M., & Kralstein, D. (2019). *Court-ordered community service: A national perspective.* New York, NY: Center for Court Innovation. https://www.innovatingjustice.org/publications/community-service

Reichert, J. (2020). *Drug testing in community corrections: A review of the literature.* Illinois Criminal Justice Information Authority, Center for Justice Research and Evaluation. https://doi.org/10.13140/RG.2.2.15643.82728

Ruhland, E. L. (2020) Social worker, law enforcer, and now bill collector: Probation officers' collection of supervision fees. *Journal of Offender Rehabilitation, 59*(1), 44–63. https://doi.org/10.1080/10509674.2019.1671571

Ruhland, E. L. (2021). It's all about the money: An exploration of probation fees. *Corrections: Policy, Practice, and Research, (6)*1, 165–84. https://doi.org/10.1080/23774657.2018.1564635

Sainju, K. D., Fahy, S., Hamilton, B. A., Baggaley, K., Baker, A., Minassian, T., & Filippelli, V. (2018). Electronic monitoring for pretrial release: Assessing the impact. *Federal Probation, 82*(3).

Spelman, W. (1995). The severity of intermediate sanctions. *Journal of Research in Crime and Delinquency, 32*(2), 107–135. https://doi.org/10.1177/0022427895032002001

Sperber, K. G., Latessa, E. J., & Makarios, M. D. (2013). Examining the interaction between level of risk and dosage of treatment. *Criminal Justice and Behavior, 40*(3), 338–348. https://doi.org/10.1177/0093854812467942

Steffensmeier, D., Ulmer, J., & Kramer, J. (1998). the interaction of race, gender, and age in criminal sentencing: The punishment cost of being young, Black, and male. *Criminology, 36*(4), 763–798. https://doi.org/10.1111/j.1745-9125.1998.tb01265.x

Taxman, F. S., & Breno, A. (2017). Alternatives to incarceration. In H. N. Pontell (Ed.), *Oxford research encyclopedia of criminology and criminal justice.* Oxford University Press. https://doi.org/10.1093/acrefore/9780190264079.013.259

Taxman, F. S., Smith, L., & Rudes, D. (2020). Putting a square into a circle: The story of boot camps—A tribute to Doris Mackenzie's work. In P. Lattimore, B. Huebner, & F. S. Taxman (Eds.), *Handbook on moving corrections and sentencing forward: Building on the record.* Routledge Press.

The Council of State Governments (2019). *Confined and costly: How supervision violations are filling prisons and burdening budgets.* The Justice Center, The Council of State Governments. https://csgjusticecenter.org/publications/confined-costly/

Tonry, M. (1998). Intermediate sanctions in sentencing guidelines. *Crime and Justice, 23,* 199–253. https://doi.org/10.1086/449271

Tonry, M., & Will, R. (1990). *Intermediate sanctions.* National Institute of Justice, U.S. Department of Justice.

United States Sentencing Commission. (2009). *2009 federal sentencing guidelines manual.* https://www.ussc.gov/guidelines/archive/2009-federal-sentencing-guidelines-manual

United States Census Bureau. (2021). *Population.* https://www.census.gov/topics/population.html

Weisburd, K., Bhadha, V., Clauson, M., Elican, J., Kahn, F., Lawrenz, K., Pemberton, B., Rikngler, R., Schaer, J., Sherman, M., & Wohlsdorf, S. (2021). *Electronic prisons: The operation of ankle monitoring in the criminal legal system* [Research Paper No. 2021–41]. *GWU Legal Studies.*

Wilson, D. B., MacKenzie, D. L., & Mitchell, F. N. (2005). Effects of correctional boot camps on offending: A systematic review. *Campbell Systematic Reviews, 1*(6). https://doi.org/10.4073/csr.2005.6

Image Credits

Fig. 5.1: Adapted from Faye S. Taxman and Alex Breno, "Probation to Prison Scale" from "Alternatives to Incarceration," https://oxfordre.com/criminology/display/10.1093/acrefore/9780190264079.001.0001/acrefore-9780190264079-e-259. Copyright © 2023 by Oxford University Press.

Fig. 5.2: Pennsylvania Commission on Sentencing, "Basic Sentencing Matrix," https://pcs.la.psu.edu/guidelines-statutes/sentencing/. Copyright © by The Pennsylvania State University.

Fig. 5.3: United States Sentencing Commission, "Sentencing Table," https://www.ussc.gov/sites/default/files/pdf/guidelines-manual/2016/Sentencing_Table.pdf, 2016.

IMG 5.2: Copyright © by Cambodia, P.I. Network (CC BY 2.0) at https://www.flickr.com/photos/magnumppi/39362224991.

IMG 5.3: Copyright © 2012 Depositphotos/OtnaYdur.

Fig. 5.4: Sarah Picard et al., "Impact of Select Defendant Characteristics" from "Court-Ordered Community Service: A National Perspective," https://www.courtinnovation.org/sites/default/files/media/document/2019/community_service_report_11012019_0.pdf, p. 12. Copyright © 2019 by Sarah Picard, Jennifer A. Tallon, Michela Lowry and Dana Kralstein.

IMG 5.4: Copyright © 2022 Depositphotos/karrastock.gmail.com.

IMG 5.5: Copyright © by Whoisjohngalt (CC BY-SA 4.0) at https://commons.wikimedia.org/wiki/File:Ankle_monitor_for_electronic_tagging.jpg.

Fig. 5.5: PEW Charitable Trusts, "Gps Is Leading Electronic Offender-tracking Technology," https://www.pewtrusts.org/-/media/assets/2016/10/use_of_electronic_offender_tracking_devices_expands_sharply.pdf, p. 3. Copyright © 2016 by The Pew Charitable Trusts.

IMG 5.6: Fluffy89502, "Anklet," https://commons.wikimedia.org/wiki/File:Anklet.png, 2019.

IMG 5.7: U.S. Navy, "U.s. Navy Boot Camp," https://commons.wikimedia.org/wiki/File:U.S._Navy_Photo._Boot_Camp,_Naval_Training_Center_San_Diego,_California,_1980._05.jpg, 1980.

IMG 5.8: Copyright © by NPGCsoho (CC BY-SA 3.0) at https://commons.wikimedia.org/wiki/File:National_Problem_Gambling_Clinic_group_therapy_session.png.

IMG 5.9: U.S. Army, "Group Therapy at the Us Disciplinary Barrack," https://commons.wikimedia.org/wiki/File:Group_therapy_at_the_US_Disciplinary_barrack.jpg.

IMG 5.10: Copyright © by Eric Chan (CC BY 2.0) at https://commons.wikimedia.org/wiki/File:Miles_Ehrlich,_judge.jpg.

Correctional Interventions

This chapter begins with a discussion of how to determine "what works" in community corrections. The issue of defining and measuring evidenced-based practices and programs is also detailed. Students are presented with a range of evidenced-based correctional interventions: risk assessment, case planning, motivational interviewing, cognitive behavioral therapy, contingency management, and medication-assisted treatment. Students are also introduced to correctional interventions that are often popular, but evidence suggests they are ineffective. The underlying reasons that lead to the use of ineffective treatments are discussed. Additionally, evidence-based correctional officer training programs designed to teach probation and parole officers communication strategies and relationship building skills are examined. Finally, the chapter ends with an overview of the research on the effectiveness of correctional interventions, with a focus on the challenges of implementing what works.

LEARNING OBJECTIVES

By the end of this chapter, students will be able to:

- Define evidence-based programs and practices and describe how we determine whether something is effective.
- Identify and describe community correctional officer training programs.
- Discuss the challenge of implementing "what works" in community corrections.

KEY TERMS

- Cognitive behavioral therapy (CBT)
- Dosage
- Evidence-based practices and programs
- Fidelity
- Motivational interviewing (MI)

CONTENT

Determining "What Works"
   ◊ Journey into the Field: Deputy Chief Charles Robinson
Evidence-Based Practices and Interventions
   Assessing Actuarial Risk: Risk and Needs Assessment
   ◊ Diversity, Equity, and Inclusion: Considerations of Race in Risk Assessment
   Enhancing Intrinsic Motivation
   Targeting Interventions
   Skill Train with Directed Practice
   ◊ Officer Work, Careers, and Wellness: Thinking for a Change
   Increase Positive Reinforcement
   Engage Ongoing Support in Natural Communities
   Measure Relevant Processes and Practices
   Provide Measurement Feedback
Summary of Evidence-Based Practices
Medication-Assisted Treatment
Community Corrections Officer Training Programs
What Does Not Work?
Summary: The Challenge of Implementing What Works
Scenario-Based Activities

What appears to be an interruption is often an intervention.

—Rich Wilkerson Jr.

Determining "What Works"

In the criminal justice system, there are many practices and programs in place that are effective, many that are ineffective, and some that do not have enough (or any!) evidence to tell us in which category they belong. Gathering evidence and studying whether what we do in the system works is critical for telling us whether a practice or program is achieving its desired goals. This is important for several reasons. First, the practices and programs used throughout the community corrections system impact people, their families, and the community; they are not just abstract statistics. Second, we have a duty to ensure we do not cause harm, just like the Hippocratic oath that the medical community takes. That is, we should do everything we can to ensure the practices and programs in place do not have unintended consequences that can negatively impact individuals and communities (e.g., increase crime, disrupt families, harm an individual's psychological functioning, etc.). Third, most people would likely prefer a society with lower crime rates, more social cohesion, and safe schools, neighborhoods, and environments. How can we make sure the practices and programs that the criminal justice system relies upon do indeed contribute to achieving this goal while also improving the life circumstances of individuals, their families, and the community?

We need to gather evidence and systematically study whether the practices and programs we have in place result in lower crime and/or contribute to improvements. Scientific research is the primary tool used to build our knowledge about effective practices and programs. A research study should be designed to answer questions about the overall effectiveness of a practice or policy and the generalizability of results. With little understanding of scientific procedures, an individual may take for granted the results of a single research study. However, a more valid approach relies on multiple studies across different populations and locations to build generalizability for a practice or program. Additionally, research studies must use appropriate methods—referred to as the research design—to ensure several things: (a) that study measures what it intends to measure (validity), (b) that the study design generates findings that are consistent and can be replicated (reliability), and (c) that appropriate variables are controlled for that could influence study outcomes. Ultimately, the goal is to use a research design and method to collect data that is unbiased, valid, and reliable so we can have confidence and trust the study conclusions. As shown in Figure 6.1, there are multiple types of research designs, each offering a different level of confidence in its ability to answer the question, "Does it work?" As shown, the level of evidence ranges from "gold" (highest confidence in conclusions) to "iron" (lowest confidence in findings). At the lowest level is "dirt," which reflects those practices that are ineffective. To identify whether a program or practice works, evidence from the "gold" category is necessary.

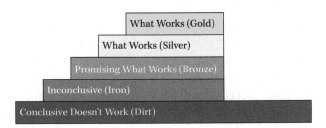

FIGURE 6.1   Research Support Gradient

GOLD

- Experimental/control research design with controls for attrition
- Significant sustained reductions in recidivism obtained
- Multiple site replications
- Preponderance of all evidence supports effectiveness

SILVER

- Quasi-experimental control research with appropriate statistical controls for comparison group
- Significant sustained reductions in recidivism obtained

- Multiple site replications
- Preponderance of all evidence supports effectiveness

BRONZE

- Matched comparison group without complete statistical controls
- Significant sustained reductions in recidivism obtained
- Multiple site replications
- Preponderance of all evidence supports effectiveness

IRON

- Conflicting findings and/or inadequate research designs

DIRT

- Silver and gold research showing negative outcomes
- Conclusively doesn't work

Over the last several decades, there has been a push to identify "what works," with the term "evidence-based practice" gaining traction across the field of community supervision. To receive the label of being an **evidence-based practice and program** requires rigorous evidence of demonstrative effectiveness, often over time. That is, if a program or practice has just one study saying it works, that is not sufficient to label it as "evidence-based." However, practices and programs with some evidence can be considered "promising." That is, there is some evidence to demonstrate that it may be effective, but we need further testing. When studies receive the label of "promising," it is often due to conflicting studies, where some indicate a positive outcome, some identify a neutral outcome (no effect), and others indicate a negative outcome. As illustrated in Figure 6.2, an evidence-based program reflects a specific intervention designed to change the behavior of individuals (e.g., cognitive-behavioral therapy), while an evidence-based practice refers to agency procedures (e.g., matching individuals to

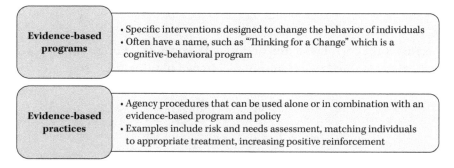

FIGURE 6.2   Evidence-Based Programs versus Evidence-Based Practices

appropriate treatment). The key similarity between evidence-based programs and practices is a high level of quality of evidence to support their use.

There are many ways to gather evidence about a practice or program. The gold standard is typically considered the *randomized controlled trial (RCT)*, which involves random assignment of study participants to the intervention group (those who will experience the policy/practice/program) and the control group (those who will not receive anything). The RCT is considered the gold standard because the randomization process reduces bias, making it easier to attribute study results to the actual intervention tried rather than differences in participants. However, RCTs are often challenging in a criminal justice context, especially in corrections. For example, it would be unethical for a judge to randomly sentence individuals to prison versus probation because one scenario has more liberty restrictions than another. In conducting an RCT (or any study), the researcher must ensure that the procedures used do not negatively impact an individual. For example, assignment to prison compared to probation would be considered a harmful research procedure because the person incarcerated is removed from their family, required to live in a cell, and has their daily existence guided by the rules of the prison.

As a result, many practices and programs are often evaluated using quasi-experimental designs. *Quasi-experimental designs* do not use randomization but rather use a variety of strategies to get a comparison group that resembles the group exposed to the intervention. Instead of randomization, quasi-experimental designs employ pre-post designs, where the pre-period is before the new program/practice is used and the post-period is after the program/practice has been introduced. For example, say a probation office implemented a new risk and needs assessment tool. To conduct a quasi-experiment, we could examine recidivism rates before this new assessment was implemented and compare them to recidivism rates after it was implemented for a group of individuals supervised by the probation office. This would be considered a pre-post design without a comparison group. A different type of quasi-experimental design would include a comparison group. That is, maybe one probation agency implemented the new assessment, but another agency did not. A nonrandomized design would compare the recidivism rates for both agencies to ascertain the differences due to the use of a new instrument. Researchers can take steps to try to ensure their groups are as similar as possible using various sampling and statistical techniques; however, without the random assignment it will be possible that some biases remain.

While RCTs are considered the gold standard for a single study, they alone are not sufficient to earn a program or practice the label of "evidence-based." Typically, evidence from several RCTs and/or quasi-experimental designs is needed. Practices and programs that have been tested using these methods across multiple time points, in different settings, and with different populations provide the most compelling evidence that the label "evidence-based" should be applied. In fact, the very best evidence we can get for whether something works comes from a meta-analysis or systematic review.

A *meta-analysis* combines the results of multiple studies using specific, statistical analyses. This approach allows researchers to estimate the effect of a program/practice across multiple studies, allowing for an estimation of the overall impacts. For example, say there are 12 RCTs examining the effectiveness of intensive supervision programs. A meta-analysis would combine the results of those studies to analyze overall patterns and trends. That is, if there are six studies that found intensive supervision programs (ISPs) to have negative effects, three found no effects, and three found positive effects, then the meta-analysis would give a rating based on a combination of these findings. A meta-analysis would allow researchers to examine the overall impact across these studies. For example, this imaginary meta-analysis might conclude that across these studies, ISP has a negative effect. One of the key requirements of a good meta-analysis is that researchers engage in a systematic search process to identify all existing research on the particular program or practice. For example, Chadwick and colleagues (2015) measured the impact of training probation officers in core correctional practices. They identified 10 studies of varying research designs by using key search terms such as "training," "core correctional practices," "officer skills," and "recidivism." Using these search terms, the authors identified the ten studies summarized in Table 6.1 that reported recidivism rates ranging from 18% to 67% for individuals of varying risk levels on supervision.

Next, Chadwick et al. (2015) created a plot that illustrates the mean recidivism rate in each study and the range of reported recidivism rates. Recidivism is a very important outcome

TABLE 6.1 Studies Included in Chadwick et al.s (2015) Meta-Analysis

Study	N	Country	Follow-up[a]	Age Group	Gender	Risk	Recidivism	Recidivism Rate[b] (%)	Training Length[c]
Pearson, McDougall, Kanaan, Bowles, and Torgerson (2011)[d]	170	United Kingdon	—	—	—	Moderate	Reoffense	41.76	—
Latessa, Smith, Schweitzer, and Labrecque (2013)	264	United States	24	Mixed	MF	Moderate	Arrest	18.18	24
Raynor, Ugwudike, and Vanstone (2014)	75	United Kingdom	24	Adult	—	Medium	Reconviction	41.33	—
Trotter (2013)	117	Australia	24	Juvenile	MF	—	Reoffense	66.67	—
Milson, Robinson, and Van Dieten (2010)	348	United States	12	Adult	F	Modert	Arrest	37.07	54
Taxman (2008)	548	United States	9	Adult	MF	Medium	Arrest	35.99	—
Trotter (1996)	366	Australia	48	Adult	MF	Medium	Reoffense	61.48	40

Study	N	Country	Follow-up[a]	Age group	Gender	Risk	Recidivism	Recidivism rate[b] (%)	Training length[c]
Lowenkamp, Holsinger, Robinson, and Alexander (2014)	406	United States	24	Adult	MF	Moderate	Arrest	45.07	28
Pearson et al. (2011)	5,929	United Kingdom	24	Adult	MF	Medium	Reconviction	44.21	—
Bonta et al. (2011)	112	Canada	24	Adult	MF	Moderate	Reconviction	30.36	24
Note. Empty cells indicate that information was unable to be obtained for that variable. MF = the sample consisted of males and females. F = the sample consisted of females.									
a. Follow-up time is presented in months.									
b. Recidivism rate presented is the rate for the total sample, regardless of training status of supervising officer.									
c. Length of training is presented in hours.									
d. Represents a pilot study embedded within the original article.									

Source: Chadwick et al., 2015.

measure for community corrections, which is explored more in Chapter 10. As Figure 6.3 reveals, the odds of recidivism varied across the 10 studies identified; however, the mean analytic average presents the mean odds of recidivism across all 10 studies. As shown in this figure, the odds ratios vary across each of the studies identified, with some higher than others (although all are positive). However, after combining all results to generate an overall effect, the mean analytic average was 1.48. This suggests that after considering all available

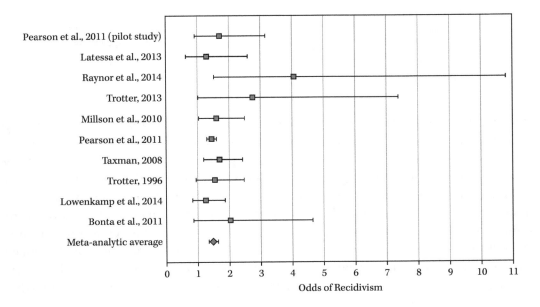

FIGURE 6.3 Individual Study Effect Sizes and Overall Meta-Analytic Average

evidence, individuals supervised by officers who were trained in core correctional practices had lower odds (1.48 times lower) of recidivating compared to individuals supervised by untrained officers.

Systematic reviews are another method of combining results across research studies. The main difference between a systematic review and a meta-analysis is that a systematic review does not involve statistical analyses to compare effect sizes. Instead, systematic reviews provide a qualitative summary of existing studies. Systematic reviews do include the same systematic search process as a meta-analysis and should include all possible studies on the topic, which allows researchers to describe and provide context for the available evidence on the program or practice. As shown in Figure 6.4, meta-analyses and systematic reviews provide the strongest evidence for whether a program or policy is effective. Methods that are listed lower on the pyramid (e.g., cohort studies, case-control studies, case reports, expert opinion) produce evidence that is less rigorous and more susceptible to bias.

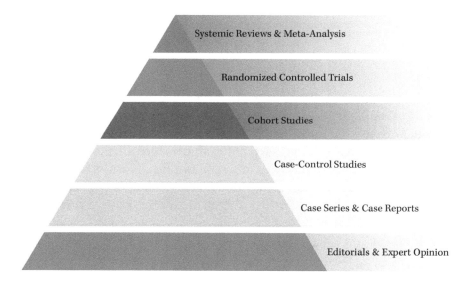

FIGURE 6.4   Levels of Scientific Evidence

There are many additional ways to gather evidence that are important for understanding the impact of a program or practice. Strong evaluation studies also include process evaluations that examine what actually happens in the new program or practice. *Process evaluations* seek to understand whether a program or practice was implemented as intended. This type of examination is important because a study might conclude that a program does not work but that may be from a failure to really implement the new program or practice, also referred to as **fidelity**. If that program or practice was implemented poorly, it is actually not accurate to conclude it did not work. Instead, we would conclude that there was not enough evidence to determine if the program or practice was effective because implementation did not result in any changes to standard practice. Process evaluation in the context of agency partnerships is provided in Chapter 12.

Fidelity is critical to evaluate because a study might find that when implemented well, a program does actually work. As a result, researchers must specifically study what happens in daily practice when people attempt to use the program or practice in real-world settings. This allows us to identify what specifically results in the success or failure of a program. Finally, a process evaluation can add insight into the experiences of those using and/or impacted by the program or practice. For example, consider a probation office implemented a new cognitive behavioral program. A process evaluation might include surveys of probation officers and clients to understand whether they liked the program, thought it was helpful, and valued its addition to existing programming. If an RCT found this new cognitive behavioral program was ineffective and the process evaluation identified that parole officers and clients did not like the program, this might help researchers and practitioners understand why the program did not work. If the RCT found the program was effective, data from a process evaluation might help shed light on specific components participants liked that may have contributed to success. Strong process evaluations often include a mix of quantitative (e.g., surveys) and qualitative (e.g., interviews and observations) data to generate an in-depth analysis of the implementation process.

JOURNEY INTO THE FIELD: DEPUTY CHIEF CHARLES ROBINSON

◇◇◇◇◇◇◇◇

Full name: Charles Robinson

Title: Deputy Chief, Probation and Pretrial Services Office, Administrative Office of the United States Courts

Charles Robinson is the deputy chief of the Probation and Pretrial Services Office of the Administrative Office of the United States Courts. Over the course of more than 20 years, he has worked in a variety of positions in both county and federal probation, including supervising a caseload of community supervision clients and serving as a chief probation officer. Deputy Chief Robinson has coauthored several widely used client and officer training programs for community and custodial correctional settings. Mr. Robinson has extensive experience as a consultant training agency leaders and staff in both juvenile and adult correctional settings. Deputy Chief Robinson has also helped leaders and agencies in the United States and other

Image 6.1

countries better align their community supervision systems with practices proven to exert a positive effect on clients and their communities. He has coauthored several articles that contribute to the research literature supporting effective practices in community supervision. Deputy Chief Robinson is passionate about the work of probation officers and believes strongly that community supervision officers are uniquely positioned to influence the lives of clients and the community through direct service interactions. These vast experiences have led him to become an advocate for the reform of the community corrections system. In the following Journey into the Field, Deputy Chief Robinson reflects on his early family influences, his mentors, his career path, and the key role that correctional interventions have in probation and parole.

I am a first-generation college graduate with lived experiences that exposed me to the shortcomings of the legal system at an early age. Those shortcomings have shaped my "why" fueled my passion and defined a "cause" (a justice system that works for all) that provides a compass for my career path. My parents, a school janitor and a fast-food worker, are my inspiration. What they couldn't provide in educational opportunity, they pushed me to seek out as a curious learner. That curiosity has allowed me to develop a deep understanding of the work and helped me make connections that allow me to continue to grow. It's my parents' "early to rise" and "do what's right" influence that fuels my work ethic, integrity, and commitment to quality work. Similarly, I have benefitted from the endless lessons of my many mentors. My mentors have modeled, provided opportunities, and coached me. My growth as a professional has been nurtured by those around me who were willing to stretch me and watch me grow.

I have nearly 25 years of experience in community corrections that includes supervising a caseload, working with problem-solving court programs, authoring and delivering cognitive behavioral programs for system-involved individuals, and serving as a chief pretrial and probation officer. I was guided into community corrections by a mentor who knew my story and believed community corrections would allow me to realize my "why"—helping others find a pathway to choosing differently. My career has shifted significantly over the past 25 years. It began with a focus on monitoring client behavior, hoping that the threat of punishment would motivate change. Mentorship and professional development shifted my career toward a more evidence-informed skill-focused model of supervision that is responsive to the individual.

Community corrections has invested significantly in testing interventions without yet realizing the maximum benefit that would come from full implementation. The collective investment and our partnership with academics have produced a body of evidence that offers a roadmap to our desired outcomes: public safety and reduced recidivism. Similarly, the partnerships between community corrections and academics have created a culture that will lead to new evidence and new ways of work that make us more efficient and improve the success rate of those we serve. New practices are in turn pushing those in leadership to consider new policies that enable systemic adoption of critical interventions and align better with the desired outcome. Similarly, diminished resources are forcing leaders to consider ways to "work smarter," including not doing things we may have done for years although they have no relationship (or in some cases have an adverse relationship) to outcomes. What we stop doing is as important as the new interventions we decide to adopt.

Simply put, the future of correctional interventions will be guided by our commitment to equitable outcomes and our willingness to build systems and provide training and support that respond to the diverse needs of the population receiving services. Putting equity at the center of correctional interventions, programs, and policies will require leaders, developers, and frontline staff to view equity as a fundamental part of the way we work and take intentional action to make equity part of the intervention's design and delivery. To get there, academics and practitioners must consider disparity data to be as essential as program efficacy when evaluating programs; system leaders must also normalize discussions about the drivers of program disparities and strategies that reduce disparities.

Evidence-Based Practices and Interventions

Correctional interventions for individuals on community supervision or incarcerated are generally aligned with the punishment philosophy of rehabilitation. *Rehabilitation* is defined as "a planned correctional intervention that targets for change internal and/or social criminogenic factors with the goal of reducing recidivism and, where possible, of improving other aspects of an offenders life" (Cullen & Jonson, 2011, p. 295). Most often, the goal of correctional interventions is to reduce recidivism, although there are other additional important outcomes to consider, such as mental health, substance use, employment, and housing. Regardless of the outcome, no single correctional intervention is always effective in every situation (we are still dealing with human behavior, which is never 100% predictable after all). However, we know that there are common factors that make programs more successful than others in most situations. There has been a great deal of research that has identified core evidence-based practices that increase the probability that correctional programs will be successful (see Figure 6.5). These practices are part of the evidence-based supervision framework that identifies how agencies can use research findings in daily practice. By adopting these practices, it signifies to probation and parole staff that these are the supervision practices that are most likely to generate positive findings.

Below we will summarize the existing state of knowledge about eight effective practices that can

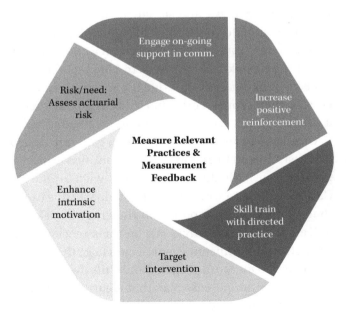

FIGURE 6.5   Core Evidence-Based Practices

reduce recidivism. These are practices that have been determined to have sufficient studies to verify that the practice "works" as well as those practices that can be considered promising, but we need more research.

Assessing Actuarial Risk: Risk and Needs Assessment

Historically, probation and parole agencies linked decisions to the perceived riskiness of individuals under supervision. Early attempts at prediction and classification relied on the subjective decisions of individual probation and parole officers. However, contemporary research highlights the challenges with this approach, especially the inconsistency in decision making and the inaccuracy in anticipating future behavior (Andrews & Bonta, 2010; Bonta et al., 2000; Gottfredson & Moriarty, 2006). Instead, the use of validated risk and needs assessment instruments can both systematize decision making and reduce disparities and inaccuracies in decision making. Today, the evidence-based practice movement prioritizes the use of a risk and needs assessment that measures an individual's static risk (risk of recidivism based on historical factors) and dynamic risk (psychosocial factors linked to recidivism, also called "criminogenic needs"). Today, probation and parole officers routinely conduct a risk and needs assessment on every new client as soon as possible. These are part of the daily activities of officers working in community corrections, as documented in Chapter 4. The results of the assessment provide data that should drive the assigned risk level the individual should be supervised at (e.g., low, moderate, or high risk). The assigned risk level should then dictate supervision requirements, including the number of office visits, home visits, collateral contacts, and drug tests required per month. The assessment also provides a detailed summary of the individual's score on a range of criminogenic needs, such as criminal thinking, criminal peers, substance use, and employment.

Officers should then target high-priority areas (e.g., those with the highest scores) with appropriate responses. For example, if a client scores high in criminal thinking, a probation officer should link that individual to a high-quality cognitive behavioral program that addresses decision making and cognition. Over time, if that client engages in the program and is successful, their score on criminal thinking should decrease. This would indicate a reduction in a risk factor (i.e., criminal thinking) for that individual.

Often, agencies require officers to generate *case plans*, or documents that outline goals and tasks linked to an individuals identified criminogenic needs. Case plans provide assessment-driven, individualized plans designed to address each client's most pressing risk factors. Case plans help to structure an individual's time under supervision to best address the factors that might place that person at the greatest risk for recidivism. Agencies typically require officers to reassess individuals on their caseloads periodically throughout the year as well as anytime a significant event occurs (e.g., the individual commits a new crime). This allows the officer to measure progress and shift their supervision approach as necessary. Below, you can find an example case plan that identifies individualized goals, tailored to the supervision client's criminogenic needs.

EXAMPLE   Case Plan

Client Information:	
ID: 123456	**Name:** James Daily
DOB: 02/08/1973	**Supervising Officer:** Jared Mullins
Risk Level: High	**Offense(s):** Aggravated Assault
Date: 03/10/2023	

Goal 1:	To abstain from alcohol and illegal drugs.		
Criminogenic Need:	Substance Use	**Need Score:**	8
Tasks:	Attend substance use treatment evaluation.		
Progress:	Complete. James was assessed as eligible for substance use treatment.		
Date:	03/17/2023		
	Attend substance use treatment.		
Progress:	Ongoing. James enrolled in treatment and attended the first session.		
Date:	04/10/2023		

Goal 2:	To find employment.		
Criminogenic Need:	Employment	**Need Score:**	9
Tasks:	Apply for 5 jobs.		
Progress:	In progress. James applied for 1 job since our last meeting.		
Date:	04/10/2013		

Progress Notes:	On 03/10/2023, I conducted the COMPAS risk assessment with James. He was assessed as high risk and having two high criminogenic needs: substance use and employment. During this appointment, we worked together to create his case plan. His first goal is to abstain from alcohol and illegal drugs. James notes that he is struggling with this. He was agreeable to attend an evaluation for treatment. We made an appointment for his evaluation during our meeting, which was scheduled for 03/17/2023.
	James attended his substance use treatment evaluation, which concluded he met the criteria for enrollment in substance use treatment programming. He was enrolled in treatment and attended the first session on 04/10/2023. His counselor verified his attendance. James will continue to participate in treatment as the clinical team recommends.
	Additionally, James scored high on employment. He notes that this is a difficult area for him. He has not had consistent employment for over 5 years and is intimidated by the process. We discussed strategies for searching for employment and applying. On 03/10/2023, we set a goal that he will apply for at least 5 jobs before our next meeting. James did not meet this goal; however, he did apply for 1 job. He will continue to apply for jobs and provide an update at our next meeting.

James Daily   04/10/2023   *Jared Mullins*   04/10/2023
Client Signature   **Date**   **Officer Signature**   **Date**

◊ Diversity, Equity, and Inclusion: Considerations of Race in Risk Assessment

Image 6.2

Racial disparities in the criminal justice system have always been a controversial topic. One issue that has been receiving increasing attention is the consideration of race in risk-assessment practices. While the main goal of risk assessments is to reduce differences in decisions across decision makers (i.e., using a risk assessment should theoretically result in different probation officers assigning the same level of risk to the same client) and reduce the potential for bias, it is important to examine how risk assessment practices promote fairness and accuracy. Risk assessment information should inform key supervision decisions, such as contact requirements (e.g., higher risk clients come into the office more frequently) and drug testing requirements. This makes it important to understand whether and how risk assessment accurately predicts the risk for clients with different characteristics, such as race.

First, let's talk about how risk assessments work more generally. *Risk assessments* are essentially predictive models that aim to predict whether someone who has committed a crime will do so again in the future (or will have future interaction with the justice system). We can make these predictions at many times throughout the criminal justice process, such as at arrest, when filing formal charges, when deciding whether to hold someone in jail pre-trial, when determining appropriate sentences, and during probation or parole supervision and case planning decisions. To provide an example, let's explore the case study of Mark.

Mark was convicted of drug possession. The judge in his case now must decide whether to sentence Mark to prison or probation. The judge will likely consider the risk Mark poses to the community if he is sentenced to probation and whether he might commit another crime. To help

Image 6.3

answer this question, the judge might use a risk assessment. Now, you might be asking, "But where does a risk assessment get its predictions from?" That is a great question! Statisticians and computer scientists develop risk assessments using data on thousands of people who have been involved in the criminal justice system and who have not been involved. They run statistical models to divide these people into categories based on characteristics such as their gender, race, age, education, employment, and criminal history. Once people are placed into categories based on characteristics, the models can predict the risk associated with each category based on criminal justice outcomes (e.g., arrest, conviction). Now, with all of this information and groups based on characteristics that identify different risk levels, the tool is ready for use (of course this is a vast oversimplification of a very complicated statistical process).

Now, let's go back to Mark. The court may now do a risk assessment before making a sentencing decision. They will input all of Mark's characteristics into the tool (the same characteristics that were used to create the original groups). The risk assessment will then identify all of the people included in its sample who are similar to Mark. Now that it has found all of the similar individuals, the tool will look at how many of those individuals were arrested while on probation and how many were not. The model then estimates the likelihood that Mark would be rearrested by calculating the percentage of people who are like Mark (e.g., same age, gender, employment) who were arrested while on probation. If 10% of people like Mark were arrested while on probation, the risk assessment might provide a result to the court that Mark is at low-risk for rearrest. On the other hand, if the model suggests 75% of people like Mark were arrested while on probation, the assessment might suggest Mark is actually high-risk. The judge can then use this information to determine whether they will or will not place Mark on probation and maybe even what type of special conditions to give Mark. Again, this is an oversimplification of the process; however, it provides a basic overview of how the risk assessment models and processes work.

Now, let's think about the information that goes into a risk assessment. Some assessments include more characteristics than others, but it is not uncommon for these to include age, gender, sex, criminal history, and even personal beliefs (e.g., indicators of criminal thinking like rationalization of behavior). Several factors have been identified as affecting the fairness of the prediction models, especially when race and gender are included. That is, people question whether risk assessments fairly assess the risk of people of varying racial groups and genders. The concerns identified typically revolve around (a) whether risk scores for different groups of people mean the same thing (e.g., if a model suggests 10% of people in a given group should reoffend but only 5% of Black individuals do, while 30% of White individuals do, this would be a major issue surrounding fairness) and (b) whether people who do (or do not) reoffend receive similar scores across different groups (e.g., Black and White individuals who do not reoffend (or do) should get the same risk score). The concerns surrounding this issue relate to the fact that some individuals may reside in areas that are overpoliced, and some reside in areas where there is a high concentration of individuals on supervision or who have been incarcerated. If a risk assessment consistently places more Black individuals who do not reoffend in higher risk groups than similarly situated White individuals who do not reoffend, this illustrates a concern about the fairness of the prediction models.

While this is a controversial topic in the field right now, it is an issue that is not easily solved. For one, part of the difficulties associated with race in risk assessment surrounds systemic disparities across the criminal justice system. Risk assessments commonly use prior criminal justice involvement, such as number of prior arrests or convictions, as a key predictor of risk. However, these variables have been identified as areas of potential bias that impact discretion throughout the system (e.g., police decision to stop and arrest someone, prosecutorial decisions to file a charge, etc.), with Black and Hispanic individuals more likely to receive negative outcomes compared to similarly situated White counterparts (e.g., Abrams et al., 2012; Goel et al., 2016; Harcourt, 2015; Wooldredge, 2012; Wu, 2016). As a result, these risk assessments end up making their predictions based on decisions made by justice actors: police who decide to arrest an individual instead of giving a warning, prosecutors who decide to prosecute instead of dropping charges, or judges who decide to accept a plea bargain instead of diverting the individual. Thus, when risk assessments rely on static (i.e., unchangeable) factors such as criminal history, this means people of color may be more likely to be classified as higher risk compared to White individuals based on the source of the data put into predictive models.

These issues surrounding race and ethnicity in risk assessment are not easy to address. This threat of bias in the data that is entered into risk assessments is not one that can be solved quickly or easily, as it would require eliminating or modifying discretion that occurs throughout the system. You might ask, "So why don't we just remove race from risk assessments altogether?" Researchers who have been digging into this issue suggest that it is nearly impossible, if not impossible, to remove race from predictive models. That is, even if we took race out of assessments, there are other related variables that are correlated with race included in the models as well (e.g., income, education, zip code, and prior encounters with police; Eckhouse et al., 2019).

According to Eckhouse et al. (2019), improvements in risk assessment tools based on predictions can be improved if the designers would follow certain key characteristics. First, they suggest using larger and more diverse samples when creating predictive models. This will increase the likelihood that prediction models will make predictions based on individuals who are more similar to the individual we are assessing. However, doing this also creates new problems; that is, the larger our sample size, the more likely we are to detect significant differences between groups, even if those differences are not meaningful. Eckhouse and colleagues give an example: Say a predictive model identifies a group with a 29% chance of reoffending and another group with a 35% chance of reoffending. In practice, it might be difficult to identify a meaningful difference between those two groups: Would we really need to treat them differently and label one as higher risk than the other? This means the differences between groups might be more accurate when we develop predictive models with very large samples.

What we are left with are complicated issues that are not easily solved. Prior to the use of data-driven risk assessments, we relied on individual decision making based on their professional or clinical experience. As you are most likely aware, humans also make decisions based on individual biases, whether intentional or unintentional. Making complicated decisions in a fair and equitable manner is not easy. There is a great deal of research that suggests pretrial and sentencing decisions made based on an individual's judgment result in disproportionate treatment of people of color (e.g., Kutateladze et al., 2014; Wooldredge et al., 2015). As a result, proponents of risk assessment argue that data-driven risk assessments are better than subjective judgments, which tend to be inconsistent and not transparent. However, this is an ongoing debate in the field that is unlikely to be resolved any time soon. Researchers, policymakers, and criminal justice practitioners should continue to evaluate and consider how racial biases impact risk assessments and how to better promote accurate prediction and fair decision making across the system.

Enhancing Intrinsic Motivation

Intrinsic motivation reflects when someone does something because it is "inherently inter-esting or enjoyable" (Ryan & Deci, 2000, p. 55). That is, if someone is intrinsically motivated, they do something because it comes naturally and because the individual enjoys it (not, for example, because someone else told them to). For lasting behavior change of any kind to occur, intrinsic motivation is necessary because the individual wants to improve themselves. One of the primary evidence-based practices implemented in community corrections agencies (and substance use treatment) is to enhance client intrinsic motivation through the use of **moti-vational interviewing (MI)**, which is a communication technique that probation and parole officers can use with individuals on their caseloads. MI requires that officers are provided in-depth training to learn and perfect the skill.

One of the main goals of MI is to address ambivalence about change through collaboration between the practitioner and client. Probation and parole officers can be trained to guide and listen to clients as opposed to simply telling them what to do to promote clients' individual motivation to make changes in their behavior. More specifically, probation and parole officers can be trained to use MI to help clients explore how they can make impactful changes in their lives while also providing encouragement that change is possible. Today, many agencies require probation and parole officers with active caseloads to complete MI training, which typically consists of several training sessions, ongoing training, and submission of taped interactions with clients for feedback. There is vast support for the use of MI in clinical settings for a variety of behaviors, including smoking cessation, drug use, alcohol treatment, gambling, and diet/exercise. While fewer studies exist in probation and parole settings, a systematic review reported use of MI in correctional settings can lead to increased motivation to change, increased retention in treatment, and reduced recidivism (McMurran, 2009). Figure 6.6 provides a

Open-Ended Questions	Affirmations	Reflective Listening	Summarize
• Allows client to do the majority of speaking • Provides opportunity for client to share their perspective and experiences • Improves officer understanding of client (experiences, thoughts, beliefs, behaviors) • Builds a trusting and respectful relationship	• Positively reinforce client behavior, accomplishment, ability, strength • Allows officer to recognize and reinforce client success • Helps to build rapport, affirm client pro-social behavior, and build their confidence and self-efficacy	• Officer rephrases client statements in their own words • Demonstrates to client officer is paying attention and understands what they are saying • Provides client the opportunity to hear their own words and reflect on them	• Typically used at the end of a conversation to paraphrase the discussion and identify key discussion points • Allows the officer and client to end discussion on the same page and often with an action plan • Improves clients ability to see the big picture and important parts of the meeting

FIGURE 6.6 *Motivational Interviewing Key Skills*

description of the key skills involved in motivational interviewing, with reference to the use of open-ended questions, affirmations, and reflective listening.

Targeting Interventions

The risk-need-responsivity (RNR) model outlines three principles designed to generate effective interventions for correctional clients: risk, need, and responsivity (as introduced in Chapter 4).

RISK
tells us
WHO

NEED
tells us
WHAT

RESPONSIVITY
tells us
HOW

FIGURE 6.7   Risk, Need, Responsivity Model

The RNR model outlines that programming should embrace a social learning environment and use cognitive and behavioral techniques to improve treatment and reduce recidivism by better targeting their intervention efforts (and thus better using their resources as a result!). The risk principle tells us who should receive an intervention: higher risk clients. The needs principle tells us what we should target in our interventions: criminogenic needs that are susceptible to change. The responsivity principle tells us how to intervene. Interventions should use a cognitive behavioral therapy (CBT) approach matched to the abilities, motivation, and learning style of each individual client. For example, placing a client who scored high in substance use and only speaks Spanish in an anger management program run by a facilitator who only speaks English would be poor responsivity. Instead, responsivity can be improved by linking the client to CBT-based substance use program led by a clinician who speaks Spanish. Figure 6.7 shows the risk, need, responsivity model.

In addition to attending to the risk, need, and responsivity principles, targeting appropriate interventions also requires attention to dosage and integration of treatment into supervision protocols. **Dosage** refers to the actual amount of time a client spends in treatment. General research guidelines suggest that treatment should occupy somewhere between 40% to 70% of an individual's time, especially in the first 3 to 9 months of supervision, with higher risk clients receiving a greater dosage (Gendreau & Goggin, 1996). If an individual does not receive an appropriate amount of treatment, that treatment can be ineffective or even harmful. Additionally, community corrections agencies should formally integrate treatment into supervision requirements. That is, clients should not only be required to abide by supervision conditions and follow rules but should also have access to appropriate treatment, and for higher risk clients, treatment should be required. Taken together, community corrections agencies can best target interventions when they adhere to risk, needs, responsivity, dosage, and treatment integration.

Table 6.2 provides recommendations, or dosage guidelines, for the number of hours of treatment recommended by risk level. As you can see, individuals who are at higher risk are recommended to receive a greater number of treatment hours.

TABLE 6.2   Dosage Guideline Recommendations

Risk Level	Hours of Treatment Recommended
Low–moderate	100–149
Moderate–high	200–249

(based on findings of Makarios et al., 2014)

Skill Train with Directed Practice

This evidence-based practice refers to the value of using techniques that are based on the principles of social learning and are cognitive behavioral in nature. **Cognitive behavioral therapy (CBT)** is a key component of improving outcomes. CBT is often cited as one of the most prominent and widely studied psychological interventions to support behavior change. The main premise of CBT is based on the idea that our thoughts, cognitions (i.e., beliefs), attitudes, and behavior are strongly connected to one another—so much so that the way we think about something can directly impact our behaviors and actions. As a result, CBT aims to help clients identify these links and how changing those initial thoughts, cognitions, and attitudes can ultimately result in behavioral changes. Practicing these skills is a key component of CBT and similar interventions. That is, if we want to help individuals learn to make decisions or assess situations, these techniques need to be ingrained in the individual.

Image 6.4

Let's use a fictional probation client named Max to illustrate how CBT works. Max has struggled with substance use but is committed to making a change. He has had three negative drug tests at his last three probation appointments. Recently, Max's mother passed away. To cope with this loss, Max began using drugs to self-medicate. At his next probation appointment, he tested positive. His probation officer asked Max to identify what he was thinking when he decided to use drugs. Max said he thought he could not handle the loss of his mother without drugs. His officer responded by asking him to think about a time he was in a difficult situation when he did not use drugs. They talked about his thoughts in those situations and how they led to a different outcome. They came up with a few coping strategies Max could use when he found himself having thoughts like "I can't do this without drugs" again, including identifying several individuals in his social support network with whom he can call and connect. Over time, Max is more confident in his ability to manage difficult situations and he can act less impulsively. While this is a very simplified explanation and CBT is often an intensive process that happens over time and with practice, it illustrates how negative thoughts, beliefs, and attitudes are challenged and clients are encouraged to develop healthier coping strategies and resulting behaviors. Figure 6.8 provides a visual guide to the theoretical underpinnings of CBT.

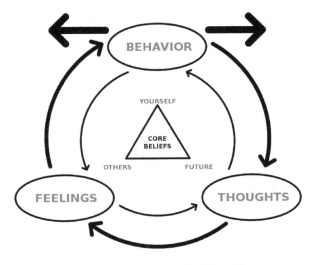

FIGURE 6.8 Theoretical Framework of Cognitive-Behavioral Therapy

CBT is a common intervention used with people on probation and parole supervision. A meta-analysis of CBT for adult and juvenile clients reported reductions in recidivism, particularly with higher risk individuals and especially among those with higher treatment quality (Landenberger & Lipsey, 2005). Examples of CBT programs used for individuals in the criminal legal system include Thinking 4 a Change (T4C), Reasoning and Rehabilitation, and moral reconation therapy. Most probation and parole departments provide training to officers on cognitive behavioral techniques. In some agencies, probation and parole officers receive training to become certified CBT facilitators. These officers then actually provide the CBT program for clients in their office.

◊ Officer Work, Careers, and Wellness: Thinking for a Change

Thinking for a Change (T4C) is a CBT program used in community corrections settings. T4C is distributed and available on the National Institute of Corrections (NIC) website (NIC, n.d.-a). The NIC provides training and technical assistance to help officers learn to use this approach in working with individuals on supervision (or in prison/jail). This program contains 25 lessons covering three primary components: cognitive self-change (e.g., teaching process for self-reflection as a means to identify antisocial thoughts, feelings, attitudes, and beliefs), social skills (e.g., teaching prosocial skills and increase awareness of how one's actions impact other people), and problem-solving skills geared to equip individuals to handle stressful situations they face (see Figure 6.9). Each lesson runs about 1–2 hours depending on how the individual agency and facilitator implements the program. Some facilitators may need two sessions to complete a full lesson of material. The recommended group size for a T4C program is 8–12 participants to allow for adequate engagement of all participants and to make it feasible for one officer or clinician to manage.

In many probation and parole agencies, probation and parole officers serve as T4C facilitators. To become a T4C facilitator, an officer must undergo a required formal facilitator training provided by the NIC (n.d.). The T4C curriculum provides tools for program facilitators. These tools include charts, handouts, scripts, slides, and videos that must be used during the program

1: Introduction	6: Thinking Controls Our Behavior	11: Understanding the Feelings of Others	16: Introduction to Problem Solving	21: Think of Choices and Consequences
2: Active Listening	7: Pay Attention to Our Thinking	12: Making a Complaint	17: Stop and Think	22: Make a Plan
3: Asking Questions	8: Recognize Risk	13: Apologizing	18: State the Problem	23: Do and Evaluate
4: Giving Feedback	9: Use New Thinking	14: Responding to Anger	19: Set a Goal and Gather Information	24: Problem Solving Practice
5: Knowing Your Feeling	10: Thinking Check-in	15: Negotiating	20: Practice Problem Solving Skills 1, 2 and 3	25: Next Steps

☐ Social Skills   ☐ Congnitive Self-Change   ☐ Problem Solving

FIGURE 6.9   Thinking for a Change Lessons

sessions. The curriculum guides facilitators in what to say and how these tools should be used during each session. This training is a hybrid model with 4 weeks of online learning and 4 days of face-to-face learning, for a total of 73 hours of training (NIC, n.d.-b)

NIC (n.d.-b) recommends agencies select officers to become facilitators who display empathy, strong teaching abilities, an ability to understand and navigate group processes, strong interpersonal communication skills, and the ability to manage a group of individuals without using coercion. The following provides an excerpt from the introductory lesson for T4C.

READING

Lesson Activities

Lesson Script	Lesson Guidance
Activity 1: Introductions and Expectations P-1-1 	P-1-1
Welcome! This program is called Thinking for a Change.	Introduce yourself and mention some personal (not private) information, such as your job or where you come from.
We'll talk about what Thinking for a Change means in a minute. First I want to introduce myself and have my cofacilitator introduce him/herself. Then, I will introduce each of you to the group.	Ask co-facilitator to introduce him/herself. Introduce each member by name to the rest of the group (where they are from—town or state, not institution/facility).
Activity 2: The Pocket Analogy	
You can be successful in this program, and this program can help us all be more successful in life. Let's take a minute to talk about how.	Dress for this lesson with clothes that have lots of pockets. Be sure all of your pockets are empty so that you can turn them out as you complete this demonstration.
	The goal of the pocket analogy is to give a feeling of empowerment to group members.

Each of us in this room probably knows how to do one thing pretty well. If it come downs to it, most of us have some skill with fighting. Some of us fight with fists, some of us fight with words, some of us may use weapons. This is a way we have learned to survive.	
I am going to use my fist to represent fighting.	Briefly hold up one fist.
Let's agree that you have the ability to fight anytime you want to. You can pull out angry words, raise your fists, or grab a weapon.	As you state this, make a fist and pull it out of one of your pockets.
You can always choose to fight. You always have this choice "in your pocket."	Put your fist back into the same pocket. Leave this pocket intact as you carry out the rest of the demonstration.
But, what do you have in this pocket?	Each time you answer, "Nothing!" turn out a pocket to reveal that it is empty. The more empty pockets, the better for this demonstration.
Nothing!	
And what do you have in this pocket?	
Nothing!	
And this one?	
Nothing!	
And here?	
Nothing!	
The Thinking for a Change program will fill your pockets with tools you can use to do all kinds of things well.	Pull your fist out of the original pocket.
We are not here to tell you what to do, but rather to provide you with choices. You can still choose to fight anytime you want to.	
But now you will have choices. You will have additional tools in your pockets.	
We will practice social skills, like negotiating, responding to anger, and giving feedback. Each of these will go into a pocket.	Each time you mention a new skill, make a show of putting a tool into a pocket. Turn that pocket back in, until all of your pockets are turned back in.
We will learn to examine our thoughts, and to recognize risk in our thinking and feelings. We'll put these tools in our pockets.	
We'll fill our pockets with problem solving skills like setting goals, brainstorming choices, and making plans.	

Your pockets will be filled to the ripping point with skills you can use to improve your chances of success. To give you an edge. You'll have more tools to choose from.

And what happens when we have more skills?

Example answers: You have more choices. More options. You have a better chance of a positive outcome.

Exactly. When you have more skills, you are better able to deal with a lot of different types of problems. You have more tools to help deal with difficult situations. You have more choices. You have more control. And you have a better chance of things going your way.

Transition
Let's take a look at the goals of this course and how we will achieve them.

P-1-2

Activity 3: Overview of Course Outcomes

The idea behind this course is that we can learn to take charge of our lives by taking control of the thoughts and feelings that go on inside us.

This idea—that thinking connects to the way we feel and act, is the main idea of Thinking for a Change.

Because our thinking controls so much about us, we can learn to control our lives by learning how to take control of our thinking.

P-1-3

Thinking for a Change has three parts: the skill of cognitive self-change, social skills, and problem solving skills.

Reinforce answers that reflect empowerment.

P-1-2

Thinking Controls Behavior

By taking charge of our thinking we can take control of our lives

P-1-3

3 Key Types of Skills

· **Cognitive Self-Change**–Paying attention to the thoughts and feelings that go on inside of us to mind the kinds of thoughts and feelings that lead us to trouble

· **Social Skills**–Behaviors or abilities we see in situations that involve other people

· **Problem solving Skills**–Skills to helps us make better choice

The models you will present in the following activities are intended to be brief introductions only. Avoid getting into details about the skills.

Increase Positive Reinforcement

Use of positive reinforcement is an important behavioral management strategy to promote behavior change. Positive reinforcement can help shape an individual's thinking pattern, which can lead to engagement in desired behaviors. That is, the use of positive reinforcements acts as a social learning process where the use of incentives disrupts the influences associated with undesirable behaviors, such as illegal behavior and substance use. These ideas date back to Pavlov's (1927) foundational work on classical conditioning that suggests behavior can be shaped through use of stimuli. Skinner (1948) expanded on this theory by testing which processes made certain behaviors more or less likely to occur. His resulting theory of operant conditioning suggests two types of responses can influence behavior: reinforcements and punishments (see Figure 6.10).

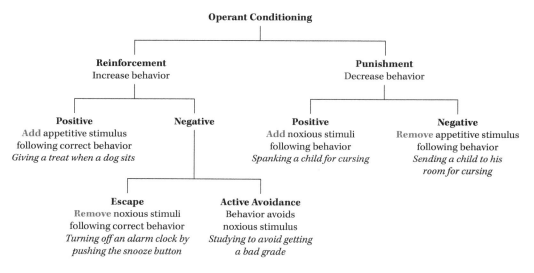

FIGURE 6.10   Principles of Operant Conditioning

Skinner identified both positive and negative reinforcement, with positive reinforcement strengthening behavior by providing a rewarding consequence and negative reinforcement removing a negative consequence. On the other hand, punishment is designed to eliminate a response rather than increase it, with either an unpleasant consequence applied or removal of a rewarding consequence for undesirable behavior. As Chapter 3 highlights, the use of a punishment as a key strategy has a long history in community corrections practice. However, research finds that the use of positive reinforcement in addition to sanctions is more effective than sanctions alone in community corrections. More specifically, research suggests that positive reinforcements should outnumber sanctions by a 4:1 ratio for interventions to be most effective (Gendreau et al., 1996; Wodahl et al., 2022).

Operant conditioning has been applied in several settings, including drug and alcohol treatment, through use of punishment (sanctions) and reinforcements (rewards or incentives) to change behavior. Research conducted in substance abuse treatment settings finds that the use of positive reinforcements helps encourage individuals to continue engaging in desired behaviors through influencing their thinking patterns (Griffith et al., 2000; Lussier et al., 2006; Petry & Martin, 2002). This research finds use of incentives can disrupt the influences associated with undesired behaviors, such as drug use, and facilitate a social learning process.

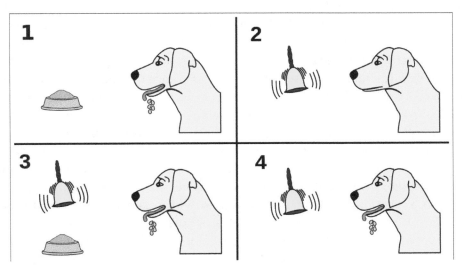

IMAGE 6.5   Classical Conditioning

In substance abuse settings, *contingency management (CM)* is a commonly used behavior modification program involving the use of incentives (positive reinforcements) to change behaviors (Petry, 2000). CM relies on the application of incentives to instill motivation and shape behavior by influencing individual thinking patterns to continue engaging in desired behaviors (Griffith et al., 2000; Lussier et al., 2006; Petry & Martin, 2002). Rather than providing a punishment for behavior, CM focuses on incentivizing desired behaviors to help the individual recognize the resulting benefits. For example, in substance abuse treatment settings, rewards are provided for abstinence, making abstinence a more attractive behavior to achieve (Griffith et al., 2000; Higgins & Petry, 1999). This system of incentives has been found to be effective in reducing use of a variety of substances, including alcohol (Miller, 1975; Petry, 2000), nicotine (Roll et al., 1996; Stitzer & Bigelow, 1983), cocaine (Higgins et al., 1994), and opioids (Bickel et al., 1997; Stitzer et al., 1984). Additionally, several meta-analyses find CM increases the likelihood of abstinence amongst drug users (Griffith et al., 2000; Lussier et al., 2006; Prendergast et al., 2006). In the criminal justice system, incentives can be used to reinforce abstinence, being drug-free, being employed, and other prosocial behaviors.

The use of CM with justice-involved populations has not been widely researched. When applied within criminal justice settings, behavioral modification interventions frequently borrow from Skinner's (1948) model of operant conditioning with interventions seeking to sanction negative behaviors while reinforcing desired behaviors (Andrews & Bonta, 2010). Of the few studies examining the use of positive reinforcement in criminal justice systems, most take place in problem-solving courts where the use of incentives is coupled with the use of sanctions (Doctor & Polakow, 1973; Marlowe & Wong, 2008; Marlowe et al., 2008). The idea supporting the use of such incentives is to increase the likelihood individuals will engage (and continue to engage) in desired behaviors (Wodahl et al., 2011).

In contrast, sanctions are frequently used to lessen the probability of a reoccurrence of negative behaviors (Wodahl et al., 2011). Friedmann and colleagues (2009) evaluated a CM intervention in which parole officers monitored specific behaviors of parolees such as abstinence, attending treatment, and applying for jobs. When parolees engaged in desired behaviors, they received rewards such as praise or financial assistance to support achievement of goals (e.g., purchasing clothing for job interviews). Findings from this study suggested the use of rewards leads to increased attendance and engagement in treatment and counseling services.

Additionally, Wodahl and colleagues (2011) examined the use of a behavioral modification program in an ISP. While ISP traditionally emphasizes close surveillance of offenders and the use of sanctions, the added behavior modification program introduced the use of rewards to encourage compliance. Wodahl et al. found that successful completion of an ISP was more likely when both sanctions and incentives were used, with greater completion rates associated with a higher ratio of rewards to sanctions. These studies highlight the importance of using reinforcements to encourage compliance amongst individuals supervised in the community while research on use of behavior modification programs in drug courts (Shaffer, 2006; Wilson et al., 2006), and therapeutic communities (Inciardi et al., 2004; Prendergast et al., 2004) suggest use of rewards can increase abstinence and reduce recidivism.

Engage Ongoing Support in Natural Communities

Prosocial support is an integral part of supporting success while on supervision. Individuals are more likely to succeed when interventions engage prosocial others in their lives, such as family members, spouses, and friends. These prosocial support networks can positively reinforce desired behaviors and progress in treatment. There is research support for restorative approaches that focus on developing and strengthening individuals' social ties and bonds to prosocial individuals within the community (Bonta et al., 2002; Clear & Sumter, 2002; O'Connor & Perryclear, 2003).

Measure Relevant Processes and Practices

To know if something works, we must study it using reliable, valid, and appropriate research designs. As discussed earlier in this chapter, it is critical that agencies collect data and track progress to determine whether they are meeting their goals. In particular, agencies must collect data in a way that they can do something with it (i.e., keeping disorganized, handwritten records is not ideal), and they must actually be able to use the data they collect in a meaningful way. This often requires planning and sometimes improvements to infrastructure (e.g., moving to electronic records) to allow for ongoing data collection.

CHAPTER 6 Correctional Interventions | 203

Provide Measurement Feedback

Once agencies have the necessary systems in place to measure processes and procedures (i.e., collect data), they must be able to analyze the data and report on outcomes. These analyses and reporting should be done regularly at the client, officer, and agency level. As such, it is critical for clients to get ongoing feedback about their progress (or lack thereof) so adjustments can be made, or achievements can be positively rein-

Image 6.6

forced. Likewise, officers also need feedback about their job performance. For agencies to have the best possible chance of improving client outcomes, it is necessary to evaluate individual officer performance and alignment with effective correctional practices. These processes can help encourage officers who display a high level of quality and fidelity to practices and programs while also identifying staff who may need additional training, support, and/or supervision. As discussed earlier, fidelity is a critical part of the RNR model, as it tells us "how well" a practice or program has been implemented. It is not possible to measure fidelity without the systems in place to collect data.

Summary of Evidence-Based Practices

Taken together, these eight principles synthesize the existing research evidence on effective practices within community corrections and provide real-world examples of evidence-based supervision. They highlight key agency procedures that inform both agency policy (e.g., requirements to conduct risk and needs assessments on all clients) and decisions regarding the type of interventions to recommend for clients (e.g., cognitive behavioral therapy). These principles also suggest specific strategies agencies can implement in order to become more evidence-based and thus have a greater likelihood of supporting successful outcomes (e.g., reduced recidivism). The following discussion outlines additional evidence-based interventions that can be used in conjunction with evidence-based supervision practices. These interventions or therapies are essential to improve outcomes on supervision.

Medication-Assisted Treatment

Medication-assisted treatment (MAT) is an evidence-based treatment that is the gold standard for individuals with opioid use disorder (OUD) and alcohol use disorder (AUD). Medication-assisted treatment is exactly what it sounds like; it is a pharmacotherapy (i.e., prescription medication) often used in conjunction with behavioral therapies. Because many individuals under community supervision often require substance use treatment, including for OUD and/ or AUD, MAT is an important best practice to discuss, as probation and parole officers should encourage and support individuals to use MAT. Not only does research strongly support the use of MAT for opioid and alcohol use but some studies also find it can lead to reductions in recidivism (Schwartz et al., 2013; Stancliff et al., 2012).

There are three types of MAT approaches that are FDA-approved for the treatment of OUDs: buprenorphine, naltrexone, and methadone. Each of these medications have been deemed to be effective. Individuals on probation or parole who are undergoing MAT are typically overseen by their probation or parole officer, substance use counselor, and a medical doctor who can prescribe the medication. Probation and parole officers who supervise a client on MAT must communicate often with treatment providers and medical professionals on client progress to best support their success.

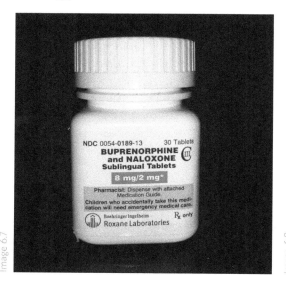
Image 6.7

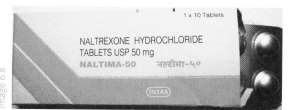
Image 6.8

Community Corrections Officer Training Programs

When implementing evidence-based practices or programs, the burden is often heavily shifted onto probation and parole officers. Because these practices often seek to realign and change the way supervision is delivered, the individuals who are responsible for supervision (i.e., officers) must put in a lot of work. Often, this involves training—usually several training programs are used. For example, say a probation agency wants to implement a new validated risk and needs assessment. The agency might require officers to participate in an initial training that introduces them to the assessment and why they are implementing it. Then, they might have to participate in lengthier trainings where they learn how to use the assessment. These trainings often involve practice and role play. After the officers start using the assessment with clients on their caseload, they might participate in monthly follow-up training to ensure they are implementing it correctly. However time-consuming it may be, research continuously documents the importance of training. Probation and parole officers specifically trained on the RNR principles demonstrate better adherence to those principles in practice, are more likely to use cognitive behavioral techniques, and their clients are more likely to be successful. To promote change and increased adherence to effective correctional practices, agencies often implement formal community corrections officer training programs.

There are several formal, specialized training programs designed to integrate best practices into community corrections settings. These include Staff Training Aimed at Reducing Rearrest (STARR; Robinson et al., 2011), Effective Practices in Community Supervision (EPICS; Latessa et al., 2013), Strategic Training Initiative in Community Supervision (STICS; Bonta et al., 2013), and Proactive Community Supervision (PCS; Taxman, 2008). All of these training programs attempt to translate the research on best practices into specific, trainable skills that then increase the application of those best practices into daily supervision work. They focus on training probation and parole officers to implement skills and techniques during their interactions with clients that are aligned with the evidence-based practices discussed in Chapter 4. These training programs teach probation and parole officers the skills to integrate cognitive behavioral techniques in their interactions to address the criminogenic needs of their clients.

While the actual content of the training programs varies by specific program, almost all include a focus on developing a similar set of skills: effective use of reinforcement, effective use of disapproval, effective use of authority, effective use of punishment, problem solving, cognitive restructuring, structured learning, and relationship skills (see Table 6.3 for a description of the skills taught in the STARR program). The focus of these skills is to change the role of the officer from one focused on punishment and reactionary responses to one that is proactive in supporting client behavioral change. As a result, they often require major shifts in the way an officer might traditionally approach their job. To promote effective and sustained change, the actual training programs are very carefully designed and often quite intense.

Each of these programs includes comprehensive training that begins with an initial multiday session that introduces the underlying theories, purpose of the program, and individual skills. This training is typically interactive, with officers learning a new skill and then spending time practicing and role playing. Following this initial session, officers participate in monthly booster sessions. These booster sessions typically focus on one specific skill to promote proficiency. Additionally, officers can become coaches once they become proficiently trained and undergo additional coaching training. All trained officers are assigned a peer coach who then reviews audio recordings of skills used with actual clients. Coaches provide feedback while identifying areas of strengths and weaknesses, with the goal of improving overall quality of skill use.

The question is whether these training programs are effective in helping officers acquire new skills and work with individuals on supervision differently. To date, there have been two meta-analyses examining the effectiveness of these programs. (Remember back to earlier in this chapter: This is an ideal way to generate evidence on whether a program works!) The earliest one, conducted by Chadwick and colleagues in 2015, examined 10 studies on community

TABLE 6.3 Description of the Staff Training Aimed at Reducing Rearrest (STARR) Skills

Relationship skills	Used by the officer to build a collaborative working alliance with clients focused on risk reduction and accountability. Many of these skills are similar to the skills taught in motivational interviewing training.
Active listening	Process of giving your total and undivided attention to understand what the other person is communicating. The goal is to obtain accurate information, send a message that you care, support client self-efficacy, and build a collaborative working relationship.
Open-ended questions	Use of open-ended questions (i.e., not something you can answer with a yes or a no) to create a conversation with the client; helps to learn about the other person's experiences and perceptions; sets a collaborative tone.
Affirmations	A skill to build motivation to change by encouraging client effort, building their confidence, and encouraging prosocial behavior.
Reflections	Repeating what you hear the client say to let them know you heard them and to check for accuracy and check if it is what they meant to say or identify discrepancies.
Summarize	A collection of reflections you can use to redirect the conversation or maintain conversation and lead into a discussion around areas for change.
Empathy	Recognizing the client's perspective as truth in a nonjudgmental manner; recognize and communicate emotion.
Giving feedback	Interactive process aimed at reinforcing positive behavior and providing specific guidelines for future behavior.
Role clarification	Provides a way for officers to begin a relationship with a client by defining supervision, expectations, and their roles. The focus is not just on the conditions of supervision but to articulate the dual role of the officer to also support client change.
Bridging skills	Skills used to help clients stop using maladaptive behaviors and develop prosocial behaviors.
Effective use of reinforcement	Identifying a prosocial behavior you would like to reinforce, tell the client what you liked about what they said/did, ask them to identify the short- and long-term benefits of continuing to engage in this behavior, and contract with them to continue using the behavior.
Effective use of disapproval	Identifying a problem behavior, tell the client in an objective manner what you disapprove of, identify the specific reasons why the behavior was unacceptable, ask them to identify the short- and long-term consequences of continuing to engage in this behavior, ask them to identify prosocial alternatives, and contract with them to use prosocial alternative in the future.

Effective use of authority	If the problem behavior persists, this skill is used to identify the problem behavior and provide a structured message that the behavior is not acceptable. This is the only skill that is used without much client involvement.
Effective use of punishment	Identify a behavior the client engaged in or failed to engage in, identify the consequences, deliver the consequences, and debrief with the client to determine how to avoid the behavior in the future.
Intervention skills	A set of skills the officer teaches to the client to help them avoid, manage, and/or cope with high-risk situations that may lead to engagement in crime. These help clients to identify high-risk situations, improve development of internal control, risk management, and relapse prevention techniques, and increase client motivation and self-efficacy.
Teaching the cognitive model	The officer teaches the client about the link between thoughts and behaviors. Officers teach clients about how thoughts are ideas that occur in response to an event. The more aware you are of your thoughts, the more control you have over your behavior. Clients may have thoughts that support criminal behavior and/or neutralize crime and safety. This skill helps clients identify the link between thinking and criminal behavior to help them analyze situations and develop the ability to replace antisocial thoughts with prosocial ones and avoid high-risk behavior.
Applying the cognitive model	After engaging in teaching the cognitive model, perhaps in the next meeting, an officer would use this skill to practice the cognitive model. Officers typically provide clients with a worksheet where they identify a problem behavior or situation, the consequences, and the thoughts that occurred during the event. Next, they identify alternative thoughts and the resulting behavior that may occur. The goal is to identify the link between how changing your thoughts can lead to less risky and even prosocial behavior. Officers contract with the clients to use the cognitive model in a future situation.
Reviewing the cognitive model	To ensure the client is practicing the skill, officers will ask clients to complete a cognitive model worksheet on their own when they encounter a difficult situation. Once the client completes this worksheet, the officer will review it with them, reinforcing or disapproving of the resulting behavior.
Problem solving	This is another cognitive skill officers teach clients that often involves a worksheet. In problem solving, officers teach clients to stop, think, and identify a problem when they encounter a difficult situation, clarify their overall goals (e.g., complete supervision successfully), generate alternative solutions to their problem that do not involve criminal behavior, develop a plan to implement that behavior, implement the plan, and then evaluate the plan to determine how well it worked for them. Often, officers will provide an example or work through an example with the client in the office before asking them to work on it on their own. Once a client tries to problem solve independently, officers review the process with them and provide feedback and reinforcement.

correctional officer training programs. They concluded that these programs were associated with a small, statistically significant reduction in recidivism. A more recent meta-analysis expanded on this earlier study by examining the impact of these training programs on a more diverse set of outcomes. In their review of 25 articles, Labrecque and colleagues (2023) found that officer training programs had several significant impacts on trained officer behavior:

- Increased the likelihood that probation and parole officers discussed criminogenic needs with clients, and were more likely to discuss more challenging subjects like antisocial thinking.
- Decreased the likelihood that probation and parole officers discussed noncriminogenic needs and supervision conditions which means the officers are more focused on crime-producing needs.
- Increased the likelihood that trained officers used core correctional practices during meetings with clients.

Additionally, Labrecque and colleagues (2023) also identified several significant impacts on recidivism. First, they found that individuals supervised by trained officers were less likely to be rearrested or reconvicted of a crime. Next, they found that those recidivism reductions were greater among individuals supervised by officers who used the skills with greater fidelity (i.e., those who used the skills the way they were supposed to). The findings of these two meta-analyses suggest that community corrections officer training programs are successful at both changing officer behavior and leading to reductions in recidivism.

What Does Not Work?

Now that we have covered what works in corrections, it is important to talk about what does not work. Often, these are programs or policies that appeal to our senses. They seem like they should work, however most of them suffer from the same limitation: They do not address criminogenic needs. That is, they do not attempt to change the underlying factors that increase

Image 6.9

an individual's risk for recidivism. They often focus on retribution or deterrence, without concern for identifying and/or supporting behavioral change. Cullen and Johnson (2017) provide an impressive summary of these seemingly plausible yet ineffective programs. Some of the most popular yet ineffective programs that fit into this category are "scared straight" or intensive supervision programs. As discussed in Chapter 5, you already know intensive supervision alone (without treatment) is ineffective. Similarly, "scared straight" programs that focus on intimidation of youth while they visited adult prisons are also ineffective—and can sometimes have criminogenic effects.

Other punishment-focused programs deemed ineffective include boot camps and wilderness programs. These programs, often military style, focus on rigid routine, structure, and breaking down participants so far that they are forced to consider a new way of life. Additionally, programs that focus exclusively on boosting self-esteem or are not structured specifically to address thinking patterns and antisocial values are also ineffective. This is because self-esteem alone is not a strong predictor of recidivism and programs that are not structured to systematically address criminogenic needs are unlikely to yield meaningful change.

SUMMARY: THE CHALLENGE OF IMPLEMENTING WHAT WORKS

This chapter provides an overview of the practices and programs currently supported by evidence for use in community corrections. In general, these evidence-supported practices and programs all have at least one thing in common: they aim to address and change an individual's underlying risk factors that are predictive of recidivism. You might be thinking they make sense and seem like a good idea if we are trying to reduce someone's chance of recidivism. However, in practice, implementing these practices and programs is often quite challenging. One of the biggest challenges in implementing what works in community corrections is associated with the fact that what works is often not more punishment or more severe punishments but is more aligned with a rehabilitative approach. This often conflicts with the longstanding culture of punishment in the criminal justice system, which influences how people do their jobs and whether/how they align with organizational change.

In probation and parole agencies, evidence-based programs and practices often require officers to shift their core ideology from a focus on monitoring, control, and authority to a more therapeutic, rehabilitative approach. There are multiple research studies that document the challenge of implementing some of the practices and programs discussed in this chapter. Multiple studies identified challenges with successfully implementing risk and needs assessments within community corrections agencies (e.g., Ferguson, 2002; Miller & Maloney, 2013; Viglione et al., 2015). For example, Viglione and colleagues (2015) found that after implementation of a validated risk assessment, probation and parole officers rarely used the assessment as intended, often circumventing results and relying on their own previous experiences and judgments to guide their supervision and case management decisions. It is not uncommon for research studies to uncover resistance to change associated with what works in probation or parole settings. These studies often identify misalignments between the new practice and the existing agency culture and/or individual staff ideologies, lack of understanding regarding the purpose/intent of the new practice, and/or poor infrastructure to support the change (e.g., limited resources, understaffed). Often, we hear about the challenges of balancing rehabilitation with punishment across the system. That is, common concerns surround adequately punishing an individual and protecting society from future harm while also rehabilitating the individual, so they do not commit another offense.

Some may even argue it is not possible to achieve all of these goals at once. However, proponents of what works suggest that it is only by providing effective treatment and using best practices that we can truly uphold public safety and prevent future crime. In general, existing research suggests that changing existing correctional practices and policies to align within an evidence-based framework is challenging and requires dedicated efforts to ensure its success. Earlier in this chapter, we discussed community correctional officer training programs. These training programs are a promising strategy to promote change. However, as we learned from the National Institute of Correction's (NIC) guidelines, agencies must also commit to measuring relevant practices and providing measurement feedback, as these are two key strategies that enable us to determine whether something is effective.

Scenario-Based Activities

	Case	Question(s)

1.	Pretend you are a probation officer supervising a new client named Jessica. You just completed a risk and needs assessment with Jessica. Her assessment results were as follows:
	
	• Risk level: moderate
	• Needs:
	  o Criminal thinking (high)
	  o Housing (high)
		Design a case plan to address Jessica's risk assessment results. Your case plan should identify a goal and tasks for each criminogenic need. How would you measure Jessica's progress on her new case plan?

2.	Congratulations! You just completed STARR, a community corrections officer training program. In this program, you learned about relationship skills, intervention skills, and bridging skills that you can now practice when you meet with clients on your caseload. First, you want to start practicing the relationship skills you learned with your client Sam. When Sam enters your office, he seems discouraged and mentions he has been having a tough time.	Review the relationship skills introduced in this chapter (active listening, open-ended questions, affirmations, reflections, summarize, empathy, and giving feedback). How might you apply these skills to try to figure out what is going on with Sam? Write down example questions and communication techniques you would use in your conversation.

References

Abrams, D. S., Bertrand, M., & Mullainathan, S. (2012). Do judges vary in their treatment of race? *The Journal of Legal Studies, 41*(2), 347–383. https://doi.org/10.1086/666006

Andrews, D. A. & Bonta, J. (2010). Rehabilitating criminal justice policy and practice. *Psychology, Public Policy, And Law, 16*(1), 39–55. https://doi.org/10.1037/a0018362

Bickel, W. K., Amass, L., Higgins, S. T., Badger, G. J., & Esch, R. A. (1997). Effects of adding behavioral treatment to opioid detoxification with buprenorphine. *Journal of Consulting and Clinical Psychology, 65*(5), 803. https://doi.org/10.1037/0022-006X.65.5.803

Bonta, J., Bourgon, G., Rugge, T., Gress, C., & Gutierrez, L. (2013). Taking the leap: From pilot project to wide-scale implementation of the Strategic Training Initiative in Community Supervision (STICS). *Justice Research and Policy, 15*(1), 17–35. https://doi.org/10.3818/JRP.15.1.2013.17

Bonta, J., Wallace-Capretta, S., & Rooney, J. (2000). Can electronic monitoring make a difference? An evaluation of three Canadian programs. *Crime & Delinquency, 46*(1), 61–75. https://doi.org/10.1177/0011128700046001004

Bonta, J., Wallace-Capretta, S., Rooney, J., & Mcanoy, K. (2002). An outcome evaluation of a restorative justice alternative to incarceration. *Contemporary Justice Review, 5*(4), 319–338. https://doi.org/10.1080/10282580214772

Chadwick, N., Dewolf, A., & Serin, R. (2015). Effectively training community supervision officers: A meta-analytic review of the impact on offender outcome. *Criminal Justice and Behavior, 42*(10), 977–989. https://doi.org/10.1177/0093854815595661

Clear, T. R., & Sumter, M. T. (2002). Prisoners, prison, and religion: Religion and adjustment to prison. *Journal of Offender Rehabilitation, 35*(3–4), 125–156. https://doi.org/10.1300/J076v35n03_07

Cullen, F. T., & Jonson, C. L. (2011). Rehabilitation and treatment. In J. Q Wilson & J. Petersilia (Eds.), *Crime and public policy (pp. 293–344).* Oxford University Press.

Cullen, F. T., & Jonson, C. L. (2017). *Correctional theory: Context and consequences.* Sage Publications.

Doctor, R. M., & Polakow, R. L. (1973). A behavior modification program for adult probationers. In *Proceedings of the Annual Convention of the American Psychological Association.* American Psychological Association.

Eckhouse, L., Lum, K., Conti-Cook, C., & Ciccolini, J. (2019). Layers of bias: A unified approach for understanding problems with risk assessment. *Criminal Justice and Behavior, 46*(2), 185–209. https://doi.org/10.1177/0093854818811379

Ferguson, J. L. (2002). Putting the "what works" research into practice. *Criminal Justice and Behavior, 29*(4), 472–492. https://doi.org/10.1177/0093854802029004007

Friedmann, P. D., Rhodes, A. G., Taxman, F. S., & Step'n Out Research Group of CJ-DATS. (2009). Collaborative behavioral management: integration and intensification of parole and outpatient addiction treatment services in the Step'n Out study. *Journal of Experimental Criminology, 5,* 227–243. https://doi.org/10.1007/s11292-009-9079-3

Gendreau, P., & Goggin, C. (1996). Principles of effective programming with offenders. *Forum on Corrections Research, 8*(3), 38–40.

Gendreau, P., Little, T., & Goggin, C. (1996). A meta-analysis of the predictors of adult offender recidivism: What works! *Criminology, 34*(4), 575–608. https://doi.org/10.1111/j.1745-9125.1996.tb01220.x

Goel, S., Rao, J. M., & Shroff, R. (2016). Precinct or prejudice? Understanding racial disparities in New York City's stop-and-frisk policy. *The Annals of Applied Statistics, 10*(1), 365–394. http://dx.doi.org/10.2139/ssrn.2572718

Gottfredson, S. D., & Moriarty, L. J. (2006). Statistical risk assessment: Old problems and new applications. *Crime & Delinquency, 52*(1), 178–200. https://doi.org/10.1177/0011128705281748

Griffith, J. D., Rowan-Szal, G. A., Roark, R. R., & Simpson, D. D. (2000). Contingency management in outpatient methadone treatment: A meta-analysis. *Drug and Alcohol Dependence, 58*(1), 55–66. https://doi.org/10.1016/S0376-8716(99)00068-X

Harcourt, B. E. (2015). Risk as a proxy for race: The dangers of risk assessment. *Federal Sentencing Reporter, 27*(4), 237–243. https://doi.org/10.1525/fsr.2015.27.4.237

Higgins, S. T., & Petry, N. M. (1999). Contingency management: Incentives for sobriety. *Alcohol Research & Health, 23*(2), 122–127.

Higgins, S. T., Budney, A. J., Bickel, W. K., Foerg, F. E., Donham, R., & Badger, G. J. (1994). Incentives improve outcome in outpatient behavioral treatment of cocaine dependence. *Archives of General Psychiatry, 51*(7), 568–576. https://doi.org/10.1001/archpsyc.1994.03950070060011

Inciardi, J. A., Martin, S. S., & Butzin, C. A. (2004). Five-year outcomes of therapeutic community treatment of drug-involved offenders after release from prison. *Crime & Delinquency, 50*(1), 88–107. https://doi.org/10.1177/0011128703258874

Kutateladze, B. L., Andiloro, N. R., Johnson, B. D., & Spohn, C. C. (2014). Cumulative disadvantage: Examining racial and ethnic disparity in prosecution and sentencing. *Criminology, 52*(3), 514–551. https://doi.org/10.1111/1745-9125.12047

Labrecque, R. M., Viglione, J., & Caudy, M. (2023). The impact of community supervision officer training programs on officer and client outcomes: A systematic review and meta-analysis. *Justice Quarterly, 40*(4), 587–611. https://doi.org/10.1080/07418825.2022.2120062

Landenberger, N. A., & Lipsey, M. W. (2005). The positive effects of cognitive–behavioral programs for offenders: A meta-analysis of factors associated with effective treatment. *Journal of Experimental Criminology, 1*(4), 451–476. https://doi.org/10.1007/s11292-005-3541-7

Latessa, E. J., Smith, P., Schweitzer, M., & Labrecque, R. M. (2013). *Evaluation of the effective practices in community supervision model (EPICS) in Ohio* [Unpublished manuscript]. Center for Criminal Justice Research.

Lussier, J. P., Heil, S. H., Mongeon, J. A., Badger, G. J., & Higgins, S. T. (2006). A meta-analysis of voucher-based reinforcement therapy for substance use disorders. *Addiction, 101*(2), 192–203. https://doi.org/10.1111/j.1360-0443.2006.01311.x

Makarios, M., Sperber, K. G., & Latessa, E. J. (2014). Treatment dosage and the risk principle: A refinement and extension. *Journal of Offender Rehabilitation, 53*(5), 334–350. https://doi.org/10.1080/10509674.2014.922157

Marlowe, D. B., Festinger, D. S., Dugosh, K. L., Arabia, P. L., & Kirby, K. C. (2008). An effectiveness trial of contingency management in a felony preadjudication drug court. *Journal of Applied Behavior Analysis, 41*(4), 565–577. https://doi.org/10.1901/jaba.2008.41-565

Marlowe, D. B., & Wong, C. J. (2008). Contingency management in adult criminal drug courts. In S. T. Higgins, K. Silverman, & S. H. Heil (Eds.), *Contingency management in substance abuse treatment* (pp. 334–354). The Guilford Press.

McMurran, M. (2009). Motivational interviewing with offenders: A systematic review. *Legal and Criminological Psychology, 14*(1), 83–100. https://doi.org/10.1348/135532508X278326

Miller, P. M. (1975). A behavioral intervention program for chronic public drunkenness offenders. *Archives of General Psychiatry, 32*(7), 915–918. https://doi.org/10.1001/archpsyc.1975.01760250107012

Miller, J., & Maloney, C. (2013). Practitioner compliance with risk/needs assessment tools: A theoretical and empirical assessment. *Criminal Justice and Behavior, 40*(7), 716–736. https://doi.org/10.1177/0093854812468883

National Institute of Corrections. (n.d.-a). *Thinking for a Change 4.0: Preliminary*. Training for Change (T4C). Retrieved from https://t4c.nicic.gov/thinking-change/thinking-change-40/preliminary

National Institute of Corrections. (n.d.-b). *Thinking for a Change: Training for Trainers*. Training for Trainers (T4T). https://t4c.nicic.gov/training-trainers-t4t/thinking-change-training-trainers

O'Connor, T. P., & Perryclear, M. (2002). Prison religion in action and its influence on offender rehabilitation. *Journal of Offender Rehabilitation, 35*(3–4), 11–33. https://doi.org/10.1300/J076v35n03_02

Palmer, T. (1975). Martinson revisited. *Journal of Research in Crime and Delinquency, 12*(2), 133–152. https://doi.org/10.1177/002242787501200206

Pavlov, I. P. (1927). *Conditioned reflexes: An investigation of the physiological activity of the cerebral cortex.* Oxford University Press

Petry, N. M. (2000). A comprehensive guide to the application of contingency management procedures in clinical settings. *Drug and Alcohol Dependence, 58*(1–2), 9–25. https://doi.org/10.1016/S0376-8716(99)00071-X

Petry, N. M., & Martin, B. (2002). Low-cost contingency management for treating cocaine-and opioid-abusing methadone patients. *Journal of Consulting and Clinical Psychology, 70*(2), 398. https://doi.org/10.1037/0022-006X.70.2.398

Prendergast, M. L., Hall, E. A., Wexler, H. K., Melnick, G., & Cao, Y. (2004). Amity prison-based therapeutic community: 5-year outcomes. *The Prison Journal, 84*(1), 36–60. https://doi.org/10.1177/0032885503262454

Prendergast, M., Podus, D., Finney, J., Greenwell, L., & Roll, J. (2006). Contingency management for treatment of substance use disorders: A meta-analysis. *Addiction, 101*(11), 1546–1560. https://doi.org/10.1111/j.1360-0443.2006.01581.x

Robinson, C. R., VanBenschoten, S., Alexander, M., & Lowenkamp, C. T. (2011). A random (almost) study of staff training aimed at reducing re-arrest (STARR): Reducing recidivism through intentional design. *Federal Probation, 75*, 57.

Roll, J. M., Higgins, S. T., & Badger, G. J. (1996). An experimental comparison of three different schedules of reinforcement of drug abstinence using cigarette smoking as an exemplar. *Journal of Applied Behavior Analysis, 29*(4), 495–505. https://doi.org/10.1901/jaba.1996.29-495

Ryan, R. M., & Deci, E. L. (2000). Intrinsic and extrinsic motivations: Classic definitions and new directions. *Contemporary Educational Psychology, 25*(1), 54–67. https://doi.org/10.1006/ceps.1999.1020

Schwartz, R. P., Gryczynski, J., O'grady, K. E., Sharfstein, J. M., Warren, G., Olsen, Y., Mitchell, S. G., & Jaffe, J. H. (2013). Opioid agonist treatments and heroin overdose deaths in Baltimore, Maryland, 1995–2009. *American Journal of Public Health, 103*(5), 917–922. https://doi.org/10.2105/AJPH.2012.301049

Shaffer, D. K. (2006). *Reconsidering drug court effectiveness: A meta-analytic review.* University of Cincinnati.

Skinner, B. F. (1948). "Superstition" in the pigeon. *Journal of Experimental Psychology, 38*(2), 168–172. https://doi.org/10.1037/h0055873

Stancliff, S., Joseph, H., Fong, C., Furst, T., Comer, S. D., & Roux, P. (2012). Opioid maintenance treatment as a harm reduction tool for opioid-dependent individuals in New York City: The need to expand access to buprenorphine/naloxone in marginalized populations. *Journal of Addictive Diseases, 31*(3), 278–287. https://doi.org/10.1080/10550887.2012.694603

Stitzer, M. L., & Bigelow, G. E. (1983). Contingent payment for carbon monoxide reduction: Effects of pay amount. *Behavioral Therapy, 14*(5), 647–656. https://doi.org/10.1016/S0005-7894(83)80057-4

Stitzer, M. L., Bigelow, G. E., Liebson, I. A., & McCaul, M. E. (1984). Contingency management of supplemental drug use during methadone maintenance treatment. *NIDA Research Monograph, 46*, 84–103.

Taxman, F. S. (2008). No illusions: Offender and organizational change in Maryland's proactive community supervision efforts. *Criminology & Public Policy, 7*(2), 275–302. https://doi.org/10.1111/j.1745-9133.2008.00508.x

Viglione, J., Rudes, D. S., & Taxman, F. S. (2015). Misalignment in supervision: Implementing risk/needs assessment instruments in probation. *Criminal Justice and Behavior, 42*(3), 263–285. https://doi.org/10.1177/0093854814548447

Wilson, D. B., Mitchell, O., & MacKenzie, D. L. (2006). A systematic review of drug court effects on recidivism. *Journal of Experimental Criminology, 2*(4), 459–487. https://doi.org/10.1007/s11292-006-9019-4

Wodahl, E. J., Alarid, L. F., & Bowman, J. H., IV. (2022). "Would you prefer jail or probation?" Differences in sanctioning preferences among White, Black, and Latinx adults. *The Prison Journal, 102*(4), 395–416. https://doi.org/10.1177/00328855221109799

Wodahl, E. J., Garland, B., Culhane, S. E., & McCarty, W. P. (2011). Utilizing behavioral interventions to improve supervision outcomes in community-based corrections. *Criminal Justice and Behavior, 38*(4), 386–405. https://doi.org/10.1177/0093854810397866

Wooldredge, J. (2012). Distinguishing race effects on pre-trial release and sentencing decisions. *Justice Quarterly, 29*(1), 41–75. https://doi.org/10.1080/07418825.2011.559480

Wooldredge, J., Frank, J., Goulette, N., & Travis, L., III. (2015). Is the impact of cumulative disadvantage on sentencing greater for black defendants? *Criminology & Public Policy, 14*(2), 187–223. https://doi.org/10.1111/1745-9133.12124

Wu, J. (2016). Racial/ethnic discrimination and prosecution: A meta-analysis. *Criminal Justice and Behavior, 43*(4), 437–458. https://doi.org/10.1177/0093854815628026

Image Credits

PART III

Community Supervision Clients

CHAPTER 7

Categories of Clients in Community Corrections

The intersectionality framework suggests that the social structure and categorizations of people by individual characteristics creates systems of discrimination. Systemic discrimination is often centered in the basic demographic constructs of age, race, and gender, where people are born into a position of disadvantage that can inhibit their experiences with the community corrections system. Other examples of vulnerable populations include youth involved in delinquency, older justice-involved individuals (e.g., over the age of 65), Black and Hispanic individuals, American Indian and Alaskan tribes, undocumented immigrants, and LGBTQIA+ populations. Juvenile delinquency is linked to adverse childhood experiences (ACEs) and developmental processes that require consideration of age. Older justice-involved individuals have unique health needs, particularly regarding mobility, quality of life, and advanced aging disorders. Individuals under the supervision of community corrections and who are undocumented immigrants may face language barriers and confusing mandates. Male and female individuals may experience different pathways toward and through community corrections that can influence outcomes. Additionally, gender identity and sexual orientation are factors that can produce discrimination and harassment. These vulnerabilities require the community corrections system to offer trauma-informed care, gender-responsive strategies, and cultural competency training. This also requires the protection of staff against the negative effects of vicarious trauma.

LEARNING OBJECTIVES

By the end of this chapter, students will be able to:

- Describe the relationships between demographic factors (age, race/ethnicity, gender) and the community corrections system.
- Understand vulnerable populations, including their unique risks and needs.
- Distinguish the dynamics of exposure to trauma, for both clients and community corrections officers.

KEY TERMS

- Adverse childhood experiences (ACEs)
- Age-crime curve
- Cultural competency
- Gender-responsive strategies
- Trauma-informed care (TIC)

CONTENT

The Intersectionality Framework
    ◊ Journey into the Field: Ms. Shirene Hansotia
Demographic Vulnerabilities
Age and Crime
    Juveniles and Delinquency
    Older Justice-Involved Individuals
Race and Ethnicity
    ◊ Diversity, Equity, and Inclusion: Cultural Competency
    Undocumented Immigrants
Gender
    Male Justice-Involved Individuals
    Female Justice-Involved Individuals
Gender Identity and Sexual Orientation
Case Study: Supervising an LGBTQIA+ Population Using Trauma-Informed Care
    ◊ Officer Work, Careers, and Wellness: Vicarious Victimization
Summary: Intersectionality and Community Corrections
Scenario-Based Activities

I talked a lot early on in my career about intersectionality and how racism and classism and sexism and homophobia and capitalism are all connected with each other, and they're these crazy systems that are feeding on each other and are also damaging. I can't even go into the whole spectrum of it. But I feel like kids today are so much more savvy about that conversation. And I'm so thrilled when I get to meet younger people who are doing that so much better than I did. I thought about it, but I didn't know how to put a lot of the theory into practice.

—Kathleen Hanna (as cited in Borders, 2013)

The Intersectionality Framework

The intersectionality framework suggests that the social structure and categorizations of people by race, class, and gender create systems of discrimination. These disadvantages can accumulate and interact with each other to create wide inequalities and life experiences. For community corrections, this is an important legal issue because the administration of justice is designed to occur in a fair, impartial, and unbiased manner. Individuals who interact with the community corrections system possess a wide range of risks, needs, previous experiences, perceptions, and expectations. Factors such as age, race, and gender (e.g., demographics) can lead to different experiences and outcomes with the community corrections system. Other vulnerable populations include justice-involved youth, older populations under supervision, Black and Hispanic individuals, American Indian and Alaskan tribes, undocumented immigrants, and LGBTQIA+ population (i.e., lesbian, gay, bisexual, transgender, queer, intersex, asexual, and other sexual and gender minorities). Individuals may also have specific pathways toward crime, incarceration, and the community corrections systems based on gender that warrant attention. These vulnerabilities often merge into needs that overlap with criminal justice, health care, and social welfare systems. Community corrections must implement strategies targeting relevant risks and needs, and to be responsive to their supervision populations.

JOURNEY INTO THE FIELD: MS. SHIRENE HANSOTIA

◇◇◇◇◇◇◇◇

Full name: Shirene C. Hansotia

Title: State Director of Root & Rebound of South Carolina

Ms. Hansotia earned her undergraduate degrees in journalism, political science, and African studies from the University of Wisconsin–Madison. She earned a master's degree in public policy and administration with a specialty in African development issues from Michigan State University. After graduate school, Ms. Hansotia moved to the San Francisco Bay Area to work for the U.S. Department of Housing and Urban Development (HUD) where she helped individuals in under-resourced communities with housing and employment opportunities.

In 2009, Ms. Hansotia earned her Juris Doctor, graduating cum laude from Charleston School of Law. In her first year after law school, she worked as a law clerk for Judge G. Thomas Cooper in Columbia, SC, where she assisted

Image 7.1

with overseeing the civil and criminal case dockets. Ms. Hansotia spent the next 5 years working as an assistant Charleston County public defender. She was awarded a 2-year grant from Nelson Mullins law firm to work with Stuart Andrews, the lead attorney on *T.R. v. South Carolina Department of Corrections*, a landmark lawsuit on behalf of seriously mentally ill people in South Carolina. From there, Ms. Hansotia worked with the South Carolina office of the ACLU (American Civil Liberties Union) as their criminal justice policy and legal counsel, before being named the state director of Root & Rebound of South Carolina, where she remains today.

These varied and often intense experiences have provided Ms. Hansotia insight into the justice system, moving from legal representation during court procedures, to the climate of jails and prisons, and the rights of the incarcerated, and then to the need for an effective community corrections system. In this Journey into the Field, Ms. Hansotia shares her thoughts on mass supervision, supervision conditions and violations, and individualizing supervision.

Much has been written about America's mass incarceration problem; however, far less ink has been spilled addressing the enormous increase in the number of Americans wrapped up in a system of mass supervision. Probation, a period of supervision in lieu of incarceration, and parole, a period of supervision after imprisonment, often begin as hopeful alternatives to jail or prison. This hope, however, often turns into despair when the myriad restrictions placed on people while living on probation or parole serve as a tripwire, sending many back to incarceration.

Rates of probation and parole have expanded over time, both in the number of people under supervision and the length of time being supervised. Between 1980 and 2020 in the United Sates, the number of people on probation nearly tripled and the number of people under parole supervision nearly quadrupled. As of 2022, more than five million people in the United States were under supervision (probation or parole). This rise in supervision has coincided with a dramatic increase in the number of restrictions placed on people on probation or parole—even though many of these restrictions do very little to increase public safety.

While under supervision, individuals must report to an officer and follow a lengthy list of conditions, such as living in approved housing, finding full-time employment, refraining from associating with anyone with a criminal record, paying court-associated fines and fees, and much more. Any infractions can, and often do, return people back to prison. A recent study by the Council of State Governments (2019) found that technical violations, meaning a failure to adhere to supervision conditions rather than the commission of a new offense, accounted for 56% of all occasions in which people on parole or probation are sent back to state prison. The fact that the United States incarcerates far more people than any other nation on earth has been woven into the fabric of American history. Community supervision systems, including probation and parole, are some of the primary drivers of U.S. incarceration rates today.

Research shows that limited state and federal resources should be focused on supervising individuals who are deemed to be at the highest risk to reoffend. In addition, studies show that simply increasing the number of conditions placed on individuals while on probation or parole does not increase public safety. Rather, the intricate web of requirements often acts as a trap, returning many individuals to prison for failing to comply with the complicated set of rules.

To make parole and probation more effective for society, judges should evaluate each case individually and attach restrictions only as necessary. Parole and probation should be goal-based rather than time-based. Goal-based supervision incentivizes positive behavior and allows individuals who are in compliance to preserve precious time and resources that can be used to succeed upon reentry into society. For example, rather than focusing on the amount of time someone needs to serve on probation, the focus of supervision would be on achieving specific goals, such as maintaining employment and stable housing. Once an individual meets their goals, they should be eligible for supervision termination. Finally, research demonstrates that the most effective way to bring people back into compliance when they are failing under supervision is to enact immediate, brief stints of reincarceration as punishment rather than sending people back to prison for the remainder of a sentence.

Demographic Vulnerabilities

While intersectionality includes a consideration of a wide range of unique characteristics that can influence a person and their experiences, the framework is often rooted in three key social demographics: age, race/ethnicity, and gender. These factors can intersect to create isolated, marginalized, and underprivileged communities that experience very different forms of justice. Members within these groups have been termed "vulnerable populations," as they may be born into systemic disadvantage that can inhibit their experiences with the overall criminal justice system, as well as their physical health, mental health, and overall well-being (Aday, 1994). Vulnerability centers on the relative risk that a minority group may experience when compared to a majority group. Aday (1994) explains that relative risk impacts disadvantaged groups through the social status of people (e.g., age, race/ethnicity, gender), the social ties between people (e.g., family structure, marital status), and the human capital in the neighborhood (e.g., schools, jobs, income, housing). These differences in risk can be seen in Table 7.1, which highlights the intersection of these various exposures.

TABLE 7.1   Comparisons of Relative Risk*

Community and individual resources	Relative risk	
	Higher risk	Lower risk
The people: social status		
Age	Infants Children Elderly	Working-age adults
Sex	Females	Males
Race and ethnicity	African Americans Hispanics Native Americans Asian Americans	European Americans

Community and individual resources	Relative risk	
	Higher risk	**Lower risk**
The ties between people: social capital		
Family structure	Living alone Female-headed families	Extended families Two-parent families
Marital status	Single Separated Divorced Widowed	Married/mingles
Voluntary organizations	Nonmember	Member
Social networks	Weak	Strong
The neighborhood: human capital		
Schools	Less than high school	High school +
Jobs	Unemployed Blue collar	White collar
Income	Poor Near poor	Nonpoor
Housing	Substandard	Adequate +

Note: The terms to designate the race and ethnicity categories in this table are used in talking about these groups in general. When presenting specific data in the text on these groups, the designations (such as Black or Asian) in the original source from which the data were derived are generally used. *Mingles* are individuals who are not married but are living with a sexual partner. Voluntary organizations include churches, volunteer interest groups, and civic or neighborhood organizations.

*Reprinted with permission: Aday, L. A. *At risk in America: The health and health care needs of vulnerable populations in the United States.* Table 1.1 p. 9. Copyright 1993 by Jossey-Bass Inc. Publishers (1).

Age and Crime

As early as 1831, scientists like Adolphe Quetelet noted a curvilinear relationship between age and crime, one that has endured and remains a predictive pattern when examining criminal behavior. As one study reports, "When age is plotted by crime rates, the slope of the relationship ascends rapidly during adolescence, peaks in early adulthood and then falls thereafter" (Stolzenberg & D'Alessio, 2008, p. 66). This pattern is so observable that esteemed scholars like Travis Hirschi and Michael Gottfredson (1983) have termed the **age-crime curve** as "one of the brute facts of criminology" (p. 552). Younger people tend to display higher engagement in delinquent behavior for a combination of reasons—one being that adolescence is a period of significant changes, with youth typically moving from having a strong attachment to parental figures toward the attainment of social status more in line with peer standards. Youth who experience disadvantage, a lack of supervision, or who reside in socially disorganized neighborhoods may be more likely to gravitate to peers who engage in delinquency. The field of neurology has recently added to our understanding of young people, with magnetic resonance imaging (MRI) revealing that the brain, particularly the frontal and temporal lobes that regulate emotion and control impulses, are not fully formed during adolescence. Puberty also brings rapid changes in hormones, body growth, and adolescent sexuality that can influence behavior.

By adulthood, crime decreases, as life-altering events like college, full-time employment, military service, marriage, parenthood, and community relationships become established. In older populations, engagement in crime declines sharply. Older people may experience physical and mental health conditions (also termed "morbidity") that limit their daily functioning, with individuals involved in lifelong offending experiencing early mortality (death), long-term incarceration, or social isolation, which decreases their opportunity and ability to engage in crime. The age-crime curve has implications for the community corrections system because 81% of those aged 24 or younger who are incarcerated and subsequently released from state prison will be arrested within 5 years after release from prison; many of these young people will be under the supervision of probation or parole during their time in society (Durose & Antenangelo, 2021). Individuals over the age of 40 display lower rates of recidivism, with 61% of those incarcerated released from state prison arrested within 5 years of release (Durose & Antenangelo, 2021). This pattern has been observed over time and in different contexts, including diverse countries.

In one famous historical example, criminologists Sheldon Glueck and Eleanor Glueck (1950) examined data on 500 boys involved in delinquency in Boston, which they compared to 500 boys not involved in delinquency in the broader Massachusetts area. The Gluecks found early differences between these two groups of boys in terms of physical traits, emotions, attitudes (e.g., hostile vs. nonhostile), intellectual expressions, and sociocultural aspects (e.g., family structure). Laub and Sampson (2003) later reanalyzed the data, including a follow up with the boys from the original Glueck study (who were now aged 70 years and older). They found that most of the youth had desisted from crime over time due to structural routines, such as a career, and the development of strong ties to the family and community, though a small subset did continue to engage in crime. Laub and Sampson showed the relationship between age and the number of offenses (see Figure 7.1).

Juveniles and Delinquency

Adolescents enter a period of the life course where risk of aggression, violence, and crime may increase. However, much like the Glueck (1950) sample, most adolescents who experiment with delinquent behavior will "age out" and cease to continue a pathway toward crime. A small percentage of "persistent" youth will engage in a lifetime of criminality, with a risk of contact with the justice system. This makes it likely that community corrections will have sizeable caseloads of younger clients—some with relatively minor crimes, and others with more serious felonies. As such, some probation and parole departments work exclusively with juvenile populations. Even in states where juvenile and adult agencies are merged, the philosophical orientations, policies, and practices are distinct to recognize the needs of youth.

Ideally, these community corrections systems engage in partnerships that link juvenile justice, child welfare, education, and other service agencies, along with judicial leadership (Kelley & Haskins, 2021). This includes integrated data systems and pooled resources where

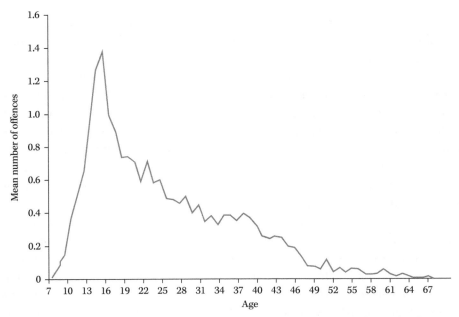

The Gluecks' delinquent sample: actual mean number of offences for total crime (total events = 9,548): ages 7 to 70

FIGURE 7.1 Age-Crime Curve

appropriate. Community corrections should also maintain effective partnerships with the court, as the state can legally intervene in cases where the juvenile is experiencing abuse or neglect from a parent (or legal guardian/caregiver; DeBellis & Soja, 1993). This is the legal doctrine of parens patriae, which is Latin for "parent of the nation" or "parent of one's country." Parens pateriae enables the state to serve as the parent of the juvenile in cases where they need protection and there is an absence of adequate or safe care at home.

A starting point for working with youthful populations under supervision is to recognize that the line between juvenile delinquency and victimization is often blurred. Significant research supports the relationship between **adverse childhood experiences (ACEs)** and juvenile delinquency. Researchers measure ACEs using three categories: abuse (e.g., physical, emotional, sexual), neglect (e.g., physical, emotional), and household dysfunction (e.g., caregiver substance use, caregiver mental illness, caregiver divorce). Exposure to these experiences increases the likelihood that a young person will interact with the community corrections system. These early exposures greatly increase the risk of a young person engaging in serious violent and chronic delinquency (Perez et al., 2018). They also led to a higher risk of general offending, gang involvement, and violent behavior involving the use of weapons (Folk et al., 2020).

There is also a cumulative effect, with a greater number of ACEs being linked to earlier onset of offending, increased number of arrests, and earlier incarceration when compared to justice-involved youth with no reported ACE exposures (Baglivio et al., 2020). ACEs are also thought to increase risk of mental illness, suicidal behaviors, substance use, unwanted pregnancy, and dropping out of school (Clements-Nolle & Waddington, 2019; Lee & Taxman,

2020). This suggests that community corrections must screen and treat existing trauma in youth and adolescent populations, as these factors may be driving delinquency and crime.

In response to the effects of trauma on young people on supervision, the field of community corrections has moved toward providing trauma-informed programs and interventions. The core element of **trauma-informed care (TIC)** for juvenile populations features three domains: clinical services, agency context, and system-level approaches (Branson et al., 2017). *Clinical services* refer to the types and characteristics of the services provided, such as screening and assessment (e.g., screening tools for mental health, posttraumatic stress disorder [PTSD], and trauma exposure), services and interventions (e.g., trauma-specific programs), and cultural competence (e.g., policies, practices, and services to avoid or reduce disparities in race/ethnicity, gender, sexual orientation, developmental level, and socioeconomic status; Branson et al., 2017).

Agency context refers to the characteristics of the service-providing organization and includes youth and family engagement/involvement (e.g., youth access to social support, involving family in planning efforts, referral to address caregiver trauma), workforce development and support (e.g., staff training on trauma-informed principles, staff skill development for working with trauma survivors, education on youth development/behavior), promoting a safe agency environment (e.g., agency policies and practices to maximize physical and psychological safety among youth, families, and staff, avoiding harsh punitive practices that retraumatized youth), and agency policies, procedures, and leadership (e.g., agency leadership and values statements that embrace a trauma-informed approach. *System-level approaches* revolve around cross-system collaboration (e.g., working with other community stakeholders to ensure that trauma-informed services/care are available), system-level policies and procedures (e.g., minimize youth contact with juvenile justice and/or keep them in the least restrictive environment, use trauma-based data for services not punitive punishment), and quality assurance and evaluation (e.g., ongoing data collection to evaluate the process and impact of implementing trauma-informed care; Branson et al., 2017). These domains can be seen in Table 7.2.

There are several benefits of trauma-informed care for juveniles. First, it involves recognition that justice-involved youth have different

TABLE 7.2 Core Domains of Trauma-Informed Care for Juvenile Justice

Area of focus	Domains within this area
Clinical services	1. Screening and assessment
	2. Services and interventions
	3. Cultural competence
Agency context	4. Youth and family engagement/involvement
	5. Workforce development and support
	6. Promoting a safe agency environment
	7. Agency policies, procedures, and leadership
System level	8. Cross-system collaboration
	9. System-level policies and procedures
	10. Quality assurance and evaluation

Source: Branson, C. E., Baetz, C. L., Horwitz, S. M., & Hoagwood, K. E. (2017). Trauma-informed juvenile justice systems: A systematic review of definitions and core components. Psychological Trauma: Theory, Research, Practice and Policy, 9, 643.

developmental transitions, physical, cognitive, emotional, and social risk factors compared to justice-involved adults. Reactions to perceived authority or stress in youth can produce short-term, impulsive decision making. As Ko et al. (2008) state, "when exposed to coercion, cruelty, violence, neglect, or rejection, a child may cope with indifference, defiance of rules and authority, or aggression as a self-protective counterreaction" (p. 400). TIC can slow this decision-making process down and allow for the regulation of emotions, the engagement of prosocial peers, and better strategies for addressing interpersonal conflict. Research suggests TIC reduces trauma-related symptoms, delinquency, and violence (Zettler, 2021). While addressing the risks and needs produced by exposure to trauma, this approach maximizes the existing strengths within the juvenile population.

Related to the need for trauma-informed services is the need for community corrections agencies to establish mentorship programs for justice-involved youth. Most acts of delinquency occur in the context of deviant peer groups, where antisocial attitudes and behaviors are encouraged. Criminologists Richard Cloward and Lloyd Ohlin (1960) explain, "the great bulk of delinquent behavior appears to occur in association rather than isolation from other like-minded persons" (pp. 41–42). Delinquency is also associated with a lack of prosocial parental figures. Mentorship can fill this gap by providing models of prosocial behaviors, offering resources for education, employment, social connections, and establishing positive peer group networks. Even in hard-to-reach groups, such as members of youth gangs, mentorship has demonstrated effectiveness.

In a Canadian study by Weinrath et al. (2016), high-risk youth involved in gangs who were also on probation supervision were guided by pro-social street mentors. The research team found that youth who received mentoring had lower recidivism rates than those who did not receive mentoring. These street mentors were perceived as "credible messengers," as they had previous experiences with gangs, and as such they were considered relatable, trustworthy, and authentic by the youth. The researchers found the mentorship program to be far more effective than the intensive supervision approaches devoid of any mentoring component that is typically offered by probation or parole service. Likewise, other studies identified beneficial effects of mentoring programs for a variety of youth outcomes, including improved social skills and academic performance (Herrera et al., 2002, 2013), reductions in internalizing behaviors (e.g., anxiety) and externalizing behaviors (e.g., aggression; Jackson, 2002), and reductions in antisocial behavior (e.g., delinquency, substance use; Tolan et al., 2014).

Older Justice-Involved Individuals

As introduced in Chapter 1, the "get tough" crime movement of the 1980s led to a significant number of individuals being charged with crime, incarcerated, and placed under the supervision of community corrections. While engagement in crime tends to decline over time, there remains a subgroup of older individuals who continue to persist with criminal activity, and there is a large group of older people who reside in our jails and prisons. For institutional corrections, particularly prisons, the "graying" of an aged resident population increases the need to shift costs to the community. In some cases, older residents have a range of complex medical conditions that require expensive technologies, specialized medical staff, as well as increased staff for transportation to the hospital. Jails and prisons use segregated housing, assisted living with support staff, and hospice units as a means of providing care to older individuals. Other efforts to move this population to community corrections included compassionate release, medical parole, and community corrections alternatives to prison. The diversion of older individuals to community settings allows for the utilization of community resources for physical and mental health needs, often while being supervised by probation or parole.

While there are disagreements about what age is considered an "older" justice-involved individual, what is clear is that community corrections interact with people who may have considerable stress on their minds and bodies. Aday and Krabill (2012) state that when considering background socioeconomic status, lifestyle choices, access to preventive health care, and institutionalization (e.g., mental health hospitals, criminal justice settings), justice-involved individuals are 10–15 years older psychologically than their chronological age. Older justice-involved individuals may have chronic psychiatric, neurological, dermatological, gastrointestinal, respiratory, musculoskeletal, and cardiovascular conditions (Fazel et al., 2004). These conditions are not only uncomfortable but can limit mobility and daily function. This suggests that community corrections agencies need to focus on the health needs of older individuals while also assessing the true risk they pose to the community.

When considering older justice-involved people, it should be noted that the concept of health occurs along a continuum. That is, a person is not healthy or unhealthy but rather functions in terms of a holistic notion of health. The World Health Organization (1948) has long defined *health* as "a state of complete physical, mental and social well-being and not merely the absence of disease or infirmity" (see Kühn, & Rieger, 2017, p. 887). Using this definition, health can be divided into the three interrelated categories of physical, mental, and social health, all of which are relevant for community corrections.

Physical Health

Older justice-involved individuals may have led lifestyles where they had little to no interaction with medical professionals and services, developed dangerous health behaviors (e.g., smoking,

drug abuse), and maintained dysfunctional coping mechanisms in response to stress (e.g., aggression, self-harm). Individuals involved in lifelong offending may have histories of violence, victimization, and neglect that negatively impact their physical health.

Community corrections can facilitate and refer individuals to appropriate medical services to address these needs. While some behaviors are solely health-related

Image 7.2

(e.g., smoking, unhealthy diets, lack of exercise), other behaviors increase direct contact with the community corrections system (e.g., illegal drug use). To develop a better understanding of people on supervision community corrections can screen for functional health status. One example is the Activities of Daily Living (ADL) assessment tool, which assesses challenges in everyday activities for older people, such as bathing, eating, and dressing. Training of officers can also motivate inquiries into the living environment of the older population (particularly the risk of slipping and falling), medication compliance, and the potential of elder abuse.

Mental Health

Common mental health conditions in older populations include depression, anxiety, alcohol/substance use, and personality disorders. However, they may also experience advanced age disorders like Alzheimer's disease and other forms of dementia (Regan et al., 2002). These conditions can impact communication with supervision officers and compliance with community corrections requirements. Officers may have to exhibit patience, empathy, and more deliberate communication strategies with these individuals who have complex behavioral health needs.

Social Health

Older individuals may have outlived their family and friend networks, they may have victimized people close to them, or they may be without employment, housing, and hobbies, resulting in little to no social interactions. Older populations have the smallest social network of any group within the justice system, which can lead to feelings of alienation, isolation, and rejection (Di Lorito et al., 2018). Community corrections can meet these needs via programming that maximizes social interactions, the endorsement of community activities, and a focus on the housing situation of the individual. Social health can also be improved by recreation, hobbies, and volunteerism.

Race and Ethnicity

Race and ethnicity differences in justice-involved individuals are frequently discussed topics in community corrections; however, this often involves confusion over terms. To be accurate, one must first acknowledge key definitions. Here, *race* refers to genetic or biological variations (e.g., skin tone, hair color, facial shape), where *ethnicity* is a socially constructed concept "based on perceptions of shared social experience or one's ancestors' experiences" (People & Bailey, 2010, p. 389). Terms like *nationality*, which become relevant when considering immigration, refer to the legal birthplace or citizenship of the individual. While recognizing that race and ethnicity can be measured using various definitions, the current text uses the U.S. Census Bureau definition, where race and ethnicity are considered separate and distinct identities. As such, race extends beyond one's genetics and biology to include social and cultural characteristics as well as ancestry, with racial and national origin often combined (Office of Management and Budget, 1997).

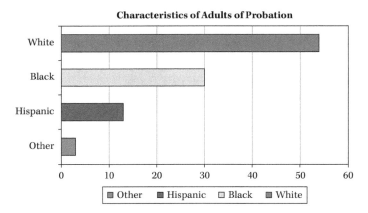

FIGURE 7.2   Characteristics of Adults on Probation
[Based on statistics from Kaeble, 2023]

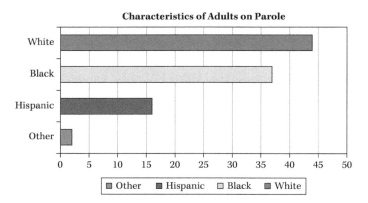

FIGURE 7.3. Characteristics of Adults on Probation
[Based on statistics from Kaeble, 2023]

Racial and ethnic minorities are overrepresented in the U.S. criminal justice system, from contact with law enforcement, to court processes, disproportionate incarceration in jail and prison, and enhanced supervision by probation and parole. Black adults are about 3.5 times as likely as White adults to be supervised by community corrections, and although Black individuals make up 13% of the U.S. adult population, they account for 30% of those on probation or parole (Kaeble, 2023). Ethnic trends are similar, though likely undercount the number of Latinx individuals under the supervision of community corrections due to a lack of consistent and quality data collection (Eppler-Epstein et al., 2016). Racial and ethnic characteristics for probation in 2021 include 54% White, 30% Black, 13% Hispanic, 3% other (i.e., American Indian/Alaska Native, Asian, Native Hawaiian/Other Pacific Islander, and persons of two or more races; Kaeble, 2023). Racial and ethnic characteristics for parole include 44% White, 37% Black, 16% Hispanic, 2% other (Kaeble, 2023). These characteristics can be seen in Figure 7.2 and Figure 7.3.

Racial and ethnic disparities in community corrections can be categorized in terms of legal sentencing and agency/officer decision making. In terms of sentencing, the community corrections system primarily responds to the legal decisions of the courts. In an assessment of 40 studies over a 30-year period on sentencing outcomes at both the state and federal levels, Spohn (2000) found that race and ethnicity played a role in the punitiveness of the sentencing decision:

> Although it is irrefutable that the primary determinants of sentencing decisions are the seriousness of the offense and the offender's prior criminal record, race/ethnicity and other legally irrelevant offender characteristics also play a role. Black and Hispanic

offenders—and particularly those who are young, male, or unemployed—are more likely than their white counterparts to be sentenced to prison; they also may receive longer sentences than similarly situated white offenders. Other categories of racial minorities—those convicted of drug offenses, those who victimize whites, those who accumulate more serious prior criminal records, or those who refuse to plead guilty or are unable to secure pretrial release—also may be singled out for more punitive treatment. (p. 481)

Differences in sentencing also occurred due to the War on Drugs, which targeted racial and ethnic minorities and increased the risk of these populations being placed on community corrections supervision. The classic example of this in action was the 100:1 sentencing disparity in federal sentencing for crack versus powder cocaine offenses. During the mid-1980s, crack cocaine came onto the market, representing a new, cheaper alternative to powder cocaine, which was much more expensive. Crack quickly grew in popularity in street markets in low-income neighborhoods led to increased competition and violence, particularly among juveniles. As a result, there was a sharp growing concern and calls for Congress to act (Blumstein, 2003). The Federal Anti-Drug Abuse Act of 1986 was passed, which implemented much harsher penalties for crack cocaine compared to powder. While crack and powder cocaine are pharmacologically identical, these laws resulted in much harsher penalties assigned to those convicted of offenses relating to crack compared to powder cocaine.

In 1995, the U.S. Sentencing Commission published a report that found White individuals were more likely to be convicted of powder cocaine offenses and Black individuals were more likely to be convicted of crack cocaine offenses. Similarly, a 2002 U.S. Sentencing Commission report found again that 85% of individuals convicted of a crack offense were Black while individuals convicted of powder cocaine offenses were primarily Hispanic (51%) and White (18%). The harsher penalties associated with crack cocaine resulted in more severe punishment disproportionately experienced by Black compared to White defendants for similar offenses (U.S. Sentencing Commission, 1995). These disparate sentencing responses directly impacted Black individuals, who constituted 80% of those sentenced under federal crack cocaine laws each year (The Sentencing Project, 2013). In 2010, the Fair Sentencing Act was passed and that reduced the penalties from 100:1 to 18:1 and eliminated the mandatory minimum sentence requirement for crack cocaine possession. In 2015, the U.S. Sentencing Commission published a report that found a reduction in the number of individuals prosecuted for crack cocaine, although the overall number remained high. Additionally, they found that while the average sentence imposed for those convicted of crack cocaine offenses were still higher compared to sentences imposed for powder cocaine offenses, which have remained relatively stable (see Figure 7.4).

While the Fair Sentencing Act is a step in the right direction, advocates for reform suggest several additional avenues. A report by The Sentencing Project (2013) called for Supreme Court decisions that recognize racial and ethnic biases throughout the criminal justice system, specifically by increasing the discretion that law enforcement is afforded and lowering the

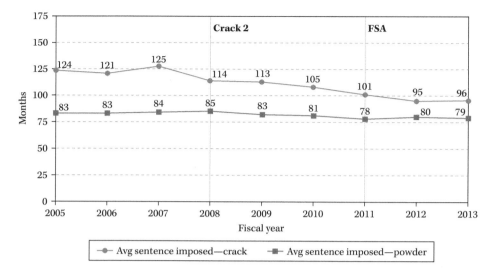

FIGURE 7.4   Average Sentences for Crack compared to Powder Cocainea

standard for indigent defense counsel for individuals convicted of a crime. The report calls for the establishment of a National Criminal Justice Commission for systematic reform, further scaling back of the War on Drugs, the elimination of mandatory minimum sentences, abolishing capital punishment, funding indigent defense agencies, adopting policies requiring the use of racial impact statements, reforming trials to recognize racial bias, addressing racial profiling through legislation, developing and implementing training to reduce racial bias for criminal justice practitioners, and adopting racial disparity-conscious policies.

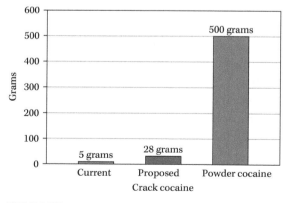

FIGURE 7.5   Amount of Cocaine for Mandatory Minimum 5-Year Sentence

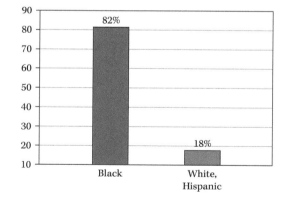

FIGURE 7.6   Crack Cocaine Offenders, 2006

The second element to address racial and ethnic disparities involves the decision-making processes of probation and parole agencies (and their officers). As Bowman (2012) states,

"The underlying characteristics of race, ethnicity, and nationality can produce language barriers, cultural misinterpretations and conflicts, mistrust, and non-maximizing outcomes for community corrections practitioners that directly affect offenders, family members, and community members" (p. 101). Community corrections agencies can promote training that supports cultural understanding, provide support for linguistic challenges, and address implicit racial/ethnic bias that officers may possess. These efforts can also include collaborations and partnerships with cultural groups in the community. Such training can be educational and interesting to officers, as they provide knowledge on the historical development of different cultures over time, leading to how certain stereotypes have manifested. Training can promote cooperative efforts that strengthen community partners. While such initiatives may appear theoretical, they should include measurement. For example, racial and ethnic disparities in parole can be measured along key points, such as parole release assessments, parole release plans and conditions, monitoring of parole compliance, and decisions to violate a parole sentence for noncompliance (Schrantz & McElroy, 2000). Areas of apparent disparity can be further reviewed by a team of parole administrators, parole commissioners, parole officers, supervisors and managers, parolee representatives, researchers, and community members (Schrantz & McElroy, 2000).

◊ Diversity, Equity, and Inclusion: Cultural Competency

The work performance of community corrections officers can be reinforced by training in **cultural competency**. Hoy-Watkins (2012) states that "in order to facilitate effective community-based interventions, services must be delivered in a culturally competent manner. It is important that community corrections staff provide services that meet the needs of their diverse offender populations" (p. 117). Strategies include having a diverse correctional staff that clients can relate to, using the preferred language of client populations when possible, and utilizing unique cultural communication behaviors (e.g., degree of eye contact, closeness of body distance). It is thought that increases in cultural competency can increase individual compliance with probation and parole requirements. One of the most important considerations is cultural differences regarding individualistic versus community interactions. While some individuals may prefer to complete their community corrections supervision period individually, others may be more culturally inclined to participate in a group, family, or community setting.

One way of explaining cultural competency is through the illustration of how the community corrections system works with American Indian and Alaska Native populations. These populations adhere to *tribal justice*, which provides sovereignty to tribal court systems, policing, and community corrections to maintain cultural values. Tribal justice involves the use of restorative justice practices that rely on community participation. This can be seen in a quote from Chief Justice Robert Yazzie of the Navajo Nation: "think of a system with an end goal of restorative justice, which uses equality and the full participation of disputants in a final decision. If we say of law that: 'life comes from it,' then where there is hurt, there must be healing" (see Sanchez, 2020, p. 70).

Tribal justice avoids the current U.S. punitive approach to justice and favors alternatives that center on dispute resolution and community mediation. As Sanchez (2020) suggests, "These justice systems are important to Indian victims to allow healing to the individual, the community, and even the offender" (p. 71). While Indian tribes are not a monolith, they generally do not differentiate between crimes that harm the community and the individual (in contrast to American legal theory), with many tribes viewing these concepts as entwined. Another difference is that American law codifies social values into texts, like the U.S. Constitution, where Indian legal systems contain oral, spiritual, and storytelling exercises that highlight social norms (Sanchez, 2020). As such, Indian legal procedures may feature circle sentencing, community participation, and a victim-centric approach. Sanchez (2020) provides insight into a peacemaking court proceeding as conducted by the Navajo Nation:

> The procedure of the peacemaking court is specific to the Navajo Nation—beginning with a prayer and asking for help from the creator for a successful ceremony. The purpose of the prayer is to bring an energy to the room that arouses focus and energizes people's intention so that they can identify the disharmony. Those who are present are encouraged to express their feelings and state what they think caused the problem. After the attitudes and feelings of the participants have been expressed and acknowledged, an elder or peacemaker gives their guidance in a form of a lecture to the disputants. When each person knows each other's feelings, and has heard the values and traditions of their people, they are ready to begin discussing how to resolve the dispute. The resolution plan should compensate and sufficiently restore good feelings to all those who are concerned. (p. 92)

While these forms of community corrections may appear unusual, they are part of the national system of justice. They serve as a reminder that cultural competency is an important skill for community corrections officers when meeting the needs of diverse and often vulnerable populations. Not only can officers be trained to recognize divergent legal and community norms and justice practices, but they can maximize outcomes for multiple parties. In the example of tribal justice, this means stressing the underlying values of traditional spirituality, self-governance, community participation, restorative justice practices (e.g., circle sentencing), and elevating the victim to be the central component of all processes.

Undocumented Immigrants

Undocumented immigrants represent a sizeable portion of society, with some placed under the supervision of community corrections. The term *undocumented immigrant* refers to foreign nationals residing in the United States without legal immigration status. This definition includes persons who entered the United States without inspection and proper permission from the U.S. government and those who entered with a legal visa that is no longer valid.

For community corrections, addressing the risks and needs of undocumented immigrants is a complex and confusing task. Undocumented immigrants on supervision may have an inherent mistrust of government agencies, particularly due to fear of deportation (as many have established families, jobs, and social ties to the United States). For community corrections officers, they may struggle between utilizing a law enforcement orientation (as the individual is not a legal citizen) and a social welfare orientation (addressing the risks and needs of the individual). For example, officers likely need to find ways to address the social welfare needs of the individual while also navigating the legal complexities related to immigration status, which may involve collaborating with immigration authorities and legal resources. Kincaid (2008) surveyed American Probation and Parole Association (APPA) members and found that state agencies did not receive budgetary assistance from the federal government to supervise individuals who may experience special difficulties such as language barriers in communication, cultural competency training for officers, and an increased need to educate immigrant populations on the basics of the U.S. justice system.

Supervision of undocumented populations, who often do not speak English, places additional burdens on probation and parole officers who may need to communicate with federal officials and work with an interpreter to conduct interviews, write reports, and attend court hearings. Chapter 4 highlights the challenging daily activities of these officers, which can become even more difficult when facing language barriers. Language becomes a very basic though crucial factor, as Jensen (2002) explains in the context of probation: "when working through an interpreter, nuances can be missed and intuition based on language clues is frequently lost. At times, cultural differences and misunderstandings by the interpreter interfere with a good interview" (p. 257). Community corrections agencies may have staff who are fluent in Spanish, though challenges arise when language needs become more diverse. Moreover, the placement of clients into community services, job training, substance use groups, and mental health treatment may also require interpreter services. One should also note that undocumented immigrants are not evenly spread across the United States. In fact, 45% of immigrants reside in three states—California (24%), Texas (11%), and Florida (10%)—and 20 metropolitan areas contain almost 64% of the nation's foreign-born population (Budiman, 2020). While larger metropolitan areas may offer greater access to English-as-a-second-language (ESL) courses, bilingual programs, and culturally competent interpreters in the community, these resources are often not easily accessible in rural and remote areas.

To supervise undocumented immigrant populations appropriately, community corrections will likely need federal-based policies for guidance. Currently, states and their political leaders have significant differences in the rhetoric, policies, and treatment of undocumented immigrants. While the federal government acknowledges that the criminal justice system is responsible for the prosecution and potential deportation of undocumented immigrants, there is little guidance, financial support, or integration with immigration systems to enforce this punitive approach. As a result, community corrections agencies and officers frequently ignore the legal status of their clients and focus on addressing risks and needs (much like any other client group) while also balancing ethical quandaries. One officer highlighted this in the following quote:

> Please note that we are dealing with human beings not "aliens." We also lack cultural understanding in order to deal appropriately with this population. Additionally, as

probation officers, we require probationers to comply with conditions which are contradictory to what they are legally able to do, e.g., to be gainfully employed. (Kincaid, 2008, p. 98)

Gender

Gender is a concept that depends on the context of social structures (e.g., gender roles) and gender identity, particularly with regard to characteristics of being masculine or feminine (Udry, 1994). Researchers have long noted a relationship between gender and crime. For example, when Robert Agnew (2012) was developing general strain theory, he found that male individuals were more likely to respond to adversity and strain by externalizing feelings of anger. Male individuals were socialized to be less concerned about angry expressions appearing to be a loss of control or harmful to relationships (Grothoff et al., 2014). In contrast, female individuals were more likely to respond to strain by internalizing emotions (e.g., guilt, fear, anxiety, depression), blaming themselves, and being more concerned with the potential to damage relationships. These generalized differences were thought to lead to differences in expressions of aggression, which in turn can partially explain engagement in violence and crime. While representing a fraction of the potential differences in gender, it does draw attention to the roles that are expected within masculine and feminine stereotypes.

Male Justice-Involved Individuals

Male individuals represent most justice-involved individuals and victims. They also disproportionately receive harsher sentencing, including greater likelihood of placement on community corrections supervision. Male individuals are often perceived as being more violent, risk taking, and less compliant with community corrections requirements. In 2020, male individuals constituted 76% of all individuals on probation, compared to 24% female individuals and 88% of all individuals on parole, compared to 12% female (Kaeble, 2023). There are now an estimated 2,251,880 male individuals on probation and 706,816 male individuals on parole in the United States, for a total of 2,958,696 male individuals under community supervision (Kaeble, 2023).

James Messerschmidt (1993), a leading researcher on gender and crime, argues that crime is essentially the act of "doing masculinity," where male individuals make efforts at establishing their masculine identifies using their available resources. While masculinity is a fluid concept, the term *hegemonic masculinity* refers to values of power, control, competition, and emotional suppression (Evans & Wallace, 2008). Such a perspective also endorses displays of strength, authority, heterosexuality, independence, and tolerance of violence (Connell, 2014). If a male individual adheres to hegemonic masculinity, then there could be poor outcomes when interacting with community corrections. This is because programs and services may oppose these values by encouraging dialogue and openness when communicating with an officer, expressing emotions and cooperation in group sessions, or avoiding the use of violence as a problem-solving strategy.

Male individuals who have previously experienced incarceration may be particularly vulnerable, as "prison is a place in which those who do not conform to these ideals are punished and forced to renegotiate their thoughts on how to be a real man" (Morse & Wright, 2019, p. 23). For officers, education and training can help with understanding expressions of masculinity, where expressions of aggression and anger (though not violence) could be interpreted as the suppression of emotions and lack of emotional language. Other barriers that officers can address are perspectives that rigid forms of masculinity tend to reduce the acceptance of support, verbal engagement in group therapies, and admissions of weaknesses (e.g., financial, educational status, housing). For some male justice-involved individuals, connections between early trauma, crime, and masculinities can also lead to breakthroughs that can facilitate openness to change, engagement in programs, and seeking prosocial connections. This can be seen in the following quote:

> If a person is a drug addict, or a person's an alcoholic, and that person maybe was abused as a child, whether sexually, emotionally, or physically, for them to deal with those emotions, it's traumatizing 'cause you have to go back to that point and deal with it. But if you've been told all along you don't deal with emotions, you don't have feelings, feelings are for girls and things like that, you got to break that barrier, you got to, 'cause you have to go back there and say, "Hey, this wasn't my fault, the person that hurt me was a bad person. It didn't have to define me though and, this is what it did to me." And then I can start moving forward and building upon that. (Morse & Wright, 2019, p. 13)

Female Justice-Involved Individuals

While male individuals constitute the majority of the justice-involved population and victims in the criminal justice system, there is increasing recognition of the presence of system-involved female individuals. There is also evidence that the number of justice-involved female individuals is growing, with 26,378 women being housed in federal and state prisons and jails in 1980, compared to 213,722 incarcerated female individuals by 2016 (Cahalan & Parson, 1986; Carson, 2018). Due to the "get tough" period of criminal justice policy, the 1980–2000 time period alone featured a 7-fold increase in the rate of female incarceration (Chesney-Lind & Pasko, 2004). Mumola (2000) highlights that most of these incarcerated female individuals (55% in state facilities and 63% in federal facilities) had a child under the age of 18, which equated to 1,498,800 children with an incarcerated mother. For community corrections, these estimates have stabilized over recent decades. There are now an estimated 711,120 female individuals on probation and 96,384 female individuals on parole in the United States (Kaeble, 2023).

Female individuals are generally associated with different types of crimes when compared to their male counterparts. Female individuals are arrested more often for sex work/prostitution (disorderly conduct and vagrancy), property crimes (larceny, embezzlement, forgery, and fraud), substance use (driving under the influence, drugs, and liquor law violations) and simple assault (Keena, 2012). While female individuals are less likely than male individuals to engage in serious personal crimes like homicide, rape, robbery, and burglary, the number of female individuals convicted of these crimes has increased in recent years. These differences reflect the unique pathways that female individuals have with crime, incarceration, and community corrections. Feminist scholar Daly (1992) studied "street women" in felony court and found a dominant female pathway:

> Whether they were pushed out or ran away from abusive homes, or became part of a deviant milieu, young women begin to engage in petty hustles or prostitution. Life on the street leads to drug use and addiction, which in turn leads to more frequent law-breaking to support a drug habit. Meanwhile, young women drop out of high school because of pregnancy, boredom, or disinterest in school, or both. Their paid employment record is negligible because they lack interest to work in low-paid or unskilled jobs. Having a child may facilitate entry to adult women's networks and allow a woman to support herself, in part, by state aid. A woman may continue lawbreaking as a result of relationships with men who may also be involved in crime. Women are on a revolving criminal justice door, moving between incarceration and time on the streets. (pp. 13–14)

Daly (1994) later added four additional pathways that justice-involved females may experience. This included harmed and harming women (e.g., women who had suggested neglect, physical and/or sexual abuse in traumatic childhood homes, and later used drugs and alcohol to cope, and engaged in aggressive or violent acts), drug-connected women (e.g., women who used or sold drugs as a component of a relationship such as family or partner), battered women (e.g., women in a violent relationships with a partner, a topic explored more in Chapter 9), and other women (e.g., not addicted to drugs nor traumatic childhoods but rather a desire for a secure, comfortable lifestyle). While not an exhaustive characterization of justice-involved females, this early typology does highlight the unique pathways that female individuals may take, especially in terms of the role of relationships with family, partners, and children.

The unique pathways to crime for female individuals are often not addressed in community corrections practice. Instead, responses are typically based on the typical risks and needs of male populations, thus creating a disconnection between theory and practice, as well as a lower chance of positive outcomes. While female and male populations disproportionately experience physical and mental health issues, there are unique needs of women. For example, female individuals on supervision require access to health care, particularly OB/GYN services with regular pap smears. Community corrections may supervise women who are pregnant, and a lack of prenatal care can place these women at increased risk for a complicated and high-risk pregnancy. The pressures of childcare can increase guilt, anxiety, and depression while also reducing opportunities to seek education and seek employment. This can reduce the likelihood of female clients to arrange required meetings with a probation or parole officer, group therapy sessions, or having the energy to actively participate, thus limiting compliance with a community correction sentence.

To address these risks and needs, the field of community corrections has moved toward the use of gender-responsive programming. This begins with policies and practices that recognize gender differences and includes training for officers and staff to provide best practices. The guiding principles of gender responsive programming can be seen in Table 7.3.

TABLE 7.3 Guiding Principles for Implementing Gender-Responsive Strategies for Justice-Involved Women

Principle 1: Gender
Acknowledge that gender makes a difference.
Principle 2: Environment
Create an environment based on safety, respect, and dignity.
Principle 3: Relationships
Develop policies, practices, and programs that are relational and promote healthy connections to children, family, significant others, and the community.
Principle 4: Services and supervision
Address substance use, trauma, and mental health issues through comprehensive, integrated, and culturally relevant services and appropriate supervision.
Principle 5: Socioeconomic status
Provide women with opportunities to improve their socioeconomic conditions.
Principle 6: Community
Establish a system of community supervision and reentry with comprehensive, collaborative services.

Source: Bloom, B., Owen, B., and Covington, S. (2003). *Gender-responsive strategies: Research, practice, and guiding principles for women offenders.* U.S. Department of Justice, National Institute of Corrections, p. 76.

For female probation or parole clients who have been incarcerated, there is an additional burden. If they are mothers, there is an expectation for them to reunify with children and immediately provide financial and emotional support. In some cases, these children may have been placed in foster care or state custody, with the mother having to demonstrate economic, housing, and childcare stability to gain custody of them. These factors become important for community corrections, as risk-assessment tools may be skewed toward male populations, thus not recognizing these unique needs. These tools may recommend a series of probation or parole obligations that are unattainable for female clients. Some agencies recognize these limitations and use different risk assessments for female clients than those used for male clients. Addressing identified risks and needs typically requires multiple systems that can offer a comprehensive range of assistance to women (e.g., education, housing, job training/ employment, transportation, family reunification, childcare, drug and alcohol treatment, peer support, and aftercare).

A critical component of gender-responsive programming is the recognition that staff require additional, specific training to successfully deliver these types of programs. The increased need of female clients to share details of their lives, including significant needs, often centers on the communication skills of the officer. Officers must balance their "listening skills" with each client, with time management skills to process their caseload efficiently. This balance is negotiated throughout the entire criminal justice system and is a skill not often learned in training, but rather on the job.

Gender Identity and Sexual Orientation

Community corrections has recently moved toward a greater understanding of the concepts of gender identity and sexual orientation. *Gender identity* refers to the personal sense of one's gender, which can correlate with a person's assigned sex at birth or differ from it (Morrow, 2006). *Sexual orientation* is defined as "a multidimensional construct encompassing emotional, romantic, and sexual attraction, identity, and behavior" (Dalke, 2022, p. 3). For community corrections, these concepts are most relevant to supervised populations who identify as LGBTQIA+ (i.e., lesbian, gay, bisexual, transgender, queer or questioning, intersex, asexual, and other gender and sexual identities that letters and words cannot yet fully describe). LGBTQIA+ populations may experience negative and inequitable treatment, including harassment, discrimination, and violence. These events can impact all domains of life, including health and access to health care services, economic and educational achievement, and family and social support.

For LGBTQIA+ populations in the community corrections system, there is a need to have trust and feelings of safety to communicate. Officers should be aware that this group has likely experienced discrimination and may be isolated from the community. Community corrections officers should be trained in the basics regarding hate crime legislation. *Hate crimes*, or bias crimes, involve an individual who enacts a crime driven by prejudice and the victim is targeted because of their membership (or perceived membership) of a certain social demographic (Streissguth, 2009). LGBTQIA+ clients will be more likely to experience victimization related to their sexual and/or gender identity. Persons who identify as lesbian or gay experience violent victimization more than twice the rate of persons who identify as straight (Truman & Morgan, 2020). Likewise, the rate of violent victimization against transgender persons is 2.5 times the rate among cisgender persons (Truman & Morgan, 2020). Bisexual people have the highest rates of victimization, with very high rates of intimate partner violence, and bisexual female individuals experience violence at rates eight times higher than heterosexual female individuals (Truman & Morgan, 2020). Victims who identify as being bisexual were also far less likely to report victimization to police, citing that the crime is a personal or private matter, not wanting to get the individual in legal trouble, or their belief that police are ineffective. This highlights the need for developing trust between criminal justice agencies and the LGBTQIA+ community. These victimization rates can be seen in Figure 7.7.

Officers have the responsibility of addressing client concerns about their safety in the community due to sexual or gender identity. This may involve protecting individual privacy and information, recognizing the need for violence prevention, and providing access to safe housing. Education of officers can improve knowledge about the differences between gender identity (e.g., the identification of a particular gender, regardless of physical sex characteristics) and sexual orientation (e.g., whom a person is emotionally and physically attracted to). This begins with the respectful use of the correct name and use of appropriate personal pronouns. Probation and parole agencies can partner with community groups to better provide medical care, advocacy, and protection from harm. For example, the advocacy group Transgender Law Center and the American Civil Liberties Union (ACLU) work with community corrections to ensure

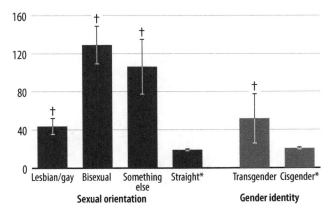

*Comparison group.
†Difference with comparison group is significant at the 95% confidence level.
Source: Bureau of Justice Statistics, National Crime Victimization Survey, 2017–20.

FIGURE 7.7   Rate of Violent Victimization, by Sexual Orientation and Gender Identity, 2017–2020

that "all individuals in community corrections be screened for sexual orientation and transgender identity in order to prevent potential harassment as well as unnecessary limitation to program involvement" (Kris Gowen, 2012, p. 417).

Community corrections can also meet the risks and needs of a particularly vulnerable populations—that is, LGBTQIA+ individuals who due to a lack of social support, resources, and access to society, may turn to "survival crimes" like prostitution, selling drugs, and petty theft as a last resort (see case study on Jasmine in Chapter 1). The Human Rights Campaign (n.d.) provides awareness, advocacy, and training regarding transgender people who turn to sex work when no other work or housing exists (Sausa et al., 2007). While transgender sex workers may encounter community corrections after being charged with prostitution and other crimes, officers should be aware that these individuals face extremely high rates of victimization, including life-threatening violence and death. This suggests that community corrections may have to extend the search for resources beyond the local community and access national-level human rights and advocacy groups to maximize outcomes for this vulnerable population. The following case study provides an example of how a probation or parole officer might provide a trauma-informed supervision approach.

Case Study: Supervising an LGBTQIA+ Population Using Trauma-Informed Care

Rebecca is a 26-year-old lesbian, transgender woman. Throughout her life, she experienced discrimination and harassment due to her gender identity and sexual orientation. One night, when Samantha was out with her friends, she was physically and verbally abused by another group

Image 7.3

of people. As a result of these experiences, Rebecca developed anxiety and depression and began using drugs as a coping mechanism. Unfortunately, this led to her arrest and subsequent placement on probation for a nonviolent drug offense. This was a wake-up call for Rebecca. She has been working hard while on probation to make positive changes in her life. She is enrolled in a drug treatment program where she is doing well. She has stable housing and is looking for full-time employment. However, her past trauma has made her self-conscious and distrusting of others, including her probation officer.

Rebecca's probation officer is trained in trauma-informed care. Since he met Rebecca, he could tell that she was not forthcoming with him. She shared very little and seemed very nervous and timid. He approached her case with sensitivity as well as respect for her identity as a transgender woman. He asked many open-ended questions and encouraged Rebecca to share her thoughts and experiences. He avoids making assumptions or judgments and tries to create a safe environment in which she is comfortable expressing her needs and concerns.

After several months on probation, Rebecca disclosed the details of the past hate crimes she experienced and how they have affected her mental health and well-being. She expressed fear and anxiety about being in public. She told her probation officer she felt like a target for violence. Rebecca also shared that she has not received any support or resources to help her deal with the trauma she experienced. Her probation officer linked her with a therapist who specializes in trauma and LGBTQIA+ clients. Next, he provided her with information on local support groups and resources for transgender individuals. Finally, he worked with Rebecca to develop a safety plan to help her feel safer and more secure when she is in public. By using this holistic, trauma-informed care approach, Rebecca's probation officer can support her to make positive changes in her life, find strategies to cope with her anxiety and depression, and increase the likelihood she will refrain from future involvement in the justice system.

◊ Officer Work, Careers, and Wellness: Vicarious Victimization

The negative impact of trauma extends beyond justice-involved individuals. In recent years, there has been growing attention to the trauma experienced by community corrections staff as well. While completing daily tasks, these staff interact with justice-involved individuals and victims who discuss traumatic events, violence, and other harmful elements of crime (Branson et al., 2017). Some officers may even respond to real-world events that have mass casualties and other highly disturbing elements. As a result, officers can experience *vicarious victimization*, which occurs when an individual witnesses or hears about the victimization of others that then induces fear of future victimization of self or others (Kort-Butler, 2010). Vicarious victimization is linked to a range of negative outcomes, such as a negative worldview, decreases in mental health, and poor job performance. These outcomes are found in staff working in law enforcement, courts, prisons and jails, community corrections, victim services, emergency medical services, fire services, and other allied professions, mainly due to their repeated exposure to people who experienced trauma. One study that included parole officers found that 80.5% of respondents had been exposed to trauma through their work and that this had impacted their personal lives in some way (Union of Solicitor General Employees, June 2017). These parole officers reported insomnia, nightmares, depression, increased consumption of alcohol and drugs, and/or unhealthy eating habits.

The Office for Victims of Crime (n.d.) has developed a toolkit for assisting officers who experience vicarious victimization. This begins with recognition that some staff will be more susceptible to vicarious victimization, particularly those with (a) prior traumatic experiences, (b) social isolation (both on and off the job), (c) a tendency to avoid feelings, withdraw, or assign blame to others in stressful situations, (d) difficulty expressing feelings, (e) a lack of preparation, orientation, training, and supervision in their jobs, (f) less tenure on the job and who were less experienced, (g) constant and intense exposure to trauma with little or no variation in work tasks, and (h) a lack of an effective and supportive process for discussing traumatic content of their work. The Office for Victims of Crime highlights that not all staff responses will be the same. Some may respond in a positive manner by developing vicarious resilience that strengthens their own mental and emotional fortitude. This may also include compassion satisfaction, which reflects a sense of meaning gained from working in the field of community corrections. In these situations, officers respond positively to trauma, resulting in transformation and/or motivation.

Other staff may respond to trauma in a neutral manner, using resilience, past experiences, support, and coping strategies to manage the traumatic material. Of course, some staff may have negative responses to vicarious victimization. This can include secondary traumatic stress (STS), compassion fatigue (CF), and critical incident stress (CIS). More specific negative reactions include emotional disturbances (e.g., anxiety, feeling numb, excessive worry, irritability, aggressiveness, outbursts), chronic fatigue and sleep disorders, physical problems or complaints (e.g., aches, pains, and decreased resistance to illness), distracted and confusing decision making, relationship problems (e.g., withdrawing from friends and family, increased interpersonal conflicts, avoiding intimacy), destructive coping or addictive behaviors (e.g., over/under eating, substance use, gambling, taking undue risks in sports or driving), and a lack of or decreased participation in activities that used to be enjoyable (Office for Victims of Crime, n.d.). Officers may become burned out and cynical at work, take more sick days, and avoid interactions with justice-involved individuals. If untreated, vicarious victimization can lead to a loss of a sense of meaning in life and/or feeling hopeless about the future, suicidal thoughts and behaviors, and a combination of symptoms that comprise a diagnosis of post-traumatic stress disorder (PTSD). This can be seen in Figure 7.8.

Solutions to addressing the negative impact of vicarious victimization are multifaceted. Education of officers, along with mental health screening, can help them recognize the warning

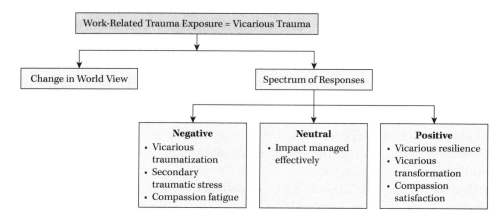

FIGURE 7.8 Vicarious Trauma Toolkit Model

signs of vicarious victimization. Also, an agency culture that endorses mental health, wellness, and resiliency responses to trauma will be more likely to encourage officers seeking help and support them prior to and following a crisis. Family members play an important role, as probation and parole officers may be reluctant to share "war stories" from work, leading to them becoming more withdrawn and isolated. Family members should be willing to engage with the officer, to share concerns, and to offer supportive feedback. The reinforcement of daily routines and work breaks to engage in social, creative, and self-care activities is fundamental (Office for Victims of Crime, n.d.). An often-overlooked component of officer well-being is the development and maintenance of social connections outside of immediate coworkers. This is a challenge in the field as there is a tendency for some community corrections officers to primarily interact with fellow officers. However, coworkers can provide a significant source of social support.

Coworkers can reach out to fellow staff, provide mentoring on the value of maintaining a work–home balance, encourage healthy habits, and support outside connections. Coworkers can also encourage officers to seek help and/or speak with their supervisors about challenges they are experiencing. Supervisors should be aware of officer needs, including their own. This may include developing physical spaces in the agency where officers can retreat to socialize, eat, and, if possible, meditate, read, and reflect. Supervisors should be trained to recognize the symptoms of vicarious victimization and have knowledge of the available resources for officer referral (e.g., both internal and external options). These external resources include large national organizations like the Vicarious Trauma Institute, which has various online resources (https://vicarioustrauma.com/).

SUMMARY: INTERSECTIONALITY AND COMMUNITY CORRECTIONS

The intersectionality framework places an emphasis on the social structure and categorizations that are placed on people and can lead to discrimination, oppression, and alienation. For the community corrections system to function effectively, these differences must be recognized and addressed. In terms of demographics, there are vulnerabilities that emerge by age, race/ethnicity, and gender. These factors create unique pathways to being justice-involved, and the community corrections response can achieve maximize outcomes by addressing these factors. For a number of justice-involved individuals, they may have experience adverse childhood experiences that changed the trajectory of their educational, social, and peer experiences. Community corrections agencies may also supervise or interact with social groups who face substantial oppression, like undocumented immigrants or LGBTQIA+ populations. Programs that reinforce cultural competency in probation and parole officer work represent one step toward sensitivity to unique risks and needs, though more comprehensive efforts are needed. Officers also benefit from programs and training that address their own risk of vicarious victimization that they may be exposed to as part of their work.

Scenario-Based Activities

	Case	Question(s)
1.	Pretend you are a juvenile probation officer. You currently have a 16-year-old on your caseload who was convicted of vandalism and assault. The youth has a history of behavioral problems and has experienced significant trauma, including physical abuse from a parent and witnessing domestic violence.	As a probation officer who provides trauma-informed care, how would you approach this case? How would you ensure the youth receives appropriate support while on supervision?
2.	Pretend you are a criminal justice researcher studying racial disparities in the crack cocaine 100:1 sentencing law. Your research shows that despite similar rates of drug use between Black and White individuals, Black individuals are disproportionately impacted by the harsh sentencing laws for crack cocaine offenses.	Using the findings of your research, develop suggestions for policymakers to address these racial disparities in the criminal justice system.

References

Aday, L. A. (1994). Health status of vulnerable populations. *Annual Review of Public Health*, *15*(1), 487–509. https://doi.org/10.1146/annurev.pu.15.050194.002415

Aday, R., & Krabill, J. (2012). Older and geriatric offenders: Critical issues for the 21st century. In L. Gideon (Ed.), Special needs offenders in correctional institutions (pp. 203–233). Thousand Oaks, CA: Sage Publications.

Agnew, R. (2012). Reflection on "A Revised Strain Theory of Delinquency." *Social Forces*, *91*(1), 33–38. https://doi.org/10.1093/Sf/Sos117

Baglivio, M. T., Wolff, K. T., DeLisi, M., & Jackowski, K. (2020). The role of adverse childhood experiences (ACEs) and psychopathic features on juvenile offending criminal careers to age 18. *Youth Violence and Juvenile Justice*, *18*(4), 337–364. https://doi.org/10.1177/1541204020927075

Bloom, B., Owen, B., & Covington, S. (2003). *Gender responsive strategies: Research, practice, and guiding principles for women offenders*. U.S. Department of Justice, National Institute of Corrections.

Blumstein, A. (2003). The notorious 100: 1 Crack: powder disparity—the data tell us that it is time to restore the balance. *Federal Sentencing Reporter*, *16*(1), 87–92. https://doi.org/10.1525/fsr.2003.16.1.87.

Borders, M. (2013, March 20). *Badass interview: Kathleen Hanna and Sini Anderson on SXSW's* The Punk Singer. BirthMoviesDeath. https://birthmoviesdeath.com/2013/03/20/badass-interview-kathleen-hanna-and-sini-anderson-on-sxsws-the-punk-singer

Bowman, S. (2012). Cultural competence. In S. M. Barton-Bellessa (Ed.), *Encyclopedia of community corrections* (Vol. 1, pp. 101–103). Thousand Oaks, CA: SAGE Publications.

Branson, C. E., Baetz, C. L., Horwitz, S. M., & Hoagwood, K. E. (2017). Trauma-informed juvenile justice systems: A systematic review of definitions and core components. *Psychological Trauma: Theory, Research, Practice and Policy*, *9*(6), 635–646. https://doi.org/10.1101/2022.07.09.22277443

Budiman, A. (2020). *Key findings about U.S. immigrants*. Pew Research Center. https://www.pewresearch.org/fact-tank/2020/08/20/key-findings-about-u-s-immigrants/

Cahalan, M. W., & Parsons, L. A. (1986). *Historical corrections statistics in the United States, 1850–1984*. U.S. Department of Justice, Bureau of Justice Statistics. https://www.bjs.gov/content/pub/pdf/hcsus5084.pdf.

Carson, E. A. (2020). *Prisoners in 2018*. Bureau of Justice Statistics, Office of Justice Programs, The U.S. Department of Justice. https://bjs.ojp.gov/library/publications/prisoners-2018

Chesney-Lind, M., & Pasko, L. (2004). *The female offender: Girls, women, and crime* (*2nd ed.*). Thousand Oaks, CA: SAGE Publications. https://doi.org/10.4135/9781452232157

Clements-Nolle, K., & Waddington, R. (2019). Adverse childhood experiences and psychological distress in juvenile offenders: The protective influence of resilience and youth assets. *Journal of Adolescent Health*, *64*(1), 49–55. https://doi.org/10.1016/j.jado health.2018.09.025

Cloward, R. A., & Ohlin, L. E. (1960). *Delinquency and opportunity*. London: Routledge. https://doi.org/10.4324/9781315007274

Connell, R. W. (2014). *Gender and power: Society, the person and sexual politics*. Stanford, CA: Stanford University Press.

Council of State Governments (2019). *Confined and costly: How supervision violations are filling prisons and burdening budgets*. Justice Center, The Council of State Governments. https://csgjusticecenter.org/wp-content/uploads/2020/01/confined-and-costly.pdf

Dalke, K. (2022). *Measuring sex, gender identity, and sexual orientation*. Washington, D.C.: National Academies Press. https://doi.org/10.17226/26424

Daly, K. (1992). Women's pathways to felony court: Feminist theories of lawbreaking and problems of representation. Southern California *Review of Law and Social Justice*, *2*(1), 11–52.

Daly, K. (1994). *Gender, crime, and punishment*. New Haven, CT: Yale University Press.

DeBellis, C., & Soja, M. (Spring, 1993). Gregory K.: Child standing in parental termination proceedings and the implications of the foster parent–foster child relationship on the best interests standard. *DePaul Law Review, 8*(2), 501–530. https://scholarship.law.stjohns.edu/jcred/vol8/iss2/6/

Di Lorito, C., Dening, T., & Völlm, B. (2018) Ageing in forensic psychiatric secure settings: The voice of older patients. *The Journal of Forensic Psychiatry & Psychology, 29*(6), 934–960. https://doi.org/10.1080/14789949.2018.1513545

Durose, M. R., & Antenangelo, L. (2021). *Recidivism of prisoners released in 34 states in 2012: A 5-year follow-up period (2012–2017).* Bureau of Justice Statistics, Office of Justice Programs, The U.S. Department of Justice.

Eppler-Epstein, S., Gurvis, A., & King, R. (2016). *The alarming lack of data on Latinos in the criminal justice system.* Urban Institute. https://apps.urban.org/features/latino-criminal-justice-data/?language=english

Evans, T., & Wallace, P. (2008). A prison within a prison? The masculinity narratives of male prisoners. *Men and Masculinities, 10*(4), 484–507. https://doi.org/10.1177/1097184X06291903

Fazel, S., Hope, T., O'Donnell, I., & Jacoby, R. (2004). Unmet treatment needs of older prisoners: A primary care survey. *Age and Ageing, 33*(4), 396–398. https://doi.org/10.1093/ageing/afh113

Folk, J. B., Kemp, K., Yurasek, A., Barr-Walker. J., & Tolou-Shams, M. (2020). Adverse childhood experiences among justice-involved youth: Data-driven recommendations for action using the sequential intercept model. *American Psychologist, 76*(2), 268–283. https://doi.org/10.1037/amp0000769

Glueck, S., & Glueck, E. (1950). *Unraveling juvenile delinquency.* New York, NY: Commonwealth Fund.

Grothoff, G. E., Kempf-Leonard, K., & Mullins, C. (2014). Gender and juvenile drug abuse: A general strain theory perspective. *Women & Criminal Justice, 24*(1), 22–43. https://doi.org/10.1080/08974454.2013.842519

Herrera, C., Vang, Z., & Gale, L. Y. (2002). *Group mentoring: A study of mentoring groups in three programs.* Philadelphia, PA: Public/Private Ventures.

Herrera, C., & M. J. Karcher. 2013. School-based mentoring. In *Handbook of Youth Mentoring.* D.L. DuBois & M. J. Karcher, Eds.: 203–220. Thousand Oaks, CA: Sage

Hirschi, T., & Gottfredson, M. R. (1983). Age and the explanation of crime. *American Journal of Sociology, 89*(3), 552–584. https://doi.org/10.1086/227906.

Hoy-Watkins, M. (2012). Diversity in community corrections. In S. M. Barton-Bellessa (Ed.), *Encyclopedia of community corrections* (Vol. 1, pp. 116–120). Thousand Oaks, CA: SAGE Publications.

Human Rights Campaign (n.d.). *Our work.* Human Rights Campaign. Retrieved from https://www.hrc.org/our-work

Jackson, Y. (2002). Mentoring for delinquent children: An outcome study with young adolescent children. *Journal of Youth and Adolescence, 31*(2), 115–122. https://doi.org/10.1023/A:1014017909668

Jensen, M. E. (2002). Reflections of a southwest border probation chief. *Federal Sentencing Reporter, 14*(5), 255–259. https://doi.org/10.1525/fsr.2002.14.5.255

Kaeble, D. (2023). *Probation and parole in the United States, 2021.* Bureau of Justice Statistics, Office of Justice Programs, The U.S. Department of Justice. https://bjs.ojp.gov/library/publications/probation-and-parole-united-states-2021

Keena, L. (2012). Female offenders and special needs. In S. M. Barton-Bellessa (Ed.), *Encyclopedia of community corrections* (Vol. 1, pp. 166–168). Thousand Oaks, CA: SAGE Publications.

Kelley, B. T., & Haskins, P. A. (2021). *Dual system youth: At the intersection of child maltreatment and delinquency.* National Institute of Justice, U.S. Department of Justice. https://www.ojp.gov/pdffiles1/ nij/255646.pdf

Kincaid, D. (2008) Community supervision of undocumented immigrants in the United States: Probation and parole's role in the debate. *Journal of Offender Rehabilitation, 46*(3–4), 91–99. https://doi. org/10.1080/10509670802143334.

Ko, S. J., Ford, J. D., Kassam-Adams, N., Berkowitz, S. J., Wilson, C., & Wong, M. (2008). Creating trauma-informed systems: Child welfare, education, first responders, health care, juvenile justice. *Professional Psychology: Research Practice, 39*(4), 396–404. https://doi.org/10.1037/0735-7028.39.4.396.

Kort-Butler, L. A. (2010). Experienced and vicarious victimization: do social support and self-esteem prevent delinquent responses? *Journal of Criminal Justice, 38*(4), 496–505. https://doi.org/10.1016/j. jcrimjus.2010.04.019

Kris Gowen, L. (2012). Sexual and gender minorities and special needs. In S. M. Barton-Bellessa (Ed.), *Encyclopedia of community corrections* (Vol. 1, pp. 416–418). Thousand Oaks, CA: SAGE Publications.

Kühn, S., & Rieger, U. M. (2017). Health is a state of complete physical, mental and social well-being and not merely absence of disease or infirmity. *Surgery for Obesity and Related Diseases, 13*(5), 887. https://doi.org/10.1016/j.soard.2017.01.046

Laub, J., & Sampson, R. J. (2003). *Shared beginnings, divergent lives: Delinquent boys to age 70.* Cambridge, MA: Harvard University Press. https://doi.org/10.2307/j.ctv1q3z28f.

Lee, J. S., & Taxman, F. S. (2020). Using latent class analysis to identify the complex needs of youth on probation. *Child Youth Services Review, 115,* Article 105087. https://doi.org/10.1016/ j.childyouth.2020.105087

Messerschmidt, J. (1993). *Masculinities and crime: Critique and reconceptualization of theory.* Lanham, MD: Rowman and Littlefield.

Morrow, D. F. (2006). Sexual orientation and gender identity expression. In D. F. Morrow & L. Messinger (Eds.), *Sexual orientation and gender expression in social work practice: Working with gay, lesbian, bisexual, and transgender people* (pp. 3–17). New York, NY: Columbia University Press.

Morse, S. J., & Wright, K. A. (2019). Imprisoned men: Masculinity variability and implications for correctional programming. *Corrections: Policy, Practice and Research, 7*(1), 1–23. https://doi.org/10.10 80/23774657.2019.1694854

Mumola, C. (2000). *Incarcerated parents and their children.* U.S. Department of Justice.

Office of Management and Budget. (1997). *A brief history of the OMB Directive 15. American Anthropological Association Response to OMB Directive 15: Race and ethnic standards for federal statistics and administrative reporting.* http://s3.amazonaws.com/rdcms-aaa/files/production/public/FileDownloads/pdfs/cmtes/minority/upload/AAA_Response_OMB1997.pdf

Office for Victims of Crime. (n.d.). *The Vicarious Trauma Toolkit.* Office of Justice Programs, U.S. Department of Justice. https://ovc.ojp.gov/program/vtt/what-is-vicarious-trauma

People, J., & Bailey, G. (2010). *Humanity: An introduction to cultural anthropology* (9th ed.). Belmont, CA: Wadsworth Cengage learning.

Perez, N. M., Jennings, W. G., & Baglivio, M. T. (2018). A path to serious, violent, chronic delinquency: The harmful aftermath of adverse childhood experiences. *Crime & Delinquency, 64*(1), 3–25. https://doi.org/10.1177/0011128716684806

Quetelet, A. (1831). *Research on the propensity to crime of different ages.* (S. F. Sylvester, Trans.). Anderson Publishing Company.

Regan, J. J., Alderson, A., & Regan, W. M. (2002). Psychiatric disorders in aging prisoners. *Clinical Gerontologist, 26*(1–2), 117–124. https://doi.org/10.1300/J018v26n01_10

Sanchez, N. R. (2020). Out with the new, in with the old: Re-implementing traditional forms of justice in Indian Country. *American Indian Law Journal, 8*(2), 70–104. https://digitalcommons.law.seattleu.edu/ailj/vol8/iss2/3

Sausa, L. A, Keatley, J., & Operario, D. (2007). Perceived risks and benefits of sex work among transgender women of color in San Francisco. *Archives of Sexual Behavior, 36*(6), 768–777. https://doi.org/10.1007/s10508-007-9210-3

Schrantz, D., & McElroy, J. (2000). *Reducing racial disparity in the criminal justice system: A manual for practitioners and policy makers.* The Sentencing Project. https://www.sentencingproject.org/wp-content/uploads/2016/01/Reducing-Racial-Disparity-in-the-Criminal-Justice-System-A-Manual-for-Practitioners-and-Policymakers.pdf

The Sentencing Project. (2013). *Report of The Sentencing Project to the United Nations Human Rights Committee: Regarding racial disparities in the United States criminal justice system.* https://www.sentencingproject.org/reports/report-to-the-united-nations-on-racial-disparities-in-the-u-s-criminal-justice-system/

Spohn, C. (2000). *Thirty years of sentencing reform: The quest for a racially neutral sentencing process.* National Institute of Justice, U.S. Department of Justice. http://www.justicestudies.com/pubs/livelink3-1.pdf

Stolzenberg, L., & D'Alessio, S. J. (2008). Co-offending and the age-crime curve. *Journal of Research in Crime and Delinquency, 45*(1), 65–86. https://doi.org/10.1177/0022427807309441

Streissguth, T. (2009). *Hate crimes.* New York, NY: Facts on File.

Sydney, L. (2005, October). *Gender-responsive strategies for women offenders.* National Institute of Corrections, U.S. Department of Justice. https://info.nicic.gov/nicrp/system/files/020419.pdf

Tolan, P. H., Henry, D. B., Schoeny, M. S., Lovegrove, P., & Nichols, E. (2014). Mentoring programs to affect delinquency and associated outcomes of youth at risk: A comprehensive meta-analytic review. *Journal of Experimental Criminology, 10*(2), 179–206. https://doi.org/10.1007/s11292-013-9181-4.

Truman, J .L., & Morgan, R. E. (2020). *Violent victimization by sexual orientation and gender identity, 2017–2020.* Bureau of Justice Statistics. https://bjs.ojp.gov/library/publications/violent-victimization-sexual-orientation-and-gender-identity-2017-2020

Udry, J. R. (1994). The nature of gender. *Demography, 31*(4), 561–573. https://doi.org/10.2307/2061790

Union of Solicitor General Employees. (2017, June). *Moving forward: A report on the invisible psychological trauma on federal public safety workers.* Ottawa, Ontarion.

United States Sentencing Commission. (1995). *Special Report to Congress: Cocaine and Federal Sentencing Policy.* Washington, D.C.

United States Sentencing Commission. (2002). *2002 Report to the Congress: Federal Cocaine Sentencing Policy.* Washington, D.C.

United States Sentencing Commission. (2015). *2015 Report to the Congress: Impact of the Fair Sentencing Act*. Washington, D.C.

Weinrath, M., Donatelli, G., & Murchison, M. J. (2016). Mentorship: A missing piece to manage juvenile intensive supervision programs and youth gangs? *Canadian Journal of Criminology & Criminal Justice, 58*(3), 291–321. https://doi.org/10.3138/cjccj.2015.E19

World Health Organization. (1947). Proceedings and final acts of the Internal Health Conference, New York 19 June to 22 July 1946. *American Journal of Public Health and the Nations Health, 37*(7), 929. PMCID: PMC1623802

Zettler, H. R. (2021). Much to do about trauma: A systematic review of existing trauma-informed treatments on youth violence and recidivism. *Youth Violence and Juvenile Justice, 19*(1), 113–134. https://doi.org/10.1177/15412040209396

Image Credits

CHAPTER 8

Special Populations and Caseloads

This chapter introduces students to special populations, a group of people who display unique risks and needs and who are under the supervision of the community corrections system. Due to the complexity of supervising special populations, there has been a movement toward practices like the use of specialized caseloads where a probation or parole officer with increased training, experience, and support is responsible for monitoring a specific group of people. At the systematic level, officers play a key role in the teamwork approach endorsed by problem-solving courts, where special populations can be identified and processed differently from other people under supervision. This includes the diversion of appropriate special populations away from incarceration and toward community care. This chapter addresses the major issues of mental illness and/or substance use for special populations under supervision as well as the supervision of special populations convicted for driving while intoxicated (DWI), intimate partner violence (IPV), and sex-based offenses. Lastly, this chapter also discusses the need for probation and parole officers to monitor their own health and workplace stress associated with supervising these higher need groups.

LEARNING OBJECTIVES

By the end of this chapter, students will be able to:

- Understand supervision strategies for special populations, including specialized caseloads and supervision practices.
- Identify and assess problem-solving courts and the appropriate linkage in programs, services, and practices with community corrections.
- Describe the various types of special populations and special considerations for probation and parole supervision.

KEY TERMS

- Intimate partner violence (IPV)
- Mental illness and/or substance use disorders

- Problem-solving courts
- Sexual offenses
- Specialized caseloads

CONTENT

Special Populations in Community Corrections
◊ Journey into the Field: Mr. Ed Hayes
Supervision Strategies for Special Populations
Specialized Caseloads
Additional Supervision Techniques
Mental Illness and Substance Use
Supervision Practices for People with Mental Illness and/or Substance Use Disorders
◊ Diversity, Equity, and Inclusion: Racial and Ethnic Disparities in Mental Health Treatment
Problem-Solving Courts
Mental Health Courts and Community Courts
Drug Courts and Community Corrections
Driving While Intoxicated Courts and Community Corrections
Intimate Partner Violence (IPV)
Sexual Offenses
◊ Officer Work, Careers, and Wellness: Employee Assistance Programs
Summary: Special Populations and Caseloads
Scenario-Based Activities

Mental pain is less dramatic than physical pain, but it is more common and also more hard to bear. The frequent attempt to conceal mental pain increases the burden: It is easier to say "My tooth is aching" than to say "My heart is broken."

—C. S. Lewis, 1940

Special Populations in Community Corrections

The intersectionality framework places emphasis on the diversity and complexity of clients who will interact with the community corrections system. It is expected that people under the supervision of the community corrections system will have significant differences in terms of their risk, needs, and responsivity factors—all of which may require additional training, sensitivity, and expertise of staff working with them. For example, probation and parole officers supervise individuals convicted of a range of offenses (e.g., sex offenses, domestic violence, white collar crime, and violent crime) as well as those with mental health and substance use disorders. The additional risk and needs associated with these individuals under community corrections supervision has led to the term "special populations," which carries the idea that these groups require more targeted, specialized approaches.

The term "special populations" does not have a singular definition across probation and parole agencies. Rather, what is defined as a special population and corresponding supervision strategy will vary depending on the goals and mission statement of each probation and parole agency. Some agencies have implemented the use of evidence-based strategies where risk and needs assessments are used to screen individuals under their supervision for referral toward specific programs, resources, or caseloads supervised by specially trained staff if they display certain characteristics. However, in many cases these decisions are influenced by staff characteristics, geographic location, agency size, supervision orientations, and other more practical realities. For example, some probation and parole agencies may not have the staffing levels and community resources necessary to support specialized caseloads. In these agencies, individuals who meet criteria for a special population may be supervised similarly to other individuals on probation or parole.

While a primary focus of the community corrections system centers on criminal sanctions and recidivism, special populations also extend into considerations of health. A failure to address the health needs of special populations can lead to negative effects for the broader community, as explained by Aday (1994):

> A community perspective on the origins of health needs focuses on the differential risks that exist for different groups as a function of the availability of opportunities and resources for maximizing their health. Poor health results because communities fail to invest in and assume responsibility for the collective well-being of their members. (p. 490)

This suggests that "health" is a holistic concept that includes physical, mental, and social aspects of wellness and functioning, as detailed by the World Health Organization definition mentioned in Chapter 7. As such, the community corrections system can function as a form of a large-scale health intervention to address social problems that are inherently tied to these special populations. It is worth considering that the criminal behavior associated with special populations is often connected to social inequalities, with minority and low socioeconomic neighborhoods often lacking adequate treatment centers and other resources needed to address issues like mental illness, substance and alcohol addiction, sexual abuse, gang violence, and intimate partner violence (IPV). There is also substantial evidence to suggest that an overreliance on incarceration to address the health aspects of special populations leads to negative outcomes (Freudenberg & Heller, 2016). Special populations have been observed to contain a mixture of criminogenic and health-based risks and needs. As a result, physical health and mental health become significant noncriminogenic factors that probation and parole agencies must address to promote prosocial change and desistance from crime.

While special populations often require additional attention, training, and resources from community corrections agencies, some of these groups may constitute a relatively small portion of the overall supervision population. For example, of all individuals under probation supervision for a violent offense, approximately 11% are convicted for driving while intoxicated (DWI) offenses, 5% are convicted for IPV offenses, and 4% are convicted for sex offenses (Kaeble, 2023). However, these relatively small percentages of total violent crime can carry significant liability for officers, as unaddressed risk in these special populations can potentially lead to serious consequences for the individual and the community (e.g., risk of future violent offense). Other factors like mental illness and substance use are ubiquitous in community corrections, with drug charges (e.g., consumption, possession, importation, distribution, and trafficking) constituting approximately one quarter of the entire probation population (Kaelbe, 2023).

JOURNEY INTO THE FIELD: MR. ED HAYES

◇◇◇◇◇◇◇◇

Full name: Edmond Hayes

Title: Assistant Superintendent, Franklin County Sheriff's Office, Massachusetts

Assistant Superintendent Ed Hayes was born in Annapolis, Maryland, but was raised in Nashua, New Hampshire. His first introduction to the criminal justice system was when he worked as a part-time adult basic education instructor in 2007 for the Hampden County Sheriff's Department in Ludlow, Massachusetts. Within a few years, Mr. Hayes was promoted to a midlevel supervisor position at this agency. In 2010, he transferred to the Franklin County Sheriff's Office, Massachusetts, where he served as director of the Education Program. In 2013, Mr. Hayes was promoted to assistant superintendent and was the director of treatment until 2023. In that role, he supervised the behavioral health, caseworker, reentry, and education teams. Assistant Superintendent Hayes is currently the director of the Opioid Treatment Program and of grants management and research coordination for the Franklin County Sheriff's Office, Massachusetts. As a lifelong learner, he is currently pursuing a master's degree in social work, and he continues to participate in the NIH/NIDA LEAP Investigators and Scholars Program. In the following Journey into the Field, Assistant Superintendent Hayes presents an interesting pathway in his career, with recognition of the changes in the field of community corrections, particularly for vulnerable populations.

When I graduated from college with a degree in biology and music, nowhere on my list of career goals was to work in the criminal legal system. I was teaching adult basic education in the community, and as the grant funding for my position was set to expire, I found a job teaching adult education in a county jail. I fell in love with the work and especially with supporting vulnerable people to find their voices and recover from trauma and addiction. Eventually, I returned to graduate school to study social work and began to do more in the world of clinical behavioral health and postrelease supervision and support.

In my opinion, if we are truly concerned with supporting the success of our clients and improving public safety goals for our community, it's indispensable to understand the dimension of our clients so we can be effective communicators who meet people where they are at. We cannot simply hover over people, hunting for faults. We all have experiences of how this feels, and it does not promote success. Each one of us is not going through life simply hoping to avoid making terrible mistakes; we are motivated by our positive goals based on our individual values. How can we understand our clients and their unique values if we don't understand their environment and cultural/social/spiritual/physical context?

One certainty in life is that the world is always changing, whether we like it or not. We can either adapt and thrive or remain frozen in time. When I started my work, the opioid epidemic hadn't yet fully materialized; now 55% of people in our program report an opioid use disorder, and it is a central focus of our efforts. We understand so much more about trauma, its debilitating effects, as well as successful interventions and treatment strategies. We know more about the brain development of emerging adults and how this affects young adult men's impulsivity and executive functioning. We know more about how marginalized populations, such as people of color, people who identify within the LGBTQIA+ community, and many other groups, suffer through discriminatory policies. We have the opportunity to reflect our growing understanding and evolve our policies and practices. We mustn't lose our curiosity or will to learn and grow.

Supervision Strategies for Special Populations

With so many differing and complex risk and needs factors that individuals on probation and parole might possess, you might be wondering what probation and parole agencies can do to provide more targeted, individualized approaches. One of the main strategies probation and parole agencies use to interact with special populations is specialized caseloads. Agencies use this approach to tailor supervision within a focused caseload, where officers can devote more time and attention to each individual while facilitating the delivery of appropriate programs and services.

Specialized Caseloads

Specialized caseloads typically consist of a smaller number of individuals who all have similar characteristics. For example, common specialized caseloads are those that focus on individuals convicted of illegal substance use, DWI, IPV, and sex crimes. The type of specialized caseloads available within each agency depends on several factors, including agency resources, staffing levels, and primary needs (e.g., some types of offenses are more prevalent in some jurisdictions than others). Specialized caseloads are supervised by a probation or parole officer who has received additional training to provide more extensive treatment and services to address the specific needs of the caseload. A hallmark of specialized caseloads is the implementation of evidence-based practices—that is, the use of current research and the best available data to guide policy and practice decisions (see Chapter 6 for more on evidence-based practice). These caseloads also typically include partnerships with external agencies that can maximize outcomes related to the specific needs of the group, such as relevant treatment providers.

Assignment to a specialized caseload typically occurs in two main ways. For one, individuals can be ordered by the court to receive more intensive forms of supervision that include more frequent contact between the individual and their assigned officer and the provision of increased structure and oversight. However, it is more common that individual agencies have their own protocols for identifying and assigning individuals to a specialized caseload. In these agencies, officers typically conduct a risk and needs assessment and if certain criteria are met, supervisors use their discretion to make assignments to a specialized caseload. However, because a key feature of specialized caseloads is the smaller caseload sizes to accommodate the increased work required of the probation or parole officer, not all who meet criteria may be placed on a specialized caseload. This is the unfortunate reality of high probation and parole supervision populations coupled with low resources.

In some agencies instead of focusing on a single risk/need factor, they focus on clusters of needs within a group. For example, the Fort Bend, Texas, Community Supervision and Corrections Department has specialized caseloads where "specially trained Community Corrections Officers supervise caseloads of 25 to 50 offenders who share similar problems, such as substance use, mental impairments, age or language barriers, or compulsive sexual behavior" (Fort Bend County, n.d., para. 1). This caseload relies on the resources of the Texas Department of Assistive and Rehabilitative Services, local mental health authorities, counseling agencies, literacy agencies, and treatment facilities. Research suggests the success of specialized caseloads rests on the creation of a solid program infrastructure with standard operating procedures and ongoing training, correct identification of a special population based on risk and needs, development of specialized supervision case plans that maintain accountability, partnerships with community resources, and the continued support of the program by tracking and promoting successes (Haneberg, 2001). When these key principles are followed, specialized caseloads for special populations can lead to fewer arrests, shorter periods of incarceration, improved outcomes, and cost savings (Haneberg, 2021).

Additional Supervision Techniques
In addition to specialized caseloads, probation and parole officers tasked with supervising special populations also engage in several additional key tasks. Some of the most common include conducting specialized screening and assessment instruments, linkage and referral

to specialty treatment providers, in-depth communication and collaboration with treatment providers, and monitoring of often extensive additional supervision conditions. In addition to, or sometimes in place of, standard risk and needs assessments, probation and parole officers may need to conduct additional screening and assessments. For example, for individuals with suspected mental health needs, a probation and parole officer might conduct a brief screening tool to determine if they should make a referral for a thorough mental health assessment. In some instances, the court may order the individual to undergo full mental health assessment as well.

For individuals convicted of a sexual offense, standard risk and needs assessment instruments are typically not used. Instead, probation and parole officers use instruments designed specifically to measure the risk and needs of this special population, with the most common including the STATIC-99, STABLE, and ACUTE. The textbox below provides an example of the STABLE-2007 scoring form to illustrate the key areas assessed. The STABLE-2007 includes 13 items that are each individually scored (only 12 items if the victim was not a child). A total score is calculated by summing all individual item scores for a total of 26 points (or 24 points if no child victim). Individuals are then classified into one of three groups based on their results: low (0–3 points), moderate (4–11 points), and high (12–26 points; Hanson et al., 2015). Probation and parole officers supervising individuals convicted of a sexual offense must undergo extensive additional training on these assessments.

When a probation or parole officer identifies a special need that requires a clinical assessment and/or treatment, they must be well trained in identifying the appropriate resources, making a referral, and monitoring progress in treatment in collaboration with treatment providers. In some instances, probation and parole officers may call and make assessment and/or intake appointments for individuals on their caseloads to assist in the process. Probation and parole agencies typically focus on identifying treatment providers in the community who provide evidence-based treatment that can best help their clients. Treatment providers working with individuals with substance use and/or mental health issues, as well as those convicted of a sexual offense, typically develop comprehensive treatment plans that include plans for clinical assessments, intervention, and medication management. Once an individual is in the care of a community-based treatment provider, probation and parole officers must develop a relationship with the provider and maintain excellent communication to stay up to date with the individual's progress (e.g., treatment attendance, participation, adherence to treatment protocols), prescribed medications, and adherence to a treatment plan. This means that individuals under supervision must provide their approval for their treatment provider to share information with the probation and parole agency, typically a requirement of the supervision process. Probation and parole officers and treatment providers typically work very closely together to monitor the progress of each individual under supervision and communicate on a frequent basis, highlighting the benefit of smaller, specialized caseloads.

In addition to conducting additional screening and assessments and collaborating with treatment providers, probation and parole officers supervising specialized caseloads typically must monitor compliance with a range of special supervision conditions. As discussed

READING

Stable 2007

Assessment ID: DOCH-STABLE-84
Assessed: 7/11/2008
Name: John Doe (SID #: A0980003)

DOB:	06/04/2057	**Sentence Date:**	10/09/1982	**Unit:**	Intake
Gender:	Male	**Offense Type:**	Indecent exposure		Svc.
Assessor:	susan@cyzap	**Assessment Status:** Pre-trial			Center
Purpose:	Initial Assessment	**Disposition:**	Pre-trial	**County:**	Hawaii
Case Number: 7332722					

Scoring Form	Score

1. **Significant Social Influences**
   A. Number of Positive Influences (Max. 8)
   B. Number of Negative Influences (Max 7)
   C. Number of Neutral Influences
   D. Total Significant Social Influences
	2

2. **Capacity for Stable Relationships**
   A. Ever lived with an Intimate Partner for at least two years?   No / Yes
   B. Currently living with an intimate partner?   With concerns
	2

3. **Emotional Identification with Children** Any child victims less than 14 years? No	N/A
4. **Hostility toward women** *Notes:* Extreme hostility	2
5. **General Social Rejection** *Notes:* anti-social	2
6. Lack of concern for others	2
7. Impulsive	2
8. Poor Problem Solving Skills	2
9. Negative Emotionality	2
10. Sex Drive/Sex Preoccupation	2
11. Sex As Coping	1
12. Deviant Sexual Preferences	0
13. Co-operation with Supervisor	1
Total Score:	20
Risk Category:	High

in Chapter 4, these supervision conditions are typically assigned by the judge or parole board and are offense-specific. Individuals with mental health and/or substance use needs typically have special conditions centered on treatment requirements and sobriety. Those under supervision for sexual offenses typically have some of the most stringent special conditions placed on them, making the job of probation and parole officers tasked with these caseloads possibly the most intense form of probation and parole work. For example, in many states these individuals must comply with special supervision plans that contain upwards of 15 special conditions. These special conditions typically vary based on whether the victim was an adult or child. If the victim was a minor, there are often additional special conditions. These conditions would likely include that the individual cannot have any contact (direct or indirect) with any person under the age of 18 years old. Additional special conditions typically include requirements such as:

- Undergo evaluation from a certified sex offender treatment provider.
- Compliance with all treatment recommendations.
- Payment for all evaluation and treatment services.
- Allow sharing of information between treatment provider and probation/parole agency.
- Submit to polygraph testing as required.
- No direct or indirect contact with victim or victim's family.
- Restricted from using any medication or supplements to enhance sexual performance, possessing, viewing, listening to, or reading any sexually explicit materials (e.g., articles, books, literature, magazines, emails, photographs, websites), using any sexual explicit services, adult stores whose primary purpose is to sell sexually explicit materials, entering massage parlors or businesses with exotic dancers, nude/partially nude entertainers, or any business that allows viewing of sexually explicit material, using sexually explicit telephone services, joining any mailing list, group, or club whose primary purpose is to promote or engage in sexual activity, and/or using sex work or escort services.
- Restricted from hitchhiking or picking up hitchhikers.
- Cannot access the internet or possess a computer with internet access.

While these conditions may vary by agency, these are common restrictions placed on those convicted of a sexual offense. As you can see there, these present a great deal of additional conditions for probation and parole officers to monitor. Typically, officers conduct more frequent home visits and make a greater number of community contacts for individuals convicted of a sexual offense to monitor compliance. For example, when conducting a home visit an officer may check for any device that would allow an individual to access the internet. As with other special populations, supervising this group of individuals is time-intensive and requires a smaller caseload to accommodate the increased workload.

Lastly, probation and parole officers supervising special populations may need to provide more assistance to help individuals overcome significant barriers to accessing treatment and employment. Many may not be aware of federal and state programs that can provide financial assistance for program participation. In some cases, special populations may lack formal education and/or face literacy issues due to limited school attendance or English being a second language (this issue was explored in the context of undocumented immigrants in Chapter 7). Literacy challenges can result in challenges with attendance at probation/parole or court dates, engagement in educational programs, and employment searches.

For some special populations, such as those convicted of a sex offense, there may be more formal barriers to the types of work and programs they can engage in. For example, individuals convicted of a sexual offense are often not allowed to accept employment where children are present (e.g., schools, day cares), while some may not be allowed to access the internet or use a computer, which can significantly reduce potential employment opportunities. Officers must be trained to approach these needs in a neutral and professional manner to maximize outcomes for both the individual and society. An effective approach is to work collaboratively with the individual to highlight the existing strengths of the individual, especially any existing familial or social relationships that can be accessed and used to facilitate achievement of identified goals.

Mental Illness and Substance Use

The largest special population that community corrections supervise are people with **mental illness and/or substance use disorders**. The high prevalence of people with mental illness and/or substance use is the result of a well-intended, though disastrous, effort toward deinstitutionalization. Originating in the 1960s, a combination of negative media portrayals of mental hospitals and asylums, plus federal versus state budgetary conflicts, and a growing emphasis on community health care and human rights sparked this movement (Smith, 2022). The goal of deinstitutionalization was to divert people with mental illness and substance use problems away from state mental health hospitals and toward more adequate care in the community, particularly through general hospitals, medical clinics, halfway houses, and other local agencies (Smith, 2022). However, like many policies and practices devised with good intentions, there were unexpected consequences.

Instead of community health care and local neighborhoods absorbing this special population, many people with mental illness filtered into jail and prison, and the criminal justice system became a default mental health system (Smith, 2022). During the 50 years prior to deinstitutionalization, the total population of institutionalized people with mental illness remained stable, with approximately 75% housed in mental health hospitals and 25% in jail or prison (Gilligan & Lee, 2013). By 2013, this trend reversed, and there were less than 5% of these individuals in mental health hospitals, while 95% were incarcerated (Gilligan & Lee, 2013). This change in the number of people with mental illness interacting with the criminal justice system also had an enormous impact on community corrections, which was now responsible for simultaneously balancing risks, criminogenic needs, and health care needs. Decades of research indicate that the prevalence of people with mental illness under the supervision of community corrections ranges between 11% and 19%, with approximately 5% having a serious and persistent mental illness (Ditton, 1999; Eno Louden et al., 2008; Kessler et al., 1999). Of these people, about half (52%–55%) also have a co-occurring substance use disorder (Lurigio et al., 2003; Skeem et al., 2008). Special populations with mental illness and substance use also have very high rates of prior traumatic experience such as physical and sexual abuse, socioeconomic challenges, previous hospitalizations for mental illness, previous suicidal behaviors, and recidivism (Prins & Draper, 2016), suggesting that programs and policies that address existing trauma and social disparities would be suitable for this special population.

Supervision Practices for People with Mental Illness and/or Substance Use Disorders

Probation and parole agencies now supervise an unprecedented number of people with mental illness, many of whom have co-occurring substance use disorders, and there is a need to understand best practices for addressing risk and need in this special population. Mental illness and substance use disorders are highly linked for several reasons, including, though not limited to, people using street drugs and alcohol to self-medicate and alleviate the symptoms of mental illness, personal histories of being addicted to substances facilitating preexisting vulnerabilities to mental health disorders, and the intersection of mental illness and substance use leading to problems like homelessness, unemployment, and poor social relationships. As a result, officers who supervise individuals under supervision with mental illness and/or substance use disorders require additional training to understand and address the significant clinical, legal, and socioeconomic challenges these populations will face. While individuals with mental health and/or substance use disorders will have similar criminogenic risk factors as other people under supervision (e.g., antisocial peers, unemployment), they often have more of these risk factors in total, and this combination of risks can significantly impact their daily functioning (Prins & Draper, 2009).

Mental illness and substance use have a profound effect on probation and parole outcomes. For example, a lack of access to therapy and medication may increase symptoms of mental illness such as depression, hallucinations, or mania. These symptoms can contribute to missed contacts with probation and parole, lead to failures due to a lack of attending mandatory meetings and treatment sessions, and ultimately result in subsequent arrests, especially when people turn to illegal street drugs to self-medicate. There may also be an indirect impact when mental illness and a related drug addiction leads to a loss of family/social support, financial stability, and housing. In line with an intersectionality framework, it should be noted that people with mental illness and/or substance use issues are not a homogenous group; rather, individuals within these groups have important differences that require consideration.

A standard practice in probation and parole is for specialized caseloads that average 30–45 people with mental illness per officer (compared to 100 or more for traditional caseloads) and with these officers receiving an average of 20–40 hours of training on mental health topics per year (Prins & Draper; Wolff et al., 2014). Recommended supervision practices include the development of a strong rapport between the officer and their assigned clients that centers on fostering "firm but fair" relationships, an orientation toward problem solving rather than threats of incarceration or negative pressures, and officers maintaining effective partnerships with community agencies and resources. This approach, if done well, produces a reduction in the burden placed on the mental health system, an increase in the likelihood an individual's mental health needs will be well-managed, a higher likelihood of successfully completing probation or parole, and, ultimately, leads to reductions in recidivism (Wolff et al., 2014).

Beyond supervision practices there are several evidence-based treatment options that strongly support functional improvements in people with mental illness who interact with community corrections. These are presented in Table 8.1.

TABLE 8.1   Six Evidence-Based Mental Health Treatment Practices (Prins & Draper, 2009, p. viii)

1.	Assertive community treatment (ACT), a service delivery model in which a multidisciplinary team of mental health professionals provides individualized treatment.
2.	Illness self-management and recovery, in which people learn skills to monitor and control their own well-being.
3.	Integrated mental health and substance use services, in which specific treatment strategies and therapeutic techniques are combined to address mental illnesses and substance use disorders in a single contact or series of contacts over time.
4.	Supported employment, in which people with mental illnesses are employed in competitive, integrated work settings with follow-along supports.
5.	Psychopharmacology, in which medications are used to treat mental illnesses.
6.	Family psychoeducation, in which people with mental illnesses and their families learn about mental illnesses, symptom management techniques, and stress reduction.

◊ Diversity, Equity, and Inclusion: Racial and Ethnic Disparities in Mental Health Treatment

Racial and ethnic disparities in mental health service use have been identified as a major public health problem. Risk and protective factors for mental illness vary not only across individuals but across race/ethnicity, gender, and culture. These factors are nested at different levels of health, which is in line with Bronfenbrenner's (1977, 1979) concept of health described in Chapter 1. At the individual level, risk factors for mental illness include genetic vulnerabilities (e.g., biological parent/s have a mental illness), neuropsychological deficits (e.g., brain abnormalities), physical illness, and low birth weight. Within the family environment, mental health is influenced by marital conflict, poverty, overcrowded living conditions, large family size, parental criminality, family members with a mental illness, and placement in foster care. Community factors like violence, community disorganization, poor school systems, and racism/discrimination also impact mental health. These risks can be balanced by resilience, which is the capacity to bounce back from adversity.

Resilience is a strength-based concept and includes a positive emotional state, supportive relationships with peers and family members, setting rules and goals, commitment to school, social cohesion, and access to health and social services. It is important to note that, overall, there are no significant differences in levels of mental illness by racial or ethnic groups; rather, disparities emerge in how people are diagnosed, gain access to services, and in overall mental health outcomes after engaging in treatment. Beyond the direct impact of tangible items that reinforce mental health, like adequate health care insurance, there are indirect effects of mistrust, stigma, and oppression. These factors can influence cultural perceptions of seeking treatment and help, compliance with medications, and coping styles.

In the highly influential *Mental Health: Culture, Race, and Ethnicity* (U.S. Department of Health and Human Services, 2001), the topics of culture, race, ethnicity, and mental health was detailed. The report focused on the concept of functioning, as the signs and symptoms of mental health are based on deviations from social norms and cultural standards of acceptable behavior. The themes of the report provide a roadmap for understanding mental health and communities. These five key themes include:

- Mental health and mental illness require the broad focus of a public health approach.
- Mental disorders are disabling conditions.
- Mental health and mental illness are points on a continuum.
- Mind and body are inseparable.
- Stigma is a major obstacle preventing people from getting help (U.S. Department of Health and Human Services, 2001, p. 4).

The goal of the U.S. Department of Health and Human Services (2001) report was to understand disparities in mental health, gather evidence on the need for mental health services, and to articulate strategies for reducing disparities in mental health. These documented systematic effects of racial and ethnic disparities in health care have significant implications for the community corrections system, which interacts with large numbers of individuals with mental health needs representing varying races, ethnicities, and cultures. Effective approaches by community corrections agencies require them to continue to be educated and stay up to date on scientific (e.g., evidence-based) knowledge regarding ethnic and cultural based mental health interventions, develop strong partnerships with mental health and primary care services to improve access to treatment (using established screening, referral, and treatment plan processes), address barriers to receiving mental health services in their supervised caseloads (e.g., including both financial and perceptual barriers such as shame, stigma, mistrust, discrimination), and build on existing strengths to improve the quality of mental health care for people under the supervision of the community corrections system.

In terms of daily practices, staff should inquire about the cultural identity of their caseloads to (a) determine their racial, ethnic, or cultural reference group, language abilities, language use, and language preference, (b) explore cultural explanations of mental illness and severity of symptoms, (c) consider cultural interpretations of social stressors, available support, and functioning, and (d) synthesize information to develop treatment plans and referrals to care (U.S. Department of Health and Human Services, 2001, p. 11). These approaches should recognize that racial and ethnic minorities are double-stigmatized, both being members of a group that faces limited access to mental health services and being placed under supervision of the community corrections system. The future of this issue can be described as such:

> The Nation is struggling to meet the needs of its most vulnerable individuals, such as those in foster care, jails, prisons, homeless shelters, and refugee resettlement programs. Accordingly, the attention being given to the development and provision of effective, culturally responsive mental health services for these populations is increasing (U.S. Department of Health and Human Services, 2001, p. 163).

In addition to providing more culturally responsive services, these services must also be high-quality and available in locations accessible to racial and ethnic minorities, such as rural communities where such services are often not available.

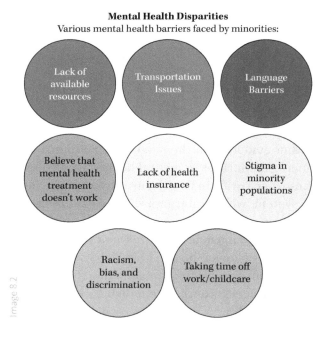

Mental Health Disparities
Various mental health barriers faced by minorities:

Lack of available resources

Transportation Issues

Language Barriers

Believe that mental health treatment doesn't work

Lack of health insurance

Stigma in minority populations

Racism, bias, and discrimination

Taking time off work/childcare

Image 8.2

Problem-Solving Courts

In addition to specific supervision practices, problem-solving courts have evolved as an innovative approach to providing care and oversight for populations with mental health and substance use needs. **Problem-solving courts** are designed to divert individuals from incarceration to a specialty court program where they will receive more intensive programming along with continued supervision by a probation officer. These are lengthy, comprehensive programs that typically center on one specific special population, with mental health courts and drug courts being two of the most common. While there are differences across various types of courts, their main approach is to provide a therapeutic environment—as opposed to the typical adversarial environment associated with the court—to address underlying risk factors and avoid incarceration. Regardless of the court type, a probation officer will typically serve as a key member of the problem-solving court team.

Mental Health Courts and Community Corrections

During the 1980s, there was increasing recognition that police and courts were placing people with mental illness in jail and prison in lieu of community-based treatment, mainly due to a lack of options and resources in the community for this special population. One of the original mental health courts was started by Judge Goodman in Indiana who frequently encountered defendants with mental illness who had criminal charges pending while also facing a civil commitment related to their mental illness. Judge Goodman developed a court within a hospital, where the defendant would become a "patient" with treatment in a state hospital before returning to have charges dropped or minimized if they complied with the established treatment plan.

By the 1990s, mental health courts were expanded at the national level. A defining characteristic of the mental health court (as with all problem-solving courts that we will discuss) is a team approach between the judge, probation officer, prosecutor, defense attorney, and mental health expert (often a case manager or treatment provider). In these team-based environments, probation officers are fundamental, as they provide detailed information on the individual participants through probation reports, presentence investigation reports (see Chapter 4 for a more thorough discussion), and progress while on supervision. In fact, the effectiveness of mental health courts is frequently measured by probation outcomes, with failures from the program determined by revocation of probation and imposition of suspended sentences.

Goldkamp and Irons-Guynn (2000) examined mental health courts across the United States, including in San Bernardino and Seattle. The San Bernardino Mental Health Court represented a unique approach, as it provided admission of defendants charged with nonviolent lower level felonies, punishable by up to 6 years in prison, as well as defendants facing misdemeanor charges, punishable by up to 1 year in jail. Compared to others, this program is more open to the inclusion of people charged with violent crimes. People with mental health issues are identified at a nearby jail, with eligible candidates signing a waiver to allow mental health information to be shared amongst the court team. Next, a probation officer is assigned to eligible candidates who agree to share mental health information. This probation officer then attends all arraignments and court hearings, collects background and criminal history information, and records information on medication and other individual needs.

The officer provides all information to the judge to make placement decisions. For defendants in crisis, they are often placed in hospitals or the psychiatric wing of the jail. For those not in crisis who pled guilty, the judge commonly assigns probation for a period of 2 years in misdemeanor cases or 3 years in felony cases, with participation in Mental Health Court ordered as a condition of probation (Goldkamp and Irons-Guynn, 2000). The interdisciplinary court team then meets regularly to discuss the treatment plan and progress of the individuals placed in the Mental Health Court. Because court participants are simultaneously on probation, they are expected to maintain compliance with supervision conditions as well as complete many of the following programs depending on diagnosis, progress, and probation conditions: anger management, socialization skills, psychotherapy, medication therapy, and chemical dependency treatment (including drug testing).

Another example of a mental health court is the King County Mental Health Court, located in Seattle. This court program was started in 1999 to address defendants with a mental illness who have offenses with maximum penalties of no more than 1 year in jail. The court focuses on people whose crimes or charges appear related to mental illness or who have been referred for competency evaluation by jail medical staff. Following acceptance into the program, along with consent to share health records and processing by the court, a team approach is initiated. Goldkamp and Irons-Guynn (2000) describe the important role of community corrections as such:

> Once the candidate opts in or formally enters the Mental Health Court, a probation officer is appointed to supervise the participant. The probation officer works as part of the Mental Health Court team and maintains close contact with the participant, whether in custody or in the community. The probation officer coordinates and communicates with the caseworker at the treatment facility handling the defendant's care and the Mental Health Court case manager. Once the treatment plan is put into effect, the probation officer and the case manager check on the participant's progress and ensure that court-ordered treatment is being provided. (p. 30)

IMAGE 8.3   The King County Regional Mental Health Court, Washington

Decades of research now indicate that mental health courts offer an effective tool for justice-involved individuals with mental health needs and that community corrections play a vital role in the success of these specialty courts. Mental health courts have been shown to reduce the number of contacts between people with mental illness and the criminal justice system, divert appropriate cases away from the negative effects of incarceration, improve symptoms of mental health to facilitate positive court interactions, develop partnerships and linkages between agencies, and protect public safety. Mental health courts are now a basic practice at the national level, with probation officers highly involved in cases from the first court date to successful completion of probation.

Drug Courts and Community Corrections

Drug courts are another common problem-solving court that uses a public health or medical approach in lieu of a criminal justice approach. With developments in science, there has been a reconceptualization of how we view addiction to alcohol and other substances. This features a rejection of theoretical explanations of addiction that describe moralistic, religious, and personal failures (e.g., laziness, lack of self-control, poverty, morals) of the individual in favor of medical explanations, where a dependency on substances is described as a "sickness" or "disease" that requires treatment. The first drug court originated in Miami-Dade County, Florida, as a response to the emerging crack cocaine epidemic (Kirchner, 2014). There are now over 3,500 drug courts found throughout the United States (Office of Justice Programs, 2023), with the collective aim of diverting people with substance use needs away from the criminal justice system and into long-term recovery. Drug courts rest on the argument that law enforcement, incarceration, and punishment produce poor outcomes for people with substance use needs. For example, an early study by Belenko and Peugh (1998) found that 70% of people sent to prison rather than a drug court or other alternative returned to drug use following release. Drug courts operate under an economic justification with reduced costs for incarceration, mental health services, and courts, as well as increases in functioning and financial stability in participants (Logan et al., 2004).

IMAGE 8.4   Senator Stabenow Meets With Administrators and Officials at the Delta County Drug Court, Michigan

Drug courts rely on a team approach where the court collaborates with community corrections, treatment providers, and other community agencies to provide clinical assessments, develop and monitor treatment placements, and review/support progress in treatment. The court may assign adult participants to intensive, supervised probation and mandatory treatment, as well as random drug testing with progress monitored by a supervising probation officer who has received specialized training. Typically, an assessment of chemical dependency is performed by a licensed addiction counselor (LAC) at a state-approved program. This may produce the recommendation of medical detoxification, where the withdrawal from substance occurs in a medical setting under the supervision of medical personnel. Most drug courts collaborate with community-based treatment providers to deliver effective treatment for court participants. This is essential for providing the gold-standard treatment for opioid use disorders: medication-assisted treatment (MAT) or medications for opioid use disorders (MOUD), as discussed in Chapter 6. If recommended by a clinician following an assessment, most participants in drug courts are allowed to use MAT that combines behavioral therapy with the use of medications (i.e., methadone, naltrexone, and buprenorphine). Probation and parole officers assigned to a drug court should focus on developing an environment of trust, though they must also verify behaviors via program attendance, drug testing, and random observations of participants in their natural social environment (Marlowe, 2012).

Driving While Intoxicated Courts and Community Corrections

An intriguing aspect of the community corrections system is that its origins are deeply connected to the issue of alcohol use. As Chapter 3 demonstrates, the "Father of Probation" John Augustus began his efforts as a member of the Washington Total Abstinence Society, with the first person he bailed out of police court being a "common drunkard." This was part of a larger movement in the United States driven by the advocacy of religious groups to criminalize alcohol—an effort that was briefly successful. In 1917, the 18th Amendment was passed by Congress leading to the prohibition of selling or consuming alcohol. The 18th Amendment was repealed in 1933 as it became clear the use of the law and criminal justice system to ban alcohol was unsustainable. Perhaps serving as a warning to future efforts regarding substance use, the criminalization of alcohol inadvertently created a high-profit industry for bootleggers and organized crime while offering no assistance for people who needed substance use treatment. Prohibition stands as a model for how the criminalization of alcohol and substance use rather than scientific and medical approaches can produce negative social outcomes.

This is not to suggest that alcohol use does not produce negative health and crime outcomes. Alcohol can take a serious toll on the body, including negative effects to the brain, heart, liver, pancreas, and immune system, and this can occur on a single occasion or over time (National Institute on Alcohol Abuse and Alcoholism, n.d.). Alcohol is also a depressant, which can disrupt the balance of neurotransmitters (chemical messengers) in the brain, affecting feelings, thoughts, and behaviors (Mental Health Foundation, 2022). This increases the risk of anxiety, depression, psychosis, suicide, and self-harm. Alcohol is a "multiplier" of crime, as it increases involvement in juvenile delinquency, sex offenses, burglary, assault, and even homicide (e.g.,

60% of people convicted for homicide consumed alcohol immediately prior to the offense; see DiLuiolo, 1996). Alcohol is so prevalent in crime that its damage and harm is more significant than all illegal drugs combined (DiLuiolo, 1996).

The negative effects of alcohol are also linked to lower level crimes that contribute to neighborhood disorder, such as public intoxication, prostitution, graffiti, vandalism, and street fights. This link between alcohol promotion and social disorder also fuels racial, ethnic, and economic disparities, as neighborhoods with higher levels of low-income, minority, and immigrant populations are often saturated with liquor stores. Rather than point to the moral failures of people who struggle with alcohol use, it is important to recognize the powerful forces that promote widespread alcohol availability and consumption. Parker and Rebhun (1995) explain this dynamic as such:

> The relative power of alcohol producers and wholesalers who supply liquor outlets, banks who loan money to store owners, and state regulators whose activities are more oriented toward the interests of alcohol industry lobbying groups than the regulation of that industry and the relative powerlessness of the poor and unemployed individuals and groups who live in greater concentration in these areas of high outlet density. (p. 51)

While alcohol operates as a multiplier of crime, there is one offense that is directly tied to the consumption of alcohol: driving while intoxicated (DWI). Depending on state laws, DWI may also be termed "operating while impaired" (OWI) or "operating while ability impaired," and "operating a vehicle under the influence" (OVI). The effects of driving while impaired or drunk are often underestimated by the public, though they represent considerable risk to the driver and others. Research dating back to the early 1990s indicates that approximately one third of all motor vehicle fatalities are the result of drunk driving, an estimate that remains stable to this day—equating to 11,654 deaths in 2020 (Centers for Disease Control and Prevention, 2008; U.S. Department of Transportation, n.d.). To address this problem, DWI courts have emerged as an effective problem-solving court strategy.

To date, DWI courts have demonstrated reductions in recidivism for impaired-driving offenders of rates between 20% and 65% (Carey et al., 2008; Fell et al., 2011; Mitchell et al., 2012). Community corrections officers play a major role in the success of DWI courts, as they work as part of the court teams to assist participants with maintaining sobriety, address housing issues, and help them develop jobs skills while also monitoring compliance with probation and parole conditions. The National Center for DWI Courts (2010) described the essential role that community corrections officers play in supervising people with DWI charges:

> Court and treatment supervision teams must extend their supervision of offenders into the home, community, and work environments of the offender. In particular, community supervision officers must conduct field and home visits frequently to identify emerging relapse patterns, to assist with the cognitive restructuring and the development of problem-solving capabilities of offenders, and to monitor the offender

for signs of substance use. Officers must relay all of the learned information regarding the offender's habits, associates, new trends, any positive urine tests, changes of circumstance, or barriers to success to the rest of the DWI court team immediately. This requires the supervision officer to be knowledgeable of the life circumstances of the offender, including both negative and positive circumstances and changes. In fact, a critical element of the community supervision piece is to catch offenders doing something right and then alerting the rest of the court team. (p. 16)

Like other problem-solving courts and specialized caseloads, probation and parole officers participating in DWI courts must first be trained on topics related to alcohol use and addiction, particularly the associated physical and mental health risks. To supervise this special caseload, probation and parole officers can follow best practices as developed by The National Center for DWI courts (2010; see Table 8.2).

TABLE 8.2 The Ten Guiding Principles for DWI Courts

Principle	Description
Principle 1: Determine the population	This involves accurate determination of the population, with differing risks and needs associated between people with first-time versus repeated charges
Principle 2: Perform a clinical assessment	This involves a clinical risk assessment function as an objective measure of the impaired-driving special population, with specific mention of alcohol use severity, drug involvement, level of needed care, medical and mental health status, extent of social support system, and individual motivations.
Principle 3: Develop the treatment plan	This requires community corrections to develop the treatment plan with a focus on the appropriate type and dosage of treatment. This special population may require a treatment plan that focuses on the nexus of substance dependence, criminal behavior, and impulse control difficulties. A holistic treatment plan will address multiple risks at the same time, with programs in self-control, motivation enhancement, cognitive behavioral theory, family therapy, and counselling. Of note, there is often a reliance on 12-step programs such as Alcoholics Anonymous (AA), Narcotics Anonymous (NA), Cocaine Anonymous (CA), Women for Sobriety, and SMART Recovery. However, reviews of these programs are controversial and subject to widely divergent interpretations, with some studies indicating effectiveness (Moos & Moos, 2006) and others finding them to be inconvenient, faith-based, and lacking any measurement benefits or actually leading to worse outcomes then no program intervention (Ferri et al., 2006; Kownacki, & Shadish, 1999). Officers should be aware that there is a lack of scientific evidence about the effectiveness of 12-step programs, with cognitive behavioral programs representing a superior, validated means of addressing alcohol dependency.

TABLE 8.2   The Ten Guiding Principles for DWI Courts (*Continued*)

Principle	Description
Principle 4: Supervise the offender	High-risk and repeat DWI offenses represent significant danger to the public, and therefore this special population requires intensive supervision. This includes, though is not limited to, frequent monitoring, random alcohol and drug testing, home and other field visits, and routine judicial review. Officers must reinforce treatment and accountability and act immediately in cases of relapse. Officers can be aided by technological developments such as drug testing devices, breathalyzers, and ignition interlocks (i.e., a device that prevents a vehicle from starting if a person's blood alcohol level exceeds a preset limit). While on a special caseload, individuals may also be subject to curfews designed to restrict their movement and risk of associating with deviant peers.
Principle 5: Forge agency, organization, and community partnerships	This requires that community corrections engage in broad partnerships to enhance credibility, bolster support, and provide resources.
Principle 6: Take a judicial leadership role	This highlights the inherent linkage between courts and community corrections, with officers responsible for maintaining strong relationships with judicial staff.
Principle 7: Develop case management strategies	This requires the special caseload to contain case management strategies that are effective, moving individuals along a continuum of assessment, planning, linking, monitoring, and advocacy.
Principle 8: Address transportation issues	Probation and parole officers with specialized caseloads of people with alcohol disorders must often negotiate transportation issues stemming from criminal charges that limit access to work, programs, and social support.
Principle 9: Evaluate the program	This requires that special caseloads and the programs that refer people to are measured in terms of outcomes and that these assessments are shared.
Principle 10: Ensure a sustainable program	Probation/parole officers are encouraged to work with their supervisors, administrators, and other stakeholders to create careful and strategic planning.

Intimate Partner Violence (IPV)

A traditional definition of *domestic violence* references forms of abuse and violence that occur in domestic settings with a focus on heterosexual, married couples where the male is the perpetrator and the female a victim. Such early definitions included outdated terms like "wife abuse," "wife battering," and "battered women." These terms are problematic, as they are limited to heterosexual relationships where married couples are cohabitating, thus not reflecting more complex, modern relationship dynamics. A more encompassing, and accurate, term is **intimate partner violence (IPV)**, which extends to various forms of physical, sexual, emotional, reproductive, and economic abuse and violence occurring in diverse relationships. This includes, though is not limited to, nonmarried, noncohabiting, LGBTQIA+, and extended family relationships (e.g., children, parents, elderly). IPV also extends beyond direct forms of violence like aggressive actions, physical abuse, and rape to include indirect or more distal acts like using technology to stalk, hack, and control a person. While "intimate partner violence" is the preferable term, legal charges, court processes, and programs in community corrections typically rely on the label of "domestic violence."

Intimate partner violence centers on interpersonal relationship conflict and coercive control. It is frequently a learned behavior that is clustered in families, neighborhoods, and social groups. IPV is also intergenerational where children who witness or experience violence are at risk of continuing the cycle as adults, mainly by finding such violence acceptable or functional. Research on IPV identified observable patterns of escalation and de-escalation (Fisher & Lab, 2010). This "cycle of abuse" (Figure 8.1) follows four phases:

1. Tension-building stage: Conflicts over children, financial problems, and other marital issues lead to the abuser feeling annoyed, ignored, or wronged.
2. Incident stage: Threats, abuse, and violence erupts.
3. Reconciliation phase: The abuser experiences guilt, makes promises the violence will never occur again, or denies the abuse took place, even showering the victim with gifts and platitudes.
4. Calm stage: The incident is forgotten, and temporary stability is maintained. (Johnson, 2006)

Due to this being a cycle, tensions soon build again, leading to repeated events of violence.

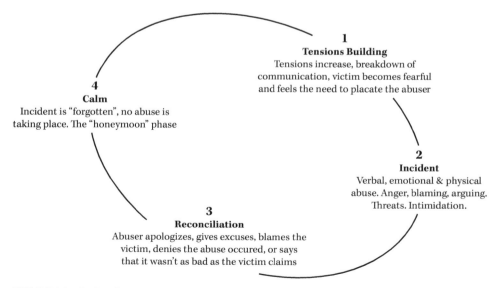

FIGURE 8.1 Cycle of Abuse

Due to legal standards, the criminal justice system has historically been reticent to intervene in IPV, even in egregious cases of violence, making arrests and prosecutions rare. The initial contact point with the abuser and victim was often law enforcement, many of whom lacked training and support to make appropriate decisions. Over time law enforcement has fluctuated between nonintervention ("hands off"), mediation (dialogue and communication) and arrest (criminal justice interventions) as a response to IPV. The colloquialism of "gaslighting" is often found in IPV, where the abuser uses coercive control to change the narrative of the abuse and violence when in the presence of law enforcement, leading to a reluctance by victims to press formal charges.

During the feminist movement of the 1970s, the lack of adequate protection for victims of IPV began to change, as activists highlighting an epidemic of violence against women created "battered women shelters," protective orders (i.e., restraining orders), and other community approaches to address IPV (Erez, 2002). As part of these efforts, there was the emergence of domestic violence courts (DVCs), which are a problem-solving court approach designed to improve victim safety and enhance defendant accountability. By using a team approach, DVCs are designed to reflect the criminal justice system's need to take IPV more seriously, with community corrections playing a large role in improving the abuser's compliance with court orders, linking trauma- and violence-informed care and advocacy, and coordinating service, programs, and partnerships to address IPV. Community corrections officers are often a major component of DVCs, working with prosecutors, defense attorneys, court clerks, police officers, mental health workers, social services professionals, and others who have specialized knowledge of and experience with IPV (Gover et al., 2021). These courts also link victims with advo-

Image 8.5

cates on the team who facilitate counseling and crisis intervention, create safety plans, aid victims with probation officer requests, provide housing referrals, explain the court processes, provide case updates, and escort victims to court procedures (Gover et al., 2021). Like other problem-solving courts, the defendant's accountability—and indeed the success of DVCs—is often measured through the person meeting conditions of probation and parole.

Not all individuals convicted of IPV will be offered the opportunity to participate in a DVC. In fact, most are likely supervised on traditional probation and parole. To effectively supervise this population, probation and parole officers must be trained in developing a professional relationship with people under supervision for IPV and know how to work toward change, recognize patterns and signs of continued IPV, access and refer to evidence-based programs and services for IPV, and respond appropriately to violations of supervision conditions. Individuals convicted of IPV will typically have special probation conditions assigned to them, with varying requirements based on risk level. For example, in California, low-risk special populations who engage in IPV are typically sentenced to a probation period of 1–3 years, though this can extend to 5 years.

Probation officers will monitor compliance with attendance at counseling, completion of a batterer intervention program, participation in community service, payment of court fines, and any related condition as imposed by the court. If the individual is deemed high risk, such as if they were convicted of a felony, then the probation sentence will typically last between 3 and 5 years and include more frequent reporting and intensive supervision by an assigned probation officer, travel restrictions, random drug testing, and payment of restitutions to the victim/s, in addition to appropriate treatment programming.

Sexual Offenses

Sexual offenses are a series of crimes that understandably generate a visceral and negative reaction from the public. In fact, of any special population supervised by community corrections, those charged with sex offenses will experience the highest degree of stigma, and this can severely limit their accessibility to work, social relationships, and rehabilitation. Individuals convicted of sex offenses are often viewed through stereotypes and myths perpetuated by the media. This is because deviant and criminal sexuality is a complex issue that is easier to comprehend and manage via simple explanations. However, these faulty assumptions can produce negative outcomes when applied to community corrections. Individuals under supervision for a sex offense are diverse. That is, there are significant differences in risks and needs among this population and a wide range of offenses classified as sexual offenses. One major misconception is that all people convicted of a sexual offense are pedophiles. Yet, pedophiles make up a very small fraction of this special population. This range of sexual offenses can be further observed in the following three cases:

- A teenage couple are dating and engaging in sexual conduct. One teenager turns 17 years old, and the other teenager is 15 years of age. A parent discovers the sexual relationship and reports them to police. The 17-year-old is charged with statutory rape, though due to "Romeo and Juliet" laws, the charges are dismissed. However, the community in which the teenagers live are now aware of the charges.
- An FBI sting operation leads to the arrest of an individual who has thousands of naked images of minors on his computer, and they are sentenced to a 1-year jail term. The individual made no effort to meet with minors in person, and the photos were not taken by him, though the individual has children in their home. Following release from jail, the individual is placed on probation for 5 years and must register as a sex offender and have all digital devices monitored.

- A series of predatory and brutal rapes have distressed a college town. An individual stalking outside a college dorm and carrying a "rape kit" is caught by campus police, and forensic reports and interrogation leads to a confession. The individual is sentenced to a 20-year prison sentence, and when released they are placed on intensive supervision while completing an additional 10-year parole period. This includes adhering to a list of over 40 conditions, such as wearing an ankle monitor, following a curfew, abstaining from alcohol, being at least 1,000 feet from a school or university, and random visits from a parole officer.

A point of confusion for the public is the intricacies of sex offense laws. For example, prostitution is illegal in every state except Nevada, and being convicted of soliciting or providing prostitution is considered a misdemeanor crime. However, in most states, prostitution does not constitute a sex offense unless the act involves a minor (though six states consider soliciting prostitution a sex offense). In contrast, innocuous acts like "flashing" one's breasts or urinating in public can lead to being charged with a sex offense. Over time, sex offenses have been expanded to include digital crimes, females as perpetrators, and thousands of new laws designed to protect public safety. However, a key point that many fail to recognize is that the vast majority of those charged with a sex offense will be returned to the community where their risk and needs must be managed. Community corrections represents a key avenue where this special population is monitored and supervised, with probation and parole officers often required to frequently check on the person's essential activities (e.g., residency, physical location, computer access) while also monitoring mandated participation in treatment and services (Baerga-Buffler & Johnson, 2006). As discussed earlier in this chapter, probation and parole officers often supervise individuals convicted of a sex offense as part of a specialized caseload, which includes increased oversight and monitoring of extensive supervision conditions. To function as effective monitors of individuals convicted of a sex offense, probation and parole officers must be aware of their own biases and stereotypical and judgmental views. This includes recognizing the impact on their own mental health and work performance and seeking help when needed or even switching to other caseloads (or transferring triggering cases to others) to avoid burnout.

As discussed earlier, individuals convicted of a sex offense should be assessed using specialized risk assessments that can guide decision-making processes specific for this population. A best practice for probation and parole officers is the use of a containment strategy, which features an integrated, multiagency approach centered around treatment, surveillance, and enforcement (English et al., 1996). A containment strategy typically follows a mix of tools, depending on the offense type and legal jurisdiction. For example, a probation officer may use a combination of Global Positioning System (GPS) tracking, home and work visits, mandatory treatment attendance records, a relapse prevention plan, curfew conditions, and strict travel restriction to monitor a person convicted of a sex offense.

A containment strategy can consist of internal control, external control, and polygraph testing (Payne & DeMichele, 2008). *Internal controls* address the treatment and interventions that this special population must meet while under supervision. It also includes the relationship between the officer and individual, with training needed to establish boundaries, recognize manipulative or deceptive behavior, and address distorted thinking, rationalizations, and excuses. *External control* centers on formal laws, policies, and practices that limit opportunities to conduct sex offenses. Officers must stay up to date on changing legal and court rulings regarding sex offenses and work to ensure that all parties working with the individual have the same knowledge. Another external control is the sex offender registration and notification (SORN), which exists at both the state and federal level. Community corrections officers are responsible for ensuring that required individuals report to local law enforcement agencies, update employment, housing, and email contact information, and, in some jurisdictions, be photographed and fingerprinted. Depending on jurisdictions, individuals may be subject to requirements for community notification (i.e., registry and notification laws requiring informing the public about the location of the individual), registration conditions, and exclusion zones (which are laws or policies that stipulate the locations that individuals must avoid, such as schools, playgrounds, daycare centers, and libraries).

It is important to note that while community corrections plays a key role in ensuring these conditions are met, there is no scientific evidence that SORN impacts recidivism and improves public safety, while there is evidence for significant negative impacts to the individual required to register, particularly surrounding stigma (Levenson & Tewksbury, 2009). Finally, polygraphs are conducted by community corrections in a minority of states, and this typically is aimed at people convicted of two or more sex offenses (Payne & DeMichele, 2008). In these states, individuals required to participate in a polygraph must either travel to the polygraph examiner's office or the examiner comes to the probation or parole office to do multiple exams in a single day. In these states, compliance with polygraphs is a part of supervision conditions.

While polygraphs lack any validity in terms of their scientific value, this category may more broadly be considered as a technology-centric strategy. Laws on GPS monitoring have been applied to people convicted of sex offenses, including those with lifetime probation or parole sanctions. GPS provides real-time monitoring of the individual's location and can alert officers when violations have occurred. Often, GPS is used to monitor compliance with travel restrictions and exclusion zones (e.g., schools). It is important to note that technological devices are tools that assist officers; however, they do not constitute programs by themselves. Additionally, they may present additional duties for the probation or parole officer, who must monitor GPS and polygraph reports frequently and address any issues that arise.

◊ Officer Work, Careers, and Wellness: Employee Assistance Programs

Working in the field of probation or parole can be challenging. Probation and parole officers are routinely asked to balance multiple goals and role orientations, and they often also supervise high caseloads while protecting public safety and supporting rehabilitation. Additionally, officers often must interact with clients who have experienced extreme trauma, putting them at risk for secondary trauma, and may need to work in environments that can make them feel personally unsafe. As a result of an often high-stress job, probation and parole officers must develop coping mechanisms. Like community supervision clients, probation and parole officers might also experience barriers to accessing necessary treatment and community-based resources. As a result, they might develop dysfunctional coping mechanisms, such as a dependency on alcohol or drugs in response to stress. Officers may experience work-related stigma that prevents them from seeking help for addressing workplace stress, daily functioning, substance use, and mental health issues.

IMAGE 8.6   Polygraph Results

Agencies with cultures where seeking help is viewed as a weakness can be particularly problematic, leaving officers and other staff with feelings of hopelessness and isolation, which can lead to additional problems. For community corrections employees who encounter a traumatic event, workplace conflicts and stress, financial issues, legal issues, family and interpersonal problems, and alcohol and substance use disorders, one avenue toward receiving professional health is employee assistance programs (EAPs). Originating as occupational alcohol programs to address alcohol use and dependency, EAPs have been extended to include all aspects of workplace productivity and organizational performance. Staff members can contact an EAP representative by phone or computer to engage in a voluntary, confidential conversation. EAPs can operate as an assessment and referral system that aims to alleviate existing challenges and problems employees face. In many cases, a staff member may contact an EAP concerned about their use of alcohol and/or substances and discover that these coping mechanisms are actually being used in response to underlying emotional and psychological issues and that they have options to support their movement toward health and recovery.

EAPs can operate as an intermediary to work with supervisors and other administrators to provide planning following a crisis. This can be particularly relevant when an employee experiences a highly traumatic event during their work, such as a client or coworker suicide, workplace violence, or a force incident. Despite common use in community corrections, there has been remarkably little research conducted on the effectiveness of EAPs. However, the goals of such programs are valuable and include improving work productivity and engagement, providing resiliency and wellness to face challenges, managing workplace stress, reducing workplace accidents, violence, and absenteeism, facilitating safe, timely, and effective return-to-work for employees, reducing health care costs, reducing staff turnover, and supporting disaster and emergency preparedness.

SUMMARY: SPECIAL POPULATIONS AND CASELOADS

This chapter examined the risks and needs associated with special populations under the supervision of the community corrections system. In line with an intersectional framework, there is an emphasis placed on diversion strategies designed to move eligible individuals away from incarceration and toward care in the community, supplemented by the supervision and monitoring of probation and parole. A key approach by community corrections is to screen special populations for specific risk and needs and place eligible individuals on specialized caseloads, where officers with additional training and expertise to develop professional relationships that facilitate successful outcomes. This includes, though is not limited to, collaboration and communication with treatment providers who implement and report progress on individualized treatment plans and conduct monitoring of special conditions. This process must consider racial, ethic, and cultural differences in special populations, particularly in terms of perceptions of mental illness, seeking help, and compliance with treatment plans.

Probation and parole officers must also assess their own risk of mental illness and substance use when working with special populations, as this workload may increase stress, frustration, and challenges. Due to the complexity of special populations, community corrections must maintain effective partnerships with multiple agencies, advocate groups, and service providers. A fundamental linkage for special populations is the interaction between courts and community corrections. A dominant approach has been the development of problem-solving courts that use a team approach to address special populations, with examples including mental health courts, drug courts, DWI courts, domestic violence courts, and sex-based offenses courts. These strategies aim to maximize effectiveness and efficiency by focusing on training, evidence-based practices, and synergy between different systems of justice.

Scenario-Based Activities

	Case	Question(s)
1.	You are a probation officer newly assigned to supervise a specialized caseload. Your specialized caseload consists of individuals with serious mental illness. There are 30 individuals assigned to your caseload.	Describe the most appropriate supervision approach for this caseload. What key strategies would you use as a probation officer? What factors would you consider in determining which strategies you selected?
2.	Madeline is a 20-year-old college student who has been struggling with substance use since she was 16. She was recently arrested for possession of a controlled substance and is facing criminal charges. The judge offered her the opportunity to participate in a drug court program. If she successfully completes the program, she will avoid incarceration and formal charges. As part of this program, the judge also sentenced her to 2 years of probation.	Pretend you are Madeline's probation officer. What key factors would you consider when designing an individualized supervision plan to address her substance use issues? What factors would you consider to reduce the likelihood of future criminal behavior?

References

Aday, L. A. (1994). Health status of vulnerable populations. *Annual Review of Public Health*, *15*(1), 487–509. https://www.annualreviews.org/doi/pdf/10.1146/annurev.pu.15.050194.002415

Baerga-Buffler, M., & Johnson, J. L. (2006). Sex offender management in the federal probation and pretrial services system. *Federal Probation*, *70*(1), 13–17. https://www.uscourts.gov/sites/default/files/fed_probation_june_2006.pdf

Belenko, S., & Peugh, J. (1998). *Behind bars: Substance abuse and America's prison population.* Center on Addiction & Substance Abuse at Columbia University. https://files.eric.ed.gov/fulltext/ED509000.pdf

Bronfenbrenner, U. (1977). Toward an experimental ecology of human development. *American Psychologist*, *32*(7), 513–531. https://doi.org/10.1037/0003-066X.32.7.513

Bronfenbrenner, U. (1979). *The ecology of human development experiments by nature and design.* Harvard University Press.

Carey, S., Fuller, B., & Kissick, K. (2008). *Michigan DWI Courts outcomes evaluation: Final report.* NDC Research. https://council.legislature.mi.gov/Content/Files/sdtcac/mi_dui_outcome_eval_final_report_0308.pdf

Centers for Disease Control and Prevention. (2008). National drunk driving crackdown—August 15–September 1, 2008. *Morbidity and Mortality Weekly Report*, *57*(31), 854–854. http://www.jstor.org/stable/23318693

Ditton, P. M. (1999). *Mental health and treatment of inmates and probationers.* Bureau of Justice Statistics. https://bjs.ojp.gov/content/pub/pdf/mhtip.pdf

English, K., Pullen, S., & Jones, L. (1997). *Managing adult sex offenders in the community: A containment approach.* U.S. Department of Justice. https://www.ojp.gov/pdffiles/sexoff.pdf

Eno Louden, J., Costino, E., Blevins, A., Fu, J., Dillman, J., & Skeem, J. (2008). *Identifying probationers with mental disorder: Validating a mental health screening questionnaire* [Paper presentation]. Annual meeting of the American Psychology-Law Society, Jacksonville, FL, United States.

Erez, E. (2002). Domestic violence and the criminal justice system: An overview. *Online Journal of Issues in Nursing*, *7*(1), 4. www.nursingworld.org/ojin/MainMenuCategories/ANAMarketplace/ANAPeriodicals/OJIN/TableofContents/Volume72002/No1Jan2002/DomesticViolenceandCriminalJustice.aspx

Fell, J. C., Tippetts, A. S., & Langston, E. A. (2011). *An evaluation of the three Georgia DUI courts.* U.S. Department of Transportation, National Highway Traffic Safety Administration. https://doi.org/10.21949/1525776

Ferri, M., Amato, L., & Davoli, M. (2006). Alcoholics Anonymous and other 12-step programmes for alcohol dependence. *Cochrane Database of Systematic Reviews*, *19*(3). https://doi.org/10.1002/14651858.CD005032.pub2

Fisher, B. S., & Lab, S. P. (2010). *Encyclopedia of victimology and crime prevention.* SAGE Publications. http://dx.doi.org/10.4135/9781412979993.n258

Fort Bend County. (n.d.). *Specialized caseloads.* https://www.fortbendcountytx.gov/government/departments/cscd-probation/about-cscd/specialized-caseloads#:~:text=Specially%20trained%20Community%20Corrections%20Officers%20supervise%20caseloads%20of,age%20or%20language%20barriers%2C%20or%20compulsive%20sexual%20behavior.

Freudenberg, N., & Heller, D. (2016). A review of opportunities to improve the health of people involved in the criminal justice system in the United States. *Annual Review of Public Health*, *37*(1), 313–333.

https://doi.org/10.1146/annurev-publhealth-032315-021420

Gilligan, J., & Lee, B. (2013). *Report to the New York Board of Correction.* National Alliance on Mental Illness Report. https://solitarywatch.com/wp-content/uploads/2013/11/Gilligan-Report.-Final.pdf

Goldkamp, J. S., & Irons-Guynn, C. (2000). *Emerging judicial strategies for the mentally ill in the criminal caseload: Mental health courts in Fort Lauderdale, Seattle, San Bernardino, and Anchorage.* Bureau of Justice Assistance. https://ojp.gov/ncjrs/virtual-library/abstracts/emerging-judicial-strategies-mentally-ill-criminal-caseload-mental

Gover, A. R., Boots, D. P., & Harper, S. B. (2021). Courting justice: Tracing the evolution and future of domestic violence courts. *Feminist Criminology, 16*(3), 366–381. https://doi.org/10.1177/1557085120987638

Haneberg, R. (2021). *Implementing specialized caseloads to reduce recidivism for people with co-occurring disorders.* Council of State Governments Justice Center. https://csgjusticecenter.org/wp-content/uploads/2021/02/CSGJC-Specialized-Caseloads_508compliantFINAL.pdf

Hanson, R. K., Helmus, L. M., & Harris, A. J. (2015). Assessing the risk and needs of supervised sexual offenders: A prospective study using STABLE-2007, Static-99R, and Static-2002R. *Criminal Justice and Behavior, 42*(12), 1205–1224. https://doi.org/10.1177/0093854815602094

Hauser, R. T. (2017). *The Allegheny County Sex Offense Court: Using evidence-based practices to increase accountability and safety.* Center for Justice Innovations. https://www.innovatingjustice.org/publications/allegheny-county-sex-offense-court-using-evidence-based-practices-increase

Johnson, S. A. (2006). *Physical abusers and sexual offenders: Forensic and clinical strategies.* CRC Press.

Kaeble, D. (2023). *Probation and parole in the United States, 2021.* Bureau of Justice Statistics. https://bjs.ojp.gov/library/publications/probation-and-parole-united-states-2021

Kessler, R. C., Berglund, P. A., Walters, E. E., Leaf, P. J., Kouzis, A. C., Bruce, M. L., Friedman, R. M., Grosser, R. C., Kennedy, C., Kuehnel, T. G., Laska, E. M., Manderscheid, R. W., Narrow, W. E., Rosenheck, R. A., & Schneier, M. (1999). *Population-based analyses: A methodology for estimating the 12-month prevalence of serious mental illness.* Center for Mental Health Services.

Kirchner, L. (2014). *Remembering the drug court revolution.* Pacific Standard.

Kirshner, S. (2014). *Officer survival for probation and parole officers.* CreateSpace Independent Publishing Platform.

Kownacki, R. J., & Shadish, W. R. (1999). Does Alcoholics Anonymous work? The results from a meta-analysis of controlled experiments. *Substance Use & Misuse, 34*(13), 1897–1916. https://doi.org/10.3109/10826089909039431

Levenson, J., & Tewksbury, R. (2009). Collateral damage: Family members of registered sex offenders. *American Journal of Criminal Justice, 34*(1), 54–68. https://doi.org/10.1007/s12103-008-9055-x

Logan, T. K., Hoyt, W., McCollister, K. E., French, M. T., Leukefeld, C., & Minton, L. (2004). Economic evaluation of drug court: Methodology, results, and policy implications. *Evaluation and Program Planning, 27*(4), 381–396. https://doi.org/10.1016/j.evalprogplan.2004.04.012

Lurigio, A. J., Cho, Y. I., Swartz, J. A., Johnson, T. P., Graf, I., & Pickup, L. (2003). Standardized assessment of substance-related, other psychiatric, and comorbid disorders among probationers. *International Journal of Offender Therapy and Comparative Criminology, 47*(6), 630–652. https://doi.org/10.1177/0306624X03257710

Marlowe, D. B. (2012). *Behavior modification 101 for drug courts: Making the most of incentives and sanctions.* National Drug Court Institute. https://www.watcp.org/wp-content/uploads/2015/03/BehaviorModification101forDrugCourts.pdf

Mental Health Foundation. (2022, February 16). *Alcohol and mental health*. https://www.mentalhealth.org.uk/explore-mental-health/a-z-topics/alcohol-and-mental-health

Mitchell, O., Wilson, D. B., Eggers, A., & MacKenzie, D. L. (2012). Assessing the effectiveness of drug courts on recidivism: A meta-analysis review of traditional and nontraditional drug courts. *Journal of Criminal Justice*, *40*(1), 60–71. https://doi.org/10.1016/j.jcrimjus.2011.11.009

Moos, R. H., & Moos, B. S. (2006). Participation in treatment and Alcoholics Anonymous: A 16-year follow-up of initially untreated individuals. *Journal of Clinical Psychology*, *62*(6), 735–750. https://doi.org/10.1002/jclp.20259

National Center for DWI Courts. (2010). *The ten guiding principles for DWI courts*. https://allrise.org/publications/the-10-guiding-principles-for-dwi-courts/

National Institute on Alcohol Abuse and Alcoholism. (n.d.). *Alcohol's effects on health*. https://www.niaaa.nih.gov/alcohols-effects-health/alcohols-effects-body

Parker, R. N., & Rebhun, L. A. (1995). *Alcohol and homicide: A deadly combination of two American traditions*. SUNY Press.

Office of Justice Programs. (2023). *Drug courts*. https://www.ojp.gov/feature/drug-courts/overview

Payne, B. K., & DeMichele, M. (2008). Warning: Sex offenders need to be supervised in the community. *Federal Probation*, *72*(1), 37–42. https://digitalcommons.odu.edu/sociology_criminaljustice_fac_pubs/13

Prins, S. J., & Draper, L. (2009). *Improving outcomes for people with mental illnesses under community corrections supervision: A guide to research-informed policy and practice*. Council of State Governments Justice Center. https://csgjusticecenter.org/wp-content/uploads/2020/02/Community-Corrections-Research-Guide.pdf

Skeem, J., Eno Louden, J., Manchak, S., Vidal, S., & Haddad, E. (2008). Social networks and social control of probationers with co-occurring mental and substance abuse problems. *Law and Human Behavior*, *33*(2), 122–135. https://doi.org/10.1007/s10979-008-9140-1

Smith, H. P. (2022). *Criminal justice and mental health: An evidence-based approach*. Kendall Hunt.

U.S. Department of Health and Human Services. (2001). *Mental Health: Culture, Race, and Ethnicity—A Supplement to Mental Health: A Report of the Surgeon General*. Substance Abuse and Mental Health Services Administration, Center for Mental Health Services. https://www.ncbi.nlm.nih.gov/books/NBK44243/pdf/Bookshelf_NBK44243.pdf

U.S. Department of Transportation. (n.d.). *Drunk driving*. https://www.nhtsa.gov/risky-driving/drunk-driving#:~:text=Risk%20Factors,-Driving%20After%20Drinking&text=If%20you%20drive%20while%20impaired,g%2FdL%20or%20higher).

Wolff, N., Epperson, M., Shi, J., Huening, J., Schumann, B. E., & Sullivan, I. R. (2014). Mental health specialized probation caseloads: Are they effective? *International Journal of Law and Psychiatry*, *37*(5), 464–472. https://doi.org/10.1016/j.ijlp.2014.02.019

Image Credits

CHAPTER 9

Experiences of Individuals on Supervision

To understand the community corrections system, it is important to examine the history, processes, and practices of agencies and their officers. However, it is also valuable to view the system through the eyes of people on supervision. In this chapter, we look at the characteristics of the supervised state and how the conditions of supervision can result in burdensome requirements and collateral consequences. The supervised state reflects the use of punitive, harsh, and controlling forms of surveillance that place unnecessary restrictions on physical movements, heightens psychological impacts, and imposes financial burden. The experiences of people on supervision reveal an accumulated effect where every point from entry and intake, to meeting the conditions of probation and parole, to acts of compliance carries risk of punishment, including further sanctions and incarceration. Many of these practices alienate and isolate people on supervision from society, creating stigma and shame while producing poor outcomes. In this chapter, we explore the notion of shame and the potential for reintegrative shaming techniques and programs that can reestablish relationships and social attachments. The chapter concludes with an examination of the ethical and legal rights that people on supervision are entitled to, such as confidentiality and privacy laws, due process and fair treatment, and other legal protections.

LEARNING OBJECTIVES

By the end of this chapter, students will be able to:

- Examine the concepts of a supervised state and the pains of supervision.
- Identify examples of collateral consequences and their impact on supervision.
- Explain stigmatization and reintegrative shaming.

KEY TERMS

- Collateral consequences
- Legal rights

- Pains of supervision
- Reintegrative shaming
- Supervised state

Nothing ever becomes real 'til it is experienced.

—John Keats

The Supervised State

In Ruben Miller's (2021) book titled *Halfway Home: Race, Punishment, and the Afterlife of Mass Incarceration*, he describes how the policies of mass incarceration and mass supervision create a "prison without walls" in the community. For people unfamiliar with community corrections, this may be an invisible or irrelevant problem, as people under supervision coexist in society and it is rare that their experiences are presented by media or public opinion. Yet for individuals who must follow the conditions of probation and parole and their families, the reality is that interactions with the criminal justice system as a whole can be daunting, inconsistent, and negative. Miller describes the modern-day community corrections systems as facilitating a supervised state, where an individual has numerous and often unnecessary restrictions imposed on their daily life. This includes where they live, who they live with, how they live, and a range of other conditions related to their behaviors (as discussed throughout this book).

Miller's (2021) **supervised state** has two components. First, the state (e.g., authorized state, justice, and welfare agencies) establishes standards of conduct that individuals must abide by to be in the community as part of their sentence. Second, the individual must feel the legal pressure of being "watched," where their daily functions are under the control of an agent of the state. In contrast to the early history of probation and parole that was discussed in Chapter 3, the supervised state moves community corrections away from rehabilitation and toward punitive responses characterized by surveillance. In Miller's assessment, in a supervised state, it is not enough to say that a person must be law-abiding, but the conditions and requirements are designed to require the individual *prove* that they are law-abiding and are deserving of having the rights of a citizen.

There are challenges associated with this supervised state. As discussed in Chapters 4 and 6, probation and parole officers are asked to engage in many rehabilitative activities, including developing a positive relationship characterized by trust, caring, and fairness. Additionally, there is an expectation that supervision rules and procedures will be uniformly applied without bias. The supervised state can also infringe upon the legal rights of individuals under supervision, particularly when surveillance, rules, and expectations are too punitive and burdensome to produce good results. For community corrections, the supervised state can undermine efforts to create a positive experience by burdening individuals with the oversight and demands that come from the pains of supervision, the burden of supervision conditions, and collateral consequences. These issues commonly appear in the narratives of individuals under the supervision of probation and parole and their descriptions of their lived experiences.

JOURNEY INTO THE FIELD: MR. TERRANCE FERRELL

◇◇◇◇◇◇◇◇

Full name: Terrance Ferrell

Title: Director of Production, Turn90 Nonprofit Organization, South Carolina

Terrance Ferrell

Mr. Terrance Ferrell was raised in the turbulent neighborhood of Echo Avenue in North Charleston, South Carolina. In 2009, *The Post and Courier* newspaper termed the broader community area of Union Heights as being the fourth worst location in the United States, as measured by crime, disorder, and poverty. These neighborhood disadvantages dated back to the 1980s and 1990s. During the 1980s, Mr. Ferrell's mother went to prison for manslaughter, and his family structure consisted of, in his words, "my grandma raising me and my brother along with a host of my uncles and people that they ran with that influenced my upbringing." Mr. Ferrell began selling drugs at age 13 and remained in school until his senior year. He received his GED the following year and attempted technical college, though he found engagement difficult due to the allure of the streets. Mr. Ferrell recounts that "selling drugs was my life and way of living. I made attempts at working, but I never spent more than a few days at it." Following release from prison in 2019, he found a sense of purpose and meaning with the nonprofit organization Turn90. He states, "I began to wonder if I could do more than selling drugs for the rest of my life. Now today I am the director of production for Turn90 Locations." Turn90 remains a key aspect of the community cor-

Image 9.1

rections system, as most participants are referred through federal and state forms of probation and parole. The organization works with men at the highest risk of rearrest by combining cognitive behavioral classes, supportive services, transitional work, and job placement to create an opportunity for success after prison where one doesn't currently exist.

Mr. Ferrell is now 45 years of age. In the following Journey into the Field, he provides his views on incarceration, probation, and finding happiness and success as an adult who has experienced adversity.

My pathway to probation began when I was very young. Growing up in a tough, drug- and violence-infested neighborhood took its toll on me as a youth—also being raised in a family that was mostly males who were older and continuously violated the law. I came from a family and community of drug dealers whom I looked up to that led to me first being on probation as a juvenile and then as an adult.

My first time on probation as an adult was for 1 year. I will never forget this experience because I felt like I was being bullied by my probation officer. He was very aggressive, and he would use his size to intimidate me. I would have an 8:30 a.m. appointment, and he would leave me in the lobby for 2 hours because he could. I have been on probation other times, and you do sometimes get that aggressiveness from most officers, but the one thing that always mattered the most was your ability to pay your monthly fee. That was the single thing from my experiences that mattered the most every time I have been on probation.

I think probation could serve a purpose if the overall department showed more compassion and concern. I think if they really focus on where an individual really needs help and provide real resources to help that individual, then it would serve a better purpose.

My life today is amazing! It is nothing short of a miracle considering what I have been through in my life. The key factor that influenced me to this point is learning life skill techniques or CBT training and getting involved with a program that provided me with the resource to understand and live my life without making choices that would interfere with my goals. I'm not saying probation is bad, but it was no factor in where I am today.

The Pains of Supervision

In 1957, criminologist Gresham Sykes conducted research in New Jersey State Prison, with his findings published in 1958 in the classic book *The Society of Captives*. As part of this work, Sykes coined the phrase "pains of imprisonment" to describe the multitude of deprivations that come with being incarcerated. These included the loss of liberty, loss of desirable goods and services, loss of heterosexual relationships, loss of autonomy, and fear of security and personal safety. To Sykes, there was not one single factor that made prison hard; it was the combination of many losses, restrictions, and rules that reduced a person's autonomy and served as "pains" in their daily life. More recently, Durnescu (2011) described a similar phenomenon in community corrections and termed this the **pains of supervision**. Durnescu argued that when an individual is under supervision, they experience an accumulation of deprivations and sanctions that lead to a restriction of their liberty. As a result, Durnescu makes an argument that the pains of supervision can move beyond negatively impacting outcomes related to community corrections and can compromise human rights. Durnescu identifies the following pains of supervision that individuals under probation and parole often experience:

Deprivation of Autonomy

Autonomy is the capacity to make an informed, uncoerced decision. Individuals on supervision tend to experience deprivation of autonomy through the constant need to reorganize their daily routine around imposed sanctions, something that can be particularly harmful for those who lack effective problem-solving and self-management skills (Andrews & Bonta, 2003). Autonomy is also impacted by the deprivation of a private or family life, as individuals are often required to share elements of their personal life with the state. Autonomy is not necessarily a single event but rather the accumulation of all facets of being under supervision. Individuals typically must make visits to the probation or parole office, participate in drug tests, inform employers and/or landlords of their status of being on supervision, limit visits to family or peers either due to the location or the status of others as being involved in the legal system, allow probation and parole officers to visit their home and place of employment without prior notice, and adhere to a lengthy list of additional conditions.

Deprivation of Time

In Sykes's (1958) conceptualization of the "pains of incarceration," it was noted that people in prison experience considerably long days where they feel bored, restless, or even anxious. For people who are incarcerated, this is the root of the colloquialism "doing time," where mental health can be influenced by the sense that time (and one's life) is being wasted in an oppressive environment with little stimuli. In the context of community corrections, this term is extended to include the wasted time that the conditions of probation or parole brings. This often involves the common challenge for supervised populations of having efficient and reliable transportation. For example, a 10-minute meeting with an officer may take several hours of travel on public transportation—or longer if the person must rely on the kindness of others. Additionally, individuals may wait lengthy periods of time in the probation and parole office lobby before being taken back to meet with their officer. This can equate to the loss of substantial time during the day just for a quick check-in. Time spent also includes the small tasks required of individuals to comply with supervision conditions. When adding these tasks together, the amount of time required can be overwhelming for the individual.

Financial Costs

Many individuals under supervision of the community corrections system are from the middle to lower socioeconomic classes. This makes any financial costs more devastating when compared to those from higher socioeconomic groups. Costs that can be measured directly include household expenses of rent, food, and clothing and the fees and fines that must be paid as part of the supervision sentence. However, these calculations can be imprecise, as they are often linked, such as taking the time off work to attend a probation or parole meeting that may lead to lost wages and travel costs. There are also multiple accumulated expenses individuals face as they move through the process, from the initial charge to the completion of a supervision sentence, which can be difficult to measure when thinking about total costs. Take the example provided in Figure 9.1, where a simple drug possession charge with a fine of $250 ended up costing the individual a total of $2,231 once the supervision sentence was complete.

FIGURE 9.1   Financial Costs of a Simple Drug Possession Charge

Stigmatization Effects

Another pain of supervision involves the labeling associated with being involved in the justice system, experiences in jail or prison and/or probation and parole supervision, having others become aware of the individual's legal troubles, and being overseen by an agent of the state. Individuals must consider who receives information of their status on supervision and how they receive that information. Some individuals attempt to hide stigmatization symbols. For example, Gelsthorpe (2007) mentions a case when a man cut off his electronic monitoring tag because he claimed that it made him "feel like a dog" (p. 495). Other individuals convicted of highly violent and/or sexual offenses may have lifelong supervision periods, with community notification, placement on watch lists, and other stigmatizing effects that are impossible to avoid.

Chapter 2 detailed the labeling process, which suggests that individuals can internalize stigma, leading to a self-fulfilling prophecy and poor outcomes, including recidivism. Take, for example, a more minor situation involving police responding to a noise complaint regarding a house party and finding an individual consuming drugs. The process of being arrested, appearing in court, being convicted, and being placed on probation supervision may convince them that they are a "drug addict" or a "criminal." Yet, stigmatization is also highly variable. Say in the previous example we add the fact that the drug was marijuana. In some states where marijuana is legal, this would result in no arrest. In other states where marijuana is decriminalized, it is unlikely to result in an arrest, although an arrest is possible. In states where marijuana is illegal, this could result in an arrest and sanctions. In this example, the offense itself becomes somewhat irrelevant. Rather, it is the response by the criminal justice system that determines if a harmful label is attached to behavior.

Forced Return to the Offense

When probation and parole agencies focus on the offense rather than addressing underlying causes of behavior or barriers toward rehabilitation, individuals may be forced to relive the original offense. Individuals on supervision who are required to recount their criminal offense may feel condemned or judged. Such an approach returns the individual to the past—that is, the time of the criminal event—and limits efforts to transform or adjust toward the future. Under the supervised state, the constant return to the offense reminds the individual that they are now considered a second-class citizen and that reintegrating with society is unlikely.

In some cases of criminal events, the individual may have a traumatic experience where the difference between being a perpetrator or victim was almost indistinguishable. A frequent example is a person who was dealing drugs when someone tried to rob them using a firearm. The resulting homicide can be a matter of impulsiveness and circumstances. Another example is when a person experienced years of violent intimate partner abuse before responding with lethal force. When these people are placed on supervision and forced to return to the offense, in many cases they are retraumatized. An analogy is a veteran of military combat who experiences posttraumatic stress following a traumatic war experience, where the mental health condition keeps them stuck in that moment in time (Falke & Goldberg, 2018). Post traumatic stress disorder and other mental health conditions do not distinguish whether a person was a perpetrator or victim (or a "good guy" or "bad guy"); they just react to a traumatic event (Falke & Goldberg, 2018). Repeatedly returning people to traumatic events without allowing for the removal of barriers to move forward can have disastrous effects on mental health.

Life Under a Constant Threat

As presented in Chapter 3, the original development of community corrections rests on the idea that the court is granting a favor by placing the individual on supervision rather than imposing a worse punishment of incarceration. As a result, many people under supervision experience constant fear and anxiety about making a mistake and being incarcerated. Research dating back 40 years has found that people on supervision perceive a disconnect between what probation and parole should do and what these systems actually do. For example, Allen (1985) found that 69% of people on probation believed that rehabilitation should be the aim of supervision, yet 78% of these same respondents agreed or strongly agreed that probation focused on surveillance. The impact of these perceptions is that the punitiveness of probation and parole may outweigh the threat of incarceration, reducing the deterrent effect of the threat of incarceration. Petersilia and Turner (1993) found that some people in intensive probation supervision found probation programs were more punitive than short prison terms. Crouch (1993) discovered that almost one third of surveyed people who were incarcerated stated that they would prefer 1 year in prison to 3 years on probation. This suggests that the pains of supervision may be more severe in some cases than the pains of incarceration.

The Burden of Supervision Conditions

The pains of supervision represent large influences on how people experience community corrections. Yet, it is important to consider the actual burden that is imposed through formal sanctions. This centers on supervisions conditions being the raison d'être (or "reason for being") for probation and parole. Restated, without conditions of supervision being placed on individuals by the state, the community corrections system would not exist. People on supervision routinely criticize supervision conditions as being burdensome, expensive, ineffective, meaningless, and invasive to their privacy. On paper, the use of 17 conditions for people under supervision might appear to be sufficient for a community punishment, as the individual is on supervision for violating the law. However, 17 conditions means that the individual is being supervised in all aspects of their lives, from where they reside, to where they work, to who they have friendships with, to what they are doing as part of social activities.

A starting point for understating this burden is to consider that the pure number of conditions violates a social work principle. In general, people can focus on and conduct up to three tasks simultaneously before they feel psychologically drained (Taxman, 2002). While three activities can be managed and juggled for most people, this does not include consideration of mental illness, substance use disorders, physical disability, and other factors that reduce this threshold. A typical set of supervision conditions produces a 6–8 times greater burden than is recommended. As a result, the burden of being supervised can overwhelm people as they must balance the challenges of everyday life.

The supervised state is apparent when one examines an actual document of conditions of supervisions. The textbox below provides an example of community corrections supervision in the state of Texas. This is a checklist that a probation or parole officer (i.e., the official government representative) would use to identify conditions and measure compliance over time. Not only is the list extensive and burdensome but it is also often vague and confusing, leaving a lot of room for interpretation for both the client and officer. Take, for example, Condition 2, which states that a person must "avoid injurious or vicious habits," a phrase that is neither defined nor has any real meaning. Condition 3 requires that a person avoid associating with an "active member of a criminal street gang, including persons with criminal records," which is unreasonable in a modern world where a person may encounter many different people (and not be aware of their gang and/or criminal history status). Most telling is Condition 7 that permits open access by the state into personal space, stating that the individual must allow the "Community Supervision Officer to visit you at your home or elsewhere, which could be digitally recorded, saved, and reproduced." Taken as whole, the conditions of supervision are broad requirements that are burdensome, not tailored to individual risks or needs, and, as a result, they are not aligned with existing evidence regarding best practices in supervision.

CONDITIONS OF SUPERVISION—TEXAS

◇◇◇◇◇◇◇◇

1. Neither commit nor be convicted of any offense against the laws of the State of Texas; or any other State; or of the United States of America.
2. Avoid injurious or vicious habits and abstain from the use of illegal drugs in any form, and not consume, transport, purchase, trade for or possess any alcoholic beverage.
3. Avoid all places and persons of harmful or disreputable character, including any person, other than a family member of the defendant, who is an active member of a criminal street gang, including persons with criminal records, (except at CSCD approved activities), persons and places where illegal drugs are possessed, used, or sold; and places where alcoholic beverages are sold and consumed except incidental to the sale of food.
4. Obtain drug/alcohol screening and/or testing and counseling as indicated under the direction of the Community Supervision Officer at own expense.
5. Report to the Community Supervision Officer as directed by the Judge and monthly thereafter unless otherwise directed by the Community Supervision Officer.

The State of Texas, Selection from "Subchapter G: Discretionary Conditions Generally," Texas Code of Criminal Procedure, 2019.

6. Participate and cooperate in the Community Supervision and Corrections Department assessment, classification, and habilation/rehabilitation programs. Obey all rules and regulations of the Community Supervision and Corrections Department.

7. Permit the Community Supervision Officer to visit you at your home or elsewhere, which could be digitally recorded, saved, and reproduced, should circumstances warrant.

8. Report any change of address, change of job, or arrest to the Community Supervision Officer within 48 hours.

9. Remain within [specified county], Texas, unless permitted in writing to depart by the Judge and/or Community Supervision Officer.

10. Not leave the State of Texas, without the written consent of the Judge filed among the papers in this cause. Comply with all requirements of the Transfer Request/Order.

11. Report by mail monthly, when transferred out of Bell County and within the State of Texas. Comply with all conditions of community supervision/probation as required by the receiving County or State. Remain in county or state of transfer unless permission from said county Supervision Officer is granted.

12. Submit to literacy testing and training as directed by Community Supervision and Corrections Department. Obtain GED or High School Diploma within year or provide proof of having.

13. Obtain and keep gainful full-time employment in a lawful occupation with referral to Texas Workforce Commission and Texas Rehabilitation Commission at any time unemployed.

14. Support dependents you now have or may acquire during the term of this community supervision.

15. Participate in substance abuse testing and submit a urine/saliva/breath specimen upon direction of the Community Supervision Officer. Do not attempt to alter, manipulate, or otherwise corrupt the test result.

16. Do not own, possess, use, or transport a firearm or ammunition, except while performing active military service with government issued weapon.

17. Do not enter into any agreement to act as "informer" or special agent for any law enforcement agency without approval of the Judge.

18. Maintain on your person at all times a current, valid State issued driver's license, or State/U.S. government issued photo identification card.

19. Attend a Victim Impact Panel at such time deemed necessary and warranted by the Community Supervision Officer.

20. Participate in and successfully complete the Cognitive Program, as directed, at own expense.

21. On or before June 15th of each year during this community supervision, defendant shall insure that his community supervision officer receives a true and correct copy of his Federal Tax Return for the previous year and a copy of all W-2's, 1099's, etc. attached thereto.

22. Pay the total of court ordered payments indicated below through the community supervision office at no less than the rate specified. All payments are effective at supervision begin date and due at the end of each month thereafter. A one-time $25.00 "time payment" fee is imposed if any part of court costs, fine, or restitution is not fully paid by the 31st day of this order. Total of court ordered payments must be paid thirty days prior to expiration. When placed in a facility in this Cause where unable to be employed and with no other source of income, all payments are held in abeyance until release.

$ Court Costs to be paid $ per month.

$ Fine to be paid $ per month.

$ Restitution to be paid $ per month. (Payable to:)

$ Texas Department of Public Safety Lab fee to be paid $ per month.

$ Court Appointed Attorney to be paid $ per month.

$ Crime Stoppers fee.

$ Life Skills program fee.

$ Pre-Sentence Investigation report fee.

$ Substance Abuse Questionnaire fee.

$ Supervision fee per month for each month of the supervision period.

$ $25.00 Substance Abuse Test fee per month for each month of the direct supervision period while on specialized caseload/ $10.00 fee per month for each month of the direct supervision period while on regular caseload.

23. Participate in and successfully complete the Life Skills program, as scheduled by Community Supervision Officer.

24. Work faithfully and satisfactorily participates in approved community service project(s) by completing _____ hours of community service at a rate of no less than _____ hours per calendar month.

Maya Schenwar and Victoria Law (2020), authors of *Prison by Any Other Name: The Harmful Consequences of Popular Reforms*, discuss how the excessive and harsh nature of supervision conditions transform community corrections into an oppressive experience that has all the trappings to keep individuals recycling through the justice system. Schenwar and Law describe experiences of individuals attempting to meet conditions of probation and parole within the supervised state. Their work describes people in a vulnerable situation because the officer (as the overseer of the state) has discretion to determine whether a person is considered compliant or not. This discretion is what makes the supervised state so difficult, as the person on supervision does not know what decisions officers will make. Given the high level of discretion available to officers, it is typically unclear which or what combination of condition violations are serious enough to warrant revocation or to be considered for reincarceration. This is highlighted in an excerpt from Schenwar and Law (2020):

> Colette Payne had been in Chicago's Cook County Jail for a week when she was offered the option of being released on electronic monitoring and house arrest. … So Payne chose the monitor—an electronic shackle that would essentially incarcerate her in her home, forcing her to stay within a certain radius, or else the police would be alerted. The monitor was presented as her only alternative to incarceration. …

Maya Schenwar and Victoria Law, Selection from "Your Home Is Your Prison," *Prison by Any Other Name: The Harmful Consequences of Popular Reforms*, pp. 1-2. Copyright © 2020 by The New Press.

What Payne hadn't counted on were the extreme restrictions that came with house arrest and monitoring. Every step beyond 100 feet of her mother's doorway had to be preapproved by her probation officer. Employees from the sheriff's department came to Payne's home to conduct inspection alerting the entire housing complex that she was being monitored. Payne was unable to take her young children to school or to the store. She knew they were affected by her confinement—her older son began to act out in school and cried often. Payne missed family barbecues. She couldn't even take the garbage out since the dumpsters were at the end of the housing complex, beyond where she was allowed to go. ... "You're basically held hostage in your own home," she said of her time on the monitor.

Being tethered to her home didn't help Payne address the reason she had been arrested in the first place—a decade-long heroin addiction. ... But electronic monitoring does the opposite—it traps people, many times isolating them from loved ones, sometimes making it difficult for them to take care of others and to feel a sense of purpose and meaning. Instead, they spend their days wrestling with boredom and the strain of captivity.

For Payne, that boredom and isolation exacerbated her desire to get high. Her cravings for heroin were ever-present. But neither the court nor the probation office offered resources to support her in addressing her addiction. In fact, she was not granted permission to leave her home to look for or attend treatment. If she attempted to do so, she would be in violating the terms of her electronic monitoring and subject to arrest and reimprisonment. (pp. 1–2)

In this narrative it is evident that the person on supervision did not lend toward noncompliance (i.e., substance use) due to one major life event or one condition of probation. Rather, it was the constant and collective burden of restrictions on movement, officer surveillance, emotional and social isolation, boredom and restlessness, and barriers to treatment that pushed her closer and closer to heroin use. This narrative can promote empathy in the reader, as one can ponder whether they could meet these conditions of probation or parole or how much these conditions would interfere with their own daily habits and activities. Upon reflection, it becomes easy to perceive a community corrections system (and court system) that mandates so many conditions that it sets people up for failure—a view that often emerges in the cynicism of people who are on supervision or who have previously been on supervision.

Collateral Consequences

It is evident that the pains of supervision and the burden of supervision conditions can have a profound effect on the lives of people who interact with community corrections. In recent years, this work has been extended to include recognition of the impact of extra-legal restrictions, known as collateral consequences. **Collateral consequences** are the indirect effects of being under supervision. For example, an individual may have to meet direct conditions for their probation sentence such as drug testing, attending program, and paying fees; these are often assigned during court procedures and during initial meetings with probation or parole. However, individuals may not consider the indirect impact that a probation or parole sentence will have on other parts of their life, like employment, housing, and public assistance.

A collateral consequence can also include nontangible factors, like stigma and shame experienced by the person and their family, which can be more common in parole where clients have previous periods of incarceration. While collateral consequences are difficult to measure (e.g., How does one measure shame in the child of a person on parole? How does one measure not having voting rights?), we know they exist because they frequently emerge in the narratives of people under supervision. It is also worth noting that while a probation or parole sentence can be completed, collateral consequences can continue indefinitely, leading to long-term harm.

Collateral consequences vary by state and individual, though we provide three examples below that individuals on supervision frequently experience: employment, housing, and public assistance.

Employment

Nearly 87% of employers conduct background checks, and most employers report that they are unwilling to hire applicants with justice involvement (American Bar Association, 2018). Many states do not allow individuals with justice involvement to be employed by public agencies. Additionally, some probation and parole officers require individuals under supervision to disclose to potential employers their current supervision status. As a result, nearly 60% of formerly incarcerated individuals remain unemployed, as reported by the American Bar Association (2018). Additionally, justice-involved individuals are paid 40% less annually than the typical employee in that job who is not justice-involved. There are also barriers to employment in some professions in some states that do not allow individuals under supervision to work in certain professions (e.g., barbers or in a position handling money). Trying to find employment and a job that pays a living wage is a challenge for those on supervision—a pattern that can continue for years after a probation or parole supervision period is completed.

Housing

Much like employment, many landlords will do a background and credit check to screen out prospective tenants with criminal records. Home ownership is an option, though experiences in the criminal justice system, either incarceration or community corrections supervision, can lead to the depletion of the necessary funds to buy a house. In terms of public housing, federal laws require a mandatory ban on access for people with certain types of convictions, although the law also gives discretion to local housing authorities to determine whether a person may be eligible. However, when used, the ban can be applied to the entire household and can result in eviction if violated. Without options, some individuals on supervision turn to public homeless shelters, though this carries instability and risk of violence and recidivism (American Bar Association, 2018).

Public Assistance

Depending on the state that a person lives in, individuals may be banned from receiving assistance for food, housing, substance use and mental health services, and other health services. Medicaid expansion, thanks to the Affordable Healthcare Act, relieved some of the challenges with access to health and behavioral health services in the states within the expanded services network. Food insecurity remains a problem, with many individuals lacking enough income to purchase foods that meet adequate dietary standards (American Bar Association, 2018). In fact, studies have found that not having enough food or nutritional food (food insecurity) affects compliance with supervision conditions of release and recidivism (Al Abosy et al., 2022; Testa & Jackson, 2019).

The Community Corrections Process

Elements of the supervised state that frequently emerge in the narrative of individuals under supervision include the high levels of surveillance, control, and harsh punishment. However, it is common to find that many individuals who interact with community corrections find the cumulative effect of punishment to occur along multiple points throughout the process. To better understand the perspective of people under the supervision of probation and parole, it is beneficial to examine the points of contact that produce the greatest resentment and negativity in these populations. While the burden of the actual conditions of probation and parole (and the related collateral consequences) have been discussed, there are real-world interactions that occur along a continuum from entry to probation and parole, meeting the conditions of supervision over time, and to state responses when noncompliance occurs.

Entry to Probation and Parole

People on supervision routinely report the entry points to community corrections as being burdensome and potentially traumatic. This may include an interaction with law enforcement, courts, and institutional corrections prior to being placed on supervision. At each point in these systems, the individual is categorized and processed, typically by moving the person along a series of punishments and sanctions.

Court Processing and Sentencing

During court processing and sentencing, the individuals must attend the court hearings. Most courts require the individual to come at the beginning of the day and wait till their case is called, possibly resulting in returning another day because the court did not get to the case. Malcolm Feeley (1979) described the court as a place where the legal processes are the punishment, meaning that the court operations implicitly serve to demean individuals through demanding multiple court appearances, not having clear rules and procedures about when a hearing or sentencing will occur, making the individual lose wages from missing work, paying bail bondsmen and attorney's fees, and wasting their time. Defendants may develop the perception that judges, prosecutors, and defense attorneys perceive their jobs as handling "social outcasts" or other negative labels, which leads to shame and stigma in these populations.

Intake

Once placed under the supervision of community corrections, individuals will find that each probation and parole agency has their own procedures for intake. Sometimes the intake unit is in the courthouse, and sometimes it is at the probation agency. Sometimes the person must go to the courthouse to initiate the process and then go to the probation agency to complete the process. The process of categorization is intensified at intake, where the individual may be required to bring the court order, present personal identification, have their picture(s) taken, report tattoos (and often have each tattoo photographed), and give a urine sample. Individuals may also be subjected to a DNA test, with the information then placed in a state and/or federal database. Often, these procedures are done in open areas where an individual's business can become public. Intake is typically impersonal and bureaucratic, involving the individual reviewing basic demographic and criminal history information for accuracy, completing a risk-need assessment tool, establishing a fee payment schedule, and reviewing supervision requirements. Intakes are typically lengthy appointments, which may run upwards of 45–60 minutes long with many different requirements to cover, often leaving little room for dialogue or discussions.

Experiencing Probation and Parole

Following intake and depending on risk category and officer discretion, the individual will be monitored by three primary methods: routine office visits, home and work visits, and via technology. People who experience probation or parole can find these forms of surveillance ubiquitous; that is, the state becomes highly involved in their daily movements, activities, and personal life.

Routine Office Visits

After the initial intake, many individuals will be required to comply with a schedule of routine office visits with their assigned probation or parole officer. These interactions also include phone conversations, and contacts with family members, employers, treatment providers, or anyone else the officer feels would be necessary to contact.

Mandated officer visits usually produce the need for individuals to inform others that they are on supervision and that the supervision officer may be contacting them for information about how the person is doing. Most probation officers operate during the normal business hours of 8:00 a.m. to 5:00 p.m., which means it is common for individuals to be required to take off work to meet this obligation.

Many individuals have additional conditions of probation and parole that require additional office visits. For example, if an individual must comply with random drug testing, visits can increase in frequency to weekly contacts (often with little to no notice to plan in advance).

In a study of people on probation in Baltimore, Maryland, Wooditch and colleagues (2013) found that individuals were required to meet their officer monthly while also being drug tested twice a week in the office. On average, these individuals spent over 2 hours each way to get to the probation office using buses and other public transportation. Since most individuals did not have a car, the frequent visits to the probation office meant the individuals could not work or had to find jobs that occurred at night. This transportation issue contributed to many individuals not showing up for drug testing and monthly visits with the officer because they could not afford the transportation costs and lost wages, find someone to give them a ride, and get permission from their employers to take off that much time.

In addition to the sheer effort of making it to office visits, there is the experience that people on supervision have once they arrive. The physical space and architecture of community corrections office spaces vary. Some offices may have dim lights, unclean restrooms, and sparse environmental resources, while others may feel more like hospital waiting rooms. Feeley (1979) argues that the probation or parole setting often speaks to the fact that individuals are being punished, and to a large extent, the individuals in this setting are considered not to be worthy of a pleasant setting. While some agencies prioritize the office environment and strive to make the waiting room feel welcoming with warm colors painted on the walls, indoor plants, and calming pictures, this is not the norm.

IMAGE 9.2   Municipal Courts and Council Chambers, Englewood Civic Center, Colorado

Differences in agencies can also be found in security procedures. Many offices have metal detectors, wands, and/or security personnel that individuals must go through before they can enter the office. This again reminds the individual that they are under the supervision of the state and must be monitored at all times. With the prevalence of personal technologies, many offices will not allow individuals to bring a cell phone. Most offices will not allow individuals to bring another person or children, which also requires the individual to secure care providers if they are caretakers for their parents, elderly grandparents, or children. This means that individuals often must wait at the supervision office by themselves (and without cell phones).

Supervision visits are typically brief, lasting around 5–10 minutes in most cases. Individuals are required to "check in" and provide an update on the status of their conditions, employment, education, living arrangements, and any other topic that the officer desires information on. Research indicates that there is a lot of uncertainty that an individual experiences during office visits since the tone and procedures during meetings depend largely on the demeanor of the officer. Some officers pursue a working relationship during these monitoring sessions, as described in Chapter 6, and some officers have an authoritarian tone. The check-ins serve the purpose of identifying if there are any compliance issues with supervision, and the individual cannot predict how the officer will respond if they fail a drug test, lose a job, have to move, or anything else that could be considered a violation to their conditions of supervision.

Home and Work Visits

Depending on the conditions of supervision and the discretion of the officer, contacts may also occur randomly at home or work. Individuals under supervision commonly report concern about whether a family member or employer will report information that may not be considered favorable. For example, if the person has been out sick from work, the employer may inform the supervision officer, and then the officer may use this information to consider that the person is not abiding by the work requirements. If the individual is not getting along with a family member or there are tensions in the house, this could also be an issue if the individual is portrayed as "threatening," "confrontational," or "aggressive." The mere presence of an officer at a home or workplace means that all the individuals in those settings are also being judged. If an officer sees something they are concerned with, they can inform law enforcement, child welfare (if it involved a child), or housing authorities (if the house was in disarray or hazardous). This extends the supervision state to not only the individual but to their support systems, home, and work environment.

Technological Surveillance

In 1949, George Orwell published his now classic dystopian fiction book titled *Nineteen Eighty-Four*, which warns of the consequences of totalitarianism and omnipresent government surveillance. The book portrays a society with little privacy, where houses are equipped with technology that allows people to be watched or listened to at any time and children are asked to report suspicious people to the government and denounce their parents. Through mass surveillance, people are compelled toward obedience and compliance. In today's community corrections system, technological advancements (e.g., electronic monitoring, GPS units, cell phones, electronic kiosks, client portals) have far surpassed anything that Orwell could have imagined. These technological advancements are continuing to evolve through biometric monitoring, digitally enabled toolkits and interventions, virtual reality, and artificial intelligence. For people under supervision, this brings concern that the state is monitoring their movements and behaviors for every minute of the day with no reprieve. This is not to say that technology is all bad; there are some recent advancements surrounding virtual reporting that may reduce barriers and improve the process for individuals under supervision. However, if used inappropriately, technology can serve to further increase the supervised state promoted by probation and parole.

Noncompliance

The community corrections process is considered complete when the individual meets one of two outcomes: they successfully meet all requirements of the supervision sentence, or they fail the supervision sentence due to noncompliance. *Noncompliance* refers to a range of behaviors, including technical violations or recidivism (see Chapter 10 for a further discussion of measuring recidivism). Within a state of supervision conceptualization, expressions of noncompliance can be viewed as a rejection, challenge, or threat toward the state. Individuals under supervision are often surprised to find that their noncompliance may be taken personally by officers, particularly officers (and agencies) aligned with a law enforcement culture. In many cases, individuals under supervision simply do not know how their officer will respond. Often, officers will not inform the individual of the consequences of noncompliance, or they will threaten to seek a warrant for the person if they do not abide by supervision rules. One defense attorney commented on this uncertainty that can occur in supervision based on the discretions of officers:

> Most probation officers, I think, will informally deal with issues before they file a violation. I think some probation officers will deal with quite a bit of issues, like a person's left treatment, but they got a new Rule 25 done, and they got back into treatment, and so they'll give a lot more leeway. I think other ones are more willing to just be like, "Well, you didn't do what I said. I'm done with you." You know, "I'm filing that violation." ... I think it's so probation officer-dependent, which can be frustrating. Sometimes I see names and some probation officers, whether it's fair or not, I'll give more credence to, because, from prior experience, I know that they really work with their people. Sometimes I see names being like, "Of course. They file a violation about everything." ... It's so based on personalities, and maybe the connection they have, or they don't have. (Mitchell et al., 2021, p. 34)

Some officers will respond with blurred roles, such as acting in the capacity of a judge who is seeking indications of shame and remorse from the individual, as seen here:

> Did they have a misconduct, they realized it, they took responsibility and they're addressing it? That's going to get a totally different response from me, as opposed to a client who is increasing their level of misconduct and non-compliance and are not responding to attempts to regain compliance. (Mitchell et al., 2021, p. 29)

To alleviate overcrowded court dockets, some community corrections systems will encourage these judicial-like processes. In fact, beginning in the 1990s, many probation agencies were extended the authority to put a person in jail for up to 30 days for violating a condition of supervision without a violation hearing by the judge. This administrative tool gave officers the opportunity to exalt more punishment on an individual if they did not follow the rules of supervision.

From the perspective of individuals on probation or parole supervision, a failure to comply is often not intended as a challenge to the state but rather a reflection of the barriers to obtaining health care, social welfare, and social support coupled with their everyday needs to meet basic human needs (e.g., food, shelter, relationships). Most supervision agencies do not have in-house support or health-related services, instead relying upon community-based services. This is particularly problematic, as individuals under supervision are substantially more likely to have a substance use disorder, mental health disorder, or a co-occurring disorder. Instead, individuals under supervision usually are given a list of approved services and told to make their own arrangements (see Chapter 4 for a discussion of passive referral system). They are then required to obtain the needed services, pay for the services, and go to services.

Taxman et al. (2007) found that on any given day, less than 10% of individuals under community corrections supervision could access services. This places the person at greater risk for being considered noncompliant, and depending on the attitude of the officer, they could be in violation. Even more importantly, the services that are available in the community are often inappropriate for the needs of the individual. This is especially true, as individuals tend to need more intensive services than the traditional once-a-week group counseling session that is most commonly available (Taxman et al., 2013). As a result, individuals under supervision do not get the treatment they need, which can further contribute to negative outcomes.

The consequences for noncompliance can be dire for the individual, a point described as the "revolving door" of the criminal justice system. In this cycle, a person is placed on probation or parole, the person violates the conditions of supervision, and the person then has their community privileges terminated and they are incarcerated. An enduring problem is that many violations of the conditions of supervision are not criminal behavior, as discussed throughout this book. Instead, they are rules of supervision that place individuals in jeopardy just as much as committing a crime. For example, if an individual does not pay child support or visits a friend in the hospital who may have been involved in the justice system, the officer has a discretion to issue a warrant for noncompliance. Since supervision is considered a form of conditional release, a violation of a supervision condition is essentially a violation of supervision, where the individual could be (re)incarcerated. Besides the numerous conditions that are required for supervision, the ever-present potential for violation and loss of one's liberties can place tremendous burden on an individual.

◊ Diversity, Equity, and Inclusion: Reintegrative Shaming

The lived experience of people under supervision presents challenges in terms of tangible elements (e.g., employment, housing, fees, health programs, treatment) and nontangible, or more emotional, components. For many people under supervision of parole and probation, these factors push them to the periphery of society. Using an intersectional framework, we must consider that a justice-involved individual may be experiencing poverty or homelessness, may be a racial or ethnic minority, and may be experiencing physical or mental health issues, all of which isolated the person from the social resources that being in mainstream society brings. In many ways, the community corrections system functions to create a conduit, or opportunity, that allows marginalized people to reintegrate with society. While tangible elements are observable and easy to measure, far less is known about the nontangible factors that limit inclusion into society. However, the narrative of people on supervision often includes the issues of shame, stigma, and alienation, suggesting that these issues require further consideration.

The topic of shame received a boost from Australian criminologist John Braithwaite (1989) when he published the now classic *Crime, Shame, and Reintegration*. Braithwaite explained that all countries have a system of justice that identifies and punishes crime, though there are differences in the way that countries reintegrate people into society. In places where there is a high degree of social integration, there is an increased use of restorative justice, where people who have committed crimes are punished and then welcomed back into the community. Examples include countries like Japan and through tribal justice in Indigenous tribes. In contrast, the U.S. criminal justice system is distinguished by a reliance on deterrence, incapacitation, and retribution (see Chapter 1), where a formal punishment relegates a person to being separated from society (and with little chance of returning). Braithwaite (1989) describes these differences as such:

> The crucial distinction is between shaming that is reintegrative and shaming that is disintegrative (stigmatization). Reintegrative shaming means that expressions of community disapproval, which may range from mild rebuke to degradation ceremonies, are followed by gestures of reacceptance into the community of law-abiding citizens. These gestures of reacceptance will vary from a simple smile expressing forgiveness and love to quite formal ceremonies to decertify the offender as deviant. Disintegrative shaming (stigmatization), in contrast, divides the community by creating a class of outcasts. (p. 55)

When one considers jails and prisons, the individual is physically isolated from society and their presence within an institution carries significant negative stigmatization. Once a person is released from jail or prison, the more they can be economically, socially, and emotionally attached to their community, the less likely they are to continue to engage in criminal behavior (Berg & Huebner, 2011). This is why the term "reintegration" is preferred over "reentry," as the former indicates a successful fusion back into society, while the latter simply refers to a change in the individual's physical location. Community corrections may offer greater likelihood of connecting people to their society as they operate within the community, engage in partnerships with other agencies, and may have a rehabilitative orientation that can address barriers to care.

In line with Braithwaite's (1989) theory of reintegrative shaming, community corrections should acknowledge that shame and stigma will be prevalent in their supervised populations.

It is not a matter of recognizing that shame exists but whether this shame is stigmatizing (i.e., disintegrative) or not stigmatizing (i.e., reintegrative). In fact, Braithwaite (1989) wrote that "it would seem that sanctions imposed by relatives, friends or a personally relevant collectivity have more effect on criminal behavior than sanctions imposed by a remote legal authority" (p. 69). In other words, it is the community that impacts crime and recidivism, not just individual choice.

Reintegrative shaming theory has been associated with restorative justice, which includes a wide range of practices, such as family conferences, victim–offender mediations, sentencing circles, victim-impact panels, and community boards. For probation and parole, restorative justice places an emphasis on using reintegrative shaming when addressing individuals. A salient example is Dollar and Ray's (2015) investigation of a mental health court, which uses a team approach involving community corrections staff. The court takes a nonadversarial approach that emphasizes treatment and relationship redevelopment. Once placed on probation or parole, the individual receives an individualized treatment plan, which is reviewed and approved by all team members. Community corrections is responsible for monitoring progress on mental health services, medical treatment, medication, attendance at group sessions, obtaining stable housing, retaining stable housing, participating in school or work-related activities, and avoiding additional criminal behaviors.

Compliance is also reinforced during open court sessions each month, which last 2–3 hours and are used to publicly evaluate each participant's compliance with treatment, service, and other court mandates (Dollar & Ray, 2015). The emphasis during these sessions is positive and designed to build relationships, with conversations about birthdays and other life events. In one session, the judge said:

> Each one of you are unique and deserve a quality life. There are no failures in this courtroom. There is an opportunity to hold your own outcome. We are here to balance accountability and support. Accountability means that you need to make your group meetings, follow the law, respect yourself and others, and be honest. Support means that you have to continue coming here for help, so that you can have the life you deserve. And what you deserve is to be safe, sober, and happy. (Dollar & Ray, 2015, p. 36)

When individuals are not compliant, such as a failed drug test or additional crime, the team follows the tenets of reintegrative shaming by disapproving the behavior but not the individual. This is evident in one judge's statement: "I hate your behavior. I hate that you used drugs. But I still love you" (Dollar & Ray, 2015, p. 37). The final stage is the use of ceremonial decertification—that is, expressions that the individual is welcome back into the community. Braithwaite (1989) states, "Reintegrative shaming is shaming which is followed by efforts to reintegrate the offender back into the community of law-abiding and respectable citizens through words or gestures of forgiveness or ceremonies to decertify the offender as deviant" (p. 101). The mental health court uses graduation ceremonies, with an announcement that formal charges have been dropped or that periods of supervision are over to meet this goal. Taken as a whole, **reintegrative shaming** represents a conduit for success in community corrections, where medication programs and addressing barriers to care can connect stakeholders like people under supervision, victims, and members of the community. Noncompliance brings a rejection of the behavior but continued support for the individual in lieu of harsh, isolating, and stigmatizing (i.e., disintegrative) responses that cause more crime.

Ethical Considerations and Legal Rights

As people on probation and parole deal with the pains of supervision, they can begin to feel hopelessness and alienation. Here, the strain of being in a state of supervision, with high levels of surveillance and continued risk of punitive responses, can make many people unwilling or unable to consider their ethical and legal rights. In some cases, an individual may be unaware or misguided when it comes to understanding their rights. In other cases, an individual may believe that expressing their rights to a probation or parole officer could result in being labeled a "troublemaker," which could produce negative responses. Another explanation is that many people on supervision have the sole aim of completing their sentence and putting the experience behind them. However, ethical considerations and legal rights are a crucial component of the experience of people on supervision, as they represent the accepted standards, practices, and procedures that reinforce the rights of the individual. They are the rule book for how the community corrections system is supposed to operate.

Confidentiality and Privacy Concerns

The rights of individuals on supervision and their protected health information (PHI) are also reinforced by the Health Insurance Portability and Accountability Act of 1996 (HIPAA). In Chapter 12 we address the data management and sharing of personal information in the context of partnerships; however, in the current chapter we will address the legal rights of the individual. It is important to note that probation and parole agencies are not defined as "covered entities." Therefore, if an individual discloses personal health information to their probation officer, that officer may share or redisclose that information without being affected by HIPAA (Petrila & Fader-Towe, 2010). However, there are local, state, and federal laws that govern what information can be shared. For example, when a probation or parole officer is determining whether an individual is complying with supervision conditions, they must have either a court order or the individual's authorization permitting the treatment provider to release the information (Petrila & Fader-Towe, 2010). In most cases, individuals must permit the disclosure of information to community correction officers, including both mental health and substance use information.

Probation and parole officers must maintain confidentiality regarding personal information disclosed by individuals on probation and parole. For example, officers will often be privy to PHI, including mental health, substance use, and physical health. State laws may require individuals under supervision to provide permission to the probation and parole agency to disclose PHI to the court. As a result, some agencies make sharing of PHI a condition of supervision. Additionally, federal laws require that individuals under supervision provide consent to treatment providers before those providers can provide PHI to their probation and parole officer. Beyond PHI, probation and parole officers are legally allowed to contact family members, employers, and friends to discuss an individual on their caseload. Typically, agency policies specify that these communications should be solely for the purpose of doing one's job.

Due Process

The Supreme Court decision in *Morrissey v. Brewer* (1972) determined that while parole revocation hearings do not trigger full due process protections, individuals under supervision do maintain rights protected under the 14th amendment (see Chapter 4 for more information). For example, this decision determined that individuals have six basic protections to protect due process during parole revocations:

- They must receive written notice of the violation(s) of parole.
- All evidence against the individual must be disclosed.
- The individual must be given the opportunity to be heard in person, present witnesses, and document evidence.
- The individual has the right to confront and cross-examine witnesses.
- There must be a "neutral and detached" hearing body (e.g., traditional parole board whose members do not need to be representatives of judiciary or lawyers).
- If parole is revoked, a written statement by the hearing body must detail the evidence and reasons for revocation.

In 1973, *Gagnon v. Scarpelli* extended these same protections to individuals on probation. Additionally, many probation and parole agencies will have their own policies in place to promote due process for individuals under supervision. For example, some agencies have grievance processes in place that allow individuals to file formal complaints against their probation or parole officer. These policies typically dictate that individuals may not issue a grievance for factors beyond the agency's control, such as state decisions, laws and regulations, supervision conditions, and violations.

Legal Rights

While on probation and parole, individuals retain access to their **legal rights** protected under the U.S. Constitution. For example, as discussed previously, individuals under supervision have the right to due process if their probation or parole is revoked. Individuals under supervision also have the right to consult with an attorney when facing legal issues related to their supervision. These may include issues related to violations, modifications made on their supervision terms, and early termination of supervision. While this can be beneficial to ensure their rights are protected and they receive appropriate guidance, this can be costly for individuals who are often already financially insecure. Additionally, individuals under supervision have the right to access necessary medical care if they are injured or ill.

However, some protected rights may be limited based on one's supervision status. Common rights that are modified during a supervision period include the freedom of movement (need travel permission, may be limited to specific areas), privacy (supervision officer can search individual and their property at any time), and freedom to own a firearm (nearly all under supervision are prohibited from owning or possessing a firearm). Additional limitations are placed on individuals depending on their charge (e.g., sex offenses, as discussed in Chapter 8). The legal rights of each individual will vary depending on the specific jurisdiction and the individual's specific circumstances.

The organization Roots & Rebound (n.d.) provides a roadmap for people under supervision that provides legal guidance, resources, and referrals at each step in the system. This includes county-level supervision (court probation, formal probation, post-release community supervision, mandatory supervision, violations and revocations), state parole, and federal community supervision (federal probation, supervised release, federal parole). Roots & Rebound (n.d.) moves along the roadmap sequentially. For example, the state parole category follows these topics in order:

1. The basics of state parole
2. After release: what to expect in your first days out on state parole
3. The length of state parole, including (a) what to do if you believe your parole term length is miscalculated, and (b) how to get off parole early
4. The general conditions of state parole
5. The extra ("special") conditions of state parole and the legal requirements for imposing these special conditions
6. The process for challenging conditions of state parole
7. Your rights as a parolee with a disability
8. Procedures for state parole violations and revocations

Roots & Rebound (n.d.) provides information that assists individuals with understanding their rights within the community corrections system. In one example, the question asked is "What is the legal standard for finding me guilty of a parole violation?" (Roots & Rebound, n.d., "State Parole Violations" section). The response is "At the parole revocation hearing, the judge must decide whether a 'preponderance of the evidence' (meaning more than half of the evidence) supports the charges. In other words, the district attorney must prove that it is more likely than not that you violated parole" (Roots & Rebound, n.d., "State Parole Violations" section). Roots & Rebound also provides forms for individuals to use for legal purposes. For example, a Petition for Writ of Habeas Corpus is a legal option available to people in custody. In this kind of petition, the individual is arguing that are being unlawfully held in custody and should be released.

READING

MC-275

Name: _____

Address: _____

_____

_____

_____

CDC or ID Number: _____

_____

_____

_____

_____

(Court)

_____	**PETITION FOR WRIT OF HABEAS CORPUS**
Petitioner	
vs.	No. _____
_____	*(To be supplied by the Clerk of the Court)*
Respondent	

INSTRUCTIONS—READ CAREFULLY

- **If you are challenging an order of commitment or a criminal conviction and are filing this petition in the Superior Court, you should file it in the county that made the order.**
- **If you are challenging the conditions of your confinement and are filing this petition in the Superior Court, you should file it in the county in which you are confined.**

- Read the entire form *before* answering any questions.
- This petition must be clearly handwritten in ink or typed You should exercise care to make sure all answers are true and correct. Because the petition includes a verification, the making of a statement that you know is false may result in a conviction for perjury.
- Answer all applicable questions in the proper spaces. If you need additional space, add an extra page and indicate that your answer is "continued on additional page.'
- If you are filing this petition in the superior court, you only need to file the original unless local rules require additional copies. Many courts require more copies.
- If you are filing this petition in the Court of Appeal in paper form and you are an attorney, file the original and 4 copies of the petition and. if separately bound. 1 set of any supporting documents (unless the court orders otherwise by local rule or in a specific case). If you are filing this petition in the Court of Appeal electronically and you are an attorney, follow the requirements of the local rules of court for electronically filed documents. If you are fifing this petition in the Court of Appeal and you are *not* represented by an attorney, file the original and one set of any supporting documents.
- If you are filing this petition in the California Supreme Court file the original and 10 copies of the petition and, if separately bound, an original and 2 copies of any supporting documents.
- Notify the Clerk of the Court in writing if you change your address after filing your petition

Approved by the Judicial Council of California for use under rule 8.380 of the California Rules of Court (as amended effective January 1. 2007). Subsequent amendments to rule 8.380 may change the number of copies to be furnished to the Supreme Court and Court of Appeal.

Page 1 of 6

Form Approved for Optional Use Judicial Council of California MC-275 [Rev. January 1, 2017]	**PETITION FOR WRIT OF HABEAS CORPUS**	Penal Code, § 1473 at seq.; Cal. Rules of Court, rule 8.380 *www.courts.ca.gov*

◊ Officer Works, Careers, and Wellness: Professional Membership Associations

Within an intersectionality framework it becomes clear that modern-day probation and parole work is complex and people on supervision have a range of risks, needs, and challenges. For staff working in community corrections, confronting social problems in the form of the clients who they interact with can be gratifying but also overwhelming and confusing. Support for the workplace can be found in professional membership associations, a primary source of governance, advocacy, training, culture, and professional development. The American Probation and Parole Association (APPA, n.d.) is the largest and most respected association in community corrections. Membership is open to all levels of the government and the private sector and include community corrections professionals, service providers, libraries and educators, research students, volunteers, concerned citizens, corporations, public policy advocates, and others (APPA, n.d.). The APPA (n.d.) aims to meet the following eight goals:

- Instilling confidence in the community corrections industry.
- Serving and engaging the more than 90,000 community corrections professionals in America.
- Providing a safe space for dialogue and resolution of the many issues facing the community corrections workforce.
- Utilizing the latest and best technology to deliver training and disseminate information.
- Assisting in the growth and professional development of community corrections and supervision professionals.
- Providing networking opportunities for students and professionals to share ideas and exchange information about what works in the field.
- Offering support, direction, and resources to jurisdictions that are grooming the best of industry professionals.
- Working continuously to define our role in public policy and expand our presence, both nationally and internationally.

The APPA (n.d.) uses several approaches to achieve these goals. First, it interacts with scholars and experts to produce research reports, technical guides, and provide webinars for information. They publish a quarterly journal called *Perspectives*, which brings together innovative work done by practitioners and researchers in the community corrections field. Second, the APPA develops professionalism in community corrections through onsite and online training. A review of upcoming training seminars shows the following topics: community corrections reform, integrating RNR with desistance, officer health, wellness and trauma-informed leadership, racial justice town hall, the use of office discretion in supervision for seriously mentally ill clients, and best practice for transgender clients. This also includes a leadership institute where senior probation/parole officers and managers engage in 12 months of training and produce a project that benefits their home agency. Third, the APPA advocates for evidence-based practices and updated policies for use in the field, organizes committees, and hosts issue-specific working groups to address current crisis and problems.

SUMMARY: THE EXPERIENCE OF COMMUNITY CORRECTIONS

Being in a supervised state means that one is not truly free to make decisions and that the individual is considered a law violator who needs to be watched (Miller, 2021). A review of the supervision experience reveals that individuals are often in a state of uncertainty: What are they to do? How will the officer respond? How will the court respond? And how can they manage their daily life with all the requirements of supervision? Individuals under supervision often experience many challenges coupled with the constant threat of incarceration that can turn into physical and psychological pains that affect the everyday decisions and movements of individuals. In the larger community, there are numerous collateral consequences related to the basics of life—housing, food, employment—and these consequences present barriers to resuming a crime-free lifestyle.

The experiences of people on supervision are systematic, and they extend from entry to probation and parole, to the burden of extensive supervision conditions, and to issues of noncompliance. Reintegrative shaming offers the potential to move isolated, alienated populations back into mainstream society, where attachments and social resources can reduce the risk of recidivism. This can make individuals feel that they are valued, have a future, and can consider their time under supervision as useful and valuable. Along with emotional and social integration, individuals on supervision can also benefit from an understanding of their ethical and legal rights. This includes confidentiality and privacy concerns, due process and fair treatment, and legal rights. For staff working in community corrections, engagement in a professional membership organization can also help with awareness of evidence-based practices, leadership, client rights, and other factors that can reinforce wellness and work performance.

Scenario-Based Activities

	Case	Question(s)
1.	Pretend you are on supervision and you are assigned an officer that is very nice but strict. You have several setbacks, such as testing positive for drugs, not having money for the bus to go to see the officer, and not being able to pay your fines and fees.	What should the person on probation do when they have a setback? When should they notify the probation officer? What steps should an officer use to help the person who is struggling? Explain how motivation enhancements might be useful.
2.	As an officer, you work at a probation agency that has not had decent furniture in over 50 years. The agency also has security officers who are more punitive than the probation officers. In discussions with your supervisor, you point out that the supervision agency does not treat individuals very well and express that you would like to improve the culture and environment.	How would you explain to your supervisor why dignity is important? How might officers benefit from treating individuals well? What type of recommendations could you make to make the supervision agency feel more like a place that values individuals?

References

Al Abosy, J., Grossman., A, & Dong, K. R. (2022). Determinants and consequences of food and nutrition insecurity in justice-impacted populations. *Current Nutrition Reports*, *11*(3), 407–415. https://doi.org/10.1007/s13668-022-00421-4

Allen, G. F. (1985). The probationers speak: Analysis of the probationers' experiences and attitudes. *Federal Probation*, *49*(3), 67–75.

American Bar Association (2018). *Collateral consequences of criminal convictions: Judicial bench book.* National Institute of Justice. https://www.ojp.gov/pdffiles1/nij/grants/251583.pdf

American Probation and Parole Association. (n.d.). *Home page.* Retrieved October 10, 2023, from https://www.appa-net.org/

Andrews, D. A., & Bonta, J. (2003). *Psychology of criminal conduct.* Cincinnati, OH: Anderson.

Berg, M. T., & Huebner, B. T. (2011) Reentry and the ties that bind: An examination of social ties, employment, and recidivism. *Justice Quarterly*, *28*(2), 382–410. https://doi.org/10.1080/07418825.2010.498383

Braithwaite, J. (1989). *Crime, shame and reintegration.* Cambridge: Cambridge University Press. https://doi.org/10.1017/CBO9780511804618

Crouch, B. M. (1993). Is incarceration really worse? Analysis of offenders' preferences for prison over probation. *Justice Quarterly*, *10*(1), 67–88. https://doi.org/10.1080/07418829300091711

Dollar, C. B., & Ray, B. (2015). The practice of reintegrative shaming in mental health court. *Criminal Justice Policy Review*, *26*(1), 29–44. https://doi.org/10.1177/0887403413507275

Durnescu, I. (2011). Pains of probation: Effective practice and human rights. *International Journal of Offender Therapy and Comparative Criminology*, *55*(4), 530–545. https://doi.org/10.1177/0306624X10369489

Falke, K., & Goldberg, J. (2018). *Struggle well: Thriving in the aftermath of trauma.* Austion, TX: Lioncrest Publishing.

Feeley, M. (1979). The process is the punishment: Handling cases in a lower criminal court. New York NY: Russell Sage Foundation.

Gagnon v. Scarpelli, 411 U.S. 778 (1973). https://www.oyez.org/cases/1972/71-1225

Gelsthorpe, L. (2007). Probation values and human rights. In L. Gelsthorpe & R. Morgan (Eds.), *Handbook of probation* (pp. 485–517). London: Willan. https://doi.org/10.4324/9781843926184

Miller, R. (2021). Halfway home: Race, punishment, and the afterlife of mass incarceration. New York: Little, Brown and Company.

Mitchell, K., Hanrath L., & Harbinson, E. (2021). *Understanding probation violations and disrupting the revocation pathway in Ramsey County, Minnesota.* University of Minnesota Robina Institute of Criminal Law and Criminal Justice. https://robinainstitute.umn.edu/publications/understanding-probation-violations-and-disrupting-revocation-pathway-ramsey-county

Morrissey v. Brewer, 408 U.S. 471 (1972). https://www.oyez.org/cases/1971/71-5103

Orwell, G. (1949). *Nineteen eighty-four.* London: Secker and Warburg.

Petersilia, J., & Turner, S. (1993). Intensive probation and parole. In M. Tonry (Ed.), *Crime and justice: A review of the research* (Vol. 17, pp. 281–335). Chicago: University of Chicago Press.

Petrila, J., & Fader-Towe, H. (2010). *Information sharing in criminal justice-mental health collaborations: Working with HIPPA and other privacy laws.* Bureau of Justice. https://bja.ojp.gov/sites/g/files/xyckuh186/files/Publications/CSG_CJMH_Info_Sharing.pdf

Roots & Rebound. (n.d.). *Roadmap to reentry*. Retrieved October 10, 2023, from https://roadmap.root-andrebound.org/parole-probation/state-parole/

Schenwar, M. & Law, V. (2020). *Prison by any other name: The harmful consequences of popular reforms*. New York: The New Press.

Sykes G. M. (1958). *The society of captives*. Princeton, NJ: Princeton University Press.

Taxman, F. S. (2002). Supervision – Exploring the dimensions of effectiveness. *Federal Probation, 66*(2), 14.

Taxman, F. S., Perdoni, M., & Caudy, M. (2013). The plight of providing appropriate substance abuse treatment services to offenders: Modeling the gaps in service delivery. *Victims & Offenders, 8*(1), 70–93. https://doi.org/10.1080/15564886.2012.747459

Taxman, F. S., Perdoni, M., & Harrison, L. (2007). Drug treatment services for adult offenders: The state of the state. *Journal of Substance Abuse Treatment, 32*(3), 239–254. https://doi.org/10.1016%2Fj.jsat.2006.12.019

Testa, A., & Jackson, D. A. (2019). Food insecurity among formerly incarcerated adults. *Criminal Justice & Behavior, 46*(10), 1493–1511. https://doi.org/10.1177/0093854819856920

Ward, A. (Host). (2019, September 8). A spotlight on mass supervision (Episode 397) [TV series episode]. In *Both Sides of the Bar*. The Fortune Society. https://www.mnn.org/watch/programs/both-sides-bars/spotlight-mass-supervision-rethinking-technical-violations

Wooditch, A., Lawton, B., & Taxman, F. S. (2013, April). The geography of drug abuse epidemiology among probationers in Baltimore. *Journal of Drug Issues, 43*(2), 231–249. http://dx.doi.org/10.1177/0022042612470643

Image Credits

PART IV

Measuring and Supporting Success

CHAPTER 10

Recidivism and Other Outcome Measures

In this chapter, students are introduced to recidivism, including the most common measures of recidivism used in community corrections agencies: technical violations, new offenses, revocation, arrest, and incarceration. This chapter discusses multiple ways to measure recidivism as well as challenges with these different approaches. More specifically, challenges that are highlighted include racial and ethnic disparities, the role of probation and parole officer discretion in responding to supervision violations, and the inconsistent measurement of recidivism across agencies. Students are encouraged to think outside of traditional measures of reoffending through an introduction to alternative measures that can be used to evaluate the success or failure of community supervision agencies. In line with intersectionality, a preferred measurement strategy involves the ongoing collection of data on multiple facets of an individual's life, specifically mental health, substance use, housing, and education. Such measures can provide a more comprehensive understanding of the desistance process and progress. By expanding the outcomes we evaluate, agencies can shift their focus from failure to positive behavioral change, recognizing that progress toward prosocial behavior and improved quality of life are critical components of the desistance process.

LEARNING OBJECTIVES

By the end of this chapter, students will be able to:

- Define recidivism and identify the multiple ways to measure recidivism.
- Identify and describe the limits of using recidivism as an outcome measure, including the challenges associated with recidivism measures.
- Classify alternative measures of success and discuss the role they can play in understanding the effectiveness of probation and parole.

KEY TERMS

- Desistance
- Recidivism

- Reconviction
- Reincarceration
- Revocation

CONTENT

In a forest of a hundred thousand trees, no two leaves are alike. And no two journeys along the same path are alike.

—Paulo Coelho

Defining Recidivism

Recidivism is one of the most frequently used terms across the criminal justice field and the most common metric used to determine the success or failure of criminal justice agencies, programs, and policies. The National Institute of Justice (n.d.) defines **recidivism** as "a person's relapse into criminal behavior, often after the person receives sanctions or undergoes intervention for a previous crime" (para. 1). It is the primary concept, or gold standard, that most agencies, policymakers, practitioners, and researchers alike are interested in. That is, agencies are often concerned with their recidivism rates and taking efforts to reduce those rates. Policymakers are often concerned with recidivism and thinking about what policies need to be in place to prevent reoffending. Practitioners often want to know if the things they are being asked to do at work will reduce the likelihood that clients will reoffend.

Furthermore, recidivism is often the outcome most research studies focus on, with researchers commonly evaluating programs and policies to determine whether they reduce recidivism. While you might often hear the word "recidivism" associated with the criminal justice system, what we actually mean by "recidivism" often varies. There are significant differences between the public use of the term "recidivism" to generally describe a person committing another crime and when scholars detail very specific methodological techniques to measure recidivism. Even the National Institute of Justice (n.d.) uses a broad definition of recidivism, yet upon deeper examination, recidivism includes a variety of different behaviors. The next section will provide an overview of some common examples of how recidivism is measured and tracked within community corrections agencies.

JOURNEY INTO THE FIELD: DR. CHRISTY VISHER

◇◇◇◇◇◇◇◇

Full name: Christy Visher

Title: Professor of Sociology and Director for the Center for Drug and Health Studies, University of Delaware.

Dr. Visher has over 25 years of experience in policy research on the topics of prisoner reentry, employment of offenders, criminal violence, crime prevention strategies, youth offenders, prisons, and probation. This work has often centered on the topic of substance abuse and its interplay with criminality and the criminal justice system. Dr. Visher previously worked as a senior scientist for the U.S. Department of Justice and as a senior associate with the Urban Institute in Washington, DC. Dr. Christy Visher is current a professor of sociology and director for the Center for Drug and Health Studies at the University of Delaware. In this Journey into the Field, Dr. Visher explains the steps she took to pursue a career in academia, along with her perceptions on the topic of recidivism in the context of community corrections.

Image 10.1

I began my career at the National Academies Committee on Law and Justice as a postdoctoral fellow working alongside the Panel on Criminal Careers, chaired by Professor Alfred Blumstein. I reviewed research on the initiation, persistence, and desistance stages of criminal behavior. That work led me to the National Institute of Justice and then the Urban Institute, where I developed and implemented a pathbreaking longitudinal study of individuals returning to the community from prison, *Returning Home: Understanding the Challenges of Prisoner Reentry*. Reentry to the community begins during incarceration, and now my research is focused on the prison climate and the challenges both incarcerated individuals and correctional staff face in the prison environment.

The majority of individuals involved in the criminal legal system want to be contributing members of society. Yet, these individuals face numerous obstacles, and there are many pathways toward desistance from criminal behavior. The current focus on evaluating an individual's progress in community corrections is to watch for repeat criminal behavior, often using imperfect measures of recidivism such as rearrest, failed drug tests, or violations of community supervision. In fact, the pathway to desistance may not be direct but may include setbacks. To assess progress, incremental measures of success such as health status, housing stability, job training, civic involvement, and educational advances, rather than only recidivism, should be included in periodic assessments by community supervision officers.

A report of the National Academies of Sciences, Engineering, and Medicine (2022) titled *The Limits of Recidivism: Measuring Success after Prison* concluded that reoffending is only one aspect of an individual's progress. A focus on measures of an individual's success in domains such as health, housing, employment, and education would shift the perspective of community supervision officers toward improvements in their life circumstances, which should be celebrated and encouraged. Such positive reinforcement reflects a strengths-based approach to community supervision. Relatedly, researchers, practitioners, and policymakers should carefully choose measures of recidivism that accurately reflect an individual's reoffending behavior. Developing a standard set of measures of success is the next step toward helping individuals on community supervision lead crime-free lives and improving our understanding of the desistance process.

Measuring Recidivism

There are many different forms of recidivism to consider when measuring the effectiveness of various criminal justice agencies. Any time you see a news article, published study, or report about recidivism, it is important to identify what specific behaviors they are measuring and discussing. There can be drastic differences in how recidivism is reported. Take, for example, one agency that is referring to recidivism relating to technical violations while a person is on community supervision, while another may be only including additional violent crimes that led to reincarceration. These are two very different outcomes that reflect different types of behaviors, with reincarceration an indicator of more serious reoffending compared to technical violations, which reflect rule violations (and not a crime). In general, measuring recidivism is not a straightforward process. First, we may not have an official record every time a crime is committed. This is due to several reasons, including the fact that not all crimes are detected, prosecuted, and convicted. Some studies attempt to address these challenges by asking people to self-report engagement in crime. However, this method also has flaws. People may not remember or report their behavior accurately, or crimes like sex offenses and domestic violence may carry shame and stigma, leading to people being reluctant to self-report events. As a result, it is critical to always consider how recidivism is being measured—that is, how and by whom the data was collected and analyzed.

Often, we track recidivism using multiple measures to accommodate for some of these limitations. Rearrest is a common recidivism measure that identifies whether an individual has been arrested since their last intervention/sanction. Again, this measure is imperfect. Not all crimes are detected, not all crimes that are detected result in an arrest, and not all people who are arrested are guilty of a crime. To address the last challenge, **reconviction** is an alternative measure of recidivism. This measure tracks whether an individual receives a new guilty conviction by the court since their previous intervention or sanction. After conviction, an individual can be sentenced to incarceration. Often, a measure of **reincarceration** will also be used to measure and track recidivism. This provides a proxy measure for more serious recidivism, as theoretically only the most serious reconvictions will result in incarceration.

In probation and parole, we often see three other measures for recidivism. The first is technical violations. This reflects engagement in the least serious form of problem behavior, as individuals receive technical violations for noncompliance with the rules of supervision. As discussed earlier in Chapter 4, these rules are not laws, and as a result, individuals who receive technical violations are not committing a new crime. However, technical violations reflect noncompliance with supervision that can potentially be grounds for more serious consequences, such as a revocation. However, probation and parole officers often have a great deal of discretion to determine how to respond to technical violations. Often, they may respond informally, especially with infrequent or less serious technical violations. Alternatively, when someone on probation or parole supervision does commit a new crime, agencies often refer to this as a "new offense violation," although this terminology will vary across agencies. These types of violations do reflect law violations and new crimes, although often someone can receive a new offense violation for an arrest (e.g., they are not necessarily convicted of a crime yet).

In the majority of circumstances, new offenses will result in the supervising officer filing a motion to revoke. When this occurs, the individual under supervision will be brought to court and/or the parole board and the judge and/or parole board will determine whether they will (a) continue on probation/parole as is, (b) continue on probation/parole but with increased requirements, or (c) receive a revocation. A **revocation** occurs when an individual's probation or parole term is terminated, and the individual is incarcerated. While it is less likely that a single technical violation will result in a motion to revoke and/or revocation, repeated technical violations may result in this more serious outcome. Sometimes studies use a more general measure of supervision violations, which includes both technical violations and new offenses. This measure of recidivism is problematic, as it combines more serious law-breaking behavior with less serious rule-breaking behavior. These differences in how recidivism is measured, along with their limitations or challenges, is provided in Table 10.1.

TABLE 10.1 Recidivism Measures

Recidivism Measure	Description	Source	Challenges
Rearrest	Official arrest made by police	Police data FBI data Self-report	• Not all crimes are detected. • Not all crimes are prosecuted. • Not all prosecuted crimes result in a conviction. • May include mistaken arrests.
Reconviction	Official guilty conviction determined by the court	Court data FBI data Self-report	• Not all crimes are detected. • Not all crimes are prosecuted. • May include wrongful convictions.
Reincarceration	Individual received a jail/prison sentence following a guilty conviction	Jail/prison data FBI data Self-report	• Not all crimes are detected. • Not all crimes are prosecuted. • May include wrongful convictions.
Technical violation	Noncompliance with one or more supervision conditions that does not include illegal behavior	Probation/parole data Self-report	• Not all violations are detected. • This is not criminal behavior.
New offense	Noncompliance with one or more supervision conditions that does include illegal behavior	Police data Probation/parole data Self-report	• Not all crimes are detected. • Not all crimes are prosecuted. • Not all prosecuted crimes result in a conviction.
Supervision violations	An overarching measure of noncompliance with supervision conditions that include both illegal and legal behavior.	Probation/parole data Self-report	• Not all crimes/violations are detected. • This combines less serious technical violations and more serious new offenses.
Revocation	Termination of an individual's probation/parole term by a judge or parole board in which the individual is often sent to jail/prison	Probation/parole data Court data Self-report	• Not all crimes are detected. • Not all violations receive a revocation. • This may combine technical violations and new offenses.

In addition to using these official measures of recidivism and self-report measures, we can also use time to measure recidivism. For example, we might measure how much time passed between two events. Let's pretend Jackie was just sentenced to probation.

Image 10.2

We might track the amount of time that passes between when Jackie begins probation and when she is rearrested. Or maybe we want to measure the impacts of a cognitive behavioral program on recidivism. We might track how much time occurs between when Jackie begins the program and when she is rearrested. Time is an important variable to consider when we think about recidivism rates. Say Meadowbrook County calculated recidivism rates for all individuals released from prison 1 year ago, but Lakeview County calculated their recidivism rates for all individuals released from prison 3 years ago. Lakeview County's rates will probably be higher because those individuals had more time to recidivate, but we might find that if we compare both Meadowbrook County's and Lakeview County's 1-year recidivism rates, they are similar.

Obtaining data on recidivism can be a challenging task. Criminal records are not always complete, and data systems are typically not linked. For example, state records often do not include criminal history from outside of their state. A Florida county probation office likely does not have easy access to arrest records in California. Local, state, and federal agencies typically do not share data with one another. As a result, even the FBI Interstate Identification Index, which records data from every U.S. state on arrests, case dispositions, and sentences, may be missing criminal history information (Cooper et al., 2014). Often, when conducting research, we have to use multiple sources of recidivism data. For example, let's say we are evaluating a contingency management program used in a probation office (see Chapter 6 for an introduction to contingency management). We might collect data on technical violations, new offenses, revocations, and reincarcerations from administrative data collected and provided by the probation office, and we might gather rearrest data from official state government data. However, every agency collects and records data differently, so the sources used to track various measures of recidivism will vary. When official data is not easily accessible, we can collect self-report data by asking probation and parole clients to report any recent arrests or technical violations, for example.

As you can see, there are many ways to measure recidivism. This often makes it challenging to compare recidivism rates between agencies. Comparing revocation rates to rearrest rates is like comparing apples to oranges, and it is not appropriate to equate them to one another. Comparing 1-year reconviction rates to 3-year reconviction rates is also like comparing apples to oranges. In practice, this makes it very difficult to compare recidivism rates across agencies and jurisdictions because there is no uniform standard for measuring and reporting recidivism. Often, agencies are limited to reporting just certain forms of recidivism because that is the only data they have access to. In fact, it is challenging for many agencies to accurately report their recidivism rates because they do not have the proper infrastructure in place to do so. As a result of these challenges and the lack of any national standards for measuring and reporting recidivism, there is no national recidivism rate.

The Limitations of Recidivism as a Measure of Success

Let's dig a little deeper into the challenges associated with using a binary measure of recidivism (yes/no) as the primary measure of success. First, the focus on recidivism places pressure on criminal justice agencies to produce data that demonstrate positive outcomes: reductions in recidivism (Klingele, 2019). Whether knowingly or not, this can result in issues with the validity of recidivism data. Agency administrators may focus on reducing statistical rates of recidivism more than they emphasize actually reducing reoffending behaviors. In this way, reductions in recidivism might reflect the behavior of practitioners rather than the behavior of individuals under supervision. To illustrate this concept, we turn to a real-world example surrounding the policies/practices of parole in California.

In 2005, California had one of the highest parole revocation rates in the country at over 66% (Grattet et al., 2009). In the case *Brown v. Plata* (2011), the U.S. Supreme Court ruled that California had to reduce its overall prison population by 37,000 people. To accomplish this, California changed the way they responded to technical violations, referring them to community-based programs rather than issuing a motion to revoke. As a result, parolee revocation results declined from 44.6% in 2011 to 7% in 2012 (Grattet et al., 2009). In this example, it is likely that the reductions in recidivism are not due to changes in parolee behavior but rather a change in the way California responded to parole violations. Additionally, while under pressure to reduce recidivism, agencies and programs will often cherry-pick participants (see Chapter 4 for a discussion of how agencies often select the "cream of the crop" to work with). That is, they will select the most compliant individuals and the ones most likely to succeed rather than those who are higher risk and could benefit more (and where we could see reductions in recidivism). Again, if these programs with cherry-picked participants report low recidivism rates, this does not mean the agency is doing better at reducing recidivism; it instead reflects their decisions on who to include in specific programs.

Next, by focusing only on recidivism, we may label programs as failures that actually may result in other positive outcomes. That is, by focusing solely on recidivism, other positive changes that can happen after someone receives a criminal sanction may be ignored. For example, desisting from crime is a process that might not happen as soon as someone is released from prison. **Desistance** refers to a gradual process of abstaining from crime. A major difference between recidivism and desistance is measurement. Recidivism is typically measured as a binary: Yes, someone reoffended, or no, they did not. A single yes reflects a failure. On the other hand, desistance is process-based with the assumption that there will be setbacks. A single reoffense is not considered a failure but an expected part of the difficult process of moving away from crime. There are many roadblocks to remaining crime-free in the community, especially for those under probation or parole supervision. For example, say a fictional individual on probation named John had three positive drug tests in his first 6 months on probation. However, after starting a treatment program John was able to secure a new job and find stable

Image 10.3

housing. Then, 8 months after he started this program, John had his first positive drug test. If we were only tracking technical violations as our primary measure of success, John would be labeled as a failure. However, this ignores the positive progress he has made in the desistance process. He has made great achievements in employment and housing and was able to remain substance-free for 8 months—a vast improvement over his first 6 months under supervision.

Remember back in Chapter 4, when we talked about how individuals under supervision often have about 19 rules they must follow at all times? These onerous conditions in conjunction with numerous barriers (e.g., obtaining employment, paying fees/fines) create tremendously difficult situations for individuals under supervision. This results in a system where recidivism is a result of a combination of an individual's behavior, institutional actions, and systemic inequalities. That is, the choices individuals make are often limited based on the opportunities or barriers they are constrained by (National Academies of Sciences, Engineering, and Medicine, 2022). As a result, when someone achieves something that ultimately will help them remain crime-free (like getting a job), this should be measured and reported as success. Additionally, because desisting from crime is a process, focusing solely on whether or not someone engages in any illegal behavior as the sole measure of recidivism ignores any progress that is made. For example, individuals may not immediately stop engaging in crime, but they may do so less frequently, or they may engage in less serious offenses.

These types of changes can indicate the individual is in the process of desisting from crime. However, recidivism is not measured as a process. It is event-based, meaning we often track and report just whether someone did or did not recidivate. This focus also ignores other good things that can happen when we implement correctional programs, such as increasing an individual's self-efficacy and motivation to change, reducing substance use, and improving problem-solving skills. If we only focus on recidivism as a measure of success, we might miss many other positive achievements and outcomes that can occur. In addition, focusing exclusively on recidivism generates an emphasis on the negative. It is almost like we are just waiting for someone to make a mistake. By thinking about alternative measures of success, we can shift toward a strengths-based approach (as discussed in Chapter 4), where we identify and reinforce positive characteristics and behaviors.

Lastly, focusing on recidivism promotes a primary focus on risk and avoiding risk (Klingele, 2019). Risk aversion is a key feature of our criminal justice system. The "tough on crime" era is a prime example of this: Despite declining crime rates during the previous 30 years as presented in Chapter 1, we continue to implement measures to increase the severity of punishment and expand the number of people who can receive harsher punishments (think mandatory minimums). If you speak to a probation or parole officer, you will often hear concerns about liability. That is, they don't want anyone they are responsible for supervising committing a new crime, particularly a violent offense that might gain media attention or scrutiny by supervisors. Klingele (2019) explains that:

> the emphasis that has been placed on recidivism rates and their reduction psychologically reinforces the idea that the job of the criminal justice system is to prevent crime at all costs, even if that means confining behind bars people whose conduct does not pose a serious risk of harm to others and those who have demonstrated that they are engaged in the process of behavioral change. (pp. 816)

As such, probation and parole officers might prefer to err on the side of caution and issue a motion to revoke for a technical violation rather than respond informally and risk that individual committing a new crime, regardless of how unlikely that is. On the other hand, recognizing the importance of alternative measures of success and using those to evaluate the success (or failure) of probation/parole agencies and programs could help shift the narrative from one concerned with risk aversion to one concerned with supporting the process of desistance. The following case study provides an example of the limitations associated with focusing on recidivism as the singular measure of success.

One year ago, Ana completed a 5-year probation sentence for a drug-related offense. While on probation, Ana complied with all her supervision conditions and successfully completed all of the goals laid out in her case plan. During her probation term, she found employment, enrolled in and successfully completed a substance use treatment program, and did not have any positive drug tests. Her probation officer, Officer Sullivan, noted that her attitude was positive, and he believed Ana really wanted to turn her life around and stay out of the criminal justice system.

Image 10.4

After Ana completed probation, she was doing well for 5 years. During this time, she maintained her sobriety, was doing very well in her job, and had a new boyfriend. However, Ana was rearrested for drug possession and placed back on probation. When Officer Sullivan found out, he was shocked and felt like he had failed in his job. When Officer Sullivan met with Ana, he learned that she had been having a tough time dealing with the recent loss of her mother. To cope with her grief, she turned to drugs. Ana was remorseful and asked Officer Sullivan to provide a referral for mental health counseling. She also expressed a willingness to participate in substance use treatment again. Officer Sullivan believes that if Ana can learn prosocial ways to cope with difficult situations, she will be able to stay on the right track.

If we were only using recidivism as a measure of success in this example, it would look like Ana was a failure. However, when we take a more detailed view of Ana's time on probation and the months following her probation completion, we see a much different picture. In this view, we would see an individual who made significant positive progress in the areas of employment, substance use, and social support. If we consider the additional factors surrounding her rearrest, we will see that it was a single relapse in a period of intense grief. This example demonstrates the limits of using only recidivism as an outcome measure while ignoring progress made in other important areas of an individual's life.

◊ Diversity, Equity, and Inclusion: Racial and Ethnic Disparities in the Measurement of Recidivism

Racial and ethnic disparities have been documented throughout the criminal justice system, including police, courts, and corrections. At the group level, disparities are evident at the initial contact between an individual and law enforcement. Police are more likely to stop (Baumgartner et al., 2018; Pierson et al., 2020) and search (Baumgartner et al., 2018; Gelman et al., 2007) people of color. Yet, research suggests searches of White individuals are more likely to result in possession of contraband (Levchak, 2017) compared to searches of Black or Hispanic individuals. Racial disparities have also been identified in police use of force. For example, Black individuals are more likely to experience nonlethal and lethal force when compared to White individuals, even after controlling for crime rates, suspect demeanor, and presence of a weapon (Kramer & Remster, 2018; Morrow et al., 2017). Additionally, after controlling for criminal activity, police are more likely to shoot Black suspects (Scott et al., 2017).

There are many research studies documenting disproportionate arrest rates for people of color. For example, a 2019 study found that Black individuals were 8 times more likely to be arrested for marijuana possession compared to White individuals (Jones et al., 2019). Additionally, studies controlling for rates of offending behavior and police presence still find racial disparities in drug-related arrest rates (Mitchell & Caudy, 2015, 2017). It is estimated that due to racial disparities in policing practices, people of color are more likely to be incarcerated (Anderson & Morash, 2015). One study estimated that racial disparities in arrest decisions may account for 70%–75% of racial disparities seen in imprisonment rates (Beck & Blumenstein, 2018).

Disparities in incarceration rates can also arise from decisions made within the courts, such as via prosecutorial decisions to file a charge and judge decisions surrounding pretrial detention, plea deals, convictions, and sentencing. For example, research finds that Black men are more likely to be detained pretrial compared to similarly situated White men (Prison Policy Initiative, n.d.). These disparities are most clearly seen when looking at imprisonment rates. For example, Black adults make up 13% of the U.S. population (U.S. Census Bureau, 2019); however, they represent over 30% of those in prison (Bronson & Carson, 2019). Data collected by the Vera Institute of Justice (2023) suggests that people of color are incarcerated in U.S. jails and prisons at much higher rates than White people (see Figures 10.1 and 10.2).

Research also suggests there may be disparities in probation and parole revocation decisions. First, like incarceration, Black adults are overrepresented among the U.S. probation and parole

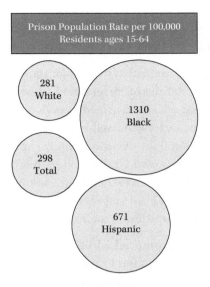

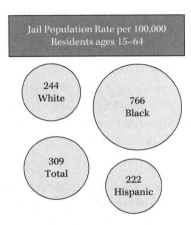

FIGURE 10.1   Jail Population Rates (2021) per 100,000 U.S. Residents aged 15–64, Vera Incarceration Trends Data

FIGURE 10.2   Prison Population Rates (2022) per 100,000 U.S. Residents aged 15–64, Vera Incarceration Trends Data

population, making up over 30% of those under supervision (Kaeble, 2023). A study conducted by Jannetta and colleagues (2016) found that Black individuals on probation were more likely to receive a revocation compared to White and Hispanic individuals. Similar research suggests that Black individuals are more likely to have their parole revoked for a new offense (19% more likely) or a technical violation (50% more likely) compared to similarly situated White counterparts (Steen & Opsal, 2007).

It is important to also consider these racial disparities that accumulate throughout the criminal justice system, as they may result in higher measurements of recidivism for people of color. Further, decisions made by actors within the system (e.g., to make a stop, to search someone, to make an arrest, to file charges) may drive higher recidivism rates for certain groups of individuals, particularly for racial and ethnic minority groups. Additionally, there is a wealth of evidence that suggests people of color also face reentry barriers in the community at higher rates, including increased challenges obtaining housing, employment, and resources, which can complicate the desistance process. The overrepresentation of people of color throughout the criminal justice system can result in discrimination and stigma, which further perpetuates the cycle.

Measures of Success or Progress: Desistance and Behavioral Change

The limits associated with recidivism have gained recent attention with a movement to shift toward thinking about more encompassing measures of success or progress in the criminal justice system. Recidivism is a very limited measure and, as shown above, can depend on decisions by the criminal justice system such as the decision to arrest, prosecute, and sentence. In a recent review, The National Academy of Sciences, Engineering, and Medicine (2022) noted:

> The measurement of success for those returning from prison has implications for the responsibilities of correctional agencies toward the persons under their supervision, the design of effective reentry policy, community-based programs and services across multiple sectors, the well-being of marginalized communities, victim satisfaction with correctional interventions, and crime control policy. Improving metrics of post-release success is a vital first step in making informed policy decisions and ensuring that taxpayer investments are spent wisely. It is also important for ensuring that the criminal legal system is accountable to those it affects directly, to their families and communities, to their victims and survivors, and to the broader public. (p. 12)

A commonly promoted additional measure of success is desistance. Desistance is process that is quite complicated to measure. Measurement of desistance requires tracking an individual's progress over time and also recognizing that there will be bumps in the road. Much like recidivism, however, there can be a multitude of ways to measure desistance from crime. One popular framework for thinking about behavior change is the "transtheoretical model." (Prochaska & Velicer, 1997). This model contains six stages of change that individuals move through as they attempt to shift from antisocial behavior. The first stage is precontemplation, where individuals are not aware of, deny, or ignore the need for behavior change. In contemplation, they are aware of needed behavior change but are often ambivalent that such change is possible. In this stage, they might think about change but have not yet committed to change. In preparation, they now start to plan for behavior change and are committed to doing so. In the action stage, the individual has started to modify their behavior with the goal of change. A critical component of this stage is that behavioral change during the action phase is often not total cessation of the unwanted behavior. Often, behavior change reflects reductions in behavior (e.g., instead of total sobriety, perhaps the individual is having fewer drinks per week).

Individuals often stay in the action stage for a while as their new behaviors become more consistent and eventually turn into new habits. It is in this stage that small bumps are likely to occur and may affect how well a person does. For example, if someone encounters challenges, such as losing a job, needing to find a new place to live, experiencing a death in the family, it can result in relapse. However, the goal is to reduce the negative behaviors that occur because of such challenges and reengagement in prosocial behaviors. When the undesirable behavior is terminated, the maintenance stage begins. Here, the individuals focus on maintaining behavior change to prevent the old, unwanted behavior from returning. This is not a short process and can take years. At any stage during this process, relapse to an earlier stage is expected. The purpose of introducing this model is to illustrate that behavioral change is a long and difficult process.

Behavior can be very challenging to modify because it is built on longstanding daily habits and routines. As such, the best way to think about behavioral change and the transtheoretical

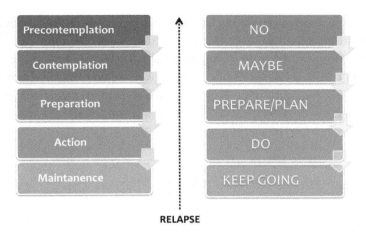

FIGURE 10.3   Transtheoretical Model

model is to consider a behavior you have tried to change in the past. This behavior could be related to diet or exercise, or perhaps related to an interpersonal relationship you were in. It could also involve issues that draw people to community corrections, like associating with antisocial peers or use of drugs and alcohol. After visualizing the issue you attempted to change in the past, think about the following three questions:

- What was that process like for you?
- Did you find you had setbacks along the way?
- What planning steps and actions did you take toward success?

So, if we agree that human behavior is hard to change, it is unreasonable to expect individuals to be able to change their criminal behavior quickly and without the help of others. Especially when we consider the number of barriers in place for those with criminal records, it is no surprise that abstaining from crime is a difficult process. Desistance from crime is highly correlated with age (Ulmer & Steffensmeier, 2014). We have years and years of data that illustrate that engagement in crime, particularly among males, peaks between 15 and 25 years old (see a discussion of the age-crime curve in Chapter 7). There is an entire subfield of criminology dedicated to studying this phenomenon, called "life-course criminology." As people age, they typically experience "turning points" that encourage an individual to desist from crime. Common turning points are marriage, having children, and obtaining solid employment. Research suggests that there are moral and emotional changes that occur in conjunction with turning points that encourage individuals to rethink their identities and, as a result, shift their behavior (Sampson & Laub, 1997). Often, individuals experience multiple turning points that then lead to a gradual movement away from criminal behavior.

Measuring success during the intricate desistance process and transitioning through stages of behavioral change is a challenging task for several reasons. First, we know that using a binary measure of whether someone is engaging in crime will not capture desistance. We would need much more information about an individual's life and behaviors. For example, if we wanted to track desistance from criminal behavior, we might start with identifying whether an individual's engagement in specific types of crimes has changed over time or whether they are engaging in crime less frequently. However, there are additional measures we can consider to understand the process of desistance and behavioral change beyond examining an individual's involvement in crime or rule breaking.

Measuring Desistance: Alternative Measures of Success

The overreliance on recidivism as the sole measure of success or failure by community corrections continues to offer little in terms of understanding the complex experiences that people encounter while on supervision. By using an intersectional approach, we recognized that clients who are under the supervision of probation or parole have a range of dynamic risk factors (i.e., criminogenic needs) related to crime and desistance as well as responsivity factors that may serve as a barrier to change. In Chapter 4, we introduced the central eight criminogenic needs, which include antisocial attitudes, antisocial associates, a history of antisocial behavior, antisocial personality pattern, problems at home, problems at school or work, problematic leisure circumstances, and substance use (Andrews & Bonta, 2010). Chapter 4 also provides insight into the basic needs of people under supervision under the risk-need-responsivity (RNR) model—namely, housing, employment, and education. Chapter 6 adds to this consideration by detailing community corrections interventions that target thoughts, behaviors, and actions, while Chapters 7 and 9 detail the need to reinforce overall well-being, health, and resiliency in people on supervision. Taken as whole, existing evidence suggests that the measurement of desistance requires a broad, holistic approach that includes consideration of a range of factors impacting one's life.

In 2022, the National Academies of Sciences, Engineering, and Medicine published a report with research-supported recommendations for alternative indicators of success throughout the desistance process. These include measuring an individual's overall well-being, overall health, mental health, substance use, engagement in health care, housing and homelessness, employment and job retention, educational attainment, social relationships, civic engagement, and neighborhood context. Table 10.2 provides a review of these items and examples of ways we might track progress and what might be considered success. A common theme throughout these measures is the recognition that small steps forward can be a positive signal for change given the complexity of human behavior.

Well-Being
Now, let's talk about why these various alternative measures of success are important for tracking progress with individuals on community supervision. First, overall well-being is an important factor in people's lives. Our well-being can be impacted by various things, such as

TABLE 10.2 Alternative Measures for Success (National Academy of Sciences, Engineering, and Medicine: The Limits of Recidivism: Measuring Success After Prison)

Alternative Measure of Success	Examples
Desistance	• Decrease in the number of activities reported in a specified time frame • De-escalation in the severity of offense categories (e.g., movement away from violent activities) • Cessation of criminal activity within broad offense categories over a specified time frame
Overall well-being	• Measure people's attitudes toward their life • Includes perceptions of their mental, physical, financial health, feelings of social and emotional support and isolation, and spiritual support • Do people perceive their life is going well?
Overall health	• Measure people's perceptions regarding their physical health • For example, asking individuals to rate their perceived health
Mental health	• Use validated instruments to identify indicators of mental health disorders • For example, the Patient Health Questionnaire-9 (PHQ-9) evaluates the severity of depression.
Substance use	• Use validated instruments to identify severity of substance use disorder, like the Addiction Severity Index • Decrease in the frequency of substance use (self-report)
Engagement in health care	• Measure whether people have a place they can go to when they need health advice and what type of place it is • Identify what type of place (e.g., clinic, doctor's office, emergency room) people go to most frequently for help • Frequency they have seen a doctor/health care professional • Frequency stayed overnight in the hospital • Frequency have seen a mental health professional
Housing and homelessness	• Measure perceived safety and satisfaction with current housing situation • Type of housing (e.g., private, renting) • Identify who they live with • Measure housing stability (e.g., frequency of moving) • Number of moves in a specified time period
Employment and job retention	• Employment status, including whether they are employed, want to keep their job, type of job, seasonality of employment, number of hours worked per week, work schedule, length of time in current job, satisfaction with job, how they obtained the job

(Continued)

Alternative Measure of Success	Examples
Employment and job retention	• Pay/wage information, including hourly age/annual salary, if pay is enough to make ends meet, satisfaction with pay, nature of pay (paycheck versus cash), benefits • Are they learning new skills on the job? • Ease to get to and from work • How long they plan to stay at current job • Do they get along with their boss and coworkers? • Do they go to work after drinking or using drugs? • Have they experienced unfair treatment because of their criminal record? • Are there career opportunities with this job? • Is the work schedule flexible? • If unemployed, what actions are they taking to identify a job?
Educational attainment	• Attainment of a degree • Number of certifications/degrees earned • Number of courses completed • Enrollment in courses for college credit • Enrollment in a certification course • Enrollment in/completion of GED • Desire for additional education • Completed paperwork for additional education • Received assistance to secure funds to obtain additional education • Available educational tutoring or mentoring
Social relationships	• Positive relationships and social engagement • Social support • Family support, closeness to family • Have friends they can go to for help • Support from faith community • If they have children, how often do serve in caregiving/parental role? • Frequency of contact with children • Engagement with children • Degree of connection to others for social support • Receipt of peer support • Involvement in peer support groups
Civic engagement	• Political participation • Political volunteering • Attending rallies, demonstrations, and other political events • Individual-level political efficacy (e.g., belief that people like me have no say about the government) • Individual-level importance of engagement in the community • Political engagement with family and friends • Legal restrictions on right to vote or other limits to civic participation

stable housing, meaningful employment, safe neighborhoods, quality relationships, emotions and resiliency, and overall satisfaction with life. Assessing an individual's overall well-being recognizes that there is more to well-being than just physical or mental illness. Instead, a more holistic measure of health and life experiences is helpful in measuring progress for justice-involved individuals. This is particularly salient, as research suggests exposure to the justice system, including interactions with police, arrests, and incarceration, can result in reductions in well-being (Sundaresh et al., 2020).

In fact, Sundaresh and colleagues (2020) found that the more exposure individuals had to the justice system, the progressively lower their overall well-being was. Measuring an individual's overall health is similarly informative. This includes an individual's perceptions of the current status of their health, taking into consideration their physical health in particular. Justice-involved individuals often experience physical health conditions at a disproportionate rate compared to the general population, have limited access to health care, and, for those who were incarcerated, often experience health declines as a result. Therefore, overall health is an important indicator for the community supervision population.

Mental Health and Substance Use

Additionally, justice-involved individuals experience disproportionate rates of mental health and substance use disorders compared to the general population. Thus, measuring and tracking indicators of mental health and substance use while on probation or parole can provide meaningful information regarding success, especially if those individuals are also participating in community-based treatment programs. The most common measure currently used to measure "success" for individuals with substance use is drug testing. However, there are a number of issues with reliance on drug testing results. First, in the context of probation and parole, drug testing tends to be implemented as a means to increase surveillance and provide sanctions rather than intervene therapeutically. However, the American Society of Addiction Medicine suggests that a single positive drug test is an expected outcome associated with substance use disorders, which is classified as a chronic health condition (Jarvis et al., 2017). Additional research suggests challenges with appropriate implementation and interpretation of drug tests, suggesting limited value in relying solely on this measure to identify progress and success. Instead, the National Academies of Science, Engineering, and Medicine (2022) suggest using measures that "define success as a progression of health-promoting behaviors over time" (p. 165), as they are more reliable indicators of improvement and can actually provide improved insight for probation and parole officers.

Health

Given the vast number of health issues many justice-involved individuals face, including physical health, mental health, and substance use, engagement with the health care system is an important indicator of success. For example, let's consider Jessica, who is a fictional individual on probation who has diabetes, a chronic health condition. In the past, Jessica did not keep up with her doctor's appointments and did not fill her necessary prescriptions on time, frequently leading to lapses in medication. This led Jessica to make multiple visits to the emergency room, including a few overnight stays. These hospital visits racked up large medical bills, which placed extreme financial pressure on Jessica. However, she is feeling so physically unwell that she cannot work. She is struggling to pay her bills and make ends meet. Now, let's say Jessica has started to make some changes. She is making and keeping her doctor's appointments. She is filling her prescriptions on time. She starts to see that her health is improving. She feels well enough to start looking for a job. Many individuals on probation or parole have similar stories. This engagement in health care can be considered a success and should be recognized and reinforced. Additionally, by measuring and tracking health care engagement, we can also start to see where individuals face barriers or challenges. This could inform larger, system-level changes that can improve access to care for this vulnerable population.

Housing

People on probation and parole (and, really, anyone with a criminal record) often face multiple challenges when looking for stable housing. For example, a housing provider may provide an application that contains a check box labeled "Check if you have ever been convicted of a felony," and they may automatically discard applications when a person responds that they have. Some states also have policies that prohibit individuals with a prior drug or felony conviction from accessing public housing. Remaining successful in the community can be challenging when also facing housing instability and homelessness. While on probation or parole, individuals are required to have an approved place to live. Probation and parole officers typically make a home visit in the first 30–45 days after someone starts supervision to review and approve their living arrangement. If at any point the individual moves, they are required to immediately notify their probation or parole officer, who will likely make another home visit to the new residence.

If an individual cannot find housing, probation and parole officers might provide resources for local shelters that can provide temporary housing. However, spaces in shelters are often limited, the living arrangements are often not ideal, and some even require individuals to check in and check out daily, leading to consistent concern regarding whether they will have somewhere to sleep each night. As you can imagine, this can place a high level of stress on an individual. Additionally, individuals with criminal records often experience discrimination by landlords, are ineligible for housing assistance programs, and cannot afford to live in certain neighborhoods. As a result, they may be forced to reside in neighborhoods ridden with crime and poverty. With unstable housing, it may be more difficult to find employment, get an ID, establish social networks, and avoid reoffending. As a result, when an individual can make positive progress toward housing and housing stability, this can serve as an indicator of success on community supervision.

Employment

Individuals on probation and parole are also required to gain employment. If unemployed, most probation and parole agencies will require that individuals are actively seeking employment (and provide proof they are doing so). Like obtaining housing, finding employment is often quite challenging for individuals with criminal records. The reasons for this are complex and often stem from a combination of factors, including difficultly obtaining employment prior to involvement in the justice system (Visher & La Vigne, 2020), an erosion of skills and/or holes in resumes, and damaged ties to previous employers due to incarceration (Western, 2002).

The research on the relationship between employment and desistance is complex. One study found that of those who had desisted from, most had already done so before they began working (Skardhamar & Savolainen, 2014). However, it is possible that individuals can form prosocial bonds at work that can help encourage desistance (Sampson & Laub, 1990). Additionally, other research suggests employment is associated with a longer period of time before reincarceration (Tripodi et al., 2010). There are multiple things to consider beyond just whether someone is employed, including the quality of employment, perceived work conditions, and type of employment (Ramakers et al., 2017). Additionally, it is common for individuals on probation or parole to experience unstable employment. That is, they may find a job and keep it for a month, be unemployed for a few months, and then find another job, and so on. As a result, it is important to also measure duration of employment as an additional indicator of success.

Education

Education presents another possible indicator of success for individuals on probation or parole. Like employment, education should also be measured in a processual manner, tracking small steps toward larger goals (e.g., enrollment in a GED probation, attaining a GED class). Justice-involved individuals often have significant educational needs compared to the general population. In 2014, approximately 30% of individuals who were currently incarcerated had less than a high school degree or equivalent compared to just 14% of the nonincarcerated population (Rampey et al., 2016). While 64% of people incarcerated in federal and state prisons are eligible to enroll in a postsecondary education program, 58% of those in prison do not complete an education program while incarcerated (U.S. Department of Education, 2014). However, research suggests that education can serve as a protective factor against recidivism: The more education an individual gains, the lower their likelihood for recidivism is (e.g., Cleere & Maguire, 2013; Zgoba et al., 2008). Measuring progress toward educational attainment can include a range of factors, such as enrolling in courses, completing courses, and completing a degree/certification—all of which can serve as indicators of success for those under community supervision.

Social Relationships

There is a vast body of research that highlights the importance of social support for justice-involved individuals. Several studies suggest that social support may impact recidivism, as it can serve as a means for effective social control (Braithwaite, 1989), result in increased parental monitoring/care (Wright et al., 2001), encourage appropriate coping mechanisms to stress (Agnew, 1999), and aid support desistance (Laub & Sampson 1993). Informal social control theory suggests that social support increases the likelihood that an individual feels obligated to family and will perceive the costs of crime as higher (Sampson & Laub, 1993). Individuals can receive various types of support from their family and friends. This can include instrumental support, which involves provision of physical support (e.g., housing, transportation, and financial support or emotional support). While increasing social support can certainly serve as an indicator of success, doing so is not straightforward. Many individuals under supervision have burned bridges with their social support networks, and some have social support networks that are also involved in crime. Thus, probation and parole officers must be able to distinguish between prosocial and antisocial support while also encouraging those who have damaged relationships. For some, they may need to work toward reinstituting contact with children and gaining back parental rights. While these may not be easy, they do all reflect processes that can be measured to identify progress.

Civic Engagement

Lastly, the National Academies of Science, Engineering, and Medicine (2022) suggest measuring civic engagement as an alternative indicator of success. They point out that while individuals with criminal records are taxpayers, volunteers, homeowners, and, when possible, voters—making them citizens although they may not even view themselves as such. You might be wondering why civic engagement matters. Civic behaviors, like voting, are associated with desistance from crime (Uggen & Manza, 2004). This means that increasing one's perception that they are a citizen and that their voice (and vote) matters can be an impactful part of the desistance process. However, many individuals with criminal records are legally not allowed to vote. As a result, the National Academies of Science, Engineering, and Medicine (2022) recommend measuring not only an individual's civic engagement but also system-level indicators of voting laws prohibiting or allowing justice-involved individuals to vote.

◊ Officer Work, Careers, and Wellness: Probation/Parole Officer Discretion and Violations

When thinking about outcomes in the criminal justice system, it is imperative to remember that what happens throughout the system is often a result of decisions that individual actors, like probation and parole officers, make. Like many practitioners in the system, probation and parole officers have a great deal of discretion in their day-to-day work. *Discretion* refers to the ability of individuals to decide how to act in a given situation. Discretion is pervasive throughout the system and is a key part of decisions made every day by police, courtroom actors (e.g., judges, prosecutors, juries), and correctional staff (e.g., probation and parole officers, correctional officers). For example, when a police officer decides not to arrest someone or a jury decides not to convict, they are using their discretion to come to those decisions. Similarly, probation and parole officers have vast discretion to determine how to supervise each client and how they will respond to noncompliance. As you can imagine, these decisions made across the system can have great implications for recidivism. That is, one person may be identified as someone who recidivated while another person was not—due not to their actions but the decisions made by the criminal justice actors they interacted with.

Now, let's think about probation and parole specifically. Remember, individuals under supervision are required to abide by a long list of conditions, most of which do not reflect illegal behavior. Noncompliance with any of these conditions can result in a violation and potentially a revocation, reconviction, or reincarceration. However, probation and parole officers do not issue violations for every single instance of noncompliance that occurs. You might be wondering why that is. Well, think about it this way: Say a probation or parole officer has 100 people on their caseload who all have to follow 18–20 conditions. It would be nearly impossible for any individual probation or parole officer to monitor compliance with that many rules for that many people. Let's say during any given week 15% of their caseload violate one condition. Now, they have 15 circumstances of noncompliance (some of which might involve more than one violation) to address. To formally violate all 15 of these individuals, a probation or parole officer would have to spend a large chunk of their time—that they likely do not have—to complete onerous paperwork and file with the court (see example below of a violation report used in North Carolina). Now, let's say this specific probation or parole agency has 20 officers. If all 20 officers were to file a formal violation for every detected instance of noncompliance, that would be 300 formal violations per week. That is a lot of paperwork that would require approval from agency supervisors, who also likely would not have time to review and approve such a high volume of violations. Courts would also likely not be able to keep up with such a high volume of violation cases.

READING

STATE OF NORTH CAROLINA

File No. County of Hearing _____

File No. County of Origin _____

In the General Court of Justice

| County | Seat of Court | ☐ District | ☐ Superior Court |

STATE VERSUS _____

Defendant

VIOLATION REPORT

G.S. 15A-1345

| *Race* | *Sex* | *DOB* |

ADMINISTRATIVE REVIEW

The violations listed on this Violation Report were reviewed with _____

Chief Probation Officer on _____ .

The State of North Carolina, Selection from "Violation Report from North Carolina," *Violation Report from North Carolina*, pp. 1-2, 2006.

STATE VERSUS _____

Defendant

| Race | Sex | DOB |

VIOLATION REPORT - Page 2

G.S. 15A-1345

SIGNATURE OF PROBATIONER

I have received a copy of this Violation Report and understand its contents and that I must appear in Court as directed by my Probation/Parole Officer.

_____

Signature of Probationer   Date

HEARING NOTICE

WHEREFORE, the undersigned requests that a hearing on the charge(s) contained in this report be conducted pursuant to G.S. 15A-1345 (e) on the date and at the time and place set forth below, that the notice of this hearing be given in any manner provided by law, and that after such hearing the Court take the action which it considers proper under G.S. 15A-1344 (d) and/or 15A-1344(el).

Hearing Date _____ Time _____ ☐ am ☐ pm   Place _____

OATH AND SIGNATURE OF OFFICER

I have read the Violation Report, and state that the contents are true to my own knowledge except those which are stated upon information and belief, and as to them I believe that they are true.

_____

Signature   Name (Type or Print)   Title   Date

SWORN AND SUBSCRIBED TO _____

Signature of Person Authorized to Administer Oaths

on _____.

☐ Deputy CSC/Assistant CSC   ☐ Superior Court Clerk

☐ Magistrate   ☐ Notary Public

Date Commission Expires: _____

The probation officer, being duly sworn, states that the defendant was placed on probation pursuant to the following Judgment Suspending Sentence.

Date of Judgment	Court	County of Origin	File No.	Offense
_____	_____	_____	_____	_____

Length of Sentence: _____

Length of Term of Probation: _____

Sentencing Judge: _____

STATE VERSUS		
Defendant		

VIOLATION REPORT - Page 3

G.S. 15A-1345

Race	*Sex*	*DOB*

Of the conditions of probation imposed in that judgment, the defendant has willfully violated:

1. Regular Condition of Probation "Report as directed by the Court or the probation officer to the officer at reasonable times and places?" in that:

2. Special Conditions of Probation "Be assigned to the Electronic House Arrest//Electronic Monitoring program for the specified period and obey all rules and regulations of the program until discharged?" in that:

3. Monetary Condition of Probation "The defendant shall pay to the Clerk of Superior Court the "Total Amount Due" as directed by the Court or probation officer" in that:

4. Monetary Condition of Probation "The defendant shall pay to the Clerk of Superior Court the monthly probation supervision fee as set by law" in that:

5. Regular Condition of Probation "Remain within the jurisdiction of the Court unless granted written permission to leave by the Court or the probation officer" in that:

6. Regular Condition of Probation "Commit no criminal offense in any jurisdiction" in that:

So, if we agree that formally responding to every individual who violates their terms of supervision is not realistic, what happens? Well, we expect probation and parole agencies to allow officers discretion in determining when to respond formally to noncompliance. There are only a few circumstances where officers do not have much discretion—namely, when an individual under supervision commits a new crime. For most other violations, probation or parole officers have discretion as to whether and how to respond. They may consider a wide range of factors to make these decisions, including (but not limited to) an individual's pattern of behavior, severity of the violation, whether the violation is related to the original offending behavior, relationship with the individual, whether the individual admits/accepts responsibility, and any other mitigating factors (e.g., client mental health). Additionally, the probation and parole officer's role orientation, as discussed in Chapter 4, can influence discretionary decision making with regard to noncompliance. For example, an officer aligned with a rehabilitative approach may be more likely to respond to a positive drug test therapeutically (e.g., referral to treatment) versus a law enforcement-oriented officer who may be more likely to respond punitively (e.g., increase drug testing requirements).

To try to guide probation and parole officer discretion in responding to violations, some agencies use graduated sanctions, as discussed in Chapter 5. In the context of community supervision, graduated sanctions provide probation and parole officers with a ladder of possible sanctions and interventions they can apply on a sliding scale. That is, as the seriousness and frequency of violations increase, officers can select responses higher on the ladder. However, even with graduated sanctions officers typically still have a choice as to which response they want to implement. Thus, this only guides discretion rather than removing it entirely. There is also some research that suggests that officers may also circumvent policies that seek to limit formally violating individuals (Rudes, 2012). Additionally, external factors may influence whether and how probation or parole officers respond to violations. For example, in some jurisdictions, community-based treatment is not readily available. Access to community-based resources is often even more strained in rural communities (Garland et al., 2013). With fewer non-incarceration alternatives, some probation and parole officers may feel like their only option is to file a formal violation.

A second piece of the issue here is that once a probation or parole officer files a violation, it now moves to the court. This introduces a whole new group of actors who will use their discretion to determine what the criminal justice response will be. Violation hearings are quite different than typical criminal hearings, with much fewer due process protections (e.g., there is no right to a speedy trial, no right to a jury trial, and guilt is not determined beyond a reasonable doubt but by preponderance of evidence). During probation violation hearings, typically the probation officer will speak about the individual's progress on supervision so far in addition to discussing the specific behavior that led to the current violation. A prosecutor(s) will also be present and will share evidence that the individual violated the terms of their probation. The individual under supervision may also be asked to speak. A judge will then determine if a probation violation happened and what the appropriate sentence will be.

If a judge determines that no probation violation occurred, the individual will continue supervision with no changes. If the judge determines a probation violation did occur, they have multiple options for responses. The most serious response is a revocation, which likely results in incarceration, although less commonly it could result in a new probation or parole term. Judges may also decide to modify probation, which may be more common for first-time violators, technical violations, or nonviolent offenses. In these situations, a judge may decide to add additional supervision conditions or extend the amount of time an individual must serve on supervision. Finally, a judge may decide to sentence the individual to a continuation of probation with no modifications, although this is uncommon. The process for parole violations is similar; however, a parole board may make outcome decisions instead of a judge.

As you can see, there are multiple stages of decision making that can determine an outcome for a single probation or parole violation. At each of these stages, the way individual actors decide to use and apply their discretion can have significant impacts on the final response to a violation. As a result, some may argue that violation and revocation rates are less indicative of the behavior of individuals under supervision, and more indicative of agency and individual officer discretionary practices. This is another compelling reason to track and measure multiple forms of recidivism and measures of success.

SUMMARY: MEASURING SUCCESS AND REDUCING RECIDIVISM

Recidivism is measured inconsistently across agencies and jurisdictions. While generally recidivism reflects engagement in a new crime after one has already received a sanction/intervention for a past crime, the actual way we measure this activity varies. For example, when we say "recidivism," sometimes we mean a new arrest or sometimes we mean a new conviction. When thinking about the way our criminal justice system works, these two different measurements are quite different. Keep in mind that the criminal justice system is like a funnel. That is, the likelihood that criminal behavior will be detected and then result in an arrest, conviction, and punishment all decrease as one moves through the process (see Figure 10.4). If Agency A measures recidivism using reincarceration while Agency B uses rearrest, it is likely Agency A's recidivism rates will look much better because reincarceration is less common than rearrest. To be able to make a true comparison, you would need to compare the same measure of recidivism. This includes both the type (e.g., rearrest, reconviction, reincarceration) as well as covering the same time period. Rearrest data reported for a 1-year time period is not comparable to rearrest data for a 3-year time period. Anytime you are reviewing an agency or program's recidivism rate, you should ask yourself a few questions:

1. How do they define recidivism?
2. What measure(s) do they use for recidivism?
3. What amount of time are they calculating recidivism for?

While there is no "right" or "wrong" measure of recidivism, it is better to use multiple measures when possible. There are a couple of benefits to doing this. Let's pretend we evaluated a cognitive behavioral program for individuals on probation. We measured both reincarceration and rearrest as recidivism outcomes. We found that program completion significantly reduced reincarceration but had no impact on rearrest. How could this happen? Well, take another look at our criminal justice funnel in Figure 10.4. Incarceration is the

FIGURE 10.4 Criminal
Justice Funnel Example

rarest outcome in the process. As a result, it likely reflects more serious behavior. On the other hand, arrest is near the top of the funnel, as it happens more frequently. It is possible that someone in the process of desisting from crime might be less likely to receive reincarceration, especially if they are engaging in less serious/frequent criminal behavior but may continue to get arrested for less serious offenses. If we had only measured rearrest, we might conclude the program was not worth the time or resources. However, by also including reincarceration, we could identify an important benefit of the program. Including multiple measures of recidivism also provides additional metrics to collect data over time as well, which is also important in determining whether a program/policy works (see Chapter 6 for more on this). Including more measures of recidivism also makes it easier to compare programs to other studies. Now, we could compare our study on this cognitive behavioral program to other studies that used rearrest and/or reincarceration.

In Chapter 6, we established the importance of engaging in ongoing data collection and analyses to determine whether programs and policies are working as intended. Unfortunately, this is something many agencies struggle with, often making it difficult to know how effective probation and parole programs and agencies are. Not all states currently measure and report on recidivism annually, and many cannot compare their current performance to past years or evaluate any policy or practice changes they implement (King & Elderbroom, 2014). Also, many agencies do not consistently track or report on the alternative measures of success discussed in this chapter. For some probation and parole agencies, the only information they might collect on mental health, substance use, housing, education, and social support comes from their risk and needs assessment. It is rare, if not nonexistent, that an agency would collect the extent of the information presented in this chapter to better understand the desistance process and alternative measures of success in their clients. However, considering the issues with relying solely on recidivism and the need to consider racial disparities throughout the system, it is critical to consider using these alternative indicators of success.

In doing so, we can better identify program and policy outcomes while also measuring reductions in criminogenic needs, which are also important targets for success. Importantly, by expanding the outcomes we evaluate, we can shift from a focus on failure to an emphasis on positive behavioral change. This is particularly salient as we consider that probation and parole is part of the "corrections" system. That is, we should determine whether correctional programs and policies result in desired behavior and not just recidivism. It is important to identify the small steps of progress individuals make toward prosocial behavior and improvements in one's quality of life. When probation and parole agencies recognize steps toward success, they are also recognizing that individuals can be successful and pursue a life without involvement in the criminal justice system.

Scenario-Based Activities

	Case	Question(s)
1.	Pretend you are a researcher who just teamed up with a probation agency. This probation agency is about to implement a new program designed to reduce recidivism among clients. The program involves several components: (a) probation officer training in motivational interviewing, (b) implementation of a validated risk and needs assessment instrument, and (c) probation officer training to create a supervision/case plan to address assessed risk/needs factors.	What outcome measures would you track and measure to evaluate the success of this program? For each outcome measure, how you would measure the outcome (including the source of the data)?
2.	You are working with a probation agency that is interested in learning more about their clients and providing more opportunities for officers to encourage client progress. They already track multiple recidivism measures, but they want to know how they can track client progress on other key desistance measures.	Describe what desistance measures you would recommend this agency begin to track. Explain why you selected each measure. Describe how the agency could feasibly track, measure, and report each measure for their clients.

References

Agnew, R. (1999). A general strain theory of community differences in crime rates. *Journal of Research in Crime and Delinquency, 36*(2), 123–155. https://doi.org/10.1177/0022427899036002001

Andrews, D. A., & Bonta, J. (2010). *The psychology of criminal conduct.* (5th ed.). Anderson Publishing.

Baumgartner, F. R., Epp, D. A., & Shoub, K. (2018). *Suspect citizens: What 20 million traffic stops tell us about policing and race.* Cambridge University Press.

Beck, A. J., & Blumstein, A. (2018). Racial disproportionality in U.S. state prisons: Accounting for the effects of racial and ethnic differences in criminal involvement, arrests, sentencing, and time served. *Journal of Quantitative Criminology, 34,* 853–883. https://doi.org/10.1007/s10940-017-9357-6

Braithwaite, J. (1989). *Crime, shame and reintegration.* Cambridge University Press.

Bronson, J., & Carson, E. A. (2019). *Prisoners in 2017.* U.S. Department of Justice, Office of Justice Programs. https://bjs.ojp.gov/content/pub/pdf/p17.pdf

Brown v. Plata, 563 U.S. 493 (2011). https://www.oyez.org/cases/2010/09-1233

Cleere, G., & Maguire, N. (2013). *Social capital and desistance: an exploration of prisoners' experiences in Ireland* [Unpublished doctoral dissertation]. Waterford Institute of Technology.

Cooper, A. D., Durose, M. R. & Snyder, H. N. (2014). *Recidivism of prisoners released from 30 states in 2005: Patterns from 2005 to 2010.* Bureau of Justice Statistics, Office of Justice Programs, The U.S. Department of Justice. https://bjs.ojp.gov/library/publications/recidivism-prisoners-released-30-states-2005-patterns-2005-2010-update

Garland, A. F., Haine-Schlagel, R., Brookman-Frazee, L., Baker-Ericzen, M., Trask, E., & Fawley-King, K. (2013). Improving community-based mental health care for children: Translating knowledge into action. *Administration and Policy in Mental Health and Mental Health Services Research, 40*, 6–22. DOI 10.1007/s10488-012-0450-8

Gelman, A., Fagan, J., & Kiss, A. (2007). An analysis of the New York City Police Department's "stop-and-frisk" policy in the context of claims of racial bias. *Journal of the American Statistical Association, 102*(479), 813–823. https://doi.org/10.1198/016214506000001040

Grattet, R., Petersilia, J., Lin, J., & Beckman, M. (2009). Parole violations and revocations in California: Analysis and suggestions for action. *Federal Probation, 73*(1), 2–11.

Jannetta, J., Breaux, J., To, H., & Porter, J. (2016). *Examining racial and ethnic disparities in probation revocation: Summary findings and implications from a multisite study.* The Urban Institute.

Jarvis, M., Williams, J., Hurford, M., Lindsay, D., Lincoln, P., Giles, L., Luongo, P., & Safarian, T. (2017). Appropriate use of drug testing in clinical addiction medicine. *Journal of Addiction Medicine, 11*(3), 163–173. DOI: 10.1097/ADM.0000000000000323

Jones, K. A., Agboh, D., Patten, M., & Chauhan, P. (2021). An examination of racial disparities in misdemeanor marijuana possession arrests following reforms in four U.S. jurisdictions. *Journal of Drug Policy Analysis, 14*(1), 41–53. https://doi.org/10.1515/jdpa-2021-0008

Kaeble, D. (2023). *Probation and parole in the United States, 2021.* Bureau of Justice Statistics, Office of Justice Programs, The U.S. Department of Justice. https://bjs.ojp.gov/library/publications/probation-and-parole-united-states-2021

King, R., & Elderbroom, B. (2014). *Improving recidivism as a performance measure.* Urban Institute.

Klingele, C. M. (2019). Measuring change: From rates of recidivism to markers of desistance. *Journal of Criminal Law and Criminology, 109*(4), 769–817. DOI: 0091-4169/19/10904-0769

Kovera, M. B. (2019). Racial disparities in the criminal justice system: Prevalence, causes, and a search for solutions. *Journal of Social Issues, 75*(4), 1139–1164. https://doi.org/10.1111/josi.12355

Kramer, R., & Remster, B. (2018). Stop, frisk, and assault? Racial disparities in police use of force during investigatory stops. *Law & Society Review, 52*(4), 960–993. https://doi.org/10.1111/lasr.12366

Laub, J. H., & Sampson, R. J. (1993). Turning points in the life course: Why change matters to the study of crime. *Criminology, 31*(3), 301–325. https://doi.org/10.1111/j.1745-9125.1993.tb01132.x

Levchak, P. J. (2017). Do precinct characteristics influence stop-and-frisk in New York City? A multi-level analysis of post-stop outcomes. *Justice Quarterly, 34*(3), 377–406. https://doi.org/10.1080/07418825.2016.1162320

Mitchell, O., & Caudy, M. S. (2015). Examining racial disparities in drug arrests. *Justice Quarterly, 32*(2), 288–313. https://doi.org/10.1080/07418825.2012.761721

Mitchell, O., & Caudy, M. S. (2017). Race differences in drug offending and drug distribution arrests. *Crime & Delinquency, 63*(2), 91–112. https://doi.org/10.1177/0011128714568427

Morrow, W. J., White, M. D., & Fradella, H. F. (2017). After the stop: Exploring the racial/ethnic disparities in police use of force during Terry stops. *Police Quarterly, 20*(4), 367–396. https://doi.org/10.1177/1098611117708791

National Academies of Sciences, Engineering, and Medicine. (2022). *The Limits of recidivism: Measuring success after prison.* The National Academies Press. https://doi.org/10.17226/26459

National Institute of Justice. (n.d.). *Recidivism*. Retrieved October 10, 2023, from https://nij.ojp.gov/topics/corrections/recidivism#:~:text=Recidivism%20is%20one%20of%20the,intervention%20for%20a%20previous%20crime.

Pierson, E., Simoiu, C., Overgoor, J., Corbett-Davies, S., Jenson, D., Shoemaker, A., Ramachandran, V., Barghouty, P., Phillips, C., Shroff, R., & Goel, S. (2020). A large-scale analysis of racial disparities in police stops across the United States. *Nature Human Behaviour, 4,* 736–745. https://doi.org/10.1038/s41562-020-0858-1

Prison Policy Initiative. (n.d.). *How race impacts who is detained pretrial*. Retrieved May 27, 2023, from https://www.prisonpolicy.org/blog/2019/10/09/pretrial_race/

Prochaska, J. O., & Velicer, W. F. (1997). The transtheoretical model of health behavior change. *American Journal of Health Promotion, 12*(1), 38–48. https://doi.org/10.4278/0890-1171-12.1.38

Ramakers, A., Nieuwbeerta, P., Van Wilsem, J., & Dirkzwager, A. (2017). Not just any job will do: A study on employment characteristics and recidivism risks after release. *International Journal of Offender Therapy And Comparative Criminology, 61*(16), 1795–1818. https://doi.org/10.1177/0306624X1663614

Rampey, B. D., Keiper, S., Mohadjer, L., Krenzke, T., Li, J., Thornton, N., and Hogan, J. (2016). *Highlights from the U.S. PIAAC survey of incarcerated adults: Their skills, work experience, education, and training: Program for the International Assessment of Adult Competencies: 2014* (NCES 2016-040). U.S. Department of Education. Washington, DC: National Center for Education Statistics.

Rudes, D. S. (2012). Getting technical: Parole officers' continued use of technical violations under California's parole reform agenda. *Journal of Crime and Justice, 35*(2), 249–268. https://doi.org/10.1080/0735648X.2012.677572

Sampson, R. J., & Laub, J. H. (1990). Crime and deviance over the life course: The salience of adult social bonds. *American Sociological Review, 55*(5), 609–627. https://doi.org/10.2307/2095859

Sampson, R. J., & Laub, J. H. (1997). A life-course theory of cumulative disadvantage and the stability of delinquency. In Thornberry, T. P. (Ed). *Developmental Theories of Crime and Delinquency,* (7th ed., pp. 133–161). Transaction Publishers.

Scott, K., Ma, D. S., Sadler, M. S., & Correll, J. (2017). A social scientific approach toward understanding racial disparities in police shooting: Data from the Department of Justice (1980–2000). *Journal of Social Issues, 73*(4), 701–722. https://doi.org/10.1111/josi.12243

Skardhamar, T., & Savolainen, J. (2014). Changes in criminal offending around the time of job entry: A study of employment and desistance. *Criminology, 52*(2), 263–291. https://doi.org/10.1111/1745-9125.12037

Steen, S., & Opsal, T. (2007). "Punishment on the installment plan": Individual-level predictors of parole revocation in four states. *The Prison Journal, 87*(3), 344–366. https://doi.org/10.1177/0032885507304526

Anderson, T. S., & Morash, M. (2015). Racial/ethnic disparities in boys' probability of arrest and court actions in 1980 and 2000: The disproportionate impact of "getting tough" on crime. *Youth Violence and Juvenile Justice, 13*(1), 77–95. https://doi.org/10.1177/1541204013515280

Sundaresh, R., Yi, Y., Roy, B., Riley, C., Wildeman, C., & Wang, E. A. (2020). Exposure to the U.S. criminal legal system and well-being: A 2018 cross-sectional study. *American Journal of Public Health, 110* (Suppl. 1), S116–S122. 10.2105/AJPH.2019.305414

Tripodi, S. J., Kim, J. S., & Bender, K. (2010). Is employment associated with reduced recidivism? The complex relationship between employment and crime. *International Journal Of Offender Therapy And Comparative Criminology, 54*(5), 706–720. https://doi.org/10.1177/0306624X09342980

Uggen, C., & Manza, J. (2004). Voting and subsequent crime and arrest: Evidence from a community sample. *Columbia Human Rights Law Review, 36*, 193–215.

Ulmer, J. T., & Steffensmeier, D. J. (2014). The age and crime relationship: Social variation, social explanations. In K. M. Beaver, J. C. Barnes, & B. B. Boutwell (Eds.), *The nurture versus biosocial debate in criminology: On the origins of criminal behavior and criminality* (pp. 377–396). SAGE Publications.

U.S. Census Bureau. (2019). *Annual estimates of the resident population by sex, race, and hispanic origin for the United States: April 1, 2010, to July 1, 2019.* Retrieved from https://www.census.gov/newsroom/press-kits/2020/population-estimates-detailed.html.

Vera Institute of Justice. (2023). *Incarceration Trends data.* https://trends.vera.org/

Visher, C. A., & La Vigne, N. (2020). Returning home: A pathbreaking study of prisoner reentry and its challenges. In B. M Huebner, F. S. Taxman, & P. K. Lattimore (Eds.), *Handbook on moving corrections and sentencing forward: Building on the record* (pp. 278–311). Routledge.

Western, B. (2002). The impact of incarceration on wage mobility and inequality. *American Sociological Review, 67*(4), 526–546. https://doi.org/10.2307/3088944

Wright, J. P., Cullen, F. T., & Miller, J. T. (2001). Family social capital and delinquent involvement. *Journal of Criminal Justice, 29*(1), 1–9. https://doi.org/10.1016/S0047-2352(00)00071-4

Zgoba, K. M., Haugebrook, S., & Jenkins, K. (2008). The influence of GED obtainment on inmate release outcome. *Criminal Justice and Behavior, 35*(3), 375–387. https://doi.org/10.1177/0093854807311853

CHAPTER 11

Agency Culture

In this chapter, organizational culture and climate are introduced as key factors that influence the way probation and parole agencies operate. Three different types of cultures are discussed, including punitive agency culture, rehabilitative agency culture, and hybrid agency culture, as well as the types of policies and practices reinforced by each. Additionally, the implications and consequences associated with each type of culture are discussed, with a focus on the harmful effects of a largely punitive culture. The current emphasis is on a hybrid culture that incorporates elements of both punitive and rehabilitative culture. However, students are introduced to the challenges of changing an organization's culture. Students are presented with information on the idea of culture change, including why agencies might want to generate change in their culture and typical tools to accomplish such change. This involves the components of leadership, training, coaching and education, human resources, and quality improvement processes. This also includes consideration of how to measure and sustain positive changes in agency culture, aided by innovation, technology, and the collective voice of executives with experience in community corrections.

LEARNING OBJECTIVES

By the end of this chapter, students will be able to:

- Identify how culture affects the policies and practices of probation/parole agencies.
- Identify how relationship building can occur in an authoritarian environment.
- Understand the importance of team-based change strategies.

KEY TERMS

- Culture
- Data-driven decision making
- Leadership
- Quality improvement process

CONTENT

Organizational Culture
    Punitive Agency Culture
    ◊ Journey into the Field: Mr. CJ Appleton
    Policies and Practices Associated with a Punitive Approach
    Rehabilitative Agency Culture
    Policies and Practices Associated with a Rehabilitative Approach
    Hybrid Agency Culture
Generating Culture Change
    Effective Leadership
    ◊ Diversity, Equity, and Inclusion: Leadership and Inclusion
    Training, Coaching, and Education
    Human Services
    ◊ Officer Work, Careers, and Wellness: Stress Management and Retention
    Quality Improvement Process
Measuring and Sustaining Change
    The Role of Innovation and Technology
    National Reform by Executives
Summary: Agency Culture and Community Corrections
Scenario-Based Activities

Until I came to IBM, I probably would have told you that culture was just one among several important elements in any organization's makeup and success—along with vision, strategy, marketing, financials, and the like. ... I came to see, in my time at IBM, that culture isn't just one aspect of the game, it is the game. In the end, an organization is nothing more than the collective capacity of its people to create value.

—Louis V. Gerstner Jr.

Organizational Culture

This chapter introduces students to the role of culture and its influence on probation and parole agencies. Culture is an important topic because probation and parole agencies are very diverse in their size, function, and operation (see Chapter 3). For example, in the United States, probation agencies can be run by a statewide agency that has field offices to provide local services, at the county level (where the state has little authority), or at the federal level (where states and counties have little authority). At each level of government administration, a mission statement defines the direction of an agency, including operational features, often with input from vital stakeholders such as the legislators and state and/or county legislative authorities. The mission sets the tone for the agency, but the actual operations are impacted by the culture of the agency, which is defined as "the way things get done" (Deal & Kennedy, 1984, p. 4).

The culture of an organization is a combination of many things: ideals, practices, routines, goals, and norms. **Culture** represents the formal and informal structures within an organization combined with intra- and interorganizational contingencies (Schein, 1990). As a result, the organizational culture of an agency creates a normative environment where organizational actors determine how to do their job, grow, and conform to informal and formal cultural guidelines. The culture of an organization is informed by three main components:

- The experiences of leaders and staff in doing their jobs
- The technical skills that staff have and are comfortable using, including risk and need assessment tools, case plans, monitoring individuals, behavioral management strategies, use of sanctions and incentives, motivational techniques, and other skills that are involved in the supervision process
- The relationship with other similar organizations and stakeholders that have expectations about the goals of probation and parole

Throughout this book, we have discussed the varying emphasis that is placed on rehabilitation and punishment in community corrections (for example, see Chapter 1). The shift between these two primary goals, which can be influenced by large-scale political, social, and economic changes tend to also drive cultural shifts within probation and parole agencies. For example, over the last decade, there has been mounting financial strain on probation and parole, coupled with increasing evidence that punitive correctional policies are ineffective, which have produced pressure for community corrections agencies to shift toward the goal of rehabilitation (Rhine et al., 2006).

Pendulum Swings in Correctional Policy

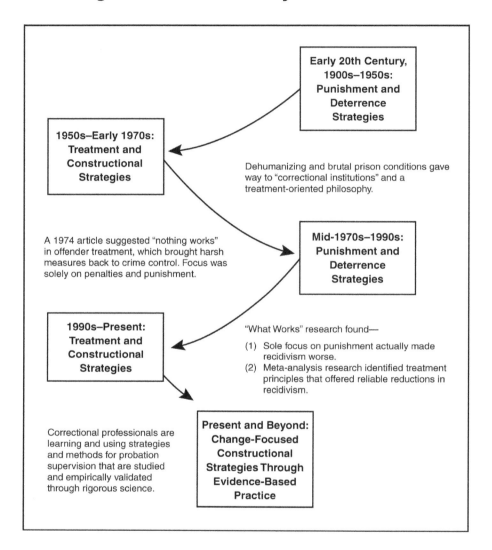

Related, there has been a movement toward the use of evidence-based practices (EBPs), discussed in Chapters 4 and 6, that focus on supporting behavior change in community supervision clients. Evidence-based practices are guided by scientific research rather than a more political and public opinion reaction toward punishment and control. The movement toward these practices, however, often requires changes in core ideologies. In some cases, this has required a shift in the culture of the probation or parole agency from the traditional focus on

Scott T. Walters, Michael D. Clark, Ray Gingerich and Melissa L. Meltzer, "Exhibit 1-1: Pendulum Swings in Correctional Policy," *A Guide for Probation and Parole: Motivating Offenders to Change*, p. 3, 2007.

control and punishment to a more therapeutic, rehabilitative orientation. There is a wealth of research, including the seminal work of Lipsky (2010), that highlights the critical role that street-level bureaucrats, like probation and parole officers, play in supporting change in the organizational culture. *Street-level bureaucrats* are civil servants, often employed by a public agency or government institution, who have direct contact with members of the public. This is relevant for community corrections because laws, policies, and practices are often devised by judges, academics, and politicians; however, it is the street-level bureaucrat who is responsible for implementing these ideas through their daily activities. Probation and parole officers are the "human face" of the community corrections system, and they have discretion, accountability, limited resources, and an increasing reliance on technology to fulfill their myriad of duties.

As a result, street-level bureaucrats are responsible for implementing policy (Lipsky, 2010) and they bring the organization's culture (ideals, practices, and goals) to life (Lin, 2000). It should be recognized that the culture of an organization significantly impacts how street-level bureaucrats conduct their daily responsibilities, as they can be a facilitator or barrier to implementing change within the agency. The following sections discuss the implications of three primary agency cultures (i.e., punitive, rehabilitative, and hybrid) that frontline probation and parole officers are likely to encounter, with references to their key differences, orientations, and outcomes.

Punitive Agency Culture

In an agency that emphasizes law enforcement, the agency culture reflects the punishment philosophies of deterrence, incapacitation, and retribution, as presented in Chapter 2. In community corrections, this approach often translates to a punishment strategy of "prison without walls" where the conditions of release assigned by the judiciary and/or parole board and the requirements of supervision are strictly enforced. The officers in these agencies place a high value on compliance, and even the smallest deviation can have serious consequences, including risk of incarceration. This punitive mission is often referred to as "nail 'em, tail 'em, and jail 'em" because the officer is strictly overseeing the conditions of release with little leeway for any noncompliance, identifying those that are not abiding by the rules of supervision and recommending to the court to return the individual to jail or prison due to violations of the conditions of supervision.

The punitive approach escalated during the 1980s when there was political pressure to "get tough" on those who violate the law. In community corrections, there was an increased focus on holding the individual accountable for their actions and behaviors using the threat of incarceration. This era produced an increase in the number of probation and parole conditions, including adding more geographical limitations through house arrest, curfews, and/or electronic monitoring to ensure that the individual was fully aware that they were being sanctioned and monitored. During this time, the limiting of the physical movements of those under supervision became an increasingly accepted practice.

Punitive supervision conditions place psychological burdens on an individual to make the individual cognizant of their supervision status; this is often reinforced by hefty monetary sanctions to repay the community for the crime committed. Some scholars refer to this punitive era of supervision as "mean supervision" given the heavy emphasis on adding more requirements, strictly enforcing these requirements, and incarcerating those who violate these requirements (Taxman et al., 2020). As a consequence of the political movement toward getting "tough on crime," the culture of probation and parole agencies also gravitated toward more punitive measures. The following section details additional policies and practices associated with this increasingly punitive approach to community corrections.

JOURNEY INTO THE FIELD: MR. CJ APPLETON

◇◇◇◇◇◇◇◇

Full name: CJ Appleton

Title: PhD candidate, George Mason University.

CJ Appleton was raised in Portland, Oregon—specifically, in North Portland, which is one of the few predominantly Black neighborhoods in the city. Mr. Appleton describes his early life as a "mixed bag" with both positive and negative influences in the neighborhood—positive influences being great people, friends, and community and negative influences being gangs, violence, and drugs. Mr. Appleton grew up in a single-family home with a mother who worked as a registered nurse and one sister. He attended private school from second grade through to his senior year of high school. Mr. Appleton was an athlete, an identity that he holds as an adult. He played sports (soccer, basketball, track, baseball) but in high school, he specialized in football and basketball. Mr. Appleton played both football and basketball in college at Lewis and Clark College in Portland. During this time Mr. Appleton encountered the community court system (detailed below), which detoured his plans. However, Mr. Appleton is now a PhD candidate in George Mason's Criminology, Law and Society program. He is also a research assistant who works for the Center for Advancing Correctional Excellence (ACE!). CJ Appleton presents a unique and fascinating Journey into the Field of community corrections, including experiences with both punitive and rehabilitative officers. The intricacies of these life events are shared below.

I was on probation for 10 years, from the time I was 18 years old until I was 27 years old. I went through a number of different types of supervision. My initial sentence was 30 days in jail with 3 years of probation. When I was on supervision, I participated in drug court, drug treatment (in-patient and out-patient), drug testing, community service, property crime court, and eventually was put on a low risk supervision caseload. I was never given an assessment, never told my risk level, never told any of my criminogenic needs, and never had an intervention given during an office visit. My typical office visit was very formulaic: What are you doing, do you have a job, where do you live, have you been in trouble, have you pissed dirty (e.g., failed a drug test), pay the fee, and come back in 3 weeks.

My supervision experience was horrible from the beginning. When I first signed my plea deal in court, it was for the expressed purpose of being able to leave the state to take advantage of a football scholarship in Utah. I went to court on a Monday, and it was a part of the language that I would check in with Portland probation the next day on my way out to Utah where I already had a new probation officer. I thought it was the end of a yearlong horror-filled journey and showed up to my check-in full of hope. I was told at my first meeting with probation that if I got on that plane to Utah, they would ensure that the police were waiting to arrest me on the other end. When I protested, showing them the explicit language in my court order that said I could leave, I was informed, "That is just a recommendation that we can take or not. We are choosing not to take it." This was the knockout blow. Just when I thought it was over, it was just the beginning of a terrible journey.

I got a probation officer who was a law enforcement–focused person who never once tried to be warm, friendly, or build any type of connection. All of it was too much for my immature mind at the time. I felt that what was happening to me was unfair, but because of the mistakes I made, no one cared how unfair I thought things were. It was all a part of a punishment I brought upon myself and thus one I deserved, no matter the circumstances. I descended into depression and drinking and smoking weed. When I failed drug tests, I was never offered drug treatment, only given jail sanctions, and this caused me to disengage with the probation process. I spent a great majority of my 10 years on supervision absconding because I did not believe they were there to help me. From 18–27 years of age, I was never out of jail longer than 6 months. Most often the stints were between 30 and 90 days on the street followed by a sanction for absconding or new charges.

Eventually, I was given a different probation officer who was more in line with a change agent. She tried to help me get into treatment many times, but I was too far gone. I did not trust her, I was combative when we would meet, and I did not trust that she had my best interests in mind whatsoever. She did not give up on me though, and although we never built much of a connection, no matter how many times I relapsed or absconded, she would offer me another chance when I was in jail to get my life together. Finally, she got me into a 90-day in-patient treatment facility, and then before graduation, she visited me and suggested I go to another 90-day outpatient treatment program afterward. I did not like the idea, but I listened to her, and it was one of the best decisions of my life. My life has taken off since then. Altogether, she got me into four in-patient and two out-patient treatment programs.

There are so many things that need to be fixed in community corrections, but I will focus on one issue. When you are in the justice system, it is difficult to distinguish between the different aspects and actors. This is in part because so many of them operate in a similar fashion. For instance, the same asshole mentality that one gets from the police, you can also feel when in jail or prison from the correctional officers and on probation from your probation officer. Moreover, each aspect of the system can feel dehumanizing, from being arrested, to being put in jail, being strip-searched, transported, taken out to the yard and watched, and then supervised on the street. The consequence of this, at least for me, was that the negative experiences I had with some areas (police, court, jail, probation) made me distrustful of the whole criminal justice system.

This is where the relationship between probation officer and client becomes so important. The probation officer carries the burden of all the dehumanizing and traumatic experiences their clients have had previously, to their next meeting. Because of this they are often already behind the 8-ball when it comes to developing a trusting collaborative relationship. Yet, I see the development of this relationship as the key to everything. Developing a relationship where the client feels respected, seen as a human being, and valued increases the likelihood they will engage in the supervision process. Additionally, developing a strong relationship between officer and client will open up additional avenues for accountability outside of sanctions and violations. For instance, when you respect and value a person's opinion, like a mentor, then letting them down can often be the biggest punishment one can receive and serves as motivation for future behavior change. Also, being valued by and building a quality relationship with a law enforcement agent can rebuild faith and trust in the system overall, which can also impact the likelihood the individual will remain crime-free in the future.

Policies and Practices Associated with a Punitive Approach

Agencies more heavily aligned with a punitive approach typically have a greater focus on policies and practices that prioritize public safety over all other goals. "Public safety" is a broad term that is used to emphasize control over the individuals under supervision to prevent crime. Many of these strategies are designed to send a message to the public that the agency is protecting citizens and their property from harm. It is assumed that strict operations can control crime by deterring individuals from participating in criminal behavior.

In community corrections, punitive practices include the addition of conditions and requirements that are placed on an individual. While the court can assign formal conditions for the supervision of individuals, probation and parole agencies often have regulations that can place added burdens or demands on the person under supervision. Some of these are statutory, and some are agency requirements. They range from how often the individual reports to the probation or parole officer, the manner in which the person reports, requirements to be employed or in school, travel permissions, who the person can associate with, where the person can live, and other conditions that can significantly impact the daily functioning of an individual. These requirements are similar to conditions ordered by the court, in that a failure to comply can result in more punishments or sanctions.

There are a number of specific ways agencies can increase the punitive nature of supervision. Below are the most frequently used practices that can constrain the individual via controlling basic behaviors and holding the individual accountable. It is important to note that the examples provided reflect essential practices that any probation or parole agency will engage in;

however, a more punitively aligned agency often uses these control-based approaches as the primary tactic without (or with very little) inclusion of additional rehabilitative approaches.

Number of Face-to-Face Contacts

The number of times an officer meets with an individual under supervision is a tool to intensify supervision and provide more oversight. The risk-need-responsivity (RNR) model suggests that higher risk individuals should receive more intensive supervision, while lower risk individuals should receive minimal supervision. As a result, many agencies have implemented graduated reporting policies aligned to the level of risk of an individual. Yet even in this context, some agencies or even some individual probation and parole officers who are more punitively minded may require individuals to report to the office more frequently than their risk level or agency policy requires. This is often done to increase control, surveillance, and monitoring in the interest of public safety. While punitive approaches argue for the need to reinforce public safety, an overreliance on face-to-face meetings can be counterproductive and lead to harm (e.g., increase recidivism and/or create barriers to finding employment, maintaining social relationships, etc.).

Drug Testing

Most individuals under supervision are required to participate in drug testing, regardless of evidence they need assistance with drug use or whether their offense involved drugs. The mismatch between criminal offenses and mandated drug testing is by nature a punitive, expensive, and largely pointless exercise, as Ms. Jenna Moll, deputy director of the Washington, DC–based Justice Action Network explains: "If you have someone who has been arrested for parking fines, with no history of substance abuse, [and] no evidence of any addiction issues, whatsoever, forcing that person to go to weekly or monthly drug tests is a huge waste of time" (as quoted in Rodriguez, 2019, "Add-Ons" section).

Agencies often allow officers to use multiple strategies for drug testing. They may require individuals to undergo a drug test during every office visit, they may use a random schedule in which the individual is typically notified the night before they must come in for a drug test the following day, or they can use a nonrandom assigned schedule that may vary (e.g., once a month to multiple times per week). Most commonly, agencies use a urinalysis and breathalyzer (for alcohol use), but they may also require a hair sample (which is more expensive for the agency to process).

Nearly all agencies require that drug testing be observed. This means that an officer must physically watch the individual as they provide a sample. In some agencies this means the officer enters the bathroom with the client, while in others they have observation windows. This observation is meant to ensure the person on supervision is not manipulating the process. Urine drug testing can be particularly punitive, as individuals may feel a sense of shame, humiliation, and mistrust, especially while having an officer observe them using the restroom. When used inappropriately, such testing may carry feelings of degradation that negatively impact the self-esteem of the individual. See Chapter 2 for a broader discussion of the internalization of negative labels process.

Curfew

A *curfew* restricts the movement of an individual during certain periods of time and/or from certain places. Officers use curfews to ensure that the individual under supervision limits their movements—again namely in the interest of public safety. When curfews are applied, the individuals may feel as if they are being treated like a child, with the agency operating in a parental capacity. Research suggests that forms of restrictive incapacitation like curfews should be limited to higher risk individuals who represent a threat to the community. A punitively oriented agency may promote the use of curfews widely for supervision violations rather than using them more judiciously only to limit public safety threats.

House Arrest

Individuals can be required to remain in their residence as part of supervision, as discussed in Chapter 5. Officers can show up at the person's residence, call the individual, or hire a subcontractor to ensure that the individual is where they say they are. House arrest is an extreme form of curfew, which has been coined "prison by any other name" (Schenwar & Law, 2021, title page), as it can negatively impact the individual's physical and mental health. Schenwar and Law (2021) also highlight the collateral consequences that house arrest has on others: "House arrest doesn't impact only those saddled with the orders of confinement or with the electronic shackle strapped to their ankle. The tentacles of surveillance extend to families and loved ones, effectively sentencing them as well" (p. 38). For example, individuals on house arrest are often unable to do things such as take their children to the doctor or school.

Electronic Monitoring

Electronic monitoring (EM) is the use of digital technology to monitor, track, and constrain an individual's movements in the community (see Chapter 5). The advantage of EM is that the individual's movements can be tracked at all times. Most modern-day EM systems are sophisticated, and the system can alert the person if they are entering an area that they should not be in, such as when an individual convicted of a sex offense is located within a school zone. Placement on EM provides 24-hour surveillance of the individual—another feature of the "prison without walls" (Schenwar & Law, 2021). Corbett and Marx (1991) argued that new surveillance technologies such as EM simply move prisons into the community, stating, "We appear to be moving toward, rather than away from, becoming a 'maximum-security society'" (p. 400).

A reliance on punitive forms of technological monitoring can be problematic when agencies budget for equipment while failing to consider the additional staffing costs. In one assessment of people under parole supervision with the Colorado Department of Corrections, Osher (2013) found that 212 paroles officers had to respond to nearly 90,000 alerts and notifications generated by EM devices over a 6-month period. As such, the increase in the intensity and severity of probation and parole surveillance has considerable implications for the workload of already overburdened probation and parole officers. In agencies aligned with a punitive approach, this often equates to the increased use of the strategies outlined above to respond to violations and noncompliance.

Probation and parole officers have significant discretion in how the agency responds to noncompliant behavior, with those working in a culture characterized by punitive goals more likely to issue violations, which can result in technical violence, revocations, and incarceration. Aside from the constant threat of incarceration, the burden of managing numerous conditions cannot be taken lightly, both at the personal level and the system level. At the personal level, the individual on supervision must bear the burden of these conditions and the limitations on their movements, psychological status, and financial conditions. At the system level, violations contribute to the size of the prison population, moving people who may be suitable for community corrections supervision toward incarceration.

Rehabilitative Agency Culture

In probation and parole agencies whose culture emphasizes rehabilitation, the focus is often more aligned with a public health, social support, and assistance approach to daily activities. In these agencies, officers are encouraged to help individuals under supervision learn and/or engage in prosocial behaviors by working closely with the individual, addressing their needs that are related to criminal behavior, and helping the person to connect with prosocial individuals, activities, and programs. A rehabilitative agency culture identifies and seeks to address the instabilities that make it difficult for individuals to be prosocial, such as having food, a place to live, and a job (to be able to pay bills). In this way, probation and parole officers often seek to intervene proactively before a supervision violation may occur to address criminogenic needs and barriers to success (such as housing and employment), and they are more likely to respond to violations in a therapeutic manner.

Key approaches to probation and parole work under a rehabilitative culture center on creating a "meaningful" supervision experience, often centering on positive officer–client interactions that can facilitate the identification of prosocial goals and objectives. Meaningful supervision is focused on relationships, quality of life, and trust, where the officer and the individual under supervision form a partnership to achieve the goals of supervision. Additional primary activities often include utilizing a service referral model where the officer screens clients and makes appropriate referrals to services that could help stabilize the individual in areas such as substance use, mental health, employment, and housing. Under a brokerage role, the officer becomes an advocate for the individual in terms of helping them understand what the available services are and why engagement in those services will be beneficial. Probation and parole officers do not rely on their authoritarian position but rather use relationship skills to engage the individual in processes of self-determination to achieve supervision goals.

Policies and Practices Associated with a Rehabilitative Approach

As mentioned earlier, even officers who work in rehabilitation-aligned agencies still must engage in the activities outlined above (e.g., face-to-face contacts, drug tests, EM). However, the way in which officers may implement these activities will be different, as the emphasis is less on control and more on supporting behavioral change using effective relationships, addressing barriers to resources, and encouraging engagement in prosocial activities. Instead of primarily responding to individual behavior through an intensification of supervision, probation and parole officers may use supervision tools to assist the individual to make long-term behavioral change. Below, we highlight how officers aligned with a rehabilitative approach may use common supervision activities.

Number of Face-to-Face Contacts

An agency aligned with a rehabilitative approach often more strongly adheres to risk-need-responsivity (RNR) guidelines surrounding the number of face-to-face contacts. As a result, they typically have policies in place that require officers to meet less frequently with lower risk individuals. In some agencies, this may be as infrequent as once every 6 months. Additionally, the purpose of face-to-face contacts will be less focused on compliance and more focused on getting to know the individual and building relationships characterized by trust and collaboration. This may be particularly relevant for people under supervision who have had previous interactions with the criminal justice system that produced cynicism, mistrust, and negativity. Agencies with a rehabilitative culture provide opportunities for officers and individuals to meet to identify and achieve goals in a collaborative nature. The interaction itself is viewed as a meaningful and productive opportunity, rather than a punishment.

Drug Testing

Under a rehabilitative approach, drug testing is more commonly used to assess the degree to which an individual is benefiting from services, with the goal of adjusting the need for drug testing based on the individual's behavior and progress in treatment. As a result, a positive drug test may not result in a violation but rather a consideration for altering treatment services. Additionally, a negative test (especially a pattern of negative tests) may result in a decrease in the frequency of drug testing. In this way, drug testing is also used to signal positive progress or the meeting of goals rather than being used for the sole purpose of identifying failures.

Referral to Services

A key component of a rehabilitative approach involves the use of risk and needs assessment results to refer individuals to appropriate services to address identified needs. As discussed in Chapter 4, the officer may provide individuals a list of services for them to select from or they may arrange a referral to a specific provider (sometimes even making the first appointment for them). This practice is heavily aligned with a rehabilitative cultural approach, with great value placed on direct referral interactions and collaboration process between the officer and client. The inclusion of the client in the process of selecting services can increase their motivation to both engage in and complete programming. When individuals take ownership of these decisions, there is a greater likelihood of positive outcomes.

A rehabilitative orientation overall focuses on building the individual's competencies in targeted areas to promote prosocial behaviors and relationships. Rehabilitative orientations also recognize that social inequities may contribute to engagement in criminal behavior. This intersectional approach recognizes that individuals are a product of their environment—either where they grew up or currently live—and this affects decisions that individuals make. For example, probation and parole officers aligned with a rehabilitative approach may recognize that individuals who live in public housing areas may have more policing of their community than others who do not live in such areas and that these enhanced surveillance policies may result in increased violations. Of course, there will still be plenty of situations where officers working in agencies with a rehabilitative culture will have to issue violations. However, the major differences are that these officers may look to identify and address underlying causes before issuing formal punishments. These officers may work to help individuals navigate supervision by pursuing appropriate services that will help the individual to be successful.

Today, many probation and parole agencies have incorporated key elements of rehabilitation goals into their mission and vision statements, as well as the agencies policies and practices. An example of this approach can be seen in the mission, vision, and values of the Harris County, Texas, Community Corrections and Corrections Department (see textbox below). In this example, we see references to the helping features of probation with the listed goals of assisting the individual on supervision to engage in prosocial activities and overcome barriers to care. There is also reference to the potential for individuals to change, the use of appropriate services, and the need to target factors that impact risk and need surrounding criminal behavior. The rehabilitative culture can be seen in the reference to treating individuals with respect and the endorsement of collaboration.

Mission, Vision, and Values of the Harris County, Texas, Community Supervision and Corrections Department

Mission Statement

Harris County CSCD is committed to using evidence-based strategies to help individuals on community supervision eliminate future criminal behavior and become productive citizens, which in turn creates a safer community with fewer victims.

Vision Statement

We strive to accomplish our mission by:

- Using interventions that are designed to effectively reduce criminal behavior.
- Using assessment to accurately identify and target criminal risk and needs.
- Recognizing the ability of individuals to change.
- Treating all individuals with respect and dignity.
- Creating an environment that encourages learning and professional growth.

> **Values**
>
> · *Respect*: We believe all individuals deserve respect and dignity.
> · *Knowledge*: We are dedicated to creating an environment that encourages learning and professional growth.
> · *Ability to change*: We recognize that all people can change regardless of their past.
> · *Collaboration*: We acknowledge the importance in understanding our role and working with other community stakeholders to help address our clients' holistic needs.
>
> Source: https://cscd.harriscountytx.gov/Pages/default.aspx

Hybrid Agency Cultures

Hybrid agency cultures can be identified by their balance of law enforcement responsibilities (deterrence, incapacitation, and retribution) with rehabilitative approaches (rehabilitation and restoration). As such, hybrid probation and parole agencies reinforce a culture that includes multiple orientations to differing degrees. The hybrid culture agency approach recognizes that supervision requires the technical skills of both enforcement and rehabilitation. That is, the goal of the hybrid approach is to magnify the behavioral management strategies by establishing boundaries that define compliance. These boundaries set guidelines for individuals to understand what compliance is and what compliance is not. The enforcer role is to establish the boundaries, whereas the rehabilitation role is to help the individual understand and engage in prosocial behaviors. As such, hybrid agencies use both "the stick" (i.e., surveillance, control, monitoring), and "the carrot" (i.e., positive reinforcement, removal of social barriers, providing service and programs) to motivate clients to meet conditions of probation or parole.

One example of a hybrid agency culture is the New York City Department of Probation (n.d.), whose website describes their mission: "Using evidence-based practices and a balance of enforcement, structure, treatment and support, we hold people on probation accountable and give them opportunities to forge new pathways so that they can move out and stay out of the justice system" (About Probation section). This blending of orientations is evident in the five main "drivers" of the New York City Department of Probation (n.d.) as listed here:

• Assess and respond to risk and needs: We evaluate all people on probation with an age-appropriate, validated risk assessment instrument. With that knowledge we calibrate the "dosage" of probation to the appropriate risk levels, and we target the needs areas most likely to keep someone involved in the justice system. This is what we call our "one size fits one" approach.
• Engaging probation clients: Using a strength-based approach, our officers spend time with the individuals they supervise to get to know their strengths and aspirations, so that the officers can use that knowledge to motivate and coach their probation clients towards a

law-abiding future. Probation officers work with the probation clients and their circle of influence to develop an Individual Action Plan (IAP). The IAP serves as a guide for every meeting, and through the IAP our officers work to develop transformational relationships with clients and keep them accountable as they work on goals and action steps.

- Engaging the communities of our probation clients: Working closely with the communities we serve is critical to client success. Our Neighborhood Opportunity Networks (NeON(SM)) offer easy access to essential services and make clients feel closer to their neighbors. This innovative and successful model of probation supervision has inspired similar efforts nationwide.
- Using data to guide decision making: Comprehensive data tracking and monitoring, increase efficiency, provide accurate reporting for the public, and improve outcomes for our clients. All DOP managers are expected to use data to guide their practice, both to improve day-to-day performance and to inform larger policy matters.
- Staff development: At the NYC Department of Probation, we are committed to the professional growth of our staff. Unified in our mission, all employees are equally essential to fulfilling our goals. We give clients a transformative experience—changing lives for the better—with trust, compassion, and personal accountability. We do it in close cooperation with the criminal and juvenile justice systems and in collaboration with our community partners and service providers. (DOP's 5 Drivers section)

The hybrid agency culture recognizes that accountability of the individual is important, but with accountability comes opportunities to assist with engagement in prosocial activities. As a result, officers help individuals understand the requirements of supervision while also offering opportunities to participate in treatment and services. In fact, the evidence-based supervision models discussed in Chapter 4 provide guidance on how to implement this hybrid approach. For example, officers use risk and need assessment tools to identify treatment and control needs, use case plans to connect individuals to services, use graduated sanctions and incentives to address compliance behaviors, and develop a working relationship among individuals and their assigned officers. Officers are often trained in motivational interviewing, communication skills, case management and planning, and how to use risk and needs assessments to drive supervision decisions.

Generating Culture Change

Throughout this book, we have discussed the larger social, political, and economic changes that have occurred in the criminal justice field over time (see Chapter 1 for an introduction). Throughout the history of community corrections, the pendulum has swung back and forth from a law enforcement orientation to a rehabilitative orientation. Depending on the larger social and political environment, cultural expectations in a probation and parole office may align more with one approach versus the other. The law enforcement approach has possibly the deepest roots in community corrections. Leaders of probation and parole agencies, the officers who work in these agencies, the training that is provided to staff, expectations of and pressures from stakeholders, and the community at large generally accept supervision as an enforcer of probation and parole conditions. Even public opinion, which is often based on media myths and stereotypes, will sway toward the notion that probation and parole should be severe. These influences can drive the culture of the agency to be more punitive, expecting officers to hold individuals accountable and enforcing the rules via hard punishment.

As a result of these long-standing expectations, changing the culture of probation and parole agencies to embrace tenets of rehabilitation can be a significant challenge. In fact, existing research documents many challenges associated with implementing and sustaining EBPs in punitively oriented community corrections agencies (e.g., Battalino et al., 1996; Rudes, 2012; Viglione, 2019). Change requires street-level bureaucrats (e.g., probation and parole officers) to implement new practices within the existing culture. Probation and parole officers do not mindlessly accept change; rather, they consider whether and how change aligns with their existing ideologies and approaches to their work (Embirbayer & Mische, 1998; Feldman, 2003). When there is a perceived misalignment, officers can resist change, which may ultimately undermine the reform process altogether (Viglione et al., 2015). As a result, generating change within an organization's culture requires specific and deliberative approaches to encourage probation and parole officers to accept, adopt, and implement new policies and practices.

In the context of community corrections, culture change typically requires probation and parole officers to learn and use updated clinical skills (e.g., assessments and use of assessment results) and relationship development techniques, which are typically ignored or undervalued in a punitive approach. For officers who have been in the job for many years, these new skills can represent substantial changes to the way things have been done in the past (i.e., the culture). There is considerable evidence that the following components are necessary to enact cultural change in the community corrections system: effective leadership; training, coaching and education; human resources; and quality improvement processes. These components will now be addressed in more detail.

Effective Leadership

Leadership within an organization often defines the priorities of the agency as well as directs how the agency will pursue those priorities. Leaders set the tone for the organization in a variety of ways, including through formal communication (e.g., definition mission statement, implementing policies, endorsing success) and informal communication (e.g., emails, small talk, social interactions). In addition to communication, leaders can signify their expectations and what they value through allocation of resources (e.g., funding new programs), decisions surrounding promotions and hiring, encouraging staff to attend special trainings or meetings, and working with stakeholders or the local community on issues that affect the probation and parole agency. Decades of research cite the importance of leadership for supporting strong officer performance (Dale & Trlin, 2010), strong workplace performance (Aarons, 2006), and positive attitudes toward adoption and implementation of EBPs (Aarons 2006; Aarons & Sawitzky, 2006).

A study done by Viglione and colleagues (2017) found that probation and parole officers were more likely to use EBPs when they received positive messages from supervisors supporting the changes. An excerpt from this study illustrates the supportive culture present in that agency:

> In particular, the leadership team within Site 2 clearly promotes and supports the culture shifts occurring within the organization. They emphasized the importance of using MI [motivational interviewing] and client-centered approaches not just between probation staff and probationers, but also between probation staff within the office, with other professionals they interact with (e.g., judges, treatment providers), and even with their family members at home. (Viglione et al., 2017, p. 52)

Another study found an increase in the adoption and implementation of EBPs when leaders were more educated regarding EBPs and had positive perceptions of training (Taxman & Sachwald, 2010). Leaders of probation and parole may be responsible for large numbers of officers and staff within an agency, which suggests that an integrated model is required to implement EBPs. Bogue et al. (2004) provide a model that merges evidence-based principles, organizational development, and collaboration to reinforce leadership in community corrections (see Figure 11.1).

Evidence-based principles are presented as the basis of effective leadership and supervision practices. *Organizational development* refers to the need to move agency culture away from traditional, punitive approaches and toward a hybrid model. Bogue et al. (2004) state, "Organizations must rethink their missions and values; gain new knowledge and skills; adjust their infrastructure to support this new way of doing business; and transform their organizational culture" (p. 1). Collaboration addresses the need for leaders in community corrections to seek internal and external buy-in, where partnerships with a range of support services and other agencies are maximized, a topic that is explored further in Chapter 12. Combined, these three components represent a holistic culture change that is shaped by effective leadership.

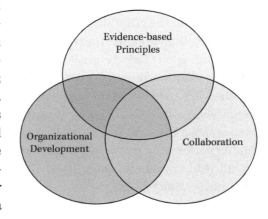

FIGURE 11.1 An Integrated Model (Bogue et al., 2004, p. 1)

◊ Diversity, Equity, and Inclusion: Leadership and Inclusion

Leaders of probation and parole agencies are responsible for the identification and implementation of evidence-based programs and policies that will filter down to the daily activities of their frontline officers. However, these leaders are often invisible from academic studies of community corrections, and they are often ignored when policymakers develop evidence-based training and other proposals. To address this gap, the National Institute of Corrections (NIC, 2020) recently initiated a four-part training series on leadership and inclusion cultures in probation and parole. The training was led by two very skilled professionals: Alfranda "Al" Durr of ALD Associates in Washington, DC, and Kari Heistad, CEO of Cultural Coach International. These trainers are certified diversity and inclusion practitioners with 40+ years of combined experience conducting in-person and virtual training on a wide range of human resources, diversity, equity, and inclusion topics.

In Part 1 of the NIC (2020) training series, the trainers examined the concepts of leadership and self-awareness, highlighting how the COVID-19 pandemic had brought increased isolation from other people and social outlets while also providing new insights into the criminal justice system (see Chapter 1 for the significance of the George Floyd incident). The concept of a "cultural eyesight" is discussed with the understanding that how we view and perceive others is impacted by our individual beliefs, cultural values, and past experiences. This exercise requires that leaders explore their own preconceptions to understand how other people see the world. It is through these personal filters that leaders are thought to best engage in dialogue, have a greater sense of awareness, and display empathy. Part 1 is summarized by the acronym HUE:

- **H**elp with cultural considerations toward effective communication in corrections.
- **U**nderstand how your preconceptions and values influence your vision.
- **E**nhance your ability to navigate shared experiences.

In Part 2 of the NIC (2020) training series, the trainers focus on building inclusion across multidisciplinary teams. The trainers state that the goal of the seminar is for leaders to develop a personal vision of what constitutes an inclusive culture in their workplace—one that promotes excellence by leveraging everyone's skills, abilities, knowledge, and workplace proficiencies. Leaders are instructed on how to best foster the workforce's diverse talents to develop a heightened awareness of each person's contribution. Ultimately, the objective of this exercise is to create a work environment where everyone contributes and feels valued, thus producing higher performing teams for problem solving. This creates a working milieu that is supported by cultural awareness, operational effectiveness, and program efficacy. The acronym of this training session is ICE:

- **I**ncrease effective communication and collaboration between teams and working units.
- **C**odify processes and behaviors that promote innovative solutions to complex issues.
- **E**xcel in the face of organizational change.

Part 3 of the NIC (2020) training series delves into the leader's role in promoting diversity, equity, and inclusion in their work culture. This session highlights that leadership is a privilege and comes with the responsibility of creating a workplace culture that values all individuals. Leaders are presented as people who are forward thinking and accepting of a changing world. This session connects leadership to organization culture and trains leaders to engage in purposeful interactions with clients, community partners, and stakeholders. It also provides guidance on how to develop emotional intelligence and how to achieve personal and professional goals. The acronym of this training sessions is LEAD:

- **L**isten: Gain a perspective or understating of the issues and opportunities people are facing.
- **E**ngage: Develop and implement strategies to drive change that is relevant and meaningful.
- **A**ssess: Sources of inclusion at the organization, leadership, and individual level.
- **D**irect and facilitate change: Based on your assessments, implement interventions and solutions to address opportunities to build and develop an inclusive culture.

Part 4 of the NIC (2020) training series provides leadership through effective communication and engagement. This moves into the need to create a culture of inclusion where everyone's voice matters. The trainers portray leaders as music producers who must direct staff, stating, "Each unique perspective has its own melody, scale, and intensity that, when combined, can lead to making an impactful DOPE sound" (NIC, 2020, "That's DOPE" section). The acronym DOPE stands for:

- **D**iverse and inclusive: Representative at all levels of the organization.
- **O**pen and fair: Transparent and equal access to opportunities.
- **P**sychologically safe place: A space where people can feel free to be themselves.
- **E**quitable: Access to shape and develop the culture of the agency.

This example of an inclusion training for leaders of community corrections shows that it can be delivered in an easily accessible, online, and free format. The design of this training also allowed participants to hear and respond to feedback from their peer leaders in other agencies and states, creating a sense of comradery and belonging. One key aspect of this type of training for leaders is the use of self-reflection, humility, and servant leadership to produce cultural change, rather than a traditional lecture pedagogy. These trainings rest on the notion that cultural change begins with the leader examining their own beliefs, thoughts, and stereotypes before creating a vision of diversity, equity, and inclusion for the agency.

Training, Coaching, and Education

The primary way to initiate change within an organization is through training, coaching, and education. In probation and parole agencies, officers may attend internal training provided by the agency or through an external agency. For many of the correctional interventions discussed in Chapter 6, probation and parole agencies could partner with experts on that intervention to provide the training. Most probation and parole agencies have access to a training academy that offers preservice (before the person becomes an officer) or in-service training. The preservice training courses are generally 2 weeks to 4 months in duration while most agencies have a mandate that an individual participate in 40 hours of training a year. As a result of the evidence-based supervision movement with a focus on rehabilitative and/or hybrid orientations, trainings today often cover specialty areas such as risk and needs assessment tool, case plans, motivational interviewing, effective communications, behavioral management strategies, and other technical topics related to more problem-solving and therapeutic approaches.

Research suggests that a single training is not sufficient to generate culture change. In reality, though, many training courses are one-time events, or they take place over 1 or 2 days. Of course, short-term training may be the only option for agencies that cannot afford to send staff out for extensive training often (both because of financial limitations and limited staffing). However, these shorter trainings are not as helpful in supporting behavior change within probation and parole officers. In fact, research suggests short-term training is not that effective in developing new skills for officers (Taxman et al., 2014). When training is done well, with ample opportunities for staff to learn about an innovation, why it is important, and practice, training can be effective. Research finds that strong training programs can result in improvements in practice, staff behavior, and fidelity to the new intervention/policy (e.g., Aarons et al., 2011; Fixsen et al., 2005).

An example of the challenges surrounding training can be seen with motivational interviewing (MI). During training, officers can learn about specific MI skills, such as the technique of summarization (repeating what the person has said). However, it is more difficult to teach more nuanced skills, such as when to summarize information, how to summarize so that it does not appear to be condescending, or what information is most important to summarize. As a result, it is common for officers to face challenges when attempting to implement newly learned skills in their everyday work when they may face more complex scenarios. This model of training ignores practical challenges associated with learning and developing new skills. Rather, most skill-building efforts require practice using various scenarios and receiving feedback—both of which are infrequently offered in training.

Officers benefit from the use of in-class mock interactions, where officers can experiment with newly learned skills. Below are two examples of motivational interviewing of people under supervision, with the first example involving a client frustrated in his search for employment and the second example showing a resistance in attending programs.

Example 1: Seeking Employment

Client: It's impossible to find a good job. Nobody wants to hire a guy with a record.

Officer 1: There are lots of jobs out there, even for people on supervision. In fact, most offenders are able to find jobs. [Confrontational—less effective.]

Officer 2: It can be much more difficult for someone on supervision to find a job, sure. How do you think you might go about that? [Reflective—more effective.]

Example 2: Program Attendance

Client: This is bullshit. Nobody told me I'd have to take those stupid classes. I got screwed by my lawyer.

Officer 1: You're the one on supervision! These classes are designed to help you with your anger—especially the kind of anger I'm seeing now. [Confrontational—less effective.]

Officer 2: You weren't expecting that you would have to attend these classes, and at this point it seems like a real waste of time. So maybe we can leave that for later. Here are the other things we've got to talk about. ... Which one would you like to talk about? [Reflective—more effective.]

In both cases, Officer 1 is not trained in MI, leading to a confrontational approach that is a less effective form of communication, while Officer 2 who is trained in MI is empowered to communicate in a more reflective style that can produce better results (adapted from Walters et al., 2007, p. 38).

To have a greater impact, training should be comprehensive, including multiple days of initial training with opportunities to practice new skills, followed by regular or booster training. *Booster sessions* are "refresher" trainings that are designed to present the information again (more abbreviated) and to offer officers the opportunity to practice. For example, in a booster session on MI, the trainer may go over the techniques of summarization or strategies to address ambivalence and then give the participants scenarios to apply the skills with a colleague. Booster sessions can be provided in a number of ways, including on- or off-site or virtually. The frequency of booster sessions varies depending on the intervention and agency. Some training programs, such as STARR (introduced in Chapter 6), provide a booster session monthly.

An additional benefit can be found with in-house coaches who can provide real-time problem solving as officers attempt to implement these new practices in their daily routines. To implement a coaching model, agencies typically identify "champions of change" staff who are fully invested in the change, display support, and demonstrate efficiency in their use of skills. These individuals often undergo extensive training to learn how to further guide and support their colleagues as they learn and practice newly trained skills. Coaches are then assigned to other officers (typically within their office) to provide support and direction.

Coaches often review how these officers use skills in their work. These reviews may be done during an observation of a meeting between an officer and a client, by listening or watching a videotape of the meeting, and/or doing role-plays with the officer where they act out different scenarios. Coaches often use a fidelity checklist to identify how well the individual did at using the skills and then use that checklist to provide supportive and helpful feedback to the officers. An example of a checklist is found in the textbox below, which provides a simple method of observing whether the officer was following appropriate screening protocols, conducting a brief intervention to address the problem behavior, referring services, and following up to determine that the person went to services (a type of proactive case management). This fidelity checklist asks the coach to indicate whether the officer used communication techniques to motivate the person. Use of a checklist like this can help coaches identify areas where officers need additional practice to strengthen their skills. Coaches often then directly provide this additional training and on-site assistance. Coaching is considered an effective strategy to improve the technical skills of staff, but it is an expensive and time-intensive culture change strategy. It is predicted that some staff may be resistant to a colleague reviewing their work. However, Labrecque and Smith (2015) found that when officers participated in training and receiving coaching after, they were more likely to use these new skills.

SBIRT Proficiency Checklist- Clinical Version

Screening (3 items)	Present	Not Present
The practitioner accurately assesses quantity & frequency of alcohol and/or drug use.	☐	☐
Practitioner accurately identifies the patient's level of risk related to their alcohol or other drug use using an appropriate evidence based screening instrument.	☐	☐
Practitioner assesses possible consequences of the patient's behavior, such as physical, psychosocial and other consequences.	☐	☐

Comments

Brief Intervention (4 items)	Present	Not Present
Practitioner asks permission to provide feedback about the patient's substance use.	☐	☐
Practitioner uses reflection and/or open-ended questions to allow patient to react to screening result.	☐	☐
Practitioner provides feedback about the risks associated with patient's substance use behavior.	☐	☐
Practitioner negotiates a goal with the patient based on steps he/she is willing to take.	☐	☐

Comments

Referral to Treatment (2 items)	Present	Not Present
Practitioner recognizes the patient's need for substance treatment based on their screening score and/or medical/behavioral factors.	☐	☐
Practitioner suggests the use of specific community and specialty resources.	☐	☐

Comments

Follow-Up (1 item)	Present	Not Present
Practitioner arranges appropriate follow-up (MD follow-up, referral to treatment, counseling, medication, etc.)	☐	☐

Comments

Motivational Interviewing Spirit (3 items)	Present	Not Present
Practitioner summarizes patient's stated reasons for change.	☐	☐
Practitioner negotiates a treatment plan in a collaborative manner.	☐	☐
Practitioner affirms the patient's strengths, ideas &/or successes	☐	☐

Comments

Total Items (13)

A third component to support culture change in probation and parole involves more formal, external sources of education for officers, such as coursework in a technical college or university. Fields of academic study that complement community corrections include criminal justice, sociology, public administration, public health, and social work. For staff who do not wish to complete an undergraduate or graduate degree, there are also certificate programs that are credentialed through colleges and universities. Current examples of certificate programs include criminal justice management and leadership, security management, mental health and criminal justice, communities and crime, human resources, women and gender studies, diversity and equity, and victim advocacy.

Many of these programs are attractive to officers working full time, as they are often offered through online formats and/or in the evenings. Pursuing education outside of the agency can lead to cultural change, as the workforce is empowered, learn about the most updated research on best practices, and become more connected to groups outside their immediate work peers and clients. Educational opportunities can also facilitate culture change as the probation or parole officer is placed in the role of being both student and expert, being able to convey their lived work experience into theoretical classroom interactions.

Human Services

One of the substantial challenges associated with culture change is accessing individuals who have been ingrained in the existing culture for their entire (sometimes extensive) careers. While training efforts can attempt to change the behavior of these individuals, in some instances it is the hiring of new staff that aligns with the emerging culture that can make a more impactful difference. This raises the crucial issues of recruiting, hiring, and retaining staff who are most suited to the culture and mission of the agency. For the last 60 years, many probation and parole agencies have hired new staff without requiring or recording any specific skills, expertise, or backgrounds. This resulted in many individuals becoming officers because the job was simply available, they had military experience, or they expected community corrections to be a step toward becoming a law enforcement officer.

With the increasing shift toward EBPs that requires the hybrid approach to supervision and thus rehabilitation skills, this has resulted in a call for the field to consider new requirements for being a probation and parole officer. Many jurisdictions have altered their hiring practices to prefer a background in social work, psychology, or other human services. Additionally, it is more common during the interview process for prospective officers to be asked questions about effective correctional practices, such as the risk-need-responsivity (RNR) model, screening assessments, and communication techniques. While these help agencies filter through candidates to identify better matches for the desired agency culture, they also send a message to prospective employees regarding the goals, expectations, and culture of the agency.

◊ Officer Work, Careers, and Wellness: Stress Management and Retention

The work of a probation and parole officer is often stressful. Not only are the caseload sizes difficult to manage but balancing the need to provide rehabilitative support while protecting the community and enforcing court orders can be challenging. Officers may often worry about individuals on their caseload who may be more likely to commit crimes, particularly those crimes that are heinous and that put the public at serious risk (e.g., robbery, sexual assault, murder). Officers may also worry that policies such as those aligned with the RNR model or that focus on behavior change may not be enough control to prevent such undesirable outcomes. For example, a person could be classified as low risk even though they routinely abuse opioids and have a serious mental illness. The low-risk category only refers to risk for future offending, which the officers often feel does not adequately consider an individual's criminogenic needs (Viglione & Taxman, 2019). As a result, an officer may be uncomfortable supervising this individual at a low level, given their substance use and mental health needs.

This example represents just one form of stress that can impact probation and parole agencies and lead to reductions in the workforce. Stress over time tends to affect the body, the mind (e.g., thoughts, feelings, beliefs), and behavior. Common effects of stress can be seen in Table 11.1. Stress management follows a public health approach that maximizes positive behaviors, such as getting regular exercise, eating a balanced and health diet, practicing relaxation techniques, keeping a sense of humor, spending time with friends and family, and engaging in hobbies. This approach also educates the workforce on poor coping mechanisms, like the use of tobacco, alcohol, and illegal drugs, as well as social isolation and avoiding health care support.

TABLE 11.1 Common Effects of Stress

On Your Body	On Your Mood	On Your Behavior
Headache	Anxiety	Overeating or undereating
Muscle tension or pain	Restlessness	Angry outbursts
Chest pain	Lack of motivation or focus	Drug or alcohol misuse
Fatigue	Feeling overwhelmed	Tobacco use
Change in sex drive	Irritability or anger	Social withdrawal
Stomach upset	Sadness or depression	Exercising less often
Sleep problems		

It is important that probation and parole agencies recognize sources of stress for officers and respond appropriately. A National Institute of Justice (2005) study points out that the following strategies can be used to maximize stress management in the workplace:

- Appoint talented and dedicated staff who can withstand the stress of helping others who experience stress. Have dedicated staff that the officers can discuss the demands of their jobs and address some of the complexities, like the assignment of certain individuals to low-risk supervision.
- Have participation by top administrators, union officers, line officers, and family members in stress-reduction programming. This is important because everyone needs to wholeheartedly participate to be successful.

- Maintain confidentiality so that officers feel comfortable expressing concerns, and these concerns will not be reflected in their performance.
- Conduct debriefs and reviews of critical incidents, such as an individual on supervision committing a heinous crime, so that everyone can express their perspectives and learn about potential warning signs.
- Train supervisors to spot and refer officers who may be experiencing stress.
- Make changes to reduce officer stress in office policy or work demands.
- Monitor program activities and evaluate their effectiveness in reducing stress.

An example of a program designed to reduce officer stress was implemented in Harris County, Texas, and is titled "Stomp Out Stress" (Glazier & Chapman, 2005). In this program, officers (and sometimes also a family member) participated in a comprehensive set of interventions designed to improve stress management and overall feelings of stress. This included a series of training classes that focus on the sources and management of stress and how to talk about stress in the home (see textbox below). In general, officers were trained in how to identify sources of stress in their work and how to respond in a healthy manner.

READING

Stress Management in Supervision Environments

"Stomp Out Stress" Among Probation Officers—Harris County (Texas)
Severe budget cuts were one reason the Harris County Community Supervision and Corrections Department developed a stress management training program for probation officers. The cuts resulted in the loss of 500 officers, causing stress even among personnel who were not directly affected.

In the first of four training modules, participants learn about the nature of stress. Because stress is viewed as having both personal and organizational sources, a module was designed for each. A fourth module on communication is intended to help officers discuss stress with their families.

One trainer called the participants "a tough, tough, paranoid audience." Afterward, participants said they believed the sessions provided practical advice. More than half had been "burned out" before training. A month later, burnout was significantly reduced in the same participants. Six months later, some burnout returned but was still less than before training.

Evaluation of this program found reductions in burnout immediately following the training, with lower levels maintained 6 months following training. Burnout is a major indicator that the officer may have intentions of leaving the job or will leave the job; therefore, burnout is a crucial factor related to retaining staff in community corrections. Turnover is a costly outcome for correctional agencies, as resources must be spent on recruiting, hiring, and training new staff while losing the expertise and experience of current employees. High staff turnover also

Alberto R. Gonzales, Regina B. Schofield and Sarah V. Hart, Selection from "Case Studies of Stress Reduction Programs," *Stress Among Probation and Parole Officers and What Can Be Done About It*, p. 9, U.S. Department of Justice, 2005.

creates additional stress for remaining employees, who must supervise additional clients and absorb new responsibilities while new officers are recruited, hired, and trained. As a result, this creates a vicious cycle that can continue to cause stress for staff and increase hardships on the agency.

Quality Improvement Processes

An effective and comprehensive change strategy involves the use of team-based **quality improvement processes**. One commonly used quality improvement process is the Plan-Do-Study-Act (PDSA), which is well documented in the field, including by the Institute for Healthcare Improvement and the Network for Improvement in Addiction Treatment. When using the PDSA, organizations create a team of 7–10 individuals (including management, officers, and support staff). In community corrections, these work teams may include key stakeholders such as a judge, prosecutor, defense attorney, treatment provider, or supervision client. The PDSA model involves four phases, as shown in Figure 11.2.

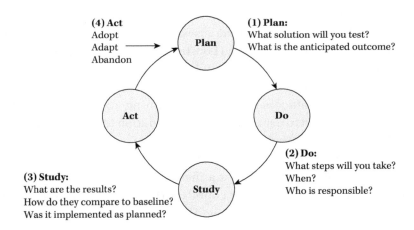

FIGURE 11.2   The PDSA Process

In the "plan" phase, the team looks at existing data, reviews the new practice/policy to be considered, discusses the agency culture, and identifies existing challenges and possible solutions. In the "do" phase, the team prepares for implementation with a plan identifying the specific desired change, identification of who is responsible for what, how will staff be prepared (e.g., training), and what type of messages should be transmitted to the agency surrounding the change. The "study" phase is devoted to implementation and measurement of the progress and outcomes. It is at this point that the agency must regularly collect data and assess how well the change process is going. In the final "act" phase, the data from the study phase is reviewed and the team determines whether the change resulted in improved outcomes, added value to existing processes, was feasible, and whether it could be implemented permanently. This PDSA process is valuable for culture change, as it utilizes a comprehensive team representing many different perspectives and experiences in the agency who can work together to deliberately attempt change.

There are several examples of the PDSA process being used in community corrections to support culture change. For example, the Medication-Assisted Treatment Implementation in Community Correctional Environments (MATTICE) study followed this process to improve the perspectives of probation and clinical staff on the benefits of medications for opioid use for drug use and recidivism (Friedmann et al., 2012). Quality improvement processes led problem-solving courts to use incentives more effectively (Rudes et al., 2021), and risk and needs assessment information to be used more frequently in case plans (Magnuson et al., 2019). The following two paragraphs provide a fictional example case study of the PDSA process.

Montclair Probation and Parole Agency identified that probation and parole officers were not using the risk and needs assessment to guide supervision and case management decisions. To address this challenge, they engaged in the PDSA process. First, they put together a team of 10 staff members, including two individuals under supervision, line officers, middle managers, and agency leaders (plan phase). During this phase, the team identified that officers were not using assessment information because they did not understand assessment results and they did not know how to explain the findings of the assessment to individuals under supervision as a result. In the "do" phase, the team developed booster trainings to help officers better understand the assessment and practice interpreting and explaining results. Additionally, they developed scripts that officers could use to help explain the results to individuals under supervision.

During the study phase, officers received this training and were given opportunities to practice using the scripts and to use assessment information to create case plans. Supervisors worked with officers to review their use of scripts and newly generated case plans, providing suggestions to improve how they talked about and addressed needs. During this phase, the PDSA team collected data and found that adherence to the risk and needs information in the case plan improved and officers were confident they understood assessment results and could explain them to clients. In the act phase, the agency incorporated scripts and increased opportunities to practice into preservice training and booster sessions focusing on risk and needs assessments and case plans became part of regular in-service training.

Measuring and Sustaining Change

To be effective in making cultural and procedural changes in how probation and parole is provided, a data-driven model that involves measurement is recommended. Data provides objective feedback on the processes of supervision. It is useful to measure before a change is made (referred to as baseline) and then routinely after change is implemented, such as every 6 or 12 months. These data can be used to see what type of progress is being made or whether progress is being made at all. Data is useful for problem solving because it helps the agency identify places where more attention is needed and where processes can be improved. This process is also referred to as **data-driven decision making**.

There are several types of measures that are important for probation and parole agencies to track. First, process measures can identify both how the change is being used in real-world practice and why changes are or are not being used the way originally intended. Often, researchers might conduct a process evaluation (as discussed in Chapter 10) to better understand what actually happened as part of the change process. Process evaluations often include observations of staff behavior and interviews with agency employees to learn about perspectives and attitudes toward change. Additionally, researchers often collect data on a variety of implementation measures to help understand why change efforts might succeed or fail. Proctor and colleagues (2011) identified the following implementation measures that are commonly included as part of a process evaluation:

- Appropriateness: perception that the change addresses the problem identified by the organization as the reason for reform.
- Acceptability: staff perception that the initiative is easy to understand and useful.
- Feasibility: staff perception that the initiative is logistically practical for day-to-day use.
- Adoptability: staff willingness to use the initiative in daily practice.
- Fidelity: staff ability to implement the innovation adhering to the principles of the innovation.

Second, agencies and researchers use outcome measures to assess change at the client, program, or system level. The outcomes measures at the client level are typically recidivism, though they can also include other measures, such as substance use behaviors, mental health, and health status (see Chapter 10 for a more thorough discussion of outcome measures in probation and parole). At the program level, agencies might track program engagement and successful completion, often looking at disparities among various groups based on race, ethnicity, and gender. System-level outcomes might include the number of people who are incarcerated.

Measuring both process and outcomes is critical for understanding the success of change efforts. If we only measured outcomes, we might find that a new correctional training program resulted in a higher number of technical violations. However, without a process evaluation we would have little clue as to why that is. Alternatively, a process evaluation might identify staff resistance to change that ultimately resulted in poor fidelity to the program intentions. These findings provide key targets to address that might help the agency to not only better implement the desired change but also improve outcomes.

While generating culture change is challenging, sustaining that change over a long period of time might be even more difficult. *Sustainment* refers to a defined period of time (usually 12 months or longer) where the new program and/or practice continue to be used. A truly sustained effort is one that resembles the original efforts and delivers similar outcomes. This is difficult to do since resources and funding changes and many agencies move from one initiative to another, therefore neglecting earlier initiatives. Sustainment means that the innovation is mostly intact and functions as it did before. In a hybrid model of supervision, this means that the emphasis is still on engaging individuals in treatments that will reduce their risk and needs and not overemphasizing accountability.

The Role of Innovation and Technology
An intersectional approach suggests that changing agency culture in a modern and complex world must include adapting to innovation and technology. In fact, a report by the RAND

corporation (see Jackson et al., 2015) identified innovation in information and technology as the foremost priority for improving the community corrections system. The primary goal of these emerging technologies for probation and parole staff is to facilitate efficiency, improve morale, maximize staff productivity, and create a supportive work culture. In many probation and parole agencies, culture can be severely constrained by staff tolling with outdated technology and administrative tasks that leave no time for evidence practices (i.e., daily activities that produce the best client outcomes).

In 2018, DeMichele and Payne conducted a survey of officers working in 24 county-level probation departments to examine their daily activities over a 1-month period. On average, these probation officers spent between 2 and 4 hours per client on risk assessment, between 5 and 6 hours on presentence investigation reports, and up to an hour or more on administrative tasks (e.g., collecting payments, drug screenings, interacting with child protective services, and completing referrals and progress reports). One experienced community corrections expert explained it as follows:

> 50 percent of a probation officer's time is sucked up by trying to find out from outside treatment providers, drug test labs, the courts, even the clients themselves, how the client is doing and then manually entering it into a case note, which is a static piece of info, in the case management system. (Rodriquez, 2019, Avoiding Bias section)

One example of technology that can address this issue is SCRAM Nexus, a dynamic decision-support engine that is showing potential for community corrections (see SCRAM systems, 2022). SCRAM Nexus is designed to support probation and parole officers by minimizing busywork, like recording attendance at meetings or tracking down client information, and maximizing real-time information on clients and best practices in response. SCRAM Nexus does not replace officer discretion, but rather it creates a portal for treatment providers and community partners to report the attendance and progress of clients, which is merged with data on supervision conditions (e.g., drug test results). This information is then compared with risk and needs assessments to provide an evidence-based response. SCRAM Nexus is essentially an automated decision tree, an innovation that has been successful in medicine and sports, mainly because they are so effective in providing positive reinforcement when clients do well.

These innovations can be effective in cultural change for several reasons. First, they free probation and parole officers of meaningless busywork so they have more time to develop meaningful relationships with their clients. Second, they provide evidence-based solutions in real time so that officers no longer rely on their "gut instincts" for decisions—a process that greatly increases uncertainty, error, and stress. Third, technology systems are transparent, as decisions are documented (and shared) rather than occurring behind closed doors or on paper worksheets in filing drawers. Overall, emerging technologies like SCRAM Nexus can reduce officer bias and reliance on punitive orientations that can limit outcomes.

National Reform by Executives

Another feature of intersectionality is the idea that society is connected. While this chapter has explored culture in community corrections, this has focused mostly on change at the individual officer and agency level. However, to generate and sustain cultural change, there is a need for community corrections executives—that is, people who have served as directors, agency chiefs, and other powerbrokers—to enact reform. The experience and knowledge in this population cannot be understated, and many hold the view that the modern-day community corrections system, with its focus on heavy fines, penalties, and even jail time for minor noncriminal infractions, is a deep-seated departure from the original philosophy of probation and parole (see Chapter 3). To reform the entire community corrections system, which is essentially an effort toward large-scale culture change, a group of more than 60 other probation and parole chiefs from around the country launched Executives Transforming Probation and Parole (EXiT, n.d.).

EXiT executives advocate for a reduction in the number of people under community supervision and endorse reforms that make the system less punitive and more equitable, restorative, and hopeful. The mission statement of ExIT (n.d.) reads:

> Executives Transforming Probation and Parole (EXiT) unites current and former community supervision executives, directly impacted people and their families, defense bar, prosecutors, and survivors of crime to build a national movement to transform probation and parole. We envision a supervision system that has a smaller and more focused footprint and values dignity, fairness, race and gender equity, community, and reintegration. We aim to shift the field away from finding failure, to focus on supporting people's success on probation and parole, by taking a fair, helpful, and reintegrative approach. Probation and parole systems should be less punitive, more effective, and focused solely on the individuals who need support in lieu of confinement in order to keep our communities safe and healthy. We believe that probation and parole should affirm the dignity and humanity of people under supervision, and should provide hope for the future, not a pathway to incarceration. (para. 1)

It may surprise the public to hear actively employed and former directors and chiefs of community corrections advocating for a reform that is more rehabilitative and supportive of clients and demonstrating a reluctance to engage in punitive strategies, though this is a valuable component of perceptions of the justice system. Moreover, it sets an example for probation and parole agencies that their executive leadership is modeling cultural change and providing evidence to support these arguments.

SUMMARY: AGENCY CULTURE AND COMMUNITY CORRECTIONS

The majority of individuals in the criminal justice system are on probation and parole supervision, and the focus on punitive strategies can result in a revolving door between the community and incarceration. While there have been shifts between punishment and rehabilitation as the primary goal of community supervision, current emphasis supports a hybrid model that prioritizes behavioral management strategies and incorporation of EBPs to support behavior change. Comprehensive training programs and quality improvement processes have been developed to assist the officers in learning and applying these skills in working with individuals under supervision. Sustaining a hybrid approach will not be easy until more staff are hired who have the skills to use these behavioral management strategies and there is a supportive agency culture and sociopolitical environment that desires probation/parole to be more than a mechanism of punishment.

Scenario-Based Activities

	Case	Question(s)
1.	You are a probation officer who has a law enforcement orientation. Your probation agency is currently implementing policies aligned with a rehabilitation model of supervision. You are being asked to develop a relationship with clients instead of using your authority to reinforce the rules of supervision.	Describe the difficulties that you may have with using relationship skills. What type of training would be helpful? How would you communicate your need to still use supervision to protect public safety?
2.	A parole agency administrator is concerned the agency has a high technical violation rate. The administrator put together a PDSA team to explore what might be causing these high violation rates.	What should the team do during each phase of the PDSA process? What data would you like to have for the "plan" and "do" phases? What type of solutions are possible? The study phase includes collecting data on case plans. What criteria should the team use to improve use of risk-need information?

References

Aarons, G. A., & Sawitzky, A. C. (2006). Organizational climate partially mediates the effect of culture on work attitudes and staff turnover in mental health services. *Administration and Policy in Mental Health and Mental Health Services Research, 33,* 289–301. https://doi.org/10.1007/s10488-006-0039-1

Aarons, G. A., Hurlburt, M. S., & Horwitz, S. M. (2011). Advancing a conceptual model of evidence-based practice implementation in public service sectors. *Administration and Policy in Mental Health, 38*(1), 4–23. https://doi.org/10.1007/s10488-010-0327-7

Aarons, G. A. (2006). Transformational and transactional leadership: Association with attitudes towards evidence-based practice. *Psychiatric Services, 57*(8): 1162–1169. https://doi.org/10.1176/ps.2006.57.8.1162

Battalino, J., Beutler, L., & Shani, A.B. (1996). Large-system change initiative: Transformation I progress at the California Department of Corrections. *Public Productivity & Management Review, 20*(1), 24–44. https://doi.org/10.2307/3380601

Bogue, B., Campbell, N., Carey, M., Clawson, E., Faust, D., Florio, K., Joplin, L., Keiser, G., Wasson, B., & Woodward, W. (2004). *Implementing evidence-based principles in community corrections: Leading organizational change and development.* National Institute of Corrections. https://www.superiorcourt.maricopa.gov/AdultProbation/docs/EBPOrgChange_Dev.pdf

Corbett, R., & Marx, G. T. (1991) Critique: No soul in the new machine: Technofallacies in the electronic monitoring movement. *Justice Quarterly, 8,* 399–414. DOI: 10.1080/07418829100091111

Dale, M. P. & Trlin, A. (2010). Leadership and probation officer practice in New Zealand. *Probation Journal*, *57*(2), 121–138. https://doi.org/10.1177/0264550510362563

Deal, T. E. & Kennedy, A. A. (2000) *The new corporate cultures: Revitalizing the workplace after downsizing, mergers and reengineering.* London-UK, TEXERE Publishing Limited.

DeMichele, M., & Payne, B. (2018). Taking officer time seriously: A study of the daily activities of probation officers. *Probation Journal*, *65*, 39–60. https://doi.org/10.1177/0264550517748358

Executives Transforming Probation and Parole. (n.d.). *Homepage.* Retrieved August 5, 2023, from https://www.exitprobationparole.org/

Feldman, M. S. (2003). Organizational routines as a source of continuous change. *Organizational Science*, *11*, 611–629. http://dx.doi.org/10.1287/orsc.11.6.611.12529

Fixsen, D. L., Naoom, S. F., Blase, K. A., Friedman, R. M., & Wallace, F. (2005). *Implementation research: A synthesis of the literature.* Tampa FL University of South Florida, Louis de la Parte Florida Mental Health Institute. *The National Implementation Research Network (FMHI Publication# 231)*, *11*, 247–266. https://nirn.fpg.unc.edu/resources/implementation-research-synthesis-literature

Glazier, B., & Chapman, B. (2000). *Stomp Out Stress.* National Institute of Justice, U.S. Department of Justice. https://www.ojp.gov/pdffiles1/nij/grants/212419.pdf

Jackson, B. A., Russo, J., Hollywood, J. S., Silberglitt, R., & Woods, D. (2015). *Fostering innovation in community and institutional corrections: Identifying high-priority technology and other needs for the U.S. corrections sector.* Rand Corporation. https://www.rand.org/pubs/research_reports/RR820.html

Labrecque, R. M., & Smith, P. (2015). Does training and coaching matter? An 18-month evaluation of a community supervision model. *Victims & Offenders*, 233–252. DOI:10.1080/15564886.2015.1013234

Lin, A. C. (2000). *Reform in the making: The implementation of social policy in prison.* New Jersey: Princeton University Press.

Lipsky, M. (2010). *Street-level bureaucracy: Dilemmas of the individual in public services.* Russell Sage Foundation.

Magnuson, S., Kras, K., Aleandro, H., Rudes, D., & Taxman, F. S. (2019). Using PDSA and participatory action research to improve use of risk needs assessments. *Corrections: Policy, Practice and Research*, *5*, 44–63. http://dx.doi.org/10.1080/23774657.2018.1555442

Mitchell, S. G., Willet, J., Monico, L. B., James, A., Rudes, D. S., Viglione, J., Schwartz, R. P., Gordon, M. S., & Friedmann, P. D. (2016). Community correctional agents' views of medication-assisted treatment: examining their influence on treatment referrals and community supervision practices. *Substance Abuse*, *37*(1), 127–133. https://doi.org/10.1080/08897077.2015.1129389

National Institute of Corrections. (2020). *Diversity, Equity, and Inclusion Series.* https://nicic.gov/series/diversity-equity-and-inclusion

National Institute of Justice. (2005). *Stress among probation and parole officers and what can be done about it.* U.S. Department of Justice Office of Justice Programs. https://www.ojp.gov/pdffiles1/nij/205620.pdf

Osher, C. N. (2013, June 8). Electronic monitoring of Colorado parolees has pitfalls. *The Denver Post.* https://www.denverpost.com/2013/06/08/electronic-monitoring-of-colorado-parolees-has-pitfalls/

Proctor, E., Silmere, H., Raghavan, R., Hovmand, P., Aarons, G., Bunger, A., Griffey. R, & Hensley, M. (2011). Outcomes for implementation research: Conceptual distinctions, measurement challenges, and research agenda. *Administration and Policy in Mental Health and Mental Health Services*, *38*, 65–76. https://doi.org/10.1007/s10488-010-0319-7

Rhine, E. E., Mawhorr, T. L., & Parks, E. C. (2006). Implementation: The bane of effective correctional programs. *Criminology & Public Policy*, *5*(2), 347–358. http://dx.doi.org/10.1111/j.1745-9133.2006.00382.x

Rodriguez, I. (2019, December 10). *Changing the culture of community supervision*. The Crime Report. https://thecrimereport.org/2019/12/10/760473/#A%20New%20Exit%20Strategy

Rudes, D. S. (2012). Getting technical: parole officers' continued use of technical violations under California's parole reform agenda. *Journal of Crime and Justice, 35*(2), 249–268. http://dx.doi.org/10.1080/0735648X.2012.677572

Rudes, D. S., Portillo, S., & Taxman, F. S. (2021). The legitimacy of change: Adopting/adapting, implementing, and sustaining reforms within community corrections agencies. *British Journal of Criminology, 61*, 1665–1683. https://doi.org/10.1093%2Fbjc%2Fazab020

Schein, E.H. (1990). Organizational culture. *American Psychologist, 45*(2), 109–119. https://psycnet.apa.org/doi/10.1037/0003-066X.45.2.109

Schenwar, M. M. & Law, V. (2021). *Prison by any other name*. The New Press.

SCRAM Systems. (2022, August 11). *SCRAM Nexus evolves into a dynamic case management system*. https://s43950.p1275.sites.pressdns.com/scram-blog/nexus-evolves-case-management-system/

Taxman, F. S. Henderson, C., Young, D. W., & Farrell, J. (2014). The impact of training interventions on organizational readiness to support innovations in juvenile justice offices. *Administration of Mental Health Policy and Mental Health Services Research, 41*, 177–188. https://doi.org/10.1007%2Fs10488-012-0445-5

Taxman, F. S. & Sachwald, J. (2010). Managing the chaos: Implementing evidence-based practices in correctional agencies. In F. McNeil, P.Raynor & C. Trotter (Eds.), *Offender Supervision: New Directions in Theory, Research and Practice* (172–192). Routledge. https://doi.org/10.4324/9780203832974

Taxman, F. S., Smith, L., & Rudes, D. (2020). From m*ean* to meaningful probation: The legacy of intensive supervision programs. In Lattimore, P., Huebner, B., & Taxman F.S. (Eds.). *Handbook on moving corrections and sentencing forward: Building on the record*. Routledge Press.

Walters, S. T., Clark, M. D., Gingrich, R., & Meltzer, M. L. (2007). *Motivating offenders to change: A guide for probation and parole*. National Institute of Corrections. https://www.innovatingjustice.org/sites/default/files/media/document/2018/Motivating%20Offenders%20to%20Change.pdf

Viglione, J. (2019). The risk-need-responsivity model: How do probation officers implement the principles of effective intervention?. *Criminal Justice and Behavior, 46*(5), 655–673. https://psycnet.apa.org/doi/10.1177/0093854818807505

Viglione, J., Rudes, D. S., & Taxman, F. S. (2015). Misalignment in supervision: Implementing risk/needs assessment instruments in probation. *Criminal Justice & Behavior, 42*, 263–285. https://psycnet.apa.org/doi/10.1177/0093854814548447

Viglione, J., Rudes, D., & Taxman, F. S. (2017). Probation officer use of client-centered communication strategies in adult probation settings. *Journal of Offender Rehabilitation, 56*, 38–60. http://dx.doi.org/10.1080/10509674.2016.1257534

Viglione, J., & Taxman, F. S. (2018). Low-risk offenders under probation supervision: risk management and the risk-needs-responsivity (RNR) framework. *Criminal Justice & Behavior, 45*, 1809–1831. https://doi.org/10.1177/0093854818790299

Image Credit

CHAPTER 12

Partnerships and Evaluations

Community corrections agencies do not operate in a silo. Instead, they rely on partnerships within the criminal justice system and the broader community. The challenge is for probation and parole agencies to establish partnerships that can help them to achieve reductions in recidivism, improve supervision processes, and help individuals who are under supervision more holistically with their needs. This chapter discusses in detail the important role of partnerships in achieving these goals. An example is provided outlining partnership between probation and parole agencies and health organizations to illustrate necessary interagency work to support effective supervision services. Additionally, researcher-practitioner partnerships are covered, with a focus on the role evaluation research plays in shaping the landscape of the community corrections field. The final summary identifies the work that needs to be done to better address gaps in the community corrections system while also recognizing the noteworthy advancements that have already been made. This final chapter aims to empower students with a hopeful perspective for the future of community corrections.

LEARNING OBJECTIVES

By the end of this chapter, students will be able to:

- Define partnerships and identify different types of partnerships.
- Understand the importance of researcher-practitioner partnerships.
- Identify and describe the limits of using program-specific and systemic partnerships.

KEY TERMS

- Cascade of care
- Memorandum of understanding
- Partnerships
- Researcher-practitioner partnerships

CONTENT

Partnership is not a posture but a process—a continuous process that grows stronger each year as we devote ourselves to common tasks.

—John F. Kennedy

The Need for Partnerships

A primary goal of the community corrections system is to serve the courts and other criminal justice systems through the provision of services in the community. Probation and parole staff working within the community corrections system often make referrals to community-based services to address criminogenic needs, as well as address factors that limit success on supervision, such as unstable housing and lack of transportation, food, and/or employment. While the community corrections system plays an important role in these tasks, it also largely depends on other agencies and individuals, both in the justice system and in the broader community, to fulfill sentencing goals and requirements.

Partnerships are essential for community corrections agencies to achieve their stated goals and objectives, particularly for helping individuals on supervision improve their lives and address risk and need factors. Partnerships can vary considerably in terms of how they are designed and implemented. According to Konrad (1996), **partnerships** can be defined as a collaboration between two or more entities that aims to improve outcomes for clients. The primary objective of these partnerships is to meet the comprehensive needs of individuals under supervision by enhancing accessibility, information systems, and efficiency while minimizing duplication of efforts, inefficiency, and costs.

The framework proposed by Konrad (1996) recognizes that partnerships can vary in terms of how much agencies collaborate or whether they integrate functions such as screening, assessment, drug testing, or other aspects that are jointly performed by community corrections agencies and other organizations (e.g., treatment providers). The degree to which organizations engage in partnerships is influenced by factors such as the decision making by leaders (e.g., who makes the decisions and whether it is autonomous or shared), the shared goals and mission (e.g., having common objectives), and the allocation of resources for certain programs and practices. The goal is to break down organizational barriers and enable organizations to see how working together toward common objectives and missions can help them both achieve their goals and objectives.

As illustrated in Table 12.1, there is a range in the level of collaboration and integration that may occur between different agencies. The level of integration reflects the degree to which two or more agencies share information, work processes, resources, and decision making. Integration can occur at the individual level where (a) two officers (from different agencies) make a mutual decision or (b) one officer makes a decision and the other officer abides by that decision. At the program level, integration can occur when two or more agencies jointly engage in processes such as intake processes, referral to services, service delivery, and resources. At the system level, integration refers to agencies that combine resources, staffing, space, and other facets to deliver a service that meets common goals. An example would be a probation agency, social welfare agency, and public health organization working together to address homelessness.

TABLE 12.1 Konrad's (1996) Levels of Integration

Type of integration	Level of integration	Dimensions
None	Independent	Operate autonomously, in parallel
Informal	Information sharing and communication	Share general information to help others understand the needs or progress of an agency. May not communicate regularly with the other agency
	Cooperation and coordination	Loosely organized autonomous agencies. Work together to change procedures or structures
Informal/Formal Hybrid	Collaboration	Shared activities: Partners are equal. Autonomous agencies work together with a common goal or product.
Formal	Consolidation	Umbrella organization with shared leadership. Some functions (e.g., administrative) are centralized; frontline authority is retained by organizations.
	Integration	Operate collectively under a single authority. Activities are blended and funding is pooled.

Adopted from Lee et al. (under review)

There are various forms of integration, varying from none to informal, hybrid, and formal integration. *No integration* means that each agency operates as their own entity by being autonomous. Examples include probation and parole agencies that screen and refer to services but do not share any information with other agencies. *Informal integration* reflects efforts to share general information that can be useful to help others understand an issue and/or problem; however, the agencies do not communicate routinely on matters at the individual, program, or system level. With informal integration, a probation or parole agency might screen and make referrals, but they share information with the screening agency or the referral agency. *Hybrid integration* occurs when there are some elements of an informal and formal integration where agencies share some activities together but are not fully integrated. An example of formal integration might be when a treatment agency physically places a mental health or substance use counselor in a probation or parole agency to screen individuals.

Finally, *formal integration* is when two or more agencies consolidate activities at various decision points, such as intake, referral, service provision, financing, and so on. With formal integration, partnering agencies jointly operate under one umbrella structure. An example of formal integration introduced in this textbook (see Chapter 8) is problem-solving courts that include a team-based approach between a judge, prosecutor, defense attorney, treatment provider, and a probation and parole officer. During pre-court staffing meetings, the court team shares information to identify how well each participant is doing in the program. The problem-solving court model is formally integrated service model on Konrad's (1996) scale because all the parties—judge, prosecutor, defense attorney, treatment provider, probation/parole—work together as a team to identify individuals eligible for the program, provide the services and make modifications as necessary, and determine when a person has successfully completed the court program.

Formally integrated agencies often have joint funding, share space, and have an electronic record system that all participating agencies can use. Shared electronic record systems are particularly useful to support partnerships, as all involved individuals can enter and review data on client progress and needs. This allows agencies to use the same information and coordinate responses to improve service provision.

JOURNEY INTO THE FIELD: DR. NANCY RODRIQUEZ

◇◇◇◇◇◇◇◇

Full name: Nancy Rodriquez

Title: Professor, School of Social Ecology, University of California, Irvine

Dr. Rodriguez received her BA in criminal justice from Sam Houston State University in 1992 and her PhD in political science from Washington State University in 1998. Dr. Rodriguez taught in the School of Criminology and Criminal Justice at Arizona

State University from 1998 to 2015. Her areas of expertise include substance abuse, juvenile court decision making, and sentencing policies. In 2014, Dr. Rodriquez was nominated by then-president of the United States Barack Obama to direct the National Institute of Justice (NIJ). Dr. Rodriquez served as director of the NIJ from February 9, 2015, to January 13, 2017. Dr. Nancy Rodriguez is currently a criminologist and professor in the School of Social Ecology at the University of California, Irvine. In this Jour-

Image 12.1

ney into the Field, Dr. Rodriquez describes her early motivations for research and the esteemed career that followed. Attention is devoted to Dr. Rodriquez's views on partnerships and evaluations in the community corrections system.

My goal in college was to work with at-risk youth. A faculty member who worked closely with criminal justice agencies exposed me to researcher-practitioner partnerships as a vehicle for knowledge development and addressing the harms of those impacted by crime and the justice system. Working on a research project as an undergraduate student interviewing justice involved persons changed the course of professional trajectory. From that moment, I knew I wanted to work alongside justice system actors and use research to guide policy and practice. Partnerships with agencies have been part of my DNA ever since.

The field of community corrections is robust and characterized by much innovation. Community corrections officials have an acute awareness of the challenges brought about by policing strategies and sentencing practices. Today, rigorous evaluations of programs that address mental health and substance abuse are needed, as is knowledge on how to ensure system involvement does not create or exacerbate social inequality.

Partnerships and evaluation in community corrections will increasingly set the agenda on criminal justice reform. This is due, in large part, to the focus on reducing the prison population but also the increasing role that community organizations and community-led initiatives on violence reduction are playing in justice system reform. Better understanding this nexus between community organizations, community corrections, and researchers will be vital in efforts dedicated to promoting safety.

Agency-to-Agency Partnerships

Community corrections agencies commonly partner with other agencies in the criminal justice system and community, particularly treatment agencies. There are many different activities probation and parole agencies can collaborate on or integrate services with treatment agencies to better serve individuals under supervision (Taxman & Bouffard, 2000). These activities are described in the textbox below.

COMMON ACTIVITIES FOR COLLABORATION BETWEEN PROBATION/PAROLE AND TREATMENT AGENCIES

Assessment: This is the process of using an instrument to screen and assess for criminogenic needs and other areas that may prevent an individual from successfully completing supervision and their own goals.

Treatment placement: This is the process of referring and placing an individual into appropriate services that will address criminogenic and noncriminogenic needs.

Treatment progress and continuum of care: This is the process of assessing progress in treatment services and adjusting requirements to accommodate the individual. Adjustments can include (a) increasing the intensity of treatment if the individual is not making reasonable progress or (b) reducing the intensity of services that a person needs based on positive progress.

Supervision/monitoring: This includes the oversight and monitoring of the individual regarding supervision conditions and service/program requirements. It can also include case management services to identify lifestyle needs, such as housing, food, transportation, clothing, or other indicators of stability in the community.

Drug testing: Urine samples, hair samples, and/or breathalyzers are taken to detect whether a person has engaged in the use of drugs and/or alcohol that are not for medical value.

Discharge/completion: This refers to assessment of the progress of the individual to determine when they should be discharged from the program, either for successful completion or an unsatisfactory discharge.

For each of the activities listed above, probation and parole agencies can determine whether they will conduct the activity by themselves, share information with another agency, and/or integrate with treatment providers to conduct some of the activities instead. The level of integration drives the extent to which information is shared and the number of activities that are a collaborative effort. Let's look at a few examples. As discussed in Chapter 8, a probation and parole officer might screen individuals on their caseload for mental health issues. If the screening indicates an area of concern, the probation and parole officer will make a referral to a mental health treatment provider for a formal assessment to make appropriate diagnoses and define a treatment plan. The probation and parole agency can collaborate with the treatment provider by sharing their screening results and the individual's progress under supervision while the treatment provider can collaborate with the probation and parole agency by sharing diagnostic information and progress in treatment. If both agencies were to conduct their own screening and assessment without sharing results and/or information on client progress, this would reflect independent actions (i.e., no integration).

Integration also applies to treatment progress where agencies have their own criteria to determine how well an individual is doing. When agencies are more fully integrated, they may jointly agree on a common definition for progress and define criteria for discharge and successful completion. Developing shared criteria for successful completion is important because various agencies could have different criteria for success, a topic explored in Chapter 10. As such, a probation agency may be dependent on the number of face-to-face contacts between the officer and the individual, while a treatment agency may be dependent on the number of times a person tested negative for drug use or number of treatment sessions a person participates in.

Formalization of partnerships is important for clearly defining goals and expectations as well as supporting sustainment of the partnership long term. When two or more agencies formalize their relationship, they often enter in a written **memorandum of understanding (MOU)** that specifies the nature of the relationship, the type of information to be shared, the activities that will be integrated, and the funding and space allocated. For example, an MOU between a probation and parole agency and a substance use treatment agency could indicate that the goal is to ensure that both agencies share information to make joint decisions regarding the type of treatment services an individual needs.

The MOU might outline (a) the role of the supervision agency; (b) the role of the treatment agency; (c) the type of services each agency will provide: (d) the criteria for determining progress in the program and the criteria to define successful completion; (e) the frequency of drug testing and that both agencies will share drug test results with one another; and (f) confidentiality requirements to protect sensitive client information (e.g., health and criminal justice information). Leaders of all participating agencies typically sign MOUs, which are often reviewed by a legal representative. Once signed, MOUs are generally considered a binding agreement, illustrating that the participating organizations are committed to this joint process. It is important to commence a partnership with a formal MOU to clarify expectations and goals/objectives. An example showing an MOU template is provided here:

READING

Memorandum of Understanding (MOU)

A Memorandum of Understanding, while not a legally binding document, does indicate a voluntary agreement to assist in the implementation plans of a grant funded collaborative project. The agreement is between the lead agency/applicant and a partnering entity. It generally defines the overall program goals and describes the collaborative nature and relationship between the identified project and MOU-referenced participant.

The initial paragraphs should contain the following information:

- Name of project
- Name of agencies involved in the MOU
- Identification of funding source
- Identification of grant period
- Project goals and key services to be provided
- Project outcomes to be addressed

The Administration for Children and Families, Memorandum of Understanding (MOU).

The body of the MOU should include the following five areas:

1. Term and conditions of the MOU should address the timeframe of agreement and, if applicable, timetable for renewing commitment.
2. Identification of roles and responsibilities of the lead agency.
3. Identification of roles and responsibilities of the partnering agency.
4. Termination clause is very important as it defines how the agreement can be ended (i.e. by written 30 day notice).
5. Signatures of the agency representatives, including date signed, is located at the end of the MOU.

◊ Diversity, Equity, and Inclusion: Leveraging Partnerships to Address Disparities

Throughout this book, we presented evidence to illustrate the racial and ethnic disparities present within probation and parole in the United States. With growing attention toward racial and ethnic disparities in other aspects of the criminal justice system—namely, policing—development of strategies to implement in the community corrections system is necessary. Remember, there are more individuals supervised on probation and parole than in any other part of the U.S. correctional system, making it a pivotal point within the system to enact change. This is an area that is in dire need of more research to provide evidence-based recommendations. However, what we do know is that this is a complicated issue that will undoubtedly require partnerships between agencies and between agencies and researchers. Below, we present several ideas for how partnerships may be able to impact diversity, equity, and inclusion in probation and parole.

First, researcher–practitioner partnerships in this area are of critical importance. These partnerships allow for analyzing data to identify existing disparities in probation and parole practice. Empirical evidence of where disparities occur can provide key information for where reform in the system is needed. For example, research finds that Black individuals on probation are revoked at higher rates than similarly situated White and Hispanic individuals on probation (Jannetta et al., 2014). This suggests policy change surrounding violation and revocation decisions is a key component of impacting change. However, making changes in violation and revocation policies is unlikely to happen without research evidence. Researchers and practitioners should continuously examine whether there are racial and ethnic disparities in outcomes and communicate those findings. They can work together to advocate for policies that address systemic racism, reduce disparities, and promote equitable and inclusive practices.

Practitioners and researchers can also work together to develop and implement culturally responsive practices that seek to reduce biases and discriminatory practices and consider the unique needs and backgrounds of all individuals under supervision (as discussed throughout this book). Some of this work could also involve development of new training and education programs for probation and parole staff. For example, some probation agencies require staff to attend cultural competency training to promote equitable supervision and effective communication with individuals of color under supervision (Janetta et al., 2014).

Second, agencies can partner with the community partners and stakeholders in a variety of ways. One such strategy involves the creation of work groups that bring together representatives from multiple different agencies (e.g., treatment agencies, judiciary, police) dedicated to addressing racial and ethnic disparities in probation and parole. It is also important these groups address disparities across the system as well (e.g., arrest, charging, and sentencing), as decisions that occur in those stages of the system can have significant effects on probation and parole outcomes (see Chapter 10). Additionally, probation and parole agencies can also focus on engaging with community partners representing marginalized communities to gain insights into the challenges faced by various racial and ethnic groups under supervision. Types of community-based agencies that may be beneficial for agencies to engage with include (but are not limited to) social service agencies, advocacy groups, faith-based organizations, educational institutions, and other community-based organizations. Additionally, soliciting input from individuals under supervision can also increase an agency's awareness of specific challenges, needs, and experiences that could help inform reform efforts.

One example involves partnerships between law enforcement and probation/parole agencies designed to address gangs. Research indicates that gangs operate as a form of community, with motivations for joining including a need for relationships, protection, support and belonging, and status (National Institute of Justice, 2013). For these reasons it is especially difficult to disrupt the flow of young people becoming members of gangs, mainly because the gang functions to provide resources (i.e., support, money, protection) that youth may be lacking at home. In its "comprehensive gang model," the Office of Juvenile Justice and Delinquency Prevention (2009; see also National Gang Center, 2023) promotes the following five core strategies to reduce gang involvement, which shows obvious overlap with the community corrections system:

- *Community mobilization:* involvement of local citizens, including former gang members and community groups and agencies, and the coordination of programs and staff functions within and across agencies.
- *Opportunities provision:* the development of a variety of education, training, employment, and reentry programs specific to engaging gang-involved youth and young adults.
- *Social intervention:* youth-serving agencies, schools, street outreach workers, grassroots groups, faith-based organizations, law enforcement agencies, and other criminal justice organizations reaching out and acting as links between gang-involved youth and their families, the conventional world, and needed services.
- *Suppression:* formal and informal social controls procedures and accountability measures, including law enforcement and close supervision or monitoring of gang-involved youth by criminal justice agencies working in collaboration with community-based service providers, schools, and grassroots groups.
- *Organizational change and development:* development and implementation of policies and procedures that result in the most effective use of available and potential resources to better address the gang problem.

In line with Chapter 8, gangs may be considered a special population for several reasons. First, despite the presence of White gangs (and interracial gangs), at the national level gangs are decidedly Black and Hispanic. Race and ethnicity is even more pronounced in jail and prison, which are often controlled by large-scale Black and Hispanic gangs (U.S. Department of Justice, 2021). This is a topic of obvious importance for people on parole supervision. Second, the preexisting risks and needs in people may be driving forces toward gang membership. Third, gang culture includes the creed of "no snitching," a mistrust of outsiders and authorities, and an obligation to protect the interests of the group, all of which greatly limit the effectiveness of interventions. When probation and parole officers encounter a person on supervision, they often lack the training, experiences, and resources to properly respond, thus suggesting that partnerships are required.

Since the 1990s there have been probation/parole-police partnerships in operation. Many were modeled on a partnership between the Boston Police and the Probation Departments that sent probation officers on nightly visits to the homes of people under supervision up to age 22 (Matz & Kim, 2017). Probation/parole partnerships with police often rely on intermediate sanctions such house arrests, curfews, drug and alcohol tests, victim restitution, mandatory school or treatment programs, and electronic monitoring (see Chapter 5). Matz and Kim (2017) conducted a national survey to assess probation/parole-police partnerships and found that community corrections officers were likely to engage in formal and informal partnerships with police agencies. The authors found these partnerships to be more common (and more supported) in agencies with rehabilitative cultures and that these interactions produced an increase in respect for probation and parole officers from both clients and police.

Matz and Kim (2017) add that effective leadership is a key component of probation/parole-police partnerships, with changes in community corrections management destroying the initiative. They also caution against the threat of mission distortion, where "the concern is to what extent working with law enforcement inadvertently sways probation officers to adopt a more compliance enforcement orientation" (Matz & Kim, 2017, pp. 485–486). This form of role conflict (see Chapter 4) can potentially merge the work duties of police and community supervision officers, creating a "polibation" officer (Nash, 2008). While more research is needed to fully measure probation/parole-police partnerships, they continue to function in a variety of community corrections settings. This includes partnerships related to enhanced supervision (i.e., joint ride-alongs, joint home visits), information sharing, fugitive apprehension, and specialized enforcement (sex offenders, domestic violence offenders, gun removal, gang interdiction, drug trafficking; Matz & Kim, 2017).

System Efforts to Promote Integration

For organizations to integrate with one another, they must understand how all related systems work and how decisions are made that impact associated functioning and processes. For example, when probation and parole agencies integrate with other organizations (e.g., substance use treatment, mental health, employment, housing, education), it is important to recognize that there are a number of complex processes that happen within each of the organizations that can impact the other. The **cascade of care** is a visual depiction of possible system-related issues that can impact the client experience and overall success in the system (Gardner et al., 2011). The cascade of care illustrates the movement of cases through the various activities or phases of care. The visual depiction of the service delivery system was originally designed for HIV, and proved to accelerate efforts to engage more individuals in need with care (Gardner, et al., 2011).

The cascade of care provides a visual depiction of how the system works, ranging from identification of individuals in need, along a continuum of care, to ultimately completion of treatment. The cascade of care also provides a depiction of the flow through various activities and stages. For example, referral and initiation of treatment are typical problem areas because they rely upon agencies to first locate and refer to appropriate programs or services, then for the individual to initiate and continue care. As a result, a greater number of individuals are typically screened compared to referred, and a greater number of individuals are typically referred than the number who initiate treatment. Figure 12.1 provides a visual depiction of the cascade considering a partnership between a juvenile probation agency and a substance use treatment agency.

In Figure 12.1, it is possible to see the areas the justice system is responsible for (in red), which activities are involved in the transition between the justice system and treatment, and

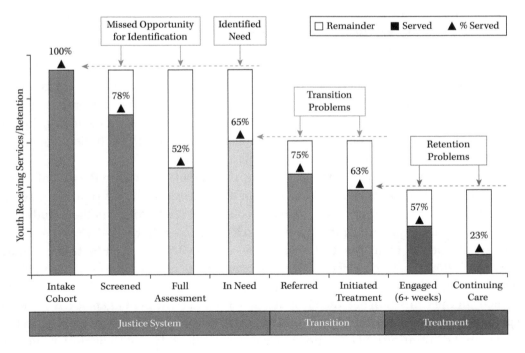

FIGURE 12.1 Cascade of Care in the Juvenile Justice System

which activities are the responsibility of the treatment agency. While this example depicts a juvenile justice agency, the same process is relevant for adult populations and for other types of services (e.g., mental health, physical health care, employment programs). By looking at the cascade of care, we can see where there are system failures that result in individuals not obtaining the care they need. For example, if we look at the responsibilities of the justice system, we can see that 22% of juveniles were not screened and 48% did not receive a full assessment. In the transition phase, 25% of individuals did not receive a referral and 37% did not initiate treatment. Lastly, activities within the treatment agency reveal that 43% of juveniles did not engage in treatment beyond 6 weeks while 77% did not engage in continuing care. Agencies can create a cascade of care for their populations to identify potentially problematic areas to pursue policies that reinforce operational procedures and successful collaborations to ensure client populations can access the services they need and are incentivized to engage in those services.

The following section introduces a systems approach to improving service delivery for youth in the justice system who have suicidal behavior and behavioral health problems. While the majority of this text covers adult probation and parole, this initiative is an innovative approach to improve integration between the youth probation systems and behavioral health care systems, which can be applied to adult systems as well.

e-Connect: A Systems Approach

Youth in the juvenile justice system are more likely to have behavioral health needs that include alcohol and substance use disorders, mental illness, and suicidal ideation. In fact, in the juvenile justice system, 10.8% of youth report a lifetime suicide attempt, which is nearly over 2.6 times greater than youth in the general population (4.1%; Elkington, Wasserman et al., 2023). Youth involved in the justice system experience disproportionately high rates of behavioral health and substance use disorders, exposure to trauma, and are at a greater risk for suicidal behavior (Wasserman et al., 2010). While youth involved in the probation system have high rates of suicidal behavior and behavioral health disorders, they also have low rates of service use. Part of this stems from a disconnect between youth probation agencies and treatment agencies in the community (Wasserman et al., 2021).

More specifically, youth needs for service are often identified within the juvenile justice system; however, necessary treatment is provided by entirely different treatment systems. Following the cascade of care, Wasserman and colleagues (2021) found in their study of over 8,000 youths entering community juvenile justice agencies that only 75% were screened for behavioral health concerns. Of those 75% screened, 50% required further evaluation; however, only 20% received a referral. Of the 20% who were referred, approximately 67% initiated treatment. This study highlights breakdowns in the system, especially in the activities that occur in the transition between justice agencies and treatment agencies. Additionally, the presence of multiple criminogenic and noncriminogenic needs (as introduced in Chapter 4) can make initiating and engaging in treatment difficult for youth on probation (White et al., 2016).

In recognition of these challenges, a team of researchers developed a systems-level program called e-Connect to promote interagency communication and coordination to improve linkage and coordination between youth probation agencies and community behavioral health providers, ultimately to improve access to and retention in treatment for youths on probation. The e-Connect program is a web-based clinical decision support application for staff working in both probation and behavioral health systems that aims to formalize their collaboration. Within e-Connect, there is a screener for suicidal behavior and behavioral health problems that is conducted by a probation officer. After generating results, e-Connect provides a script to the probation officer to inform the youth and their caregiver (e.g., parent) of the screening results.

Based on the screener results and level of care needed, e-Connect guides the officer to contact the appropriate provider based on the results of the screener to either requires a follow-up assessment, request transport to a local provider (if the youth is in active crisis), and/or make a referral to a treatment provider. The probation officer may make an appointment with the treatment provider with the youth and caregiver present or make a specific plan for the family to make an appointment that same day. Probation officers then recorded screening results, their actions, and outcomes of the meeting into the system. Figure 12.2 provides an illustration of the activities probation officers conducted in e-Connect.

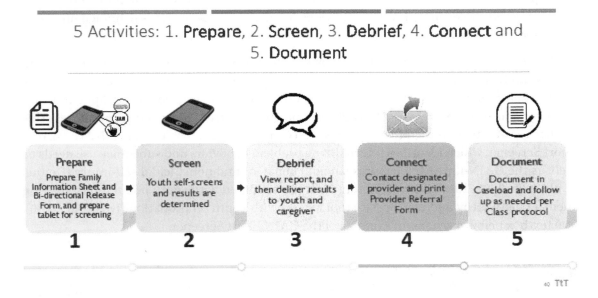

FIGURE 12.2   5 Activities that the Probation Officer Does in e-Connect (Elkington, Wasserman et al., 2023)

To determine the appropriate steps probation officers should take after completing a screening tool, representatives from probation, behavioral health, and academic researchers held "pathway meetings" to make recommendations on how to best respond to the youth in a timely fashion (Wasserman et al., 2021). These pathway meetings were designed to integrate the two systems and to ensure that both probation and behavioral health systems had consistent protocols and procedures in place to allow for the seamless transition to care from probation services. Wasserman and colleagues (2021) outlined the pathway meetings:

> The objectives of the Pathway Meetings were to determine referral processes and the destination settings for youths screened and classified as demonstrating risk of suicidal behavior; to do so, the meetings also arrived at interagency agreement on the steps needed to support service access and information exchange. The Pathway Meetings reviewed what is known about risks for suicidal behavior to ensure that there was consensus about what features should prompt action for justice-involved youths. Similarly, the mapping of the survey findings allowed for identification of points where youths commonly "fall through the cracks." The meeting also allowed the academic partner to facilitate discussions about the planned approach to screening and risk classification. If both agencies' worksheets differed regarding the preferred destination for a particular class of youths, discussion initially focused on defining the best option(s) and then achieving consensus across agencies. When both partners' worksheets identified the same destination, this was reinforced. Working backward from the agreed-upon destination, the group was challenged to consider the logical precursor to each step. Next, participants considered contingency planning if the steps on a referral Pathway could not be followed (e.g., family refusal, immediate service unavailability). (p. 5)

The two main issues the team worked on during the pathway meetings involved agreeing upon a valid screener and the appropriate level and type of response based on screener results. First, when probation agencies screen individuals under supervision, it is important that behavioral health agencies trust the information obtained from those tools. The address this challenge, e-Connect integrates a well-respected and validated instrument called the GAIN-Short Screener, which identifies internalizing problem behaviors and substance use needs as well, as the GAIN-I, which measures suicidal behavior and nonsuicidal self-injury (Dennis et al., 2006, 2008, 2013). Both screening tools are validated with youth populations, making them a trustworthy and appropriate tool for use with youth on probation (Ives et al., 2010). The textbox below provides an example of the GAIN-Short Screener.

READING

GAIN Short Screener (GAIN-SS)
Version [GVER]: GAIN-SS ver. 3.0.2

What is your name? a. _____ (First name) b. _____ (M.I.) c. _____ (Last name)

What is today's date? (MM/DD/YYYY) ☐☐ / ☐☐ / 20 ☐☐

The following questions are about common psychological, behavioral, and personal problems. These problems are considered **significant** when you have them for two or more weeks, when they keep coming back, when they keep you from meeting your responsibilities, or when they make you feel like you can't go on. After each of the following questions, please tell us the last time, if ever, you had the problem by answering whether it was in the past month, 2 to 3 months ago, 4 to 12 months ago, 1 or more years ago, or never.	Past month	2 to 3 months ago	4 to 12 months ago	1+ years ago	Never
	4	3	2	1	0

IDScr 1. **When was the last time** that you had **significant** problems with …

a. feeling very trapped, lonely, sad, blue, depressed, or hopeless about the future? 4 3 2 1 0

b. sleep trouble, such as bad dreams, sleeping restlessly, or falling asleep during the day? 4 3 2 1 0

c. feeling very anxious, nervous, tense, scared, panicked, or like something bad was going to happen? 4 3 2 1 0

d. becoming very distressed and upset when something reminded you of the past? 4 3 2 1 0

e. thinking about ending your life or dying by suicide? 4 3 2 1 0

f. seeing or hearing things that no one else could see or hear or feeling that someone else could read or control your thoughts? 4 3 2 1 0

EDScr 2. **When was the last time** that you did the following things **two or more times**?

a. Lied or conned to get things you wanted or to avoid having to do something 4 3 2 1 0

b. Had a hard time paying attention at school, work, or home 4 3 2 1 0

c. Had a hard time listening to instructions at school, work, or home. 4 3 2 1 0

d. Had a hard time waiting for your turn 4 3 2 1 0

e. Were a bully or threatened other people 4 3 2 1 0

f. Started physical fights with other people 4 3 2 1 0

g. Tried to win back your gambling losses by going back another day. 4 3 2 1 0

SDScr 3. **When was the last time** that …

a. you used alcohol or other drugs weekly or more often? 4 3 2 1 0

b. you spent a lot of time either getting alcohol or other drugs, using alcohol or other drugs, or recovering from the effects of alcohol or other drugs (e.g., feeling sick)? 4 3 2 1 0

c. you kept using alcohol or other drugs even though it was causing social problems, leading to fights, or getting you into trouble with other people? 4 3 2 1 0

d. your use of alcohol or other drugs caused you to give up or reduce your involvement in activities at work, school, home, or social events? 4 3 2 1 0

e. you had withdrawal problems from alcohol or other drugs like shaky hands, throwing up, having trouble sitting still or sleeping, or you used any alcohol or other drugs to stop being sick or avoid withdrawal problems? 4 3 2 1 0

(Continued) After each of the following questions, please tell us the last time, if ever, you had the problem by answering whether it was in the past month, 2 to 3 months ago, 4 to 12 months ago, 1 or more years ago, or never.	Past month	2 to 3 months ago	4 to 12 months ago	1+ years ago	Never
	4	3	2	1	0

CVScr 4. **When was the last time** that you...

a. had a disagreement in which you pushed, grabbed, or shoved someone? 4   3   2   1   0

b. took something from a store without paying for it? 4   3   2   1   0

c. sold, distributed, or helped to make illegal drugs? 4   3   2   1   0

d. drove a vehicle while under the influence of alcohol or illegal drugs? 4   3   2   1   0

e. purposely damaged or destroyed property that did not belong to you? 4   3   2   1   0

5. Do you have other **significant** psychological, behavioral, or personal problems that you want treatment for or help with? (**Please describe**) ....

     Yes   No

      1   0

    v1. _____

    _____

6. What is your gender? (If other, please describe below)   1 - Male   2 - Female   99 – Other

    v1. _____

7. How old are you today?   ☐☐ Age

7a. How many minutes did it take you to complete this survey?   ☐☐☐ Minutes

Staff Use Only
8. Site ID [XSITE]: _____ Site name v. _____
9. Staff ID [XSID]: _____ Staff name v. _____
10. Client ID [XPID]: _____ Comment v. _____
11. Mode: 1 - Administered by staff   2 - Administered by other   3 - Self-administered
13. Referral: MH ____ SA ____ ANG ____ Other ____ 14. Referral codes: _____
15. Referral comments: v1. _____
Observation   Value   [XOBS]:   _____   Local   Site   Name   [XSITEa]:

		Scoring			
Screener	**Items**	**Past month (4)**	**Past 90 days (4, 3)**	**Past year (4, 3, 2)**	**Ever (4, 3, 2, 1)**
IDScr	1a – 1f				
EDScr	2a – 2g				
SDScr	3a – 3e				
CVScr	4a – 4e				
TDScr	1a – 4e				

Second, the probation and behavioral health agencies had to work together to decide what to do with results from the screener used in e-Connect. As a result, the team grouped scores into three levels: Class I–crisis, imminent risk, do not leave youth unattended; Class II–crisis, not imminent risk, do not leave youth unattended; and Class III–in need of behavioral health service need (but no crisis). More information regarding each of these classes and the associated behaviors used to define each class are provided in the textbox below. One should note that adults in the justice system have similar problem behaviors with mental illness, suicide risk behaviors, and substance use (see Smith et al., 2019). The pathway meetings are designed to bring together two independent systems to engage in shared decision making and collaboration to determine how to respond to screening information collected by probation agencies. While typically probation would work in a silo, this process required the two systems to work together to create a seamless process from probation to behavioral health care. In the pathway meetings, both systems indicate their preferred method, and these are then discussed to come up with an agreed-upon response to improve linkage to care for youth on probation.

RISK CLASSIFICATION SYSTEM FOR YOUTH SUICIDAL BEHAVIOR

Class I: Crisis, Imminent Risk

Suicide attempt in the past 4 weeks <u>OR</u>
Suicidal ideation (in the past week) <u>AND</u>

- A suicidal plan (in the past 4 weeks) <u>OR</u>
- A suicidal attempt (prior to the past 4 weeks)

Class II: Crisis, Nonimminent Risk

Suicidal attempt (in the past year) <u>AND</u>

- High internalizing disorder symptoms (in the past year) <u>OR</u>
- Moderate internalizing disorder symptoms (in the past year) <u>AND</u> high substance use disorder symptoms (in the past year) OR
- Suicidal ideation (in the past month) <u>OR</u> suicidal ideation (in the past month) <u>AND</u>
- High internalizing disorder symptoms (in the past year) <u>OR</u>
- Suicidal plan (in the past month) <u>OR</u>
- Suicidal ideation (in the past week) <u>OR</u>
- Nonsuicidal self-injury (in the past 3 months)

Class III: Noncrisis, in need of behavioral health services

Suicidal attempt (in the past year or in lifetime) <u>OR</u>
Suicidal ideation (in the past month) <u>OR</u>
High internalizing disorder symptoms (in the past year) <u>OR</u>

Moderate internalizing disorder symptoms (in the past year) and high substance use disorder symptoms (in the past year) <u>OR</u>

High substance use disorder symptoms (in the past year) <u>OR</u>

Suicidal plan (in the past year) <u>AND</u>

- High internalizing disorder symptoms (in the past year) <u>OR</u>
- Moderate internalizing disorder symptoms (in the past year) <u>AND</u> high substance use disorder symptoms (in the past year) <u>OR</u>
- Suicidal ideation (in the past year)

Source: Wasserman et al., 2021

Case Study of e-Connect

To understand the processes that drive e-Connect, we present a case study of Jimmy, a youth who has recently been assigned to probation. During an interview with his probation officer, Jimmy indicates that he attempted to commit suicide a month ago, that he has had problems in school and with his parents, he started to smoke marijuana, and he experiences long periods of sadness and withdrawal. Jimmy's probation officer uses the screeners in e-Connect, which suggests that Jimmy is in Class 1 because his plan for suicide was less than 4 weeks ago, and he has several other symptoms that suggest he is in crisis. Jimmy's probation officer used e-Connect to guide them on what to do next, revealing that there was no mental health clinic within a 45-minute drive. Instead, both the probation agency and mental health agency decided that for youth who are in Class 1 (in need of immediate care), the Emergency Management System (EMS) would transport the youth to the emergency room. As a result, e-Connect instructed the probation officer to call EMS who then transported Jimmy to the hospital for a complete assessment and observation.

The e-Connect system was tested in 10 counties in New York state. Each county has a different mental health system with various types of programs and services. In some counties there are crisis services like a drop-in center for those in need of immediate services or emergency response teams. In other jurisdictions, the programs have flexibility to admit clients into care almost immediately. There are variations on how one can access care too. In some counties, the crisis center does a phone evaluation, a probation officer can walk the youth to a center (if it is within walking distance), and/or law enforcement agency can take the youth to the crisis services. In other counties, these options are not available.

Initial evaluation of the e-Connect model found that leaders from probation and behavioral health agencies successfully collaborated with one another in each of the 10 counties to create agreed upon pathways to care for youths on probation (Wasserman et al., 2021). While research on the outcomes of e-Connect are preliminary, initial evidence suggests these processes have resulted in improvements in linkage to care. At baseline (before the introduction to e-Connect), 49% of the youth on probation were referred to mental health services and 26% of the youth initiated some type of care (Wasserman et al., 2021). After the introduction of e-Connect, 92% of youth screened into Classes I, II, and III were referred to services and 85% initiated care. Overall, there was a 43% increase in referrals and a 59% increase in service initiation (see Figure 12.3) (refer to Wasserman, et al., 2021).

Even more importantly, early research suggests e-Connect also addresses equity issues in the referral process (Elkington, Wasserman et al., 2023). As shown in Figure 12.4 below, boys and girls who are White were more likely to be referred to care compared to youth of color. However, after e-Connect was implemented, the

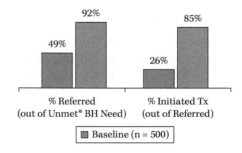

FIGURE 12.3   Impact of e-Connect on Referral and Treatment Initiation Rates

referral rate was similar for boys and girls, although boys of color tended to have slightly lower referral rates. Still, this illustrates that the e-Connect process can have a positive impact on decision making in order to equity. This is critically important given the disparities that exist in typical referral processes where probation officers do not use sufficient information to guide their treatment referral decisions. Overall, this research suggests that the e-Connect model is a promising strategy for promoting integration between two different systems that both serve youth on probation to improve linkage to care.

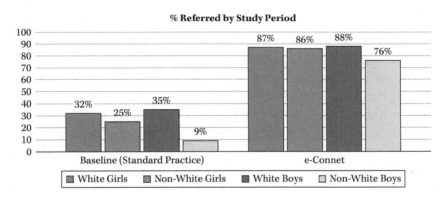

FIGURE 12.4   Impact of e-Connect on Equity Issues

One-Stop Shop Services

More recently, communities have begun to open "one-stop" shops that are often a single building where multiple service providers co-locate. The goals of these one-stop shops are to increase collaboration and sharing of information, to ease the transportation problems for clients, and to help the individuals in the community corrections system realize that obtaining services is normal. These centers provide immediate access to community-based services. In some communities, probation and parole officers may be able to walk an individual under supervision to the service center to expediate initiative into service (also referred to as an active referral process).

An example is the One-Stop Shop in the Community Corrections Center (CCC) in St. Mary's County, Maryland Sheriff's Office Corrections Division. This One-Stop Shop has multiple treatment services located within the same building, including mental health, substance use, employment, housing, transportation, and community services. This allows individuals under supervision to travel to one location to access one or more services based on their needs. An integrated service center such as this provides easy access and awareness of what the available services are in the community, which can help probation and parole officers make appropriate linkages to treatment. Mary Ann Thompson said the following in an interview published by the Southern Maryland News in 2022:

> Our community partners have always played a powerful role in recovery and rehabilitation for our offender population. During the pandemic, these partnerships played a critical role of providing services in the new normal. On the one-year anniversary of the CCC's One-Stop Shop it is a great time to reflect on the power of partnerships and what may be accomplished as working as a team to have the best possible safety net of services from incarceration to community. We look forward to continuing public safety and addressing gaps in services for the best possible outcomes for our offenders. (para. 2)

◊ Officer Work, Careers, and Wellness: Systems Efforts

Partnerships are a means to give probation and parole officers support to be able to respond more holistically and realistically to the needs of individuals by having direct relationships with services, educational, and nonprofit organizations. Partnerships can give officers reassurances that they can provide the services a person needs regardless of the resources of their own agency, which usually does not have enough funds to acquire the services directly. In some ways, this can reduce officer stress as well as provide them with more connection to service providers to better serve individuals on their caseloads.

Breno and colleagues (2023) found that when probation officers work with community providers, it increases their knowledge about various evidence-based practices and improves their perception about the effectiveness of these practices. Exposure to other experts and integration with treatment providers improved staff understanding surrounding why they should use best practices as well as how to use them. When agencies can improve their integration with external providers, such as through an MOU, systems like e-Connect, or community centers like a one-stop shop, this increases the exposure of probation and parole officers to community-based services while also increasing their access and, hopefully, likelihood to refer clients to needed services. These established processes can also send a message to supervision clients that the agency values their well-being and engagement in services. This is a double win, as it helps the probation and parole officers and it helps the individuals under supervision.

Let's look at an example. Officer A has some individuals on their caseload who are experiencing homelessness. The probation agency does not have any vouchers to help an individual obtain housing. The officer is frustrated because the individuals who are homeless tend to miss their appointments. The officer knows that the city has some shelters, but the individuals do not want to stay in the shelters, and the shelters have policies that require everyone to leave by 8:00 a.m. The officer does not want to issue a violation, but the repeated missed appointments create a problem. The officer went to the supervisor and complained that the agency did not have housing resources for people on supervision. The supervisor told the officer that there is a task force in the city titled "Housing for the Homeless" and they are looking for people from various agencies to participate in meetings. Officer A agreed to go to the meetings and represent the probation and parole agency. As part of these meetings, Officer A learned about grant programs that exist for city agencies. The officer also presented the problem of homelessness for individuals on probation and parole supervision—and how not having a place to live usually results in poor outcomes, including technical violations and potentially incarceration.

In response, the task force provided a range of resources that no one at the probation and parole agency was aware of. The officer also developed some additional resources and networks through connections made in the task force meetings that can help individuals on supervision. The task force also made the officer feel more relieved that there were some resources that were available, thus reducing his sense of guilt and frustration. Furthermore, the officer felt valued as he was able to voice his concerns to the task force on the issue of homelessness for supervised populations. The officer was commended by his agency when the task force made a recommendation to the city to develop housing options for individuals in the legal system. The officer felt that the time spent on this task force was very rewarding, and it gave the officer a new perspective on how to make changes in the system.

Researcher-Practitioner Partnerships

The prior discussion focused on service-related partnerships of probation and parole agencies with other organizations. We now turn to another partnership: researcher-practitioner partnerships that can help probation and parole agencies assess effectiveness of supervision services and programs, provide feedback on operations, and engage in quality improvement efforts. Researcher-practitioner partnerships are often long-term, mutually beneficial collaborations that promote the production and use of research to address specific community needs and/or agency challenges. These partnerships serve to connect agency interests with external researchers to achieve a shared goal to understand a problem, implement a solution(s), and assess the impact of the solution(s).

Researcher-practitioner partnerships are relationship-focused collaborations that often navigate hard-to-address issues (Rudes et al., 2014). Usually, the researcher is more familiar with the research literature on a specific topic area, whereas the practitioner has vast practical experience and is highly vested in the success of their own organizations. Partnerships with researchers, often academic partners or research organizations, are important because they serve to (a) provide an outside (objective) set of eyes; (b) increase access to the academic literature on "what works" and; (c) provide research methods to answer questions such as "Did it work?" "How did it work?" and "What was done?" Researchers can help agencies to assess the problem, identify evidence-based strategies, assist with strategic planning of strategies, assess implementation progress, and evaluate impact (Rudes et al., 2014). This translates into problem analyses, identification of evidence-informed practices or policies, provision of monitoring and feedback on progress using objective measures, and conducting impact analyses at the client, program, and/or system level (see Rossi et al., 2014).

Researcher-practitioner partnerships can help narrow the gap between research and practice. Instead of researchers sitting in their office crunching numbers, they actively work with practitioners to develop ways to translate existing evidence into practical knowledge applicable for real-world work. At the same time, these partnerships can result in evidence to support practitioner efforts. For example, say an agency has been using a cognitive behavioral program for the last 5 years but has never evaluated its effectiveness. This agency needs to make budget cuts, but staff would like to keep this program. The agency partners with a researcher at a local university to determine whether this program is effective. After an evaluation, the researcher concludes that the program does work. As a result, agency leaders decide it is worth keeping the program and find other ways to trim their budget. Of course, this could go the other way. If the evaluation concludes the program is not effective, this may result in the termination of the program. However, if the program is not working, this is not necessarily a negative outcome.

An additional benefit of researcher-practitioner partnerships is the increased ability to leverage funding. Many agencies support various interventions and efforts with grant funds. However, obtaining grant funding is not easy. It typically involves a lengthy application process, including written narratives that often must rely on theoretical frameworks and the most recent research evidence to support the request for funding. Researchers can be an asset to agencies interested in applying for this type of funding due to their training and experience (many researchers write grants frequently) and their expertise with the research literature.

Strong researcher-practitioner partnerships share several common characteristics. First, they involve mutual respect and trust. All participants should value and trust one another's expertise, perspectives, and experiences. Second, partnerships must involve strong communication that occurs frequently. Researchers should listen to the concerns and perspectives of practitioners and vice versa. Researchers can help to solve problems, but it is important that the researcher and practitioner are on the same page. This means that the researcher must share information about research studies in each area and the practitioner can highlight the efforts undertaken by their own or other agencies. The agency partner should recognize that they need to educate the researcher about the agency, county, or state laws and/or regulations and other key factors that may impact how an innovation can be implemented in their organization. Researcher-practitioner partnerships almost always require agencies to share data to help the researcher answer key questions.

Third, partnerships should seek to identify shared goals and objectives. When the partnership is defined by a common purpose, it is more likely to be successful. Fourth, decisions should be made collaboratively. Researchers should not try to dominate the partnership by dictating what the agency should do. Instead, a strong partnership involves joint decisions surrounding research questions and goals, research design, interpretation of findings, and a plan for sustaining change. Fifth, a strong partnership is flexible and adaptable. In real-world practice *and* research, things evolve constantly. Researchers and practitioners must be open to new ideas, feedback, and be willing to adjust either research protocols or agency practice and policies.

Overall, a strong researcher-practitioner partnership can result in co-creation of knowledge, use of rigorous research to inform agency practice, and production of knowledge to improve practice and policy. Researchers must value the expertise of the partnering agency and seek to understand how new programs or policies might best fit within the unique environment of each agency. This type of approach, in addition to open communication, leads to the development of mutual trust, which is critical for a successful partnership.

Types of Researcher-Practitioner Partnerships

Researcher-practitioner partnerships may focus on a variety of different efforts. The focus of the partnership should be determined in a collaborative fashion to ensure the partnership meets the needs of both parties. That is, both parties should select the research goal and then identify what type of research will answer that question. Researcher-practitioner partnerships can provide an agency with the perspective of an outsider individual or group. This "outsider" perspective is valuable since it provides insight from individuals who do not have a vested stake in the agency as an employee would. Additionally, several research studies confirm that programs evaluated with an outside researcher are more likely to achieve better outcomes and more likely to adhere to the program activities (Landenberger & Lipsey, 2005). Additionally, practitioners benefit from partnering with researchers, as it gives them access to individuals with specific expertise who want to help the agency identify ways to improve their organization. These partnerships are also very beneficial to researchers. Many researchers are in their current line of work because they enjoy working with practitioners, and scholars can learn what trends, practices, and dilemmas that probation and parole are expected to experience in the near future.

Despite these benefits, researcher-practitioner partnerships can encounter several common challenges. First, the quality and availability of agency data is usually limited. As discussed in Chapter 10, agencies often do not have the infrastructure in place to collect ongoing data that effective research evaluations may require. Furthermore, some practitioners have had difficult experiences with researchers, particularly when communication has been limited and researchers do not share clear information about their findings. In some cases, the researcher and practitioner have not agreed on how the data can be shared, used, or presented to various stakeholders (thus highlighting the need for an MOU). There are also methodological issues that can affect the relationship, such as the time to design the research project, the need for human subject review and approval by a university internal review board (IRB), and the time to collect data, analyze data, and produce a report or findings. Practitioners prefer shorter periods of time to obtain results and may not understand the research process and the amount of time each part of the process may take (which can be quite lengthy).

Despite these challenges, researcher-practitioner partnerships can succeed if there is open communication, an effective MOU in place, and strong relationships characterized by trust. A researcher-practitioner partnership must often identify the most appropriate approach or technique for studying the issue at hand. Figure 12.5 provides a loose categorization of methodological approaches within researcher-practitioner partnerships.

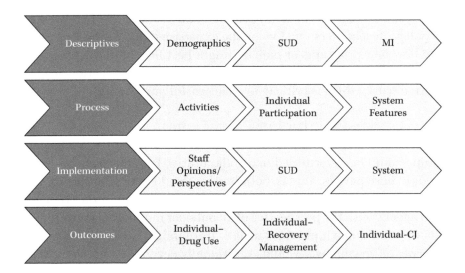

FIGURE 12.5   Methodological Approaches in Researcher-Practitioner Partnerships

To better understand the types of researcher-practitioner partnerships, we provide a brief overview of each research approach with a real-world example. Many of these examples include the direct language, descriptions, and findings reported in peer-reviewed, published journal articles. Students should note that these categories are not strict, and many examples they encounter may overlap several categories; however, it is important for students to have a sense of basic differences in these methodologies and also review and understand the literature when assessing the community corrections system.

1. *Descriptive studies:* Describes the population, staff, and/or organizations involved in the initiative. This can include demographics (e.g., age, gender, race or ethnicity, geographical information), and/or specialized needs like mental health and/or substance use disorders. These demographics can be of the individuals impacted by the project, staff, and/or the organizations. Descriptive analyses answer questions about who is involved in programs or processes. While descriptive studies may offer the most basic level of data collection, they can be very effective. Many times, a probation or parole agency may have a program that they believe is effective, yet it often takes the partnership with a researcher to specify the basic components (e.g., demographics of participants, starting and end date for participants to graduate, number of staff

involved in the program, datasets of program "failures," and information on other agencies involved in the program). Descriptive studies can provide crucial information to multiple stakeholders, such as agency leaders, political and legislative representatives, and grant funders. These stakeholders are often busy, and presentation of descriptive data are appealing and useful.

<u>Example from Suttmoeller & Keene (2012):</u> Suttmoeller and Keene (2012) sent a survey to treatment providers across Missouri to learn about their perspectives on probation and parole. In this study, the authors provide a descriptive analysis of their results. They identified that treatment providers in the state held positive perceptions towards probation and parole. Additionally, they found that treatment providers perceived probation and parole officers to be open to communication, and professional and courteous in their interactions (Suttmoeller & Keena, 2012).

2.   *Process evaluations:* strategies to examine how the agencies implement a program or policy. Process evaluations include questions about what is implemented and how it was implemented. Process evaluations can contain multiple components, including needs assessments to identify gaps in services, monitoring activities, formative evaluations, and participatory and summative evaluations. The emphasis is on the term "process," indicating a focus on the steps that occurred during implementation and the lessons learned. Process evaluations required that clear objectives for the program have been established, typically involving considerable meetings and planning between stakeholders. Due to process evaluations occurring over time, they allow the practitioner the opportunity to absorb findings from the researcher and adjust for future phases of the project.

<u>Example from Murphy & Turner (2009):</u> This study reflects a process evaluation of the Parole Violation Decision Making Instrument (PVDMI) Pilot Project that was implemented in four counties in California. The PVDMI sought to improve consistency in parole violations by providing recommended responses to each type of parole violation based on the individuals' risk level and the severity of the violation. In this evaluation, Murphy and Turner analyzed interviews, surveys, agency documents, and administrative data to evaluate the process of implementation. Through analysis of these data, the research team identified parole officer support for the tool and believed its use resulted in greater consistency in responses to parole violations.

3.   *Implementation studies:* focus on understanding the perspective of staff and stakeholders in terms of their knowledge and/or opinions of individuals involved in or affected by the innovation. Various types of implementation outcomes can be assessed including staff perception of the acceptability, appropriateness and feasibility of the innovation, perception of value added by the innovation, fidelity, and penetration in the system. Implementation studies use evidence-based knowledge and research findings to assess

programs and practices. They present a clear linkage between the knowledge and expertise of the researcher and best practices for real-world applications. These studies can be replicated in other locations or settings, producing further evidence that supports or does not support implementation processes. It should be mentioned that a lack of support for a program or policy is not necessarily a reason to disband the entire project, as a key strength of implementation research is the potential to identify systematic blockages, gaps, or resource deficits.

Example from Viglione (2019): In this study, Viglione (2019) studied the implementation of evidence-based practices aligned with the risk-need-responsivity (RNR) model. She used 1,074 hours of observational data with probation and parole officers to examine how probation staff implemented these practices. Her work found identified barriers to successful implementation, including an emphasis on protecting public safety and concern for liability should an individual under supervision violate their terms of supervision. These concerns lead officers to resist new practices, which served as a key implementation barrier.

4.   *Outcome studies:* are also termed "effectiveness studies" and are used to identify whether there are improvements in various key outcomes, such as stable housing, employment, education, and food security. Outcomes studies are often used to assess reductions in adverse outcomes such as rearrests, substance use behaviors, symptoms of mental illness, and return to prison (see Chapter 10). Outcome evaluation measures program effects in the target population by assessing the progress in the outcomes or outcome objectives that the program is to achieve. Outcome research is the most general of the categories presented here, though they generally refer to the measurement of outcomes related to services, interventions, and programs. Outcomes studies typically move beyond a simple measure of recidivism to include differences in health, quality of life, and functioning for participants. Since outcome studies usually take place after people have graduated from programs or interventions, they may also include consideration of the financial costs of the program in relation to the benefits. A cost-benefit analysis is a common technique used to identify the best practice for practitioners while preserving savings.

Example from Yeh (2010): In this study, Yeh (2010) examined the impact of electronic monitoring (EM) and home detention. They used data from a national survey of state prison inmates to estimate the total number of crimes that would have been committed by individuals on parole and probation if EM and home detention was not available. Yeh (2010) found that the availability of EM and home detention had savings in terms of financial costs and crime prevention. In fact, their analyses found that society would actually gain $12.70 for every dollar spend on EM or home detention.

Data Sharing Agreements

An important part of a partnership is to have formal documentation outlining expectations of the partnership, especially when agencies will be sharing sensitive data with external individuals. These agreements can be in the form of an MOU, discussed earlier in this chapter, or as a data sharing agreement, which focuses on outlining the requirements surrounding sharing and use of agency data. These documents are a useful tool to ensure that there are common agreements about the role of the researcher, the role of the partner, the data to be shared, the requirements for reporting data findings, and the process to ensure the confidentiality of the data and/or participants in the study. Of critical importance, these agreements typically outline that the researcher cannot share information with other agencies or use the data for another purpose without asking the permission of the practitioner agency.

A key area of concern with data sharing agreements involves the protection of information regarding personal data, particularly mental illness and substance use. Due to the variation in state laws, many specific questions raised by probation and parole agencies will require answers from local, county, or state counsel. Yet, Petrila and Fader-Towe (2010) explain:

> Federal law shapes what is permissible at the state or local level, primarily through the basic privacy rules for "protected health information" (PHI) under the Health Insurance Portability and Accountability Act of 1996 (HIPAA), and substance abuse treatment information under 42 CFR Part 2, a portion of the Code of Federal Regulations addressing public health. (p. vii)

The Health Insurance Portability and Accountability Act of 1996 (HIPAA) contains two elements, the first involving "privacy rules" discussed as individual rights in the previous chapter and the second being "security rules" focused on data sharing, data management, and information technology (IT). HIPPA establishes certain conditions or permission for the sharing of information and the circumstances under which they apply. Behavioral and physical health care providers are "covered entities" under HIPPA, with no distinction between general providers, hospitals, or specialty mental health providers (Petrila & Fader-Towe, 2010). Data sharing with these providers, or "covered entities," means that they must be clear on who is asking for the information and for what purposes the information will be used. In some criminal justice activities, HIPPA permits the disclosure of information without the client's written consent (e.g., child abuse, intimate partner violence, victims of violence or abuse). However, in most cases, an individual must consent to have their protected health information (PHI) shared.

The Confidentiality Of Substance Use Disorder Patient Records (2017) federal regulation provides the following requirement for written consent to share personal health information.

- The specific name or general designation of the program or person permitted to make the disclosure
- The name or title of the individual or the name of the organization to which disclosure is to be made
- The name of the patient

402 | Community Corrections: An Intersectional Approach

- The purpose of the disclosure
- How much and what kind of information is to be disclosed
- The signature of the patient (or that of a guardian for minors, or an authorized person for individuals who are incompetent or deceased)
- The date on which the consent is signed
- A statement that the consent is subject to revocation at any time except when the program has acted "in reliance on" the consent. For example, if a clinician provided treatment after obtaining consent to disclose the treatment information to the patient's insurance company, the patient loses the right to revoke their consent to sharing the information on this occasion.
- The date, event, or condition upon which the consent will expire if not revoked before. This date, event, or condition must ensure that the consent will last no longer than reasonably necessary to serve the purpose for which it is given.

Following client consent to share information, many probation and parole agencies have manual processes or management information systems that bring together behavioral health and criminal justice information. These information systems can be used when researchers are measuring the effectiveness of diversion and treatment programs, such as the use of the SMART system in Maryland:

> The Statewide Maryland Automated Record Tracking (SMART) system is a web-based tool that provides a client tracking system for state agencies and private treatment providers. Used by treatment providers and drug courts as a management information system, SMART enables collecting substance abuse treatment data, tracking drug court client services, and analyzing program data. SMART is based on the Web Infrastructure for Treatment Services platform. (Petrila & Fader-Towe, 2010, p. 26)

Concern over how protected health information (PHI) is shared between researchers, community corrections, and health care providers is estimated to continue in line with technological advancements and the continued growth in researcher-practitioner partnerships. The goal is to balance protecting the privacy of the client while allowing researchers and practitioners the opportunity to analyze data and improve outcomes. This tends to refer to a standard of providing and sharing personal client data to the degree that is "minimally necessary." Data management and sharing must adhere to transparent and established protocols, including self-reporting of data breaches and errors. It is projected that with increased attention on finding alternatives to incarceration for people with mental health and substance use issues and with these special populations now a component of all community corrections caseloads, the use of data management and sharing will remain an important topic.

Production of Reports for the Agency

Most partnerships will involve several analyses and the production of reports that are of value to the agency. However, issues can occur with these reports if the findings from the study are not favorable, indicate that the program or innovation did not improve the outcomes, and/or identify issues that need attention. These are the perils of partnerships: being the deliverer of negative information. However, researchers should be sure to provide the collaborating agency with information as soon as it is produced and work with the partnership team to understand the findings and determine appropriate next steps. These conversations can help address negative information and provide some information and context that can be useful in both interpreting the findings and in explaining the findings to others. It is the responsibility of the researcher to be honest, and that includes having the integrity to present difficult information. It is also good practice to have the agency partner review any written reports or presentations; they may have insights into how to explain the findings. These processes illustrate the necessary respect that define partnerships.

SUMMARY: PARTNERSHIPS AND EVALUATIONS IN COMMUNITY CORRECTIONS

Partnerships strengthen community corrections agencies by providing access to resources that are not available within the agency. Partnerships can provide access to needed services and can help the agency improve their ability to address criminogenic needs. Partnerships can also ensure that agencies have knowledge of and access to the varied types of services needed to be responsive to individuals within the justice system. Using Konrad's (1996) model of integration, this chapter illustrated different types of integration that occur at the program and system level. Partnerships are important for promoting integration with external agencies that can better help agencies meet the needs of individuals that are being supervised. Partnerships also provide opportunities to develop new efforts to improve service delivery through measuring the cascade of care, providing clinical decision supports to integrate services, and offering one-stop shops.

Another critical partnership involves the researcher-practitioner working together to understand the impact of a program or system. These partnerships can help supervision agencies understand how things work and how to make improvements. Researchers give immediate access to scientific literature on prior studies and new trends in the field. Practitioners give researchers opportunities to test out new ideas, to develop new innovations, and to improve policy and practice. The researcher-practitioner partnership brings new skills to an organization and provides new effects to improve performance at the individual, program, and system level.

Partnerships create the opportunities that community corrections agencies need to be successful, even when they do not have the resources themselves to provide certain services. Moving forward with partnerships can assist community corrections agencies to achieve their mission of helping individuals change and protecting public safety. A strong network of partnerships and integration with a variety of community-based agencies can provide the resiliency that is needed for community corrections agencies to be a vital and effective justice entity.

Scenario-Based Activities

	Case	Question(s)
1.	The probation and parole agency you work for does not have the expertise to screen individuals for mental health issues, and the risk-needs assessment tool does not have specific questions regarding suicide or trauma issues.	What are the strategies that the probation and parole agency could use to acquire screening and assessment services at the probation agency? What type of information should they include in a MOU for either approach?
2	You are a probation and parole officer who is interested in providing individuals under supervision with employment services, but your agency has no funding to provide such services.	How would you address the need for employment services for individuals on supervision? What type of partnership would be advisable to ensure that all individuals supervision with the type of services needed? How does the agency ensure that needed services are provided?

References

Breno, A., Carter, T., Vechinski, J., Molfenter, T., Clark, K., & Taxman, F. S. (under review). *Better together: Exploring staff perceptions of MOUD treatment across agencies.*

Confidentiality Of Substance Use Disorder Patient Records, 82 F.R. 6115 (2017). https://www.ecfr.gov/current/title-42/chapter-I/subchapter-A/part-2

Dennis, M. L., Feeney, T., & Titus, J. C. (2013). *Global appraisal of Individual Needs–Short Screener (GAIN-SS): Administration and scoring manual, version 3.* Chestnut Health Systems.

Dennis, M. L., White, M., Titus, J. C., & Unsicker, J. (2008). *Global appraisal of Individual Needs: Administration guide for the GAIN and related measures, version 5.* Chestnut Health System.

Elkington, K., Wasserman, G. A., Ryan, M., Sichel, C., Sarapas, C. C., Dennis, M., & Taxman, F. S. (2023). e-Connect: Linking probation youth at risk for suicide to behavioral health services. *Journal of Consulting and Clinical Psychology, 91*(9), 547–557. https://doi.org/10.1037/ccp0000824

Janetta, J., Breaux, J., & Ho, H. (2014). *Examining racial and ethnic disparities in probation revocation.* The Urban Institute.

Konrad, E. L. (1996). A multidimensional framework for conceptualizing human services integration initiatives. *New Directions for Evaluation, 1996*(69), 5–19. https://doi.org/10.1002/ev.1024

Landenberger, N. A., & Lipsey, M. (2005). The positive effects of cognitive behavioral programs for offenders: A meta-analysis of factors associated with effective treatment. *Journal of Experimental Criminology, 1*(4), 451–476. https://doi.org/10.1007/s11292-005-3541-7

Lee, C., Mackey, B. J., Johnson, J. E., & Taxman, F. S. (under review). *Justice and behavioral health service integration: Examining organizational structure variation in all 50 United States.*

Matz, A, K., & Kim, B. (2017). A national survey of chief probation/parole officers' perceived interest in and impact of partnerships with police. *Corrections, 2*(4), 269–292. https://doi.org/10.1080/23774657.2017.1310004

Murphy, A., & Turner, S. (2009). *Parole Violation Decision-Making Instrument (PVDMI)*. Center for Evidence-Based Corrections, The University of California, Irvine.

Nash, M. (2008). Exit the polibation officer? Decoupling police and probation. *International Journal of Police Science and Management, 10*(3), 302–312 https://doi.org/10.1350/ijps.2008.10.3.86

National Gang Center. (n.d.). *Comprehensive gang model: Core strategies*. Retrieved June 1, 2023, from https://nationalgangcenter.ojp.gov/sites/g/files/xyckuh331/files/media/document/CoreStrategies.pdf

National Institute of Justice. (2013). *Race and ethnicity: What are their roles in gang membership?* https://nij.ojp.gov/topics/articles/race-and-ethnicity-what-are-their-roles-gang-membership

Office of Juvenile Justice and Delinquency Prevention. (2009). *OJJDP comprehensive gang model: A Guide to assessing a community's youth gang problems*. U.S. Department of Justice. http://www.national-gangcenter.gov/Comprehensive-GangModel/Assessment-Guide

Petrila, J., & Fader-Towe, H. (2010). *Information sharing in criminal justice-mental health collaborations: Working with HIPPA and other privacy laws*. U.S. Bureau of Justice. https://bja.ojp.gov/sites/g/files/xyckuh186/files/Publications/CSG_CJMH_Info_Sharing.pdf

Rossi, P., Lipsey, M., & Freedman, H. E. (2004). Evaluation: A systematic approach (7th ed.). Thousand Oaks, CA: SAGE Publications.

Rudes, D. S., Viglione, J., Lerch, J., Porter, C., & Taxman, F. S. (2014). Build to sustain: Collaborative partnerships between university researchers and criminal justice practitioners. *Criminal Justice Studies, 27*(3), 249–263. https://doi.org/10.1080/1478601X.2014.947808

Smith, H. P., Kaminski, R. M., Power, J., & Slade, K. (2019). Self-harming behaviors in prison: A comparison of suicidal processes, self-injurious behaviors, and mixed events. *Criminal Justice Studies, 32*(3), 264–286. https://doi.org/10.1080/1478601X.2019.1602044

Southern Maryland News. (2022, July 12). *One-Stop-Shop deemed a success one year later*. https://southernmarylandpr.com/2022/07/one-stop-shop-deemed-a-success-one-year-later/

Suttmoeller, M., & Keena, L. D. (2012). Treatment provider's perceived effectiveness of probation and parole: A case study. *International Journal of Offender Therapy and Comparative Criminology, 56*(1), 153–168. https://doi.org/10.1177/0306624X11405957

Taxman, F. S., & Bouffard, J. (2000). The importance of systems in improving offender outcomes: New frontiers in treatment integrity. *Justice Research and Policy, 2*(2), 37–58. https://doi.org/10.3818/JRP.2.2.2000.37

U.S. Department of Justice. (2021, April 29). *Prison gangs*. https://www.justice.gov/criminal-ocgs/gallery/prison-gangs

Viglione, J. (2019). The risk-need-responsivity model: How do probation officers implement the principles of effective intervention? *Criminal Justice and Behavior, 46*(5), 655–673. https://doi.org/10.1177/0093854818807505

Wasserman G. A., Elkington K. S., Robson G., & Taxman F. S. (2021). Bridging juvenile justice and behavioral health systems: Development of a clinical pathways approach to connect youth at risk for suicidal behavior to care. *Health Justice, 9*(1), Article 36. https://doi.org/10.1186/s40352-021-00164-4

Wasserman, G. A., McReynolds, L. S., Schwalbe, C. S., Keating, J. M., & Jones, S. A. (2010). Psychiatric disorder, comorbidity and suicidal behavior in juvenile justice youth. *Criminal Justice and Behavior, 37*(12), 1361–1376. https://doi.org/10.1177/0093854810382751

White, L. M., Lau, K. S., & Aalsma, M. C. (2016). Detained adolescents: Mental health needs, treatment use, and recidivism. *Journal of the American Academy of Psychiatry and the Law, 44*(2), 200–212. PMID: 27236176.

Yeh, S. S. (2010). Cost-benefit analysis of reducing crime through electronic monitoring of parolees and probationers. *Journal of Criminal Justice, 38*(5), 1090–1096. https://doi.org/10.1016/j.jcrimjus.2010.08.001

Image Credits

Index